D1281957

Peter Townsend

Sociology
and
Social Policy

Allen Lane

Copyright © Peter Townsend, 1975

First published in 1975

Allen Lane
Penguin Books Ltd
17 Grosvenor Gardens
London SW1W 0BD

ISBN 0 7139 0780 0

Printed in Great Britain by
Lowe & Brydone (Printers) Ltd, Thetford, Norfolk

For Matthew

Acknowledgements

Sixteen of these papers have been written since 1968, ten of them since 1970. I owe many debts to friends and colleagues for help in their preparation, in particular to Brian Abel-Smith, Tony Lynes, Dennis Marsden, Adrian Sinfield and the late Richard Titmuss, but also, for generous help with certain papers, to Tony Atkinson, Muriel Brown, Colin Bell, David Bull, Nicholas Bosanquet, Susan Ferge, Guy Fiegehen, David Gil, Chelly Halsey, Hilary Land, Alan Harrison, Audrey Harvey, Geoffrey Hawthorn, Michael Mann, Michael Meacher, Pauline Morris, Della Nevitt, Ray Pahl, Tom Ponsonby, Martin Rein, John Rex, Hilary Rose, Ann Shearer, Alvin Schorr, Malcolm Wicks, John Veit Wilson and Stephen Winyard.

Sue Best and then Marion Haberhauer gave unstinting and superb secretarial help. Jo and Walt Jaehnig gave sound and detailed advice at proof stage. Finally I owe a general debt to the intellectual vitality and social consciousness of three organizations in which I have worked in recent years: the Department of Sociology at the University of Essex, the Child Poverty Action Group and the Social Policy Advisory Committee of the Labour Party.

Five of the papers have not previously been published. Other papers were first published in the *Royal Institute of British Architects' Journal* (Chapter 6); *Political Quarterly* (Chapter 22); *The Times* (Chapter 24); the *New Statesman* (Chapters 18, 19 and 23); *Put Away* by Pauline Morris, Routledge & Kegan Paul (Chapter 10); Proceedings of the Manchester Statistical Society (Chapter 9); *New Society* (Chapters 3, 4 and 13); *Tribune* (Chapters 16 and 21); the *Guardian* (Chapter 12); and pamphlets and books of the Fabian Society (Chapters 7, 8, 14 and 20). Permission to include these papers in this collection is gratefully acknowledged.

Contents

Preface

In the last twenty-five years social policy in Britain has failed to make much impact on the related problems of poverty and social inequality. When all that is good and indeed noble in British social life is sensitively described and fully digested that conclusion must abjectly stand. This book aims to discuss this failure and to suggest what sociology might begin to contribute towards the understanding and reformulation of that policy.

Despite a substantial increase in the absolute purchasing power of the population there is, paradoxically, no evidence of marked reduction in inequality in the last twenty-five years and some evidence of new or increased forms of deprivation — of more unemployment, and insecure employment, especially among school-leavers, the disabled, the middle-aged and women; far more people prematurely retired; the acceptance of poor conditions of work and terms of service in some reorganized or marginal industries; the growing scope, especially for migrant workers, of means-tested benefits and limitation of the rights of the poor; the squalor, danger and cramped environment of some new urban estates, especially high flats; the development of more systematic discrimination against immigrants; the rise in homelessness; weaker security of tenure of families and individuals living in rented property. Other societies with predominantly capitalist economies, 'mixed' economies and even State economies share some of the same problems and some of the same negative trends to set against their positive achievements.

No one has yet taken the full measure of this paradox and a primary task for the social policy analyst is to explain it. Accordingly, the first introductory chapter discusses at some length the meaning of social policy and the relationship between sociology and social policy. It argues that social policy is still conceived too narrowly and that any worthwhile social objectives — for example, educational equality, the elimination of overcrowding and squalor, the reduction of ill-health, and social integration — depend on the use and control of institutions like the fiscal system and the wage and fringe benefit systems of industry and not just the conventional group of public social services (education, health, social security, housing and welfare). But any attempt to study the objectives shows how important it is to define them as clearly as possible and to search for criteria by which they may be weighed and priorities determined. That means applying a stricter theory of social change, which can also be translated into a programme of action. This programme amounts to something which is a distinct alternative to existing social policy. References are made in Chapter 1 to other chapters where the argument is developed and examples given. Chapters 2 to 5 apply the general argument for an alternative plan to the social services as a whole and to the problem of reorganizing the responsibilities of Government and local authorities.

The main body of the book (Chapters 6 to 17) deals in greater detail with specific policies and the construction of specific alternatives — on housing, means-tested services and negative income tax, mental handicap and mental illness, comprehensive schools, community welfare and pensions for the elderly.

The final group of chapters relates policies more directly to the achievement and fulfilment of political power and traces the formation and expression of some parts of the Labour Party's social policy in the late 1950s and early 1960s as well as after 1964. These chapters, written at successive dates, reveal a growing awareness of the present limits of Labour's potentiality. The essays suggest that ministerial control in the development of social policy is often overrated. In the absence of control by the Labour movement and in the absence of institutional forms of cohesion and planning, the leadership proved to be indecisive and ineffective. But that merely calls attention to the contradictions and inconsistencies in society at large. The emphasis placed upon moral values in society, in shaping social policy and hence greater or lesser equality, particularly within the Labour movement, including its leadership, seems to me to have lost none of its force between, say, 1959 and 1970. The penultimate chapter turns to an examination of the Tory record in social policy between 1970 and 1974. It concludes that the Government strengthened the rich, emphasized hierarchical and managerial values and resurrected the most abrasive nineteenth-century principles of conditional welfare for the few.

The final chapter attempts to sum up ways in which the essential structure and changes in society might be analysed and controlled in the interests of social 'growth'.

1 Sociology and Social Policy *

In our eventful time, just as in the sixteenth century, pure theorists on social affairs are found only on the side of reaction and for this reason they are not even theorists in the full sense of the word, but simply apologists of reaction.

Frederick Engels, in the Preface to Book III of *Capital,* by Karl Marx, Lawrence & Wishart, 1972, p.2 (written in 1894).

When I was appointed in 1963 to the Department of Sociology in the University of Essex and became its first chairman, a number of fellow social scientists were very critical. They regarded me as fitting much more easily, in British terms, into a department of Social Administration than into one of Sociology. As it happened, I had read for Part II of the Social Anthropology Tripos after getting my degree in Philosophy at Cambridge, had studied as a sociology graduate in the Free University in Berlin, had undertaken family and community studies for more than three years at the Institute of Community Studies at Bethnal Green in the mid 1950s before doing research on institutional care and then teaching social policy for six years at the London School of Economics, and was deeply interested in social gerontology, medical sociology and the sociology of institutions — specialities which were at the time, and to a large extent still are, sadly underdeveloped. But what was correctly recognized was that this scatter of interests was held together by a commitment to social policy, and this was felt to be improper in a sociologist.

The separation of the study of social policy from sociology is, I believe, wrong. It arises in part because the concept of social policy, perhaps unconsciously for political reasons, has been confined narrowly by many scholars and others to that of welfare administration: in part because the pursuit of sociology has been wrongly believed by many to be 'value-free'; and in part because many sociologists have adopted unduly optimistic and facile theories of social change. Unlike Marx, they have been concerned to trace the progress or the achievements of modern society rather than its inadequacies and have concentrated more on the problems of social order and equilibrium than on those of the

---

* First prepared as a lecture given in the Department of Sociology, University of Aberdeen, 1973.

identification and exploration of social change. While social problems have formed part of the university curriculum they have been examined in an over-generalized way, usually from a functionalist standpoint, which does not explain incidence or degree and offers no indication of the mechanisms by which they might be reduced or eliminated. Theories of change have been insufficiently exact to furnish clear and inescapable implications for policy.

The study of social policy is the study of the means whereby societies prevent, postpone, introduce and manage changes in structure. According to the customary, if supercilious, distinction ordinarily made, such study is therefore not an applied but a 'pure' social science. It is as necessary as the study of social structure to the development and exposition of theories of social change. This is the theme of this paper and I will discuss in turn the concepts of social policy and social change.

The Definition of Social Policy

There are many different definitions of social policy. Perhaps most commonly social policy is defined as policy concerned with the public administration of welfare, that is, the development and management of specific services of the State and of local authorities, such as health, education, welfare and social security services, to remedy particular social problems or pursue social objectives which are generally perceived and agreed as such. Thus, Professor T.H. Marshall describes social policy as 'the policy of governments with regard to action having a direct impact on the welfare of citizens, by providing them with services or income' — the central core of which includes 'social insurance, public (or national) assistance, housing policy', education and 'the treatment of crime'.(1)

Most historians and social scientists do in fact adopt some such definition.(2) But it is very limited. The possibilities of outlining an approach in elementary functional terms does not seem to have occurred to the sociologists among them.(3) Thus the activities of government might be classified and analysed in terms of their functions rather than their formal administrative divisions — rather like recent approaches in systems analysis.(4) Unfortunately this is what few radical sociologists are currently doing. This would have at least two results which would transform the conception of social policy and transform too the character of any explanation of social change. First, the activities of government would be grouped more in terms of similarity of intention or of effect than of administrative convention.(5) Part of the problem is our failure, and the Government's failure, to acknowledge and even recognize similarities of function because of the rigidity of our assumptions and thought patterns. The conception would therefore go beyond that comprising health, education, welfare, housing and social security services. Measures to meet the needs of dependency or of the low paid, for example, might be introduced into a Government's tax policies or income policies and not only into its administration of a system of social security. Why should the latter and not also the former be discussed in relation to the pursuit of social objectives? Aren't the former a significant part of a Government's social policy, and hence a legitimate and necessary part of the study of social policy? At the time of writing the British Government has been applying a complex programme to control inflation, but one of its three principal aims is 'to improve the position of the low paid and pensioners'.(6) Inevitably, therefore, the series of documents published by the Government (7) and the evidence of the social effects of the programme, if any, deserve to attract as much scrutiny as, say, an increase in State retirement pensions or a change in housing subsidies in the overall examination of 'social policy'. Some policies also have to be scrutinized when they have no avowed social objectives. There may be unintended social by-products or effects of Government policies in defence, industrial ownership, industrial relations, trade, employment and the administration of law. These could either reinforce or undermine social service policies. They cannot be ignored in any discerning account or application of social policy.(8)

Secondly, the conception would include policies of institutions other than government. Government policy is no more synonymous with social policy than Government behaviour is synonymous with social behaviour. Institutionalized social policies cover a wider range than those promulgated and administered by central and local departments of Government and include the indirect as well as direct welfare policies of industry, religion, voluntary associations and private companies or employers. Religious and voluntary bodies have pioneered some services later institutionalized by the State. Today they often run services resembling those run by the State or in more or less satisfactory partnership with those run by local authorities. One use of cross-national studies is to reveal how in some countries employers offer an elaborate system of benefits in kind which in other countries are offered by the State. Such employer-administered services have similar, if more restricted, goals. Medical benefits are sometimes provided by the State under social insurance systems, but sometimes by private insurance schemes which are partly if not wholly controlled in their operation by State legislation. Again, it is impossible to understand council housing and systems of public subsidy without being aware of the structure of the housing market and the activities of the private developer and property speculator. These examples show how absurd it would be to draw a distinction between services run by the State and those run by other institutions of society and to refer only to the policies of the former in discussing social policy.

An extended conception of social policy has a number of disadvantages and advantages. It covers so many activities that there are difficulties in arranging component information as well as ideas into comparable form. Even if attention is concentrated upon different Government activities they are hard to relate. For example, only in recent years have there been any official attempts to show the respective contributions made by gross earnings, direct and indirect taxation, and direct and indirect benefits of the social services to the distribution of income.(9) The first publication of the annual *Social Trends* in 1970 was a significant development but the series has not yet given much impression of reflecting a broader conception of social policy or even an 'objective' conception of social policy. A lot more work remains to be done if the social effects of any change in levels of earnings, taxation or social services are to be traced in detail.(10) Again, it is hard to compare Government services with equivalent activities of industry and voluntary and private bodies. Little statistical information is collected and issued routinely about the latter and rarely is it presented in a form which is comparable with Government statistics. The existing fragmentation is very understandable. Civil servants and local authority officials are employed primarily to administer services for which they are publicly accountable. It is natural that they should concentrate on these services and give little heed to those outside their jurisdiction, and that statistical output and other information should reflect the history and administrative organization of government. It is also natural that the public should have been encouraged to concentrate their attentions on 'public' services which are not only so defined but financed directly by them through taxation and administered directly by Government servants. There is therefore wide agreement in principle that extensive information should be made available about these 'public' services. But it is also natural that so-called 'private' industry should be reluctant to produce some kinds of corresponding information about the welfare services of industry. That might appear to be encroaching upon public responsibilities, demonstrate too clearly how privileges are conferred on certain sections of personnel and assist competitors. It would be difficult too to get information produced in a standardized form. So even if we were to attempt to adopt a broad policy perspective it could not be sustained without great difficulty. The problem of converting society's definition of the scope and categories of social policy into one which is broader and functionally more consistent is huge. Again and again, through lack of appropriate information and of the efforts and agreement to produce it, the task is likely to be frustrated. The structure of inequality frustrates attempts even to document it. Discussion in academic journals as well as the mass media will tend to revert to more reassuring administrative concepts and will concentrate on areas about which there is information.

A related disadvantage is that the policy analyst will be overwhelmed by the sheer magnitude of his task. Any attempt to invest a conception with elaborate sub-divisions of meaning and a very broad range of subject-matter is bound to cause strain. It is difficult to preserve a sense of balance and context, not only because of the lack of good statistical data for many parts of the conception, but because so much knowledge is brought into play and, moreover, needs to be graded and weighed. For example, in reducing poverty is fiscal policy more important than price control, or employment policy more important than social security? Different Government agencies, and non-Government as well as Government agencies, serve similar social objectives. Criteria have to be evolved to settle the list of agencies which are contributing, and the degree to which they are contributing, to specific social objectives. When the information which is circulating about agencies varies in amount and accessibility this is extraordinarily difficult. And the conception becomes more difficult to communicate. Many laymen feel they can at least come to terms with experts who are talking about a set of centrally or locally administered welfare services — within which are included education, health, social security, housing and the care of children, the disabled and the old. It is an interest or a commitment which they can respect, even when it does not seem to them to be ideologically paramount. But a social policy analyst who is as much preoccupied with the social benefits of possible extensions of the public ownership of industry as he is with improving the housing facilities of the aged, or with the social benefits of a different earnings or tax structure as he is with transformations of social security, may appear to them to be more elusive, and perhaps more disconcerting. Too easily he can give the impression of being some kind of intellectual imperialist, gobbling up areas of expertise believed previously to be remote from his interests and competence.

Against these disadvantages, which have to be conceded, certain advantages have to be recognized. Social realities, and especially inequalities, are more likely to be perceived by rulers and ruled. Improvements in State unemployment insurance might be more than counter-balanced by an increase in structural unemployment leaving more families living in conditions of deprivation. So the student of social policy must seek knowledge about the structural causes of, and remedies for, unemployment as well as about the means of meeting the needs of those who are unemployed. Selective increases in indirect taxation may wipe out hard-won improvements in levels of low pay, pensions or family allowances. So the social effects of different tax policies have to be disentangled. The extension of employers' welfare benefits in kind for high-income groups may quickly neutralize the effects of the introduction of a more progressive system of taxation. Or again, the gradual development of private systems of welfare for privileged groups of the population, whether in education, medical care, housing or pensions, may undermine equality of rights, benefits or opportunities that governments fondly believe have been introduced through State legislation. So employer welfare cannot be ignored.

Policy analysis must therefore depend on a broad sociological perspective about both objectives and means. Social policy is best conceived as a kind of blueprint for the management of society towards social ends: it can be defined as *the underlying as well as the professed rationale by which social institutions and groups are used or brought into being to ensure social preservation or development*. Social policy is, in other words, the institutionalized control of services, agencies and organizations to maintain or change social structure and values. Sometimes this control may be utterly conscious, and consciously expressed by Government spokesmen and others. Sometimes it may be unspoken and even unrecognized.

In this sense of the term, then, all societies have social policies. In identifying the different policies of developing and advanced societies the sociologist may gradually call attention to the fact that policy analysis is independent of planning. The difference is essentially one between a subjective orientation, even when that is expressed collectively by a community, a city or a nation, and one that strives to be objective. Policy analysis is the task of unravelling and evaluating the policy of society, or, more correctly the policies of different social groups and agencies, with government and industry being the predominant agencies in advanced industrial societies. Planning, by contradistinction, is best conceived as the search for alternative policies. It is the definition of goals on the basis of measured needs among (and between) populations and the development of a rational strategy and of appropriate means to fulfil those objectives most quickly. This begs further questions about choosing goals, measuring needs, defining what is rational and what is appropriate, but, as discussed later, a planning perspective can be regarded as arising from the analysis of social conditions, with inequality and deprivation as the guiding concepts. A 'plan' may be adopted and put into effect as policy, but it is normally distorted in the process by the subjective interpretations and emphases of Government and officials, concessions to interest groups and limitations imposed by external forces. Whether 'planning' and research units of local and central Government and universities are planning units in an objective sense of the word rather than instruments of social policy is very doubtful. Their detachment or impartiality is of dubious validity, if only because of the influences upon them of the research foundations, professions, universities or employing departments to which in some measure they owe allegiance.

I said above that there may not be a single social policy but rather the policies of different social groups, overlapping each other in the objectives and methods which they adopt, and one or sometimes two of the groups (State and industry, or State and Church) being predominant. They are controlled by public and professional perceptions of their functions and usually operate much less independently than their direct-ors realize. Social policy is the rationale by which societies are steered towards social ends, and the rationale according to which different ends are combined together and weighed. Policy depends on a definition of needs that are perceived rather than measured, and upon administrative agencies or services that have been set up and have become familiar, rather than alternative agencies or services that might be created. It also depends, it may be said, on a concept of social change as it is perceived within society rather than as something absolute or 'objective'. So the policy analyst has to remember that the discussion of social problems is biased, whether in Parliament, the press, Government publications or even the social science journals. There are intellectual fashions in each phase of history when some problems are illuminated and others ignored, and this applies, though in different degrees, to all the contending interest groups of the policy system. It also applies to the perception of strategies.

Different interest groups see problems differently of course, and present different kinds of evidence and different policy solutions. This is as true of respected scientific foundations, bureaucratic establish-ments or professional scientists working in universities as of political campaigners, though the former usually express things more subtly. The scope, definition and presentation of official statistics, for example, depend in large part on perceptions of the functions of the civil service by its members. Such statistics will tend to be presented in forms which are favourable to past administration, do not portray any need for administrative or political upheaval and seem to heal conflicts within society. (See Chapter 22 for fuller discussion.) The research studies of academics may in some respects achieve more detachment, for example, by considering social conditions in relation to standards which are differ-ent from those of the bureaucratic establishment, in particular the stan-dards sometimes adopted in overseas countries, but they are also deeply influenced by contemporaneous university and disciplinary dictates. The university ethic of scientism and political neutrality drives academics towards topics which are neither contemporaneous nor contentious. The ivory tower is often reflected in choice of subject and manner of inquiry. And disciplinary conventions may encourage research selected more for its historical or theoretical status than its theoretical or practical worth. In Britain at the time of writing a large proportion of university and college courses in sociological theory, and a surprisingly large number of academic papers and books, are devoted to the history of sociology, and especially to the early rather than any modern applications or developments of the work of Marx, Durkheim and Weber.

An example of how the growth of sociology as an academic discipline has been drawn away from policy is provided by the United States. At the turn of the century a number of the pioneers of American sociology were deeply involved in the policy issues of their day — including city welfare, planning, and government. This changed, it is said, because sociology rapidly became an academic discipline and its representatives devoted more of their time to teaching, because attempts were made to create a scientific sociological method and because professional bureaucrats secured control from any outside interference.(11)

Societies find means of reconciling or managing the different policy standpoints of major contending interest groups. An overall social policy is usually identifiable as well as policies which are departmental, agency, employer-financed, union or otherwise specific. In theory the sociologist can characterize and describe the policies of different societies, taking account in many of them of the contributions of institutions other than the State, such as the Church and industry. In doing this some independent standard of comparison is helpful. That standard can be derived from the different policies of other societies. It throws into relief the special perception of needs and goals and the value attached to particular institutions and strategies by one society. But this cannot be a complete perspective, because there may be needs unperceived, institutions undeveloped and strategies untried in any society, and these deserve to be considered. Another standard of comparison is that supplied by some conception of 'need', fed by the legitimation of defined objectives of social change (discussed more fully elsewhere in this book, for example, Chapters 2 and 14). This presumes either consensus about those objectives or at least tacit acceptance that there are alternative objectives to those being pursued, or alternative means to those being employed, which are unobjectionable. Whether such a perspective differs in principle or only in degree from that adopted by society it is sufficiently distant or independent to justify the epithet of 'planning'. Through the method of international comparison and the operationalization of some concept of measured need, which can be regarded fundamentally as the application of the comparative method to the study of inequalities between the component sub-systems, structures and groups of society, social policy can be better understood.

Social Objectives and the Policy System

How might this approach to social policy be developed? One of the sociologist's tasks will be to identify the goals or objectives which are either explicitly proclaimed or implicitly adopted or favoured in policy, and attempt to place them in rank order. Thus, in relation to particular measures, he can show what objectives, like the abolition of poverty, abolition of squalor, equality of educational opportunity, harmony between races, integration of the community, restoration of health and prevention of disease, and equality of treatment before the law, have in fact been proclaimed publicly and may have been spelt out in legislation, and administrative regulations. Through content analysis of politicians' speeches and professional journals, or measures of the allocation of resources, he can begin to show the relative importance that has been or is attached to different (and sometimes conflicting) objectives. He can show how ministers, civil servants, members of the professions and others interpret general objectives in their specific decisions and actions.

Similarly, by analysing specific decisions and actions he can reveal objectives or values which are implicitly held. Proclamations are rarely made in public about some values which are strongly held and pursued. For example, the preservation of social control by educated élites, the conferment of markedly different rewards upon people of equal skill and ability, the preferment of those with private property, and the protection of male privileges and domination, can each be shown to be objectives being pursued institutionally. Fundamentally, some independent standard or assessment of society has to be postulated if the objectives being pursued by a society are to be identified, and that pursuit evaluated. As policy analyst, the sociologist cannot be just a servant of society — whether in the capacity of servant of the government, local authority or private agency. He cannot but also be its judge. However hard he strives for detachment, particular values and selected standards of comparison are inevitably built into his work. This is best acknowledged openly and discussed. He must therefore recognize the desirability as well as necessity of identifying the alternative objectives, rank order of objectives, and means towards the fulfilment of either existing or alternative objectives which his analysis of social conditions or needs suggest should be adopted.

In analysing the policy system its structure has to be formally identified. There are at least six headings:

1. *The organizations, agencies and services* set up formally to promote

social objectives — such as the health, education, social security, housing and welfare services; and the organizations, agencies and services in fact serving implicit objectives. The organizational network and interconnections, and the internal structure and functions of each organization or agency.

2. *The body of laws, statutes, and regulations* and the administrative procedures governing the operation of these agencies and governing too the relations between them and their recipient populations.

3. *Professional and other staff* attached to the agencies, wholly or semi-independently. The structure of the professions, and the qualifications, characteristics and ideology of professional and other groups of staff, and the processes of recruitment.

4. *The source and allocation of financial resources,* including internal distribution within services and departments as well as between them.

5. *The recipients or beneficiaries* of services, and any collective organization among and between them, including unions and consumer associations.

6. *The information* distributed about the objectives, procedures and values of the policy system, including that supplied to the public directly by advice and information bureaux and units and in a range of agency-sponsored booklets and leaflets, but also directly and indirectly through the mass media; and specialized information in research, statistical and planning journals.

These six factors and their interrelationship have to be examined in analysing the history and effect of individual and general policies.

Much of the specialized work in sociology is in practice policy-oriented. Contributions to the sociology of education in the United States and Britain make this abundantly clear.(12) Educational sociologists, criminologists and medical sociologists, for example, are conscious of the relevance of their work to developments in policy and often actively contribute to them. However, an overall policy perspective in sociology is lacking — as various attempts to synthesize discussion of social problems show.(13) One source of trouble lies in the tendency of research on social stratification to concentrate on status and status mobility rather than on either the unequal distribution of income and wealth or the ways in which the organizations and agencies which distribute these resources operate.(14) There are various explanations for the failure in sociology to adopt a thorough-going policy perspective: including the shortage of 'hard' information about the allocation of resources (for example, industrial welfare benefits and the social effects of the activities of insurance companies); the difficulties of unravelling the complex intervention of different public and private institutions in determining the final allocation to households and individuals of resources; the difficulties of mounting survey research on a national scale or of undertaking research at all into institutions such as the Board of Inland Revenue, the Treasury, the Banks, Building Societies and even the Supplementary Benefits Commission, because the research is felt to have threatening political implications; and the apparent ease with which data about attitudes rather than about conditions, or about subjective rather than objective deprivation, can be secured.

In recent years some sociologists have begun to formulate integrated conceptions. In his book *The Active Society* Amitai Etzioni, for example, discusses the historical circumstances under which societies acquire self-control, that is, become responsive to their changing membership and are engaged in an intensive and perpetual self-transformation.(15) Through an exploration of the barriers which deter societies from realizing their values he suggests that sociologists can investigate ways to accelerate their fulfilment. Self-control is exercised through the development of knowledge, the relationship between knowledge and control, the distribution and reallocation of knowledge, the promotion of social self-consciousness, strategies of decision-making, namely rationalism, incrementalism and mixed-scanning, the mobilization of collectivities and resources, the reduction of alienation and the formation of consensus. His is a normative view which does not discriminate between different values.(16) He seems to be more interested in means than ends. For this reason the management of society becomes a very broad function and encompasses all spheres of activity — including defence, foreign affairs and the control of the economy. It becomes a rather bureaucratic and mechanistic process — because the diffusion of knowledge, responsiveness to new ideas and the communication of control are paramount. And it plays down the existence of conflicting or competitive social networks having their own alternative goals and even methods of accountability. The awkward problem of choosing goals, or even of reconciling the conflicting goals of contending groups, which might be resolved only by appealing to evidence about the condition of society and in particular social inequalities, tends to be avoided. Indeed, the question of social structure and especially social stratification is muted. Nonetheless, Etzioni shows the importance of policy control in the analysis of society.

Similarly, Herbert Gans in the United States, and sociologists like Norman Dennis and Ray Pahl in Britain, have contributed to our understanding of urban development because they have insisted on the need for policy or planning analysis.(17) In illustrating the uses of sociology Gans has argued that the sociologist should participate directly in action programmes, and particularly that he can help to develop a theoretical scheme to guide the planning, help to determine goals, help to develop means and programmes, and finally evaluate action.(18) Surprisingly he assumes that the sociologist will now for the first time have to exercise value judgements. He does not offer any intellectual framework according to which the sociologist might understand and evaluate the policy-maker's perceptions, estimates of need and proposals for action. He seems to subscribe to an interpretation of the sociologist's role which makes him the lackey of any policy-maker's values, incapable of independent assessment and alternative planning. Thus, in suggesting how the sociologist might assist the various proposals for what he describes as 'guided mobility', he puts forward a timid theoretical scheme which subscribes to, and does not presume to question, and confirm or reject, the thesis of lower-class disorganization. By contrast with much American writing on urban planning, the work of Pahl, Rex and Dennis in Britain has given far more attention to social inequality, particularly to occupational and housing classes, and hence to questions of equity and equality in policy.(19)

The first problem, then, is to achieve an integrated conception of social policy as it has been developed and is operated in any society. Such policy could be flatulent, slow-moving and conservative, or it could be revolutionary, depending on the standard applied. The point is that some external standard has to be applied. Thus, a symposium on 'Approaches to Social Policy Plans' was held in Geneva in November 1969, under the auspices of the International Institute for Labour Studies. According to one contributor, social policy in the future was likely to be centred on the adaptation of societies to accelerated changes in economic and social structures and values. With affluence social policy would grow rather than decline in importance because instead of the former problems of integrating the manual working population emphasis would have to be given to raising social levels and improving social mobility — by reducing inequalities of opportunity, education, environment, and 'influence on social decision-making'.(20) The image seems to be of a meritocratic, highly-organized society committed to a high rate of economic growth and therefore to strong hierarchical control and gross inequalities in earnings and incomes even if there were to be a double shift of population — of younger adults to the relatively more numerous managerial, professional and other white-collar jobs in the middle and upper ranks of the occupational distribution, and of the elderly, disabled and middle-aged redundant to the dependent 'underclass' of the distribution. (See Chapter 24.) An alternative image would of course be a society committed to equal distribution of resources — even if this had the consequence, which it might not, of restricting economic growth. But how do these images come to be held? How is it that the former tends to reign? I would suggest that it is partly, though only partly, by default of those sociologists who have presented limited and usually over-optimistic interpretations of social change, at least for capitalist industrial societies. Among other things the particular balance of value-orientations in social policy has not been analysed and described, and the recommendations about social structure, especially stratification, which are implicit in social policy have not been made explicit.

The Sociological Treatment of Social Change

It is therefore as important to review carefully our concepts of social change as it is the corresponding concepts of social policy. Inconsequential changes have been misrepresented as being of major structural significance and an impression has been conveyed of continuing qualitative advance, when deep-seated inequalities in the distribution of resources, power and opportunities have remained in many societies, and in certain respects, and in some if not many societies, have become wider. By the criterion of inequality the recent history of industrial societies might be said to be remarkable for the absence of change. Mere reflection about this possibility gives previous sociological theories of social change fresh perspective.

Previous approaches to the conception of social change need to be critically discussed because they provide the basis for clearer thinking about policy. There appear to have been three predominant themes in sociological analysis of change. Most important is the theme of *homogeneity to heterogeneity*. Herbert Spencer said that this change 'was multitudinously exemplified; up from the simple tribe, alike in all its parts, to the civilized nation, full of structural and functional unlikeness.' Durkheim used the division of labour as his basic explanatory concept in the process of social change. A job which involved two or more major functions would tend to be split into two, and in time a more specialized occupational structure would develop. Parsons, Smelser and others have generalized the same theme into one of structural differentiation, or the establishment of more specialized and more autonomous social units as time goes on.

Linked closely with this theme are two other themes, that of *community to organized society* and of *social progress*. While these themes have of course been given different weight by different sociologists, they are continually drawn upon to describe the process of industrialization, modernization and development. To spurious biological or physiological models of change has been added the notion of the mechanical rationalization of society and the notion, too, of the steadily advancing superiority of contemporary society over all previous forms.

The extent to which nineteenth-century sociologists were captives of the prevailing ideologies, and social structure of their day, should not be neglected. This is how their contributions might best be understood. And, considering the time when they wrote, the crudity of their descriptions of social change can be forgiven. In his account of *Gemeinschaft und Gesellschaft,* for example, Tönnies represented much of the early sociological writing about urbanization and industrialization. The folk or rural culture was doomed to dissolution. Instead of relatively spontaneous, closely-knit communities there were to be relatively contrived, specialized and loosely-knit social units under formalized political control. The *Gemeinschaft* was characterized by the social will, he said, as concord, folkways, mores and religion, and the *Gesellschaft* as convention, legislation and public opinion.

By making rural community and industrial or urban society polar opposites, or at least distinct types, and declaring that the latter were replacing the former some early sociologists tended to convert discontent with contemporary industrial and urban conditions into generalized nostalgia for a way of life which was also represented as no longer possible. They were thus playing an essentially conservative and compliant role.(21) They did not really *investigate* contemporary society or try to identify in the rural community those kinds of relationships and structural characteristics which it was desirable to preserve and which *could* be preserved. Some modern sociologists are wrestling with the task of replacing the Tönnies approach to theory. By rejecting the rural-urban continuum they are calling attention to the fact that in two different *locales* modern and traditional, large and small-scale, and national and local systems of relationships are each manifest but have different weight and mix.(22)

It was very understandable that the early sociologists should have expressed these three themes crudely. They lacked precise empirical evidence. They were eager to proselytize the claims of an embryonic science. They felt compelled, if only unconsciously, to respond to the demand for a justification of nineteenth-century empire-building and nineteenth-century industrial developments. It is *less* easy to forgive some modern adaptations of these theories. Structural differentiation as a more generalized conception of 'the division of labour' has been given a major place in the history of sociology. But it has limited possibilities. Smelser, for example, states that the concept of structural differentiation can be used to analyse the marked break in established patterns of social and economic life in periods of development. It refers, he goes on, to the evolution from a multi-functional role structure to several more specialized structures, and he gives certain examples: (i) in the transition from domestic to factory industry, the division of labour increases, and the economic activities previously lodged in the family move to the firm; (ii) with the development of formal education the training functions previously performed by the family and Church are established in a more specialized unit, the school; and (iii) the development from tribal factions to modern political parties again transfers certain functions from kinship and religious systems to a different and more complex structure.(23) In his *Social Change in the Industrial Revolution,* he defines structural differentiation as a process whereby *'one* social role or organization . . . differentiates into *two or more* roles or organizations which function more effectively in the new historical circumstances.' (24) He does not realize, as discussed below, that the process is often tantamount to the creation of gross inequality.

The antithesis that is frequently made between the starting and finishing points in a period of change begins to break down upon analysis. There are three categories of evidence, which can only be sketched in barest outline here. First, historical. Laslett and others have shown that there were in fact few extended families living as households in pre-industrial England, France and America.(25) The nuclear family was by no means cohesive, since many children went to work and lived in the households of strangers at the age of eight, nine or ten. Such education as children received from the family or church rarely resembled anything in the modern sense of the word. And the relatively flimsy data on occupation suggest that only about 40 per cent of employed or occupied adults could be said to be within the field of family production or the 'domestic' economy.

Secondly, there is evidence from contemporary pre-industrial societies, much of which suggests, *depending crucially on the size of population of such societies,* that usually there are embryonic 'modern' organizations not strictly tied to the kinship structure, and a more specialized role-structure than is suggested in the differentiation model.

Thirdly, there is evidence from present industrial society. This shows that primary group associations flourish widely, not only in terms of the survival or re-generation of extended family relations in urban areas but also in clubs and relations between neighbours which flourish in suburban areas of many cities. Specialized units and roles are sometimes shown by the evidence to coalesce. Sometimes altogether new functions seem to be generated.

A very early sociologist, Adam Ferguson, writing in 1767, believed that the division of labour was an index of a society's decline. He developed a cyclical theory of history and found evidence of a greater division of labour in ancient Greece, Rome and China than in the societies which succeeded them. The division of labour, he argued, corresponded with a decline in the conception of citizenship, where everyone is concerned with public welfare. The nineteenth-century theorists of simple progress failed to learn from him.(26)

Sociological Themes of Change Applied to the History of the Welfare State

Histories of the 'Welfare State' faithfully incorporate the three themes identified above, and can therefore be criticized for the same reasons. All-purpose social services are believed to have gradually sub-divided into a variety of specialist sub-units on the model of structural differentiation. One example is the development of specialized institutions (hospitals for mothers, for children, and for those suffering from particular disease, including mental diseases, and welfare homes for children, the disabled and the aged) from the general mixed workhouse between the early part of the nineteenth-century and the middle of the twentieth-century. Another is the sub-division of specialized units specifically within medicine, the penal service, and the evolution of a more specialized role-structure in social work. From the rather condescending amateur lady visitors with hats and furs from the Charity Organization Society developed a range of specialist caseworkers: psychiatric social workers, child-care officers, and probation officers. Again might be instanced the evolution of a 'specialized' system of schools, culminating in the tripartite educational system formally established in 1944 in Britain. But, as this last example suggests, the structural differentiationist has failed to note that 'specialization' is normally a euphemism for 'ranking' or the division of an institution into grossly unequal elements. There have been recent pressures to end or at least minimize or counterbalance forms of ranking or streaming, through the comprehensive school, the district general hospital, the health centre and the generic social worker. There have been reactions too to social specialization when it has involved physical segregation of the mentally handicapped, physically disabled and aged from the 'ordinary' population or of the educationally backward from ordinary schools. Differentiation is therefore far from being the whole story. As a process it can be represented, to the discomfiture of its progenitors, as the creation of inequality in society. As a set of assumptions it is deeply imprinted in the consciousness of current policy-making.

The second theme abounds in the mythology of the Welfare State. It is widely assumed that the Welfare State, making provision from cradle to grave, has been taking over the functions of the family. Individuals were becoming less self-reliant and were having less freedom and the aged, instead of being cosseted by their families, were being thrown on to the mercy of the Welfare State and admitted to Homes and hospitals. More children were taken into care. In becoming professionally more efficient, services which substituted for the family and community were becoming impersonal. This widespread public belief about many of the changes taking place feeds not only on the writings of the early sociologists but also on the perennial misgivings of old men, whatever point in history they live. Even notable sociologists seem sometimes to mistake old age for unfavourable social change, especially when they themselves have lacked children.(27) It would be possible to document for different centuries the complaints of many middle-aged and elderly people that children no longer respect their elders like *they* did, that the family has become less cohesive and that life has lost its social intimacy and warmth. In part such statements are presented as accounts of social change when they should be presented as views about individual ageing. In part they serve the function of binding families more tightly together by favouring the maintenance of family obligations. However, this part of the theory of structural differentiation has grave limitations. In Britain and other industrial countries new services for the chronic sick and aged, such as home help, visiting and chiropody services, have grown up rapidly since the war and in some countries now cover fairly substantial minorities. A cross-national survey in the United States, Britain and Denmark which was carried out in 1962 showed that some of these services were *substituting* for the family chiefly in instances where there was no family.(28) Either the old person had no children, or if he had one or two children they were mentally handicapped or in hospital, or living far away. A majority of those receiving services had no family or none available. The welfare services are not *replacing* the functions of the family so much as providing them when the family does not exist. For these people lacking family the welfare services supply a substitute family. But there are other complications. The study also pointed out that certain services, like home nursing or chiropody, were skilled services provided by professionally trained people. These functions the family could never have provided. They could be said to augment or add to the functions performed by the family. The evolution of skilled services does not so much *displace* the functions that the family performs as refine and complement them. Moreover (a third point), the growth of a network of institutionalized services usually obliges the family to review the functions it performs. Knowledge about the importance of warmth and diet and the significance of particular ailments is diffused. Family services are in some respects intensified and their standards of care are raised.

The general conclusions that may be drawn from this illustration could be repeated many times over in reference to the theory of structural differentiation put forward by Smelser and Parsons. There is indeed a process of differentiation but there are also processes of adaptation, augmentation, coalescence and independent generation.(29)

Finally, most histories of the growth of the social services, like Bruce's *The Coming of the Welfare State,* take our third theme of social progress for granted. Continuing social advance is represented usually either by recounting the dates on which parliamentary bills were finally enacted, or by listing additions to buildings and staff, such as nurses, teachers and social workers. Searching notions of relativity — about the quality of services actually delivered by the education, health and welfare services, compared with ten or twenty years previously, the relationship of social services to changes in population numbers and structure and whether the services are, in the process of development, keeping up with the emerging disservices of industrialization and urbanization — are not applied. This explanatory strategy can be traced to writers like Herbert Spencer and Auguste Comte. The more pessimistic theories of Spengler and Toynbee, envisaging a cyclical series of ups and downs, or a long process of growth, fruition and eventual disintegration, are not seriously applied to Welfare State history, and Marxist applications are rare as well as undeveloped.(30) And yet there have been periods in history not only when social policy has been relatively stagnant, as in Britain in the 1920s, but when policy has regressed, in the sense that measures and resources have not been introduced on a scale sufficient to offset new inequalities and deprivations. It is possible to argue that Britain became more polarized, torn by conflict and mistrust between minorities, or divided between the haves and have nots as a direct consequence of social policy in the 1830s, 1840s, 1870s and 1930s, and even late 1960s and early 1970s than in the periods immediately preceding these watersheds. And particular measures in history, like the over-zealous building of workhouses, then asylums, then orphanages for children and now residential hostels for the handicapped and aged; streaming in primary and secondary schools and the post-1944 tripartite division of schools; and the 1961 and 1973 earnings-related pension schemes, might all be castigated as socially regressive.

The Definition of Social Change
1. Objectivity
Past theories of social change, even when they have been vague and implicit in argument, have therefore governed our conceptions of social policy and, as we have seen, have usually limited our vision. How can an alternative theory begin to be constructed? What can we mean by social change? Subjective perceptions of change have to be distinguished from change which can be objectively assessed. A man who gets older may lament the loss of things passed. Yet he may be lamenting lost youth rather than changed social structure. The perception of change is an important datum for the sociologist and from the start he must be aware

that subjective and collective perceptions of change may be out of phase with any objective evaluation of change. During the last hundred years, for example, changes in the consciousness of various élite groups and of the general public about the extent to which women are unequally treated have not been consistent with assessable objective situations — as might be expressed by relativity of earnings, access to different occupations, role in political decision-making, equality with men in legal rights.

Quite why levels of public consciousness of change are erratic in relation to objective trends of change must be an underlying preoccupation of the sociologist. Consciousness of deprivation may lead to demands for change. Sometimes it seems that structural changes prompt change of consciousness; sometimes changes of consciousness seem to arise despite structural stability. By examining different examples we can perhaps learn under what conditions attempts to influence public consciousness — by disseminating information or propaganda, for example — are likely to accelerate the introduction of structural changes. But by distinguishing between perceptions and the actuality of change we demonstrate the need to collect data systematically about both.

The problem of distinguishing subjective and objective change is very subtle. The measurement of change is not just a technical problem. Sociologists have to strive to adopt measures which are independent of those used by society. I do not mean that they are all or sometimes suspect, but just that they are incomplete and culture-bound. Thus official statistics do not always cover subjects which arouse controversy or conflict and are very sparing about social inequality. Bureaucracies and governments have a vested interest in demonstrating social progress. The politician presents those statistics about his government's course which put that course in the most favourable light. Because the civil servant has to play a compliant role and has little interest in demonstrating needs which imply administrative upheaval he will offer indirect support to the politician in the presentation of information. So the statistics we use to assess trends may differ at different points in time in their relevance to reality. Administrative measures may become out-of-date and although 'objective', 'scientific' or merely alternative conceptions that are brought into circulation by social scientists have an influence on the administrative or social definition, collection and presentation of statistics, these conceptions tend to be distorted in the process of adaptation to social use and are rapidly outdated. There is then a kind of running battle between objective and social definitions of change for the possession of men's allegiance. The upshot of this argument, then, is not merely that shrewd technical definitions or measures of change need to be invented but that such definitions or measures have to be established independently of bureaucratic or political control. To some extent too they have to be established independently of the conceptions and techniques which happen to be fashionable among any group of social scientists.(31)

2. Structure

A second distinction has to be made between changes of style or scale, and those of structure. Changes in styles of living — in mode of dress, housing and furnishings, type of diet or entertainment and styling of cars and buses, for example — are not necessarily symptomatic of deep-seated change in the social system. In themselves they are not therefore of much sociological interest. It is easy for us to agree that changes of appearance — whether in dress, make-up, architecture or the change from one type of transport to another — may belie the persistence of attitudes, behaviour and social organization. In fact, of course, there are connections between style and structure, and the distinction must be regarded as a starting point for analysis. There are many ways in which changes of appearance can convey the illusion of change. Governments sometimes seem to accept arguments for change, but legislation which is introduced falls short of expectations and there is little result. Traditional practices and institutions may merely be given new labels and not new functions. Change may be more nominal than real. For the sociologist the criteria of change have to be applied with sophistication. Slaves may become servants, asylums become mental hospitals and workhouses become residential homes; women may get the vote and education may be extended to all children. Yet when documentary evidence can be scrutinized for the periods immediately preceding and immediately following these watersheds the quantitative and even qualitative difference between the two situations so far as the system of social institutions and the hierarchical structure of roles is concerned, may be infinitesimal.

Yet in looking for change we have to do more than look behind the façade of appearances. By social change the sociologist is referring to differences in time of social structure, relationships, norms, roles and statuses. He is looking for differences in the number, type and balance of the sub-systems composing society, such as the relationship between family, community and urban society, the relationship between different ethnic and racial minorities, or a significant increase or decrease in social inequality. The fact that new towns are built is of no sociological interest in itself. Throughout history settlements and towns have always been built. What is of interest is why a concept of the new town which involves certain social objectives comes to be formulated, and whether it has been or can be applied in practice — for then a social change will have been introduced. Nor can we take some indices of change as demonstrating change in social structure. Thus in demography there are rates of population growth, fertility and marriage. These may or may not lead to, or correspond with, changes of structure. A population can double its size without society changing its type. The proportion of married couples having four or more children can decline considerably without leading to much change in the norms of child upbringing or family life. Again, to take a third example, a society may gradually become more affluent, but if the affluence is distributed proportionately there are grounds for asking whether there is any evidence of corresponding social change.

All of this is intended to sharpen our consciousness of the importance of asking what is meant by social change, so that hypotheses can begin to be formulated and policies of intervention evaluated and realistic alternatives devised. Like other conceptions a sociological conception is not ready-made. In writing about social change Radcliffe-Brown argued that there were internal readjustments in society which did not affect structural form. In his book *Social Change* Robert Nisbet follows suit. Thus, through marriage, two former family groups were reorganized and a new family group formed.(32) While there was change from the viewpoint of the family groups involved this did not imply change in the larger society. This is, of course, similar in principle to the sequence of changes experienced by the individual during his lifetime. The changing composition and number of sub-groups must not be mistaken, any more than individual ageing, for social change. But there remains a logical dilemma which is difficult to resolve. Societies are part of world society and may be changing in ways that are analogous to the formation, ageing and fusion of nuclear or immediate families. Without more knowledge than we possess of the criteria by which we can disentangle the continuities and discontinuities of form it would be difficult to press this analogy to its logical conclusion. We know something about stages in the life-cycle of the immediate and extended families. We know next to nothing about the stages in the life-cycle of societies as defined in their interaction within world society.

3. The Underlying Conception

Even when understood sociologically change may be very different in scale or importance. Thus although the reduction in average sizes of the immediate or nuclear family may represent a change in structure which has certain ramifications, the ramifications may not be very extensive. Inequalities between the sexes, rich and poor, black and white, rural and urban, may be little affected. Again, there may be shifts in time of the status of particular roles and occupations and while these may be of intrinsic importance they may not have much effect on class structure. But if society can be analysed and understood primarily in terms of the concept of inequality, say, then social change has to be measured principally in terms of changes in the pattern of inequality. And social policy has to be evaluated primarily in terms of the effectiveness of the design and realization of the reduction or increase of inequality.

I am suggesting that we cannot rate all discernible social changes, of whatever type, as of equivalent value. Our studies become indiscriminate and unco-ordinated, and the relatedness of structural effects is neglected. Some changes are of more importance, in terms of scope or degree or ramifying effect, than others. The organizing principles which we choose to illuminate social structure will be the ones which must also be used to test change. On grounds of both potentiality for operational definition and measurement, and the need to study the interrelationship of different aspects of social structure and organization, I choose 'inequality' as the distinctive universal feature of social structure. I should point out, however, that this thematic concept should not be treated only in terms of economic class or social hierarchy, although these are principal components of meaning. There is inequality in degree of social integration or isolation as well.

By insisting on criteria of importance in studying social change we are making major as well as minor claims. Thus the concepts of evolution, progress, modernization, development and revolution must be regarded as different versions of, or subordinated to, the concept of social change. They embody notions of scale and regularity or irregularity which have to be tested. Darwin's *Origin of the Species* was built on the idea of slow, gradual and continuous modifications. Some of the work in modern genetics conflicts, of course, with that idea. Early sociologists applied the idea to the development of human society. Durkheim was one of the first, however, to demonstrate that 'the antecedent state does not produce the subsequent one . . . the stages that humanity traverses successively do not engender one another.'(33) Much social change is discontinuous. Therefore we have to distinguish between, and account for, revolutionary and gradual change.

This implies minor claims too. At the very least we have to apply appropriate comparative measures in studying social change. The most straightforward is a simple comparison between two situations at different points in time. Thus, whether studying the abolition of slavery, the introduction in the nineteenth century of sanitary services, the movement for prison reform or the control of drug addiction, two separated points in time can be chosen and different situations specified and accounted for. But without a wider perspective this model can be very misleading. Thus if social change is defined very broadly then change can be said to be a normal state of affairs for most societies, and what may become important to identify are accelerations in the rate of change or marked differences in the rate and kind of change between one society and another. Thus nearly all societies have a positive rate of economic growth, and it is less interesting to establish this fact than to identify and explain periods when Britain, say, greatly exceeds or falls short of its 'normal' rate, or why Japan or West Germany have for several years at a time experienced quite exceptional rates of growth. Sociologists have to begin developing methods of measuring rates of change. Perhaps annual surveys showing changes in the incidence of isolation or poverty and distribution of income or of wealth represent the eventual objective. Measures of social mobility exist but are still very crude. Thus, Bendix and Lipset found remarkable similarity in rates of mobility between different societies when they concentrated only on the division between manual and non-manual workers. But some studies of particular societies were very deficient or were carried out at widely different points in time, and when S.M.Miller and others examined finer categories of social class much greater differences among societies could be seen to exist.

Conceptions, operational measurement and explanations of social change therefore have to be developed simultaneously.(34) In the pursuit of understanding and clarity they are mutually reinforcing. But each of them also incorporates prescriptions for, or assumptions about, social policy just as each of them incorporates assumptions about social structure. And in elucidating these, sociology confronts its most important and constructive challenge.

Notes

1. Marshall, T.H., *Social Policy in the Twentieth Century*, Hutchinson, 2nd ed., 1967, p.6 (also see p.166).

2. Beales, H.L., *The Making of Social Policy in the Nineteenth Century*, Hobhouse Memorial Lecture, 1945, O.U.P., 1946; Carr, E.H., *The New Society*, 1951; Polanyi, K., *The Great Transformation*, 1944; Bruce, M., *The Coming of the Welfare State*, Batsford, 1961; Robson, W.A., *The Welfare State*, Hobhouse Memorial Lecture, 1956, O.U.P., 1957; Gregg, P., *The Welfare State*, Harrap, 1967.

3. For example, Marshall, T.H., op. cit.

4. See the account of the history and scope of social systems accounting by Bertram M. Gross in Bauer, R.A. (ed.), *Social Indicators*, Cambridge, Mass., The M.I.T. Press, 1966. What is surprising is the failure until recently to grasp the implications of such work for the conceptual foundations of teaching about social policy. While a vast range of literature in economics, sociology and political science might be cited to illustrate a general 'systems' approach, including that of Talcott Parsons, Gabriel Almond, Daniel Lerner, Robin Williams, David Easton, and Bruce Russett and his colleagues, the recent work on output budgeting, cost-benefit analysis, Planning Programming Budgeting

System, social indicators, public expenditure forecasting and so on illustrate in different ways the importance and value of devising categories which are not just administrative categories for the purposes of improving the quality and cogency of social analysis and planning. For a severely critical account of some modern applications, however, see Hoos, I.R., *Systems Analysis in Social Policy*, Research Monographs, no. 19, The Institute of Economic Affairs, 1969. See also Self, P., 'Nonsense on Stilts: Cost-Benefit Analysis and the Roskill Commission', *Political Quarterly*, July-1970; and Perman D., *Cublington: A Blueprint for Resistance*, Bodley Head, 1973.

5. Richard Titmuss called attention in 1955 to three categories of welfare: social welfare, fiscal welfare and occupational welfare. 'The definition, for most purposes, of what is a social service should take its stand on aims; not on the administrative methods and institutional devices employed to achieve them.' Titmuss, R.M., *Essays on 'The Welfare State'*, Allen & Unwin, 1958, p.42.

6. *The Programme for Controlling Inflation: The Second Stage*, Cmnd. 5205, H.M.S.O., January 1973, p.3.

7. ibid.; *The Price and Pay Code: A Consultative Document*, Cmnd. 5247, H.M.S.O., February 1973; *The Counter-Inflation Programme: The Operation of Stage Two*, Cmnd. 5267, H.M.S.O., March 1973.

8. A number of social scientists have in recent years adopted implicitly or explicitly a broad definition of social policy. They have all drawn heavily on the writing of Richard Titmuss, particularly his *Essays on the Welfare State*, Allen & Unwin, 1958. Among the most important are Schorr, A.L., *Explorations in Social Policy*, Basic Books, New York, 1968; Miller, S.M., and Roby, P., *The Future of Inequality*, Basic Books, New York, 1970, and Rein, M., *Social Policy: Issues of Choice and Change*, Random House, New York, 1970. For an interesting discussion of the definitions adopted by writers in different countries, see also Gil, D.G., *Unravelling Social Policy*, Schenkman, Cambridge, Mass., 1973, Chapter I.

9. Each year a special analysis of the incidence of taxes and social service benefits, based on data from the Government's Family Expenditure Survey, is published in *Economic Trends*. See, for example, *Economic Trends*, no. 229, November 1972. For a recent review of such material see Webb, A., and Sieve, J., *Income Distribution and the Welfare State*, Bell, 1970.

10. Some of the developments in public discussion about social security suggest that in the future statistical predictions of effects of alternative policy proposals will play an increasingly influential part. The recent history of concern about 'clawback' and the 'poverty trap' are examples.

11. Gans, H., 'Urban Poverty and Social Planning', in Lazarsfeld, P.F., *et. al.* (eds.), *The Uses of Sociology*, Basic Books, New York, 1967, pp. 438-9.

12. Coleman J.S., *Equality of Educational Opportunity*, Washington D.C., U.S. Dept. of Health, Education and Welfare, 1966; Douglas J.W.B., *The Home and the School*, MacGibbon & Kee, 1966; Peters, R.S. (ed.), *Perspectives on Plowden*, Routledge & Kegan Paul, 1969.

13. Merton, R.K., and Nisbet, R.A. (eds.), *Contemporary Social Problems*, 2nd ed., Harcourt, Brace and World, New York, 1966; Smigel, E.O. (ed.), *Handbook on the Study of Social Problems*, Rand McNally, Chicago, 1971.

14. Miller, S.M., 'Comparative Social Mobility', *Current Sociology*, vol. 9, 1960; Hope, K. (ed.), *The Analysis of Social Mobility*, Clarendon Press, 1972.

15. Etzioni, A., *The Active Society*, The Free Press, New York, 1968.

16. 'The study of the active society is, therefore, the study of a society engaged in realising *its* values and an exploration of the barriers which deter societies from realising these values and investigating ways to accelerate their fulfilment.' Etzioni, A., op. cit., p.13.

17. Gans, H.J., *People and Plans*, New York, Basic Books, 1968; Dennis, N., *People and Planning*, Faber, 1970; Pahl, R., 'Poverty and the Urban System' in Chisholm, M, and Manners, G., *Spatial Policy Problems of the British Economy*, Cambridge University Press, 1972; and Pahl, R., 'Social Processes and Urban Planning'. (Forthcoming.)

18. Gans, H.J., 'Urban Poverty and Social Planning', op. cit.

19. Rex, J. and Moore, R., *Race, Community and Conflict: A Study of Sparkbrook*, O.U.P., 1967 (esp. Chapter 1); Dennis, N., *People and Planning: The Sociology of Housing in Sunderland*, Faber, 1970.

20. Gunter, H., 'Future Social Policy Requirements of Modern Societies: A Postscript', *Bulletin of the International Institute for Labour Studies*, no. 8, 1971, p. 135.

21. In some of his recent work (cited earlier) Ray Pahl has enlarged my understanding of the conservative functions of sociology.

22. See the historical account of theories of community in Chapter 2 of Bell, C., and Newby, H., *Community Studies*, Allen & Unwin, 1971; and Stacey, M., 'The Myth of Community Studies', *British Journal of Sociology*, 20, 1969; Pahl, R., 'The Rural-Urban Continuum', in his *Readings in Urban Sociology*, Pergamon Press, 1968; Warren, R., *The Community in America*, Rand McNally, Chicago, 1963.

23. Smelser, N.J., 'Towards a Theory of Modernisation', in Etzioni, A., and Etzioni, E., (eds.), *Social Change*, Basic Books, New York, 1964, p.261.

24. Smelser, N.J., *Social Change in the Industrial Revolution*, Routledge & Kegan Paul, 1959.

25. Laslett, P., *The World We Have Lost*, Methuen, 1965.

26. I owe this reference to Michael Mann. See Ferguson, A., *An Essay on the History of Civil Society*, 1767.

27. The later writings of Ernest Burgess afford an example.

28. Shanas, E., *et al.*, *Old People in Three Industrial Societies*, Routledge & Kegan Paul and Atherton, New York, 1968, especially Chapter 5.

29. See, for example, Etzioni's brief outline of an alternative theory of epigenesis in his *Studies in Social Change*, Holt, Rinehart & Winston, New York, 1966.

30. One of the best attempts so far by a British sociologist to discuss theories of the rise of the Welfare State is by Dorothy Wedderburn in her paper, 'Facts and Theories of the Welfare State', in Miliband, R., and Saville, J. (eds.), *Socialist Register for 1965*, Merlin, 1965. An interesting account of the bearing

of the work of Durkheim, Spencer, Marx and Weber upon social policy and the rise of the Welfare State is given by Pinker, R., *Social Theory and Social Policy,* Heinemann, 1971, Chapter 1.

31. Gunnar Myrdal has called attention to some of the dangers of identifying too readily with intellectual fashions: 'The scientists in any particular institutional and political setting move as a flock, reserving their controversies and particular originalities for matters that do not call into question the fundamental system of biases they share . . . The common need for rationalization will tend . . . to influence the concepts, models and theories applied; hence it will also affect the selection of relevant data, the recording of observations, the theoretical and practical inferences drawn explicitly or implicitly and the manner of presentation of the results of research.' He argues that 'objectivity' can be understood only in the sense that however elaborately a framework of fact is developed the underlying set of value premises must also be made explicit. 'This represents an advance towards the goals of honesty, clarity and effectiveness in research . . . It should overcome the inhibitions against drawing practical and political conclusions openly, systematically and logically. This method would consequently render social research a much more powerful instrument for guiding rational policy information.' Myrdal, G., *Objectivity in Social Research,* Duckworth, 1970, pp. 53 and 72.

32. 'The word "change" . . . is ambiguous in relation to society. I want to differentiate two totally different kinds. One goes to a primitive society, witnesses the preliminaries to a marriage ceremony, the ceremony itself, and its consequences: two individuals, formerly unrelated or in a special relationship, are now in another, that of husband and wife; a new group has been organized, which develops into a family. Obviously, you have here something which you can call social change or 'process'. *There is change within the structure. But it does not affect the structural form of society* . . . These two types of change it is absolutely necessary to distinguish and to study separately. I would suggest that we call the first kind "readjustment". Fundamentally, it is a readjustment of the equilibrium of a social structure'. Radcliffe-Brown, A.R., *A Natural Science of Society,* Free Press, New York, 1957, p.87. Quoted in Nisbet, R., (ed.), *Social Change,* Basil Blackwell, 1972.

33. Durkheim, E., *The Rules of Sociological Method,* p.116.

34. I have tried to clarify this in *Poverty in the United Kingdom.* (Forthcoming.)

2 The Future of the Social Services *

One of the contributions which the sociologist can make towards a better understanding of the social services is in analysing their functions. In Britain at least three misconceptions are held about them. Among one influential section of the population the social services are still conceived rather like an offshoot of the established Church, as something for which you have, or might have, a calling. They are thought of as personal, social work, services. Compared with Victorian times some professional training is advised, but you still tour the parish, doing good works. The services are felt to be a form of institutionalized benevolence to those who have fallen on hard times. This view of the social services disassociates them from social conflict and political life and invests them with a moral or religious purpose like that of saving souls. Teaching problem families the good life seems sometimes to have been elevated to the highest goal of the social work profession. This view can be dangerous. Traditional values of hierarchical superiority may be reinforced. Social workers may not simply tighten the controls of conformity, but may even become unconscious instigators instead of the conscious opponents of deprivation. Intent on saving the souls of their witches they may pursue them so relentlessly that they fail to see that the faces of the children are becoming more pinched.

A second view of the social services is that they are subordinate to the economy. They are believed to be of marginal and not central concern to the serious business of earning a living and raising production. To some extent they may serve various purposes ancillary to productive employment — for example, protecting those who fall out of work or helping people to get well quickly so that they can return to work — but in the main they are felt to dispense economic surplus as welfare, sharing out paternalistically, if more equitably, the fruits of production. It follows from this view that in periods of economic difficulty expenditure upon them can be reduced. Although the caricature is a shade unfair, it is this 'public burden' model of the social services which has been incorporated into the thinking of the British Treasury — as shown in such publications as the National Plan of 1965,

* Based on a lecture first given in Colchester on 24 February 1970 and revised for a Shotton Hall Conference at Madely College of Education on 4 April 1970.

the Green and White Papers of 1969 on public expenditure and the occasional papers on output budgeting and similar topics which the Treasury publishes. (1)

A third view, which takes something from each of the other two, is that the services are a modern tool of capitalism. As the uncritical servants of capitalist society they repair some of the worst ravages of the system, divert revolutionary ardour and ingratiate the working class into the Welfare State. Instead of helping and being part of the wholesale reconstruction of society, they help to prevent an outmoded contraption from falling apart. If capitalism did not exist in its present form the need for the bulk of the social services would not arise. This view of the social services as a kind of ambulance service for capitalism is also shared ironically enough by some liberal and conservative thinkers. (2) The services are regarded as a convenient philanthropic device for relieving minority poverty during the initial and middle stages of the industrial revolution. They can help to overcome certain temporary social problems during the early stages of the development of an efficient market economy. With the growth of prosperity they can be dispensed with.

Each of these views is powerfully represented in British opinion and each is stultifying in terms of radical social change. Yet without ruthless exposure of these superficial and inadequate views we cannot arrive at a full appreciation either of the complexity of social policy and administration or of the potentiality of social planning. For welfare organizations and services can be regressive or redistributive, totalitarian or democratic, disruptive or integrative — like other social institutions. Our job as social scientists is to illuminate the complex structure and show how elements and entire parts may change with time. In what senses can advances in medicine make a free health service more unequal? How does the evolution of specialist professions undermine the elementary rights of the people? Do some voluntary bodies become mouthpieces of the establishment after going through a pressure-group phase? These are examples of the questions that must be asked from a fuller perspective.

We must begin with the assumption that the social services are those means developed and institutionalized by society to promote ends which are wholly or primarily social. The ends include social justice; freedom from oppression; prevention of disease; abolition of poverty and squalor; integration of the community; harmony between races; equality of educational opportunity; full employment and especially social equality.

The services may be public or private and may extend beyond the conventional interpretation. The implications of this should be made clear. We must include not just the public social services like free or subsidized health services, education, housing, social security and welfare, but also fiscal means of promoting social ends (such as tax allowances for wives, children and other dependants), fringe benefits offered by employers (such as occupational pension schemes, sick pay, educational fees, free or subsidized housing), and private and voluntary services (such as life assurance, the services of organizations like the British United Provident Association, the London Clinic and clubs and services organized by voluntary associations). The ambit is wide but deliberately so. If we were to ignore certain services, such as fringe benefits and fiscal welfare, we would run the risk of ignoring major sources of conflict and inequality or major alternative means of attaining particular social ends. If the needs of old people are held to include the need for a subsistence pension upon retirement at roughly the level of a fifth of average industrial earnings,(3) then we have to ask why a different conception of need may be adopted in many occupational pension schemes of a pension of two thirds of final individual earnings, the receipt of which is not subject to retirement. The development of two sets of principles and methods may represent a waste of resources as well as a widening gulf in standards of living and social relations between two sections of the population. Narrower conceptions of the social services, like that adopted by T.H. Marshall, (4) are in my view distorting, since they imply more consensus about social problems, more uniformity of social values and a more integrated development of institutions than is in fact the case. Incidentally, these conceptions help to convey the impression that social services are entirely or principally for the working classes.

If this broad conception of the social services is accepted, then social policy is the underlying as well as the professed rationale by which they are controlled and used to bring about social development. Social policy is the institutionalized control of the social services towards implicit or explicit social objectives. Some may be implicit, of course, at the same time that others are made explicit, and there may be conflict between the two. Part of the sociologist's task is then to reveal what social policy is, in contradistinction to what it is supposed to be. And, following the broad conceptions that might be adopted, all societies, therefore, have social policies, even if they are not formulated in any comprehensive or integrated form, and all societies have social services. This paves the way for a more realistic understanding of the functions of social services in modern society and allows better comparisons between nations and between services. We can begin comparing the health and educational services in relation to employment and recognize complementary functions. We can ask to what extent different social security services achieve greater equality, as compared with educational services. We are more likely to pay respect to institutionalized modes of social control in the developing societies and not only bemoan the lack of public education services on Western lines.

This view of social policy is very broad but not so broad as to totally absorb economic institutions and policies as well. No doubt there are many economic measures which have social effects, just as there are social measures which have economic effects. It would be a mistake to subsume one under the other. Our criteria for evaluating means to certain ends and for constructing a programme for social administration as well as one for social research would be hopelessly compromised. Insofar as economic institutions are also social institutions then of course they must be studied. Insofar as economic policies also fulfil social policies, whether peripherally or centrally, then they must be studied. But this trespasses not at all over many fields of economics. Right at the heart of this conception of social policy, therefore, is the definition of social objectives.

There is one further implication. If we begin defining social services less in terms of administrative entities of government and more in terms of collective, if sometimes sectional institutions, services and practices which are designed to promote social developments of different kinds, we become more aware of the need for planning machinery. In the United States the influence of economists has been considerable in recent years in causing the Government to adopt new forms of planning. Some of it is pernicious, in the sense that attempts have been made to apply output budgeting, cost-benefit-analysis and similar techniques to matters for which they are inappropriate. The criterion of efficiency, interpreted in very limited terms of monetary saving, has been applied to the exclusion of criteria of need and quality of effect, for example. Those without demonstrable knowledge of social stratification, social security and social administration have pressed the illusory advantages of negative income tax so hard that they have persuaded President Nixon to disguise what is essentially a new and not very generous public assistance programme as a major bill to reduce poverty. In the words of Alvin Schorr, 'The President's programme thus incorporates a trade-off: it raises [assistance] levels in four or five states, but diminishes the tendency for levels to continue to improve in other states.' (5) But no one can deny that the efforts of bodies like the United States Committee for Economic Development to describe the sweep and objectives of American Government give an exciting illustration of the means we might find of evolving a more coherent social policy, which can be submitted to a more systematic rather than random public discussion. A good example is the amalgamation in Britain of the Ministries of Social Security and Health into a single department. It would not be impossible to foresee the further amalgamation, in some suitable federal form, of this department with the Department of Education, the Department of Environment and part of the Home Office. There could then be an associated Central Planning Office, concerned with producing forward plans and concerting manpower and administration. Linked with this planning office might be an advisory council of experts whose job it was to keep a watch on the social condition of the nation and issue annual reviews.

So far, then, my argument is that we need to free ourselves from conceptions of the social services and of social policies which are extremely limited. They are limited, for example, because they are so fragmented. Not only is there a tendency to concentrate attention on *public* as distinct from private and occupational services, but also on *individual* as distinct from pairs or groups of public services.

Their subtle interconnections, repercussions and conflicts are not adequately explored. We need a theory of social development. In his famous wartime report, Lord Beveridge captured the imagination of the public when he declared that the report was part of an aim to remove the five giant obstacles lying in the path of social reconstruction — want, ignorance, disease, squalor and idleness. This was an important method of achieving public agreement on social objectives, though, perhaps wisely, Beveridge did not specify the criteria required to measure degrees of success in removing the obstacles. It is easier some thirty years later to see how this might be done, even if public support is harder to secure for exactly — than for loosely — formulated proposals. We need to acquire some imaginative conception of the total effect of many different services on the structure and quality of social life and understand the direction in which they are leading us.

Objectives of Policy

But distinct from the objectives that society can be *shown* to be pursuing is there any means of determining the objectives that it should pursue? We have to adopt a view about the condition of society and how it might be improved. Characterizations of English society, for example, have been plentiful. The most interesting have been based on the theme of inequality. Although these might be said to have achieved notoriety rather than a lasting influence on the day-to-day management of social affairs they provide perhaps the most promising precedents for future approaches to planning. I propose in the rest of this paper to suggest how these might be used in creating a framework for planning.

For the first half of the nineteenth century one of the most effective statements was Engels' analysis of the effect on the lives of the labouring classes of the Industrial Revolution. He documents the degradation of the poor in cities and countryside in frightening detail. Writing a dedication at the end of the book to the working classes, he asks,

> Have the middle classes ever paid any serious attention to your grievances? Have they done more than paying the expenses of half a dozen commissions of inquiry, whose voluminous reports are damned to everlasting slumber among heaps of waste paper on the shelves of the Home Office? Have they even done as much to compile from those rotting blue-books a single readable book from which everybody might easily get some information on the condition of the great majority of 'free-born Britons'? Not they indeed, those are things they do not like to speak of − they have left it to a foreigner to inform the civilised world of the degrading situation you live in.(6)

There is a view here about the function of official committees of inquiry and official statistics which social scientists have been slow to elaborate. There have been many accounts since, notably by Charles Booth, Seebohm Rowntree and Charles Masterman, but none which perceives so clearly the structural relationship between privilege and want. Much of the British liberal tradition in the social sciences involves the portrayal of the poor relative to the secure working class, rather than the full range of social stratification.(7)

It would, of course, be possible to trace at great length changes in the pattern of social inequality in Britain. Information from the nineteenth century and the first decades of this century is tantalizingly incomplete and only in the last thirty years have the data collected on incomes and expenditure, earnings, nutrition, morbidity and so on begun to provide a framework sufficient to allow some very rough quantitative generalizations about short-term changes. In principle, however, the sociologist has the opportunity of applying the comparative method systematically to different groups, communities and classes in society so as to reveal, in an objective fashion, the inequalities that exist. I am thinking not simply of differences of consumption in similarly constituted families in Glasgow and Colchester, but comparisons between disabled and other people, in income, housing and conditions of employment, including earnings; comparisons between highly qualified coloured and white applicants for vacant jobs; or comparisons between salaried and wage-earning employees in their working conditions and treatment of sickness. Applied consistently, this approach can tell us a great deal about what actually goes on in our own society.

It is possible to compare areas: countries, regions, local authority areas, districts and wards; services: both different parts of the same service as well as different services; administrative sectors: public and private, voluntary and public, central and local authority, communal institutions and private households, fiscal, occupational and public welfare; and a wide range of different elements of social structure: age-groups, the sexes, ethnic groups, types of family, social minorities, groups of different employment status or class, persons receiving and not receiving services, and one category of clients or consumers compared with others.

It is one thing to state the broad principles of the comparative approach and another thing to apply these principles sharply and uncomfortably to the privileges and poverty we see around us. The work of Barbara Wootton, who has been one of the foremost critics of social complacency for over fifty years, is studded with examples. Arguing for family allowances in 1941, she said, 'For ten days' war, a weekly payment of upwards of five shillings could be made throughout the year for every child under the age of fifteen.' (8) The work of Richard Titmuss is also rich in examples. In 1938 he showed that if deaths in a group of northern counties (Durham, Northumberland, Cumberland, Westmorland, Yorkshire, Cheshire and Lancashire) could be brought down to the levels of the Home Counties 53,951 people who died in 1936 would not have done so. (9)

It is only when we rupture stereotyped categories of thought and discussion that we even begin to grasp the magnitude of inequality. To give a contemporary example, here are two descriptions of schools. The first is Dean Close school, not perhaps among the most widely known private schools, as described in its prospectus:

The school, surrounded by its own playing fields of 70 acres, stands on high open ground on the outskirts of Cheltenham . . . Each of the five Senior Houses has its own Studies, Common Room and Dormitories, Classrooms, Library, Music School, House Rooms, Assembly and Dining Halls, are centrally situated, in the main buildings, while nearby are the Chapel, Laboratories, Workshops, Swimming Bath and Gymnasium, as well as a Changing Room Block with baths and lavatories. In 1951 a new organ and organ chamber was built and the east end of the Chapel was panelled. In 1953 a new block of buildings was completed for metal work, mechanics and geometrical drawing, which will offer unusual opportunities to boys whose interests lie in the technical side of industry, engineering and farming. In 1955 a Music School was built. In 1956 a new C.C.F.

H.Q. was built, and the Chapel Fabric was completed by a large Vestry Block embodying a Chaplain's Classroom. In 1957, with aid from the Industrial Fund for the Advancement of Scientific Education in Schools, a block of four Laboratories with ancillary rooms and three new Classrooms was added. In 1959 another large block adjoining the last was built; it contains a new Library, an extra laboratory, 4 classrooms, 2 Common Rooms, and studies for 3 masters and 40 boys. In 1960 thirteen more rooms for Music were added making 21 in all, in addition to the Music School built for the Junior School. In 1961 two new Houses were opened, 'Yearlings' in the Senior School, and 'Wilton' for the smaller boys of the Junior School. In 1963 a new indoor 25 metre heated Swimming Bath and a Gymnasium fitted for a full-size Basket-Ball Court, or four Badminton Courts or an Indoor Tennis Court was built.

The second school is a typical secondary modern school described in the Newsom Report:

A very old building with 7 classrooms of 480 sq. ft. each, one of which is at present used for art and music as there is no teacher for the class. Four are separated by movable wood and glass partitions. There is no hall, gymnasium, dining room or special room of any kind. There is a small roof playground, very exposed to wind and weather but no fixed P.E. equipment. Netball is played in the courtyard of nearby tenements. Science has to be based on one corridor cupboard.

In order to anticipate and plan for the future, it is, of course, necessary to have information about progress. But there are three cautions. One is to guard against false optimism about progress. Remembering our childhood, it is natural to suppose that those who are younger than ourselves are having a much easier time than we did; but it seems that this feeling can be documented for every generation in history. Partly as a consequence of this feeling, however, we adopt fixed ideas about poverty. As time goes on and the country becomes more prosperous, we suppose the numbers in poverty must be dwindling to zero. But poverty is relative deprivation and every society and every generation of society creates its own patterns of needs which the population finds and feels itself compelled to meet. The labouring classes of England whom Engels describes were prosperous by contrast with many millions of people living in the cities of India today. Although the purchasing power of the poor in the United States may be greater than that of skilled manual workers in England, they are no less poor or deprived in the conditions of their own environment.

Consciousness of the relativity to social structure of living standards, needs and conditions is going to take time to acquire.

Secondly, the methods we employ to measure progress have to be changed. The yardsticks we use have to be modified and eventually changed altogether. Living standards depend more today on the resources that are distributed via employers' fringe benefits and public social services than they did twenty years or a hundred years ago. Therefore, we could not take at their face value simple comparisons of cash incomes as between wage-earners and salary-earners. Sensitivity to the emergence of new sources of inequality is also going to take time to acquire. One consequence of this concerns the nature of poverty. For example, one young widow may be bringing up two children in a slum house with a dilapidated school (of the type described in the Newsom Report) and an ex-workhouse hospital round the corner. Another family of the same kind with an identical cash income may be living in a new council house in a new town, with a modern school and hospital nearby. Plainly, the living standards of these two families are widely different.

Thirdly, the descriptions we can offer about inequality are still terribly crude. It is difficult to piece together information about the incomes of tax-payers, the expenditure of a sample of households, earnings of individuals, assets of families and utilization of social services. For all the minute scrutiny of class and social mobility, there is no comprehensive integrated account of social stratification in Britain upon which we might base a really informed analysis of social policy.

But, bearing in mind these three vital qualifications — our hazardous conceptions of progress, the need to update our methods of measuring it and our inability to document it thoroughly — what can we say about the structure of inequality? In recent British history, it seems possible to identify two phases: first, the levelling of standards that took place in the war, maintained in the first few years after the war by the Labour Government: secondly, a partial reversion to former inequalities, slow at first but probably quite fast by the end of the 1950s. In aggregate, the country was becoming more prosperous, but some minorities were losing ground and poverty was again growing. By the mid-1960s, a new, third, phase may have begun, but it is as yet too soon to be sure of it. The emphasis on economic growth, together with the disproportionately large increase of dependants in the population, has set in motion a structural drift of growing inequality which may occupy a period of some years. All these changes could be regarded as short-run cycles within a more stable and continuing inequality. No one who studies Routh's book on the occupational and pay structure in Britain between 1906 and 1960, (10) or who studies figures of income distribution over periods of ten or twenty years for different countries, can fail to be impressed by the *durability* of inequality. Important changes in the relative position in the earnings structure of some types of household or some percentiles can be traced. But the occurrence in the long term of countervailing trends which restore previous differentials is impressive.

These generalizations have to be fully documented, not just in terms of trends in personal incomes and earnings, but in the ownership of assets, the impact of taxation, the use of the public social services and employers' fringe benefits. (11) The accompanying table, prepared by R.J. Nicholson on the basis of official estimates, only establishes in small part a story which must be carefully revised and added to. The proportion of income after tax received by the top 10 per cent of income-recipients decreased at some stage during the period 1949—57 but, with minor fluctuations, the proportion remained about the same in the subsequent ten years. The middle-income groups gained to a small extent, and the incomes of the bottom 30 per cent of income recipients diminished during both periods.

TABLE 1   Percentage of income received after tax by different income groups

Group of income-recipients	1949	1957	1963	1967
Top 1 per cent	6.4	5.0	5.2	4.9
2 — 5 per cent	11.3	9.9	10.5	9.9
6 — 10 per cent	9.4	9.1	9.5	9.5
11 — 40 per cent	37.0	38.5	39.5	39.2
41 — 70 per cent	21.3	24.0	23.5	24.5
Bottom 30 per cent	14.6	13.4	11.8	12.0
Total	100	100	100	100

Source: Nicholson, R.J., 'The Distribution of Personal Income', *Lloyds Bank Review,* January 1967, p.16. For 1967 I am grateful for permission to use some as yet unpublished estimates made by the author. The table is based on data published annually in the National Income and Expenditure Blue Book, which have been converted by a method described in Nicholson, R.J., *Economic Statistics and Economic Problems,* pp.294 and 303. Like most income statistics the estimates must be used cautiously. For example, only 85 per cent of personal income is distributed by range.

However, there is some reason to believe that the upper-income groups have increased and not just maintained their share of overall resources. (12) The data for fringe benefits, capital gains and ownership of assets provide evidence of gains on the part of the middle classes in the late 1950s and early 1960s. For 1954, Lydall and Tipping estimated that one per cent of British adults owned 43 per cent of total net capital and 10 per cent owned 79 per cent. (13) For 1960, Revell estimated that the wealthiest one per cent owned 42 per cent of total net capital and the wealthiest 5 per cent (not 10 per cent) owned 75 per cent. (14)

At the lower end of the distribution of incomes we have to become conscious of a number of factors making for greater inequality. Despite a decrease in the proportion of people in unskilled occupations, there has been an increase in the proportion of persons in low-paid semi-skilled occupations and generally some signs of a failure on the part of the low-paid to keep step with the average increases in earnings. There is a disproportionate increase in the number of elderly pensioners – in common with many other societies. This is due not just to the disproportionate increase in the numbers of people of pensionable age, from 13.2 per cent in 1948 to 15.4 per cent in 1967 and 16.2 per cent in 1980 (though expected to decrease in the latter part of the century to 13.6 per cent in the year 2000). (15) It is due also to the rapid increase in the number of people retiring at a relatively early age – a development which is not approved by a majority of them and perhaps might have been avoidable. In 1959, about 47 per cent of men retired at sixty-five, but by 1964 the figure was 57 per cent and by 1968 70 per cent. (16) Given what we know about the sources of income of retirement pensioners, this tends to increase the proportion of people with incomes below or just above the supplementary benefit rates. Although much smaller numbers are affected, an increase is also taking place in the numbers of disabled persons in the population, particularly in middle age. For example, Professor J.N. Morris has shown in a recent paper that in the age-groups 40-55, the proportions absent from work because of sickness or disability for more than three months increased by 20-25 per cent from 1957 to 1967.(17) In some regions the likelihood of redundancy and prolonged unemployment is also increasing. When combined with the fact that there are relatively more families with three or more children – possibly promoted in part by the trends towards parity of numbers between the sexes in early adult life, more marriage, earlier marriage and a longer term of marriage – the impact of dependency upon the social structure can be recognized to be very great. Indeed, unless an *expanding* share of resources is devoted to social security and the other social services, the proportion of the population living in poverty is likely to increase. A differentiated 'under-class' is evolving. The term seems appropriate because many of the persons in this under-class are not in paid employment or they are in occupations which are marginal to the purposes for which the organizations for which they work exist; their incomes are depressed and they comprise a heterogeneous collection of minorities who lack collective consciousness, though some of them show signs of incipient organization. (18)

There is a second kind of inequality which tends to be neglected in analyses of the condition of society. Individuals vary in the extent to which they are integrated into families, occupational groups, other social groups and communities. In applying our comparative method, it would be possible to reveal which and how many people can enjoy the facilities of family, group and community membership. This is a kind of 'horizontal' inequality in society, compared with the vertical variety that we have been considering. Plainly there are important connections between the two. In addition to the division of society into strata, or classes, there is the division of each stratum into groups which are unequally integrated. How do people compare in their access to partners, friends, persons of the preceding and succeeding generations, persons who can offer them help and advice? How do they compare in their opportunities to command household facilities and social pursuits and sustain, make or dispense with social relations? The most obvious example of this kind of inequality is the extreme isolation of some elderly people, but there are also younger single persons and married couples, especially without children, whose lives have somehow become locked in narrow compartments — the lodging-house dwellers and the mentally ill and handicapped, including those living in vast institutions or isolated private residential and nursing homes. While it would, of course, be possible to regard vertical inequality as the dominant conception and the differential access to material resources as the key to understanding not only poverty and low incomes but also certain forms of social isolation, it seems difficult to explain inequalities in degree of social integration wholly in these terms.

The conception of the condition of society and its needs that I have sketched can be expressed in terms of vertical and horizontal inequality, or the inequalities of class and of resources, on the one hand, and of stultifying isolation on the other. It offers both a basis for assessing social policy and building a social plan. Let me give one brief example. A survey of old people in the United States, Denmark and Britain showed that they have a dual relationship with society. (19) On the one hand, there is informal association, or integration. The great majority are involved in a dense network of personal or 'privatized' relations, based on reciprocity, common interests, inculcated loyalties and affection. Their age as such is inconsequential. What matters to them are their roles as grandparents, parents, friends and neighbours. On the other hand, there is the development of a process of formal dissociation, of retirement from employment, categorization as retirement pensioners, members of old people's clubs, inhabitants of old people's bungalows or residential homes, half-price passengers on public transport or seaside holiday-makers in May or October. A series of political actions is being taken to accommodate them, rather than integrate them. The values being applied to the elderly are those of inferior ranking in resources (and status) and social segregation — the two aspects of inequality on which I have concentrated.

Future Issues of Policy

What does this analysis allow us to say about the issues of the future? I will give three illustrations: first, of community development as an example of the problems of horizontal inequality, or the division of social strata; secondly, of education, and thirdly, of poverty as examples of the problems of vertical inequality, or the division into strata.

First, community development. Here part of the conception has been supplied in Britain by the Seebohm Committee, whose conclusions have now been largely incorporated in Government legislation.(20) The committee proposed an administrative amalgamation of local social services departments for children, the physically and mentally handicapped, the old and others. However, the committee did not clearly formulate the objectives, the extent of unmet need, the priorities of development and hence the type of manpower required. Another way of expressing the shortcomings is that the committee did not fully discuss the kind of services that could be offered, and the enormous dependence of any local department upon the basic social services of health, social security and housing. There is a danger that the new local department will reflect a very narrow interpretation of social work and will stress the functions of an individual rescue service. It could become the agent of hierarchical society, unconsciously penalizing those problem families and so-called 'scroungers', 'idlers' and 'women with loose morals' in the interests of social control and conformity.(21) Much depends on the future conception of social work. It could emphasize material facilities; home help services; and sheltered housing in urban and rural centres to bring the isolated elderly and disabled into touch with society and drastically reduce the numbers of persons obliged to belong to artificial communities in mental illness hospitals, hospitals for the mentally handicapped, residential homes and nursing homes. The objective, in terms of equity and opportunity to lead a normal social life, is clear. There are some very real and exciting possibilities — some pioneered by imaginative medical superintendents of mental hospitals, others by individuals, as for example in the Responauts Society. But there are at least two other functions required of the social worker — to act as a bridge of communication between bureaucracy and people, not just to inform about regulations on housing, rent rebates and supplementary benefits, but also, in the reverse direction, to inform the bureaucracy of need. Some of the activities of pressure groups like the Birmingham Claimants' Union, Mothers in Action and the Child Poverty Action Group in informing the poor about their rights and taking test cases to tribunals illustrate this function. National systems of local information centres going far beyond the present Citizens' Advice Bureaux, and of welfare law offices, based on the extension of legal aid and advice from the present preoccupation with matrimonial proceedings, are required. Social workers can also act as expert advisers and consultants in the formation of tenants' associations, community associations and complaints committees. They can safeguard and even stimulate the expression of dissent, in the necessary pursuit of the good society.

It is possible to foresee the community welfare department (as some would prefer to call it for, after laboriously establishing the term 'social service' for the whole range of education, housing, social security, health and welfare, it would be retrograde now to restrict the term to certain parts of welfare) expanding rapidly to take its place alongside the National Health Service, education, housing and social security as one of the major social services.(22) That would depend on a clear statement of objectives, rapid expansion of resources, a controlled programme to shift resources in money and manpower from hospitals and other institutions to community and protect and substantiate individual rights. The danger is in adopting stigmatizing functions, through means-tested services and the unconscious if not conscious imposition of middle-class values, in preference to the extension of rights and the deliberate expansion of preventive services. This applies particularly to racial minorities. Services based on rights, and accessible to all, irrespective of race or means, are more likely to be effective as methods of aiding integration of racial minorities and reducing conflict, than measures designed exclusively for certain racial minorities. Policies designed solely for certain stigmatized groups sometimes harm them, by further segregating them from the social structure and allowing prejudice and pinchpenny treatment an easier target.

Secondly, education. There is an absence of planning of an effective kind, and especially in the strategic choice of priorities. The British

Government is operating within an unreal conception of the expansion, not just of education but of all the social services. A recent White Paper purports to give estimates of public expenditure on education, health, housing, welfare and social security for the period up to 1974. The international evidence shows that the percentage of national income being spent on these services is growing remorselessly, irrespective of the Government's political orientation, and in eleven countries is now larger than in the United Kingdom. The increase is partly due to the existence of more dependants in the population and to the growing costs of medical care, including medical technology, but also to educational expansion. In 1965, the abortive National Plan made the mistake of assuming a rate of growth in the services of up to 4 per cent per annum. But the Government failed to digest either comparative experience or undertake an analysis of the internal situation. The services grew in real terms by 5 per cent per annum in the period 1964-9.(23) It would have been more but for the restraints imposed by the Government during the protracted economic crisis. Certainly this rate of expansion is greater in some other countries. Yet, astonishingly, the Government has proposed that the social services should grow by only 4 per cent a year up to 1972 and by less than 3 per cent in 1972-4.(24)

The annual growth in expenditure allowed on education is 3 per cent, compared with 5 per cent in recent years. If present policies are projected, however, the current rate or a higher rate of expansion seems inescapable. A careful study by a group of experts concluded that 'only by going back on present plans to reduce class sizes and by refusing to expand higher education beyond existing plans, regardless of increased demand, can we keep the rate of increase down to 4½ per cent'.(25) The plan to raise the school-leaving age would need to be abandoned, and developments in comprehensive reorganization, further education and higher education would have to be restricted if the reduced percentage proposed by the Government were to be achieved. A successful economy drive is more likely to affect the schools than the universities and colleges, because the forces in favour of the expansion of higher education are very powerful.

In fact, the pressure to expand higher education is intense in nearly all industrialized countries. This pressure tends to increase inequality, for it is likely to push up artificially the numbers staying on to take graduate courses, and emphasizes the educational gap between most working-class people and an increasingly substantial section of the middle class. There are, of course, close connexions between techno-logical developments in industry or the quick expansion of some professional groups and the recent expansion of higher education.

But how far is education to be the compliant servant of the industrial or professional hierarchy and how far a countervailing force to establish a high basic level of education and a society better equipped for internal communication and co-operative endeavour? Partly as an indirect result of research into education by economists, educational qualifications are increasingly seen as tickets to high salaries and coveted social status. The functions of education are probably viewed more cynically today than in any previous period of Britain's history. Yet this perception and the stresses induced by expansion have helped to illuminate the real policy options. The big choice is between accepting the pattern that has become established in the last ten years and radically changing the scale of priorities in favour both of those who will be leaving school in the future at sixteen and who have in the past left at fifteen or fourteen. I am thinking of compulsory day release for sixteen- to eighteen-year-olds, rapid expansion of further education and adult education, especially short courses for adults in their twenties and thirties who have missed a decent schooling; but also a programme of nursery schooling for the under fives, teachers' aides in primary schools, and better facilities and staffing in secondary schools. In other countries the structure of the choice may be a little different but the underlying dilemma will be much the same. Without broad balance and control the expansion of education can deepen and not merely perpetuate social inequalities.

Finally, poverty. The problem is more ingrained in industrial societies than many suppose. In Britain the Minister of State for Social Security, Mr David Ennals, claimed in February 1970 that there were only 'pockets' of poverty(26) although the estimates of Atkinson(27) and others suggest a figure of up to five million in poverty and another two or three million living on the margins of poverty. Like previous Administrations the Government clearly believes that it has been more successful in reducing poverty than a dispassionate examination either of its record or of the facts about the structure of poverty would justify.(28) Thus, while it would be perfectly correct for the Government to draw attention to a list of constructive social reforms enacted between 1964 and 1969, such as redundancy and earnings-related unemployment and sickness payments, some protection from eviction, bigger improvement grants for old houses, rate rebates for poorer tenants and help for poor regions, these measures cannot be said to have had a marked effect. Strategies have not been co-ordinated and measures of achievement kept free of bureaucratic as well as party ideology. New sources of inequality have not been spotted and relative falls in living standards scrutinized. This can be shown for each of the main groups known to be in poverty five years ago — the long-term unemployed, the disabled, fatherless families, old people and low-paid wage-earners with children. The principal data, while admittedly incomplete, are drawn from official earnings surveys, income and expenditure surveys, the National Food Survey and analyses of trends in prices and taxation.

The main choice in social security policies in Britain rests between an expansion of means-tested and universal schemes. The former include familiar schemes such as free school meals, rate and rent rebates, and supplementary benefits, and, given current political pressures, might later include income-tested allowances for the low-paid. Examples of new universal schemes would be a percentage disability pension scheme for people in employment as well as outside employment; the extension of such a scheme to the infirm aged or the introduction of a supplementary pension for people aged seventy-five and over; a special allowance for families with a handicapped child; special benefit for one-parent families; increases in family allowances and their extension to the first child in the family, and reduction in some tax allowances. Given present trends, and a possible association with the Common Market countries, more of the cost could be met by earnings-related contributions from employees and employers and less from general taxation. It is arguable that this might be no bad thing if society wishes to pursue a really expansionist, and therefore very costly, policy in education and health. The growth of universal social security would not be enough, of course. To reduce poverty means changing the distribution of other resources — particularly assets, through a wealth tax; housing, through a more effective policy on new building, improvement of old buildings, control of property speculation and social ownership; employer fringe benefits through, for example, introduction of the legal obligation upon employers to pay full wages for the first two weeks of sickness; and earnings, through a more concerted attempt to rationalize wages and salaries and introduce a minimum wage.

Inegalitarian Social Services

In this paper I have tried to deal briefly with conceptions of the social services, conceptions of society and its needs and the kind of social planning that would have to be related to those conceptions. I have argued that like other social institutions the social services can be repressive, inegalitarian or manipulatory and not just gently or radically reformist. Once properly grasped this idea is immensely disturbing but liberating. It has repercussions on all our thinking about policy. It forces us as concerned social scientists and lay participants to search again for criteria of achievement and failure. More important, it forces us to accept that the objectives being pursued in any nation's social policy may not be the only objectives or even the right objectives in relation to its conditions and needs. It forces us to realize too that the methods being adopted to pursue those objectives may have effects which are the opposite of what they are supposed to be. The social policy of a nation must therefore be differentiated in principle from social planning. It is a special kind of blueprint which has to be re-constructed to explain current social activities, and therefore one which may be governed more by traditional practice and distributions of power and resources than by measured needs. It may be a compromise struck by competing interests and values or even a system of disparate policies having inconsistent effects. Social policy is the rationale for what a nation is doing in pursuing its social objectives, while social planning is more the detached preparation of measures to meet demonstrable needs.

According to such a conception, then, the social policies of the United States, Britain, Sweden, Tanzania and Ceylon could be carefully compared. They could all be distinguished in principle from social plans, drawn up to meet certain identified and measured inequalities, which could incorporate objectives not yet being pursued and means for achieving these objectives which have not yet been contemplated or discussed.

Notes

1. *A National Plan for 1965,* H.M.S.O., 1965; *Public Expenditure — A New Presentation,* Cmnd. 4017, H.M.S.O., 1969; *Public Expenditure 1968-1969 to 1973-1974,* Cmnd. 4234, H.M.S.O., 1969; Williams, A., *Output Budgeting and the Contribution of Micro-Economics to Efficiency in Government,* H.M.S.O., 1967.

2. See, for example, Peacock, A., *The Welfare Society,* Unservile State Papers, no. 2, Liberal Publications Department, 1960.

3. When the social insurance scheme was introduced after the First World War the pension for the single or widowed person was fixed at a rate just below 20 per cent of the average industrial earnings of men aged twenty-one and over and the rate has remained roughly the same ever since.

4. 'Social policy . . . is taken to refer to the policy of governments with regard to action having a direct impact on the welfare of the citizens, by providing them with services or income.' Marshall, T.H., *Social Policy,* Hutchinson, 1965, p.7.

5 Schorr, A., 'The President's Welfare Programme and Commission' (unpublished), conference of the American Public Welfare Association, Dallas, 10 December 1969.

6. Engels, F., *The Condition of the Working Class in England* (new introduction by E.J. Hobsbawm), Panther, 1969, p.324. The original German edition was

published in 1845.

7. Rowntree's survey, for example, 'did not extend to the servant-keeping class'. Rowntree, B.S., *Poverty: A Study of Town Life,* Macmillan, 1901, p.14.

8. Wootton, B., *End Social Inequality,* Routledge & Kegan Paul, 1941, p.55.

9. Titmuss, R.M., *Poverty and Population,* Allen & Unwin, 1941.

10. Routh, G., *Occupation and Pay in Great Britain,* Cambridge University Press, 1965.

11. An introductory chapter of a forthcoming book on poverty in Britain, by the author, summarizes the evidence on each of these.

12. 'Indeed if, as is sometimes suggested, certain "tax avoidance" incomes and other claims on wealth outside personal income have increased over the last decade and are concentrated more among higher income-recipients, it is possible that the distribution of incomes on some wider definition may have moved towards greater inequality.' Nicholson, R.S., op. cit., p.18.

13. Lydall, M.F., and Tipping, D.G., 'The Distribution of Personal Wealth in Britain', *Bulletin of the Oxford University Institute of Statistics,* XXIII, 1961.

14. Revell, J., 'Changes in the Social Distribution of Property in Britain during the Twentieth Century', International Economic History Conference, Munich, 1965.

15. Department of Health and Social Security, *National Superannuation and Social Insurance,* Cmnd. 3883, H.M.S.O., 1969, p.10.

16. In 1964 73 per cent of men in the age-group 65-9 and in 1968 80 per cent were retired. Department of Health and Social Security, *Report by the Government Actuary on the Financial Provisions of the National Superannuation and Social Insurance Bill,* Cmnd. 4223, H.M.S.O., 1969, p.21.

17. Morris, J.N., 'Tomorrow's Community Physician', *Lancet,* 18 October, 1969.

18. The development of claimants' unions, squatters' groups, and even of retirement pensioners' groups in recent years marks an important difference in mood from, say, the 1950s and early 1960s.

19. Shanas, E., *et al, Old People in Three Industrial Societies,* Routledge & Kegan Paul, and Atherton, New York, 1968, especially pp.424-6.

20. The Local Authorities Social Services Act, June 1970.

21. The professionalization of social work and the bureaucratization of local departments seem to be strengthening the functions of social control, as, for example, in initial referrals for non-conformity. See Handler, J., 'Controlling Official Behaviour in Welfare Administration', in Ten Broek, J. (ed.), *The Law of the Poor,* Chandler, 1966.

22. See *The Fifth Social Service: A Critical Analysis of the Seebohm Proposals,* the Fabian Society, 1970.

23. Estimates based on detailed information furnished by the Central Statistical Office, see p. 309.

24. *Public Expenditure 1968-1969 to 1973-1974.*

25. *Planning for Education in 1980,* Fabian Research Series, no. 282, February 1970, p.29.

26.*Tribune,* 13 February 1970, p.5.

27.Atkinson, A.B., *Poverty in Britain and the Reform of Social Security,* Cambridge University Press, 1969.

28.See the Child Poverty Action Group, *Poverty and the Labour Government,* 1970, and Townsend, P. and Bosanquet, N. (eds.), *Labour and Inequality,* the Fabian Society, 1972.

The creation of a concerted social policy is perhaps the most important single task for the British Government. It is as important for a Labour Party ruefully trying to understand the lessons of five and a half years of office as it is for the new Tory Government. I do not mean something limited to social work or even the five major social services — social security, education, health, housing and community welfare. I mean a national plan, specifying the principles and stages by which not only the combined social service policies but also fiscal, incomes and industrial relations policies might be related in order to achieve social objectives.

In the short term, an overall social policy is needed to restore stability and cohesion (in employment, race relations, housing and school structure, for example), from which greater national vitality and higher productivity might develop; to provide a rationale for the allocation of national resources and control of public expenditure; and to make incomes policy more acceptable to the unions and hence economic problems more manageable. In the long term, social policy is required to prevent the strong from gaining most of the fruits of economic growth at a time when the weak — the disabled, the unemployed and the sub-employed, the retired and the old — are increasing in proportion to the overall population. More positively, it is necessary to construct a just society when powerful multi-national corporations and trading areas, expensive technology and arrogant professionalism, are increasingly liable to undermine traditional democratic procedures and endanger individual and community rights.

I will try to illustrate this argument briefly from the recent history of incomes policy, and the discussions about public expenditure and fiscal policy.

First, the Labour Government's incomes policy. Economic objectives were paramount in this policy and, perhaps because they were paramount, that policy failed. The only incomes policy that seems likely to work is one with clear social objectives applying to the whole population. In his absorbing and carefully argued Fabian pamphlet, *Labour and Inflation*, Thomas Balogh leads up to this conclusion but

* First published in *New Society*, 22 October 1970.

does not plunge into it — largely because he does not set out the social context within which the incomes policy operated. He rightly concludes that 'a peaceful transition to a more balanced social system demands a policy package of which an incomes policy is one of the most essential elements'. But he does not quite understand why the trade unions came to view Labour's policy with such distrust.

The policy was restricted largely to the control of wage increases in order to curb inflation. Salaries, dividends and profits escaped close scrutiny. Wealth was not taxed, and industry was left largely free to determine prices. In these circumstances it is not surprising that the policy was felt to be socially selective and unfair. Indeed, huge increases of pay had been made to ministers, M.P.s, judges, senior civil servants and general practitioners just before the unions were asked to limit wage demands to between 3 and 4 per cent per annum. Events such as these were not calculated to breed confidence.

It would also be hard to deny that the problems of the low-paid attracted little serious attention. No detailed programme of action to help them was developed in the years 1964-70, even at the time of devaluation. Though a valuable national survey of earnings was made in 1968, no attempt to collect information about the industrial and family situation of the low-paid, even for a few industries, was made until 1970. The existing machinery of wages councils, which cover three million workers, was not reviewed. Because it was passed to an inter-departmental committee, the challenging task of finding practical methods of introducing a minimum wage was not seriously taken up.

The unions themselves bear some responsibility for not pursuing the implications — for wage policy as a whole — of commitment to a minimum wage, but it must be admitted that they received very little hard evidence of the Government really giving the priority traditionally accorded by Labour to the underdog. And this applied to the non-working poor as well. After certain measures were introduced in 1965-6, progress in social security was slow and disconnected. The incomes of pensioners and others either receiving social insurance benefits or supplementary benefits, or both, for a time kept pace with wage increases and then fell behind. The numbers of unemployed grew, and provisions for them in some respects grew worse. Rents of low-income families rose faster than average. The strong calls of the unions for much higher family allowances were not answered.

The full history of these events is of course complex and it would be wrong to expect too much of either our existing state of knowledge or capacities for planning. Nonetheless, it is fair to conclude that success in one area of policy seems to depend more on success in others than we had believed hitherto, and is probably contingent on overall planning. Had the Labour Government attempted systematically, or been allowed, to relate in its policy-making the different sources of income; had the unions been given more tangible evidence of efforts to limit salaries, dividends and profits; or had the public been convinced of the Government's determination to give priority to people with low incomes, the story might have been very different. Someone might even have begun to ask on what principles income differentials (wages, salaries *and* social security benefits) should in future be based.

A second example is the control of public expenditure in the social services. The Heath Government is facing a cluster of problems, partly of its own making; but some are problems which are real enough. It has committed itself to reducing public expenditure before finding out that it must automatically rise. There is the problem of spending proportionately more, even without any improvement in standards, to accommodate the growing proportion of dependants — retirement pensioners, disabled and children — in the population. But this problem was as serious ten or twenty years ago as it is now. There is the expensive impact of science and technology on the social services, particularly health and education. New drugs, new forms of surgery and new aids, whether for schools or the disabled, are forcing up costs. Such innovations are popular, and politically difficult if not impossible to resist. To make them available only to those who can pay for them would be to set in reverse a whole trend in medical and educational ethics.

There are, too, the effects of upward social mobility on public expenditure. The growth of the secondary school population, the slow introduction of comprehensive schools, the extension of the school leaving age and the expansion of further and higher education — all are adding enormously to public expenditure. What is sometimes forgotten is that the corresponding disproportionate increase in middle-class jobs is an in-built cause of inflation and rising expenditure. To all other increases in earnings is added the net cost of each middle-class salary which replaces a working-class wage.

What would be a more controlled strategy of educational expansion? How can costs be related to the needs of the other social services, industry and the professions? Are some of the jobs that are filled by university graduates too highly paid for the qualifications that are demanded and could they be filled more cheaply by non-graduates? Might some of the expenditure on the increased number of graduates have been better spent on improving the education of the mass of the school population? These are not easy questions to answer but since so many government decisions on the social services are taken implicitly or by accident, it is reasonable to insist, at least, that the wider ramifications of past decisions should be studied and the ugly choice of priorities brought into the cold light of day.

When cuts in public expenditure are made, whether under Labour or the Conservatives, they are usually made by introducing charges for goods and services which were previously free or subsidized and by cutting back on planned expansion. The relationship between projected public expenditure and projected private consumption is rarely examined. Nor is the relationship between the different components of public expenditure. One example is the allocation of resources to health services in hospitals instead of to such services in the community. Another is allocation of resources to staff (in the form of salaries and fringe benefits) instead of to consumers (in the form of benefits and general amenities).

Substantial awards have been made to doctors, teachers, nurses and other staff to help them catch up with, or move ahead of, other occupations. No doubt a good case can be made on behalf of some of these groups. But there are double standards operating. On the one hand, staff demand comparability in earnings with people outside the public services. On the other, they are subject to political judgements of what 'ceiling' of public expenditure can be afforded. The result is usually to chop expansion of staff numbers and to impoverish conditions and standards for consumers rather than review the distribution of future work between different kinds of grades of staff — or even to compare living standards of staff and consumers in the same group of services.

During the summer of 1970, two increases in income happened to be announced. The Kindersley committee recommended a pay award, costing £83 million a year for about 60,000 doctors (of which the Labour Government conceded £57 million), and the Government promised increases in allowances amounting to £70 million a year for 4,000,000 people dependent in whole or in part on supplementary benefits. These decisions are not wholly unrelated, and perhaps should be taken sometimes, if not always, in conjunction. Incomes and man-power policies should form part of any policy seeking to 'control' public expenditure.

One of the big surprises of Labour's administration was that social planning was not put into operational effect and in fact gave way to restrictive Treasury control over public expenditure. During the last years of the previous Conservative administration, ten-year plans for the hospital and community care services were worked out and published; there was the Robbins report on higher education; research units and programmes were established at some, though not all, of the social service ministries; digests of statistics and fuller annual reports, like that of the National Assistance Board, were published. The Labour Party had made preparations for streamlining government machinery. It was eager to strengthen economic planning and had policies, like those for national superannuation and comprehensive schools, which implied the need for an ambitious consolidation of planning machinery and procedures.

A number of proposals were carried into effect. The Department of Economic Affairs and the National Board for Prices and Incomes were established. The Ministries of Health and Social Security were amalgamated. Government surveys of the living standards of pensioners and families with children were carried out. The Central Statistical Office was reorganized and new statistical reports appeared. But there was extraordinarily little forward planning of a concerted kind on the allocation of resources. The National Plan of 1965 was not followed by further plans and planning seemed to have been discredited in government eyes. Certainly the social planning in the 1965 document was poor in its historical understanding as well as its judgement. Again, the promised series of hospital and community care plans were strangled in early life. Not at any time during the late 1960s was an attempt made to present a general view of future plans in social security in relation to social needs, despite the enormous growth of public interest in and concern about poverty. The amount and quality of information about payments of supplementary benefit actually declined − as can be seen by comparing the annual report for 1965 with that for 1969. Cabinet ministers like R. H. S. Crossman (see his 1967 Fabian Tract, *Socialism and Planning*) plainly never expected the information and planning services to crash or fragment like this. They expected them to gather momentum.

What remained of central social planning was an uninformed attempt by the Government to predict the course of public expenditure. All highly industrialized countries, whatever their political complexion, have been spending an increasing share of national income on the public social services, for the reasons I have already discussed. Countries as diverse as France, Italy, Sweden, Denmark, Austria and Japan have had annual rates of increase of expenditure on their social services, after allowing for price increases, of between 8 per cent and 13 per cent in recent periods.

But comparative experience does not appear to have been sought, and a searching internal analysis of the real reasons for the increases in public expenditure was not made. Partly as a consequence a White Paper on future public expenditure, published in December 1969, proposed a much lower rate of growth in expenditure on the social services for the period up to 1974 at constant prices, than had occurred during the preceding ten years.

Although parts of the White Paper were hedged around with qualifications, the fact remains that the estimates are irreconcilable with either national experience or reasonable expectation. To conform with the annual increase of 3 per cent allowed to education, for example, the rate of expansion of further and higher education would have had to be cut back drastically and the plans to raise the school-leaving age and reduce class sizes deferred. Presumably the Heath Government is working with these unrealistically low estimates and may even be emboldened to take some of the administrative steps which would be necessary to put them into effect.

All this suggests how important it is for guidelines on the allocation of resources to the services to be worked out in conformity with a social plan. It also suggests that just as incomes policy makes no sense if it is confined to wages, so the policy allocation of resources to social ends makes no sense if policy is confined to the traditional public social services.

A third example is taxation in relation to social dependency. The functions of fiscal policy are surprisingly little researched. The social implications of alternative budget strategies are not fully worked out, nor the consequences of each budget examined. There is not even any really precise information on the distribution of incomes among households before and after tax. Using the expanded government Family Expenditure Survey, a team at the Central Statistical Office has begun to produce valuable data on the relationship between social service policies and tax policies.

For example, the latest analysis in *Economic Trends* (February 1970) shows that between 1961 and 1968 there was virtually no change in the structure of incomes, even taking into account earnings, taxes and the value of social service benefits in cash and in kind. There was a very slight improvement in the average post-tax incomes of the poorest couples with one child or two children, by comparison with other couples with the same number of children, but a slight deterioration in the levels of the poorest among other families (namely, couples with three children, couples with four or more children, and households comprising three adults and one child, three adults and two children and four adults). The study also showed that some high-income groups benefit more in absolute money value from the public social services than do low-income groups. Thus, families with three children earning over £3,100 received £457, on average, during 1968 from the social services, while similar families with an £800-£1,000 income received £440.

Poor and rich families were found to be paying very similar proportions of gross incomes in tax. This can of course be changed. Action to change tax rates can reinforce or conflict with social service policies. Action to introduce or adjust tax allowances, in particular, can help families with dependants, or people with special needs, like the old and disabled, in the same way as social security allowances. Clearly, the two should be related (though this does not mean the purposes of both could be achieved by merging them).

The Labour Government took up a proposal of the Child Poverty Action Group to balance the cost of a general increase in family allowances by withdrawing part of the tax allowances and so concentrate the net cost of the increase on poor families. However, the measures were not synchronized. The implications for tax equity, between people with and without children, of progressive withdrawal of child tax allowances, without making the corresponding increases in family allowances tax-free were not worked out or understood. One of the original proposals of the group was to make family allowances tax-free and thus restore one of the functions of child tax allowances, which is to provide different tax thresholds for people with different numbers of children.

Just before the election in June, Edward Heath stated on behalf of the Tories, 'We accept that, as Mr Macleod said in his budget speech, the only way of tackling family poverty in the short term is to increase family allowances and operate the claw-back principle.' However, the Government might resist the temptation either to tax the increase, or to extract in tax, from the family who are living on a low income but not in poverty, as much or nearly as much as the value of the increase. Family allowances are an important adjunct of a policy to reduce wage inflation and they have a positive function both for those in hardship if not in poverty and for middle-income families trying to do their best for their children.

Tax relief on allowances must also be treated as a form of public expenditure, as in parts of Scandinavia. The Government is believed to be planning the introduction of new charges for public services. Withdrawal of tax allowances should be regarded as the fairest form of charge that could be devised since it does not penalize the poorest families. Thus, the value to tax-payers of tax-free interest on mortgages rose sharply from £95 million in 1963-4 to £215 million in 1969-70. It is a very costly form of housing subsidy going mainly to middle-class owner-occupiers. Its withdrawal, or partial withdrawal, would help finance a flat-rate housing subsidy to every disabled person and every medium-sized or large family.

The examples which I have discussed help to make the case for changes in government machinery, information and research services.

How far do the proposals put forward in the new White Paper on *The Reorganization of Central Government* meet that case? The administration of children's services is to be transferred from the Home Office to the Department of Health and Social Security. This falls a long way short of a federal department amalgamating the Department of Education, the Ministry of Housing and the D.H.S.S., which will eventually be required. A small multi-disciplinary policy review staff is to be set up in the Cabinet Office under the Prime Minister. It is difficult to know quite what this will mean. It will be essential to formulate a distinctive *social* policy and build up a substantial staff for research and information. With direct responsibility to the Prime Minister, a Social Advisory Council might be set up, possibly overlapping with an Economic Advisory Council, which recruited expert members from the social services, the unions, the research institutes and the universities and was responsible for converting the social objectives of government into an operational programme. This council would need to be served by a well-staffed office or department of social planning which might incorporate the existing Central Statistical Office. It would undertake wide-ranging research on social conditions and needs, monitor the social effects of changes in fiscal, incomes and social service policies and produce regular forward plans in cooperation with individual departments.

This conception of social policy and administration will require hard discussion if it is to become reality. Its intellectual or academic base will also have to be strengthened. For example, I believe it must be linked with conceptions of development. Development can be conceived either as primarily social or as primarily economic. It so happens that up to the present most people have regarded it as primarily economic. Against this there is a strong as well as a weaker sociological argument. The weaker argument is that the social factors in strictly economic development are much more important than usually appreciated.

In his book on *Economic Development,* Kindleberger points out that although a few economists, like Hagen, regard social or cultural variables as fundamental in explaining development many, like Adelman, regard them as additional or peripheral to a string of economic variables, including physical or land resources, labour, capital, managerial capacity and economies of scale. Kindleberger says he takes 'a reasonable middle position in which social and cultural factors are only two variables among many, including the economic, and in which there is inter-action between economic factors, on the one hand, and social and cultural, on the other'. While recognizing that the social factors have not been given sufficient weight, some sociologists would accept this.

The stronger sociological argument would be that in treating development as primarily economic, and by interpreting the term in its conventional sense, precedence is given to the wrong values. By accepting it into our political and social thinking, whether about the future of Britain, Europe or the developing countries, we accept too readily the precedence of economic institutions and the distribution of human resources in accordance with narrowly economic assumptions. It asserts the pre-eminence of Western societies and imposes a distribution of world resources which is relatively unchanging. If societies were compared more in terms of their social integration, vitality or freedom from petty conflict or individual deprivation instead of gross national product *per capita*, the ranking of nations would be radically different. Again, if national progress were measured more against social objectives like the removal of poverty, the establishment of an effective system of civil rights, and the integration of racial groups, instead of the rate of economic growth, different priorities for political action would be produced. Whatever direction the argument takes, sociology has a major contribution to make to the coherence and force of social policy.

The creation of a concerted social policy also requires more recognition of government shortcomings in meeting social problems and introducing change. The shortcomings, I suggest, arise from unwillingness to perceive how different policies — incomes, fiscal and social service — interlock. They are as inseparable from each other as are individuals and their opinions from social relationships and values. While government can give priority to particular objectives, success in any area depends on having a structural framework of policy, rather than having any single departmental programme of action. This framework also depends as much on the establishment of receptive public opinion — in terms of trust, confidence and tolerance in racial questions and over those who receive state benefits — as it does upon government machinery and special expertise. What counts in the end is the morality of government.

4 The Need for a Social Plan*

Most social planning in Britain is narrowly departmental; it is conceived within administrative and not functional boundaries. Rarely is the risk taken to spell out its logic to the general public, on grounds either that this might reveal administrative ignorance and ineptitude or encourage criticism of central thinking and action. Planning is also gravely subservient to traditional interpretations of what is good for the economy. The National Plan of 1965, the Hospital Plan of 1962, the collected plans for health and welfare services of the local authorities, and the Ministry of Health's presentation of these, the occasional utterances of Treasury spokesmen − all could be quoted in substantiation.

The National Plan seems to have been inspired partly by the aim of restraining public expenditure in the interests of economic growth. The same aim seems to underlie the latest pronouncements of the Treasury. A spokesman recently concluded: *'Unless there is a marked change in governmental policies,* social service expenditure in the next decade or so is virtually certain to rise relative to G.N.P.' (my italics). Perhaps the Treasury needs to know that, in all industrial countries for which information exists, the proportion of national income allocated to the social services has been steadily rising. It has been rising swiftly in countries which have experienced the swiftest economic growth, such as West Germany. The Canadian Royal Commission on Health Services discovered recently that, in nearly all advanced industrial countries for which data are available, the proportion of resources devoted to health services is rising so swiftly that an extra 1 to 2 per cent of the gross national product is absorbed by these services every ten years.

Such relative increases in social expenditure appear to have little connection with the political complexions of governments and appear to be remorseless in face of the demands of some sections of opinion for the return of public services to the private market. They are due partly to the ageing of populations and the maintenance of high post-war birth rates. But they are also due to the accelerated costs of surgery and of drugs; the relative increases in the numbers staying on at

* Part of a paper presented to a Government conference on the social services at Lancaster House, London, on 2 December 1967, and first published in *New Society,* 14 December 1967.

school and college; the recognition by the public that nurses and other staff have a rightful claim to higher pay; the rising industrial costs of redundancies, retraining, resettlement and retirement; and the demands of a better educated public for secure homes, jobs and incomes. Television helps to foster the public's sense of greater accessibility to its civil rights.

It may well be that, in a general sense, more welfare may mean more rather than less economic vitality. This argument could be developed in a number of ways by the sociologist. The poor who are dependent on the social services are not a separate section of the population, like some tribe of untouchables living on the other side of a canyon. Many have known prosperity or may expect to know it soon. A substantial part, and possibly a majority, of the population have known poverty at some time.

Adversity is something which might strike universally and many people who are prosperous and healthy are glad of the security of the social services. Many of their nearest and dearest (such as parents and grandparents) are dependent on these services. Security for oneself and one's family can strengthen morale and provide incentives at work. The web of social services is enmeshed with the daily life and thought of the nation.

The membership of the economically 'productive' and 'non-productive' sections of the population is constantly shifting and the distinction at any point in time is far from being as clear as many economic textbooks infer. The work of housewives and other 'dependants' releases men for industry and it would be improper to claim that they make no real contribution to production. The continuing increase in the number of married women who enter paid employment is largely attributable to the growing number of middle-aged and elderly grandmothers who share with them the tasks of caring for young children and homes.

Certainly the mis-assumptions of the defunct National Plan cannot easily be forgiven. Not only were transfer incomes and the cost of resources combined in ways which prevented rational discussion of public expenditure. And not only was little attempt made to spell out social objectives. The Plan apparently intended, even without any extension in the scope of social security, that the level of living of social security beneficiaries would fall behind that of wage-earners. Contrary to international experience, it planned no increase in the health services relative to the gross national product. It seemed to suggest that expenditure on pensions, schools, sick pay, medical services and equipment was meritorious if it was private but extravagant if it was public. The planned rate of increase in social service expenditure was, as Brian Abel-Smith has shown, lower than had been experienced in previous years and lower in most respects than in other prosperous countries.

The really big development in the social sciences which has not yet been absorbed in the thinking of government and social service departments and the Treasury is the growing use of a comparative frame of reference. This derives from recent work in comparative sociology and comparative politics. By adopting a 'comparative frame of reference' in studying and appraising British society not only do I mean comparing Britain with other countries in aggregate terms but comparing different internal regions, localities and communities and even types of family or household, comparing conditions experienced by young and old and by succeeding generations or cohorts, and comparing sections of the population and persons with different employment status, race or ethnic origin, and different health or disability. The comparisons may be made between countries as well as within them. For the health service, Table 1 gives an elementary example.

Table 1   Cost per bed-day of hospitals other than general as a percentage of the cost per bed-day of general hospitals

Type of hospital	U.S.	England and Wales	Sweden	Israel	Czecho-slovakia
General	100	100	100	100	100
Chronic disease	26	45	52	61	57
Tuberculosis and other chest disease	49	84	72	75	81
Mental hospitals	19	32	38	33	46

Some valuable lessons can be learnt from the plans for hospitals and health and welfare services published by the Ministry of Health in 1962 and 1963. The ministry assumed that up to 1975:

1. The number of chronic sick and geriatric beds for every 1,000 people aged 65 and over would diminish from 10.8 for every 1,000 of that age-group to 9.4.
2. The number of beds in psychiatric hospitals occupied by the over-65s would diminish by 40 per cent. Instead of there being about eleven beds in psychiatric hospitals for every 1,000 persons of this age, there would be five for every 1,000.
3. The number of places in residential homes would increase from 13.5 per 1,000 persons aged 65 and over in 1960, to 14.8 in 1963 and 18.9 in 1974. On revision the last figure has become 21.6 for 1976.

Are these rational assumptions? A careful reading of the plans reveals surprisingly little background information and analysis of the 'base-line' kind which is badly needed for all the social services — about social conditions, users and non-users and the different experiences of different types of users. The passages on geriatric beds contain general references to improved turnover and the requirements suggested in the light of 'experience'. A series of papers by G. C. Tooth and Eileen Brooke form the basis for the projected reduction of the need for accommodation in psychiatric hospitals. These papers, however, do not claim to present much information about the elderly persons who comprise nearly two fifths of the patients in such hospitals. And the ministry, presenting estimates of accommodation in residential homes, appears to have done little more than accept the extraordinarily diverse proposals put to it by 145 welfare authorities (174 by 1965) and comment mildly that 'experience so far would suggest that most authorities may find a ratio between 15 and 25 places per 1,000 population aged 65 and over appropriate to their areas.'

The ministry's early approach to planning was therefore tentative, and perhaps understandably tentative, but even by 1966 planning was not yet based on an assessment of the impact upon all the services of the much larger number of persons in the population aged 80 and over, nor on a careful statistical review of the possible interrelationships between residential and different kinds of hospital provision either nationally or in specific areas or regions. It had failed to persuade its sister department, the Scottish Home and Health Department, to accept its reasoning.

The Scots seem to attach greater importance to institutional care. They do not believe that the proportion of mental illness beds should be reduced, even though they start with larger relative numbers of those beds than the English. They believe that there must be 'a substantial increase' in geriatric beds (from 10.8 to 13.3 per 1,000 aged 65 and over) and a larger ratio too than in England and Wales of residential home places to population. Local authorities in Scotland have not been requested to produce development plans for community care.

Although the appearance of the Ministry of Health's plans in 1962 and 1963 was extremely hopeful there has as yet been no sign of effective consolidation or of a desire to foster public discussion of difficult issues. It has been left to organizations such as the National Institute of Economic and Social Research *(Health and Welfare Services in Britain in 1975,* by Deborah Paige and Kit Jones) and Political and Economic Planning *(Psychiatric Services in 1975,* by G. F. Rehin and F. M. Martin) to push the discussion a stage further.

Are there any general techniques of social planning which have been tried overseas which might be imported into Britain? On 25 August 1965, President Johnson announced that a new form of decision-making called the 'planning-programming-budgeting system' (P.P.B.S.) would be introduced into each agency of his cabinet. This is a system of grouping together under one rubric all services administered by different departments but with similar functions and making comparisons of objectives and programmes to see which are more 'effective'.

The technique was developed from the studies at the Rand Corporation of the location of military bases and applied to various programmes in the American Defense Department. Its intellectual heirs are cost-benefit analysis and systems analysis. 'Once in operation,' the President said, 'it will enable us to (i) identify our national goals with precision and on a continuing basis; (ii) choose among those goals the ones that are most urgent; (iii) search for alternative means of reaching those goals most effectively at least cost; (iv) inform ourselves not merely on next year's costs − but on the second, and third, and subsequent year's costs − of our programmes; (v) measure the performance of our programmes to insure a dollar's worth of service for each dollar spent. This system will improve ability to control our programmes and our budgets rather than having them control us. It will operate year round.'

In 1966 the research and policy committee of the U.S. Committee for Economic Development put out a statement on national policy. This was remarkable for its forthrightness. For example, the committee stated that the platform pronouncements of American political parties 'range from meaningless generalities to detailed positions on minor issues; in either case they provide poor guidance in setting major long-range goals.' And it suggested that this change in budgetary planning should be pushed even further. There had been too little attention given to longer-range planning, too much stress on detail and not enough on the broader picture, too little emphasis on functions performed. Organizational objectives were poorly defined and not enough use had been made of the budgetary process to improve operational effectiveness. With much of this British observers could wholeheartedly agree.

William Gorham, the assistant secretary for programme co-ordination in the U.S. Department of Health, Education and Welfare, has recently commented on some early attempts to apply the system to his department *(Public Interest,* Summer 1967). The studies range from programmes for controlling disease (cancer, arthritis, syphilis and T.B.) to possible programmes for improving both maternal child health care and income maintenance services.

Gorham finds four impediments to feeding health, education and welfare programmes into a computer. There is the technical problem of a lack of data, and follow-up information is difficult and expensive to collect. There are real conceptual problems of deciding what it is that needs to be measured. Is educational 'benefit' measurable in terms of subsequent earnings, literacy, conformity to the law, or what? There is the problem of *weighting* benefits between different members of the population—say between a young widow and a pensioner.

Finally,

'even if benefits of different programmes can be identified and measured and weighted, they cannot always be measured in the same units. Educational benefits may be measurable in terms of achievement test scores, and health benefits in terms of lives saved or days of sickness averted, and welfare benefits in terms of families rescued from poverty. When these benefits are forced into monetary terms, a great deal of violence is inevitably done to their inherent heterogeneity, and useful information is suppressed. The incommensurability of the benefits makes it difficult for cost-benefit analysis to contribute greatly to the choices that must be made among major categories like health, education and welfare.'

But . . . 'while the big choices may not be greatly illuminated by cost-benefit analysis, the narrower ones can be.'

These recently developed techniques have to be tried with a full sense of their technical limitations and of their attractions to the politically astute. Cost-effectiveness, cost-benefit analysis and now P.P.B.S. are attractive because they assist the central control of spending and make inevitable the moral subservience of spending departments to the Treasury. Doubt is cast on any programme whose benefits cannot easily be translated into units of money and, given a universal application of the method, resources may eventually be withheld from such programmes. But socially they may be the most desirable programmes and, economically, possibly the most productive.

Like simple accounting and arithmetic before them, these newest techniques must not be allowed to dominate our decision-making. They have to be kept strictly in their place. Studies based on efficiency criteria are much needed and increasingly useful but are only a small part of a rational approach to planning. Misjudgements can easily be made about which of two alternatives is most efficient unless both of them can be related to the distribution of resources in society. And, with Aaron Wildavsky, 'I would feel much better if political rationality were being pursued with the same vigour and capability as is economic efficiency' ('The political economy of efficiency: cost-benefit analysis, systems analysis and programme budgeting.' Symposium on P.P.B.S., *Public Administration Review,* December 1966).

Britain is failing to identify social objectives and failing to translate objectives into effective policy programmes. The management of our social services is being allowed to be controlled by narrowly economic criteria which are not even of the 'functional' type being introduced extensively in the United States. We are obsessed with an unreal concept of 'public expenditure'. And we are so obsessed with the idea of economic growth that we fail to give serious attention to the questions of what the growth is for, and fail to ask what social objectives can be reached without any growth at all.

The problem is complex and various solutions need to be considered. One possibility is the creation of a Department of Social Planning, guided by consultative committees recruited from the social services, research institutes and the universities, which would be not so much a co-ordinating instrument as a long-term planning instrument and a source of information about the social programmes of the Government and the local authorities. It might incorporate the existing Central Statistical Office. What could the department do?

First, it could help to furnish a dense network of comparative information of the kind described earlier. Apart from cross-national data, this would include information about the distribution in Britain of all resources, and not just money incomes, both regionally and sectionally. It would also include information about people receiving help, and the amount of help they receive from the three systems of public, fiscal and occupational welfare. If needs are to be met they must first be perceived. If fiscal and other systems of welfare are to be modified, their present effects must first be made known.

Secondly, the new department might undertake a continuing review of standards of deprivation. The rates actually paid by the Ministry of Social Security and by the Supplementary Benefits Commission have a long history and derive from the rates recommended in the Beveridge Report of 1942. No expert study or review has been made of the underlying logic of the relativity between different rates or of the relativity between all the rates and earnings levels. Definitions of 'slum', 'substandard housing', 'overcrowding', 'inadequate living facilities', 'oversized classes', 'disability', 'disease', 'inadequate diet', deserve continuing study.

Thirdly, the department would be responsible for preparing and publishing five-year and ten-year plans. These would be of a more functional kind than the hospital and local authorities' plans published by the Ministry of Health and would incorporate discussion of national objectives as well as some kind of rationale for the allocation of resources as between different services. How can we decide priorities between, say, health and education? Table 2 shows some of the changes that have been taking place in expenditure in recent years.

Table 2 Changes in current and capital expenditure on the Social Services 1958-9 to 1965-6

Service	Expenditure (1965-6) as % expenditure (1958-9)		Expenditure as % of total expenditure			
	Current	Capital	Current		Capital	
			1958-9	1965-6	1958-9	1965-6
Education	206	192	22	25	28	24
National Health Service	171	292	24	22	7	9
Local Welfare Services	204	442	1	1	1	2
Child Care	184	1,100	1	1	0	0
School Meals and Milk	174	189	2	2	2	1
Welfare Foods	158		1	1		
National Insurance and Industrial Injuries	194		33	35		
War Pensions	121		3	2		
Non-Contributory Old-age Pensions	35		1	0		
National Assistance	203		4	5		
Family Allowances	118		4	3		
Housing	135	227	4	3	63	63
All 'Public' Services	182	223	100	100	100	100
Tax Allowances for Children	230					
Roads and Highways		240				
Gross Domestic Fixed Capital Formation		179				
Total Personal Income	156					
National Income	168					

Primary Source: Annual Abstract of Statistics for 1966

Within services there have been other striking changes — capital expenditure on universities, for example, jumping from 12 per cent of total capital expenditure on education in 1958-9 to 30 per cent in 1965-6.

President Johnson's research and policy committee, quoted earlier, concluded that, despite their enthusiasm for P.P.B.S. the 'puzzling problem of achieving rational balance in allocating scarce resources among competing functional fields . . . remains unsolved. In the executive branch such issues rest finally upon presidential judgement after searching staff review.' The problem is no less puzzling in Britain — though a comprehensive analysis of relative deprivation would at least suggest what deficiencies in resources contributed most to such total and partial poverty as prevails in this country.

Finally, the department might be the centre for the continuing discussion and formulation of national objectives. And although the implications of this for large-scale bureaucracy may annoy or frighten us, it can be argued that it is no more than a logical development in an advanced industrial society which seeks to preserve democratic values and weigh human needs carefully.

A more rigorous description of the social structure and of the internal distribution of resources would reveal the gaps and inconsistencies in social policies and highlight certain types of need. I am assuming that such knowledge would help to consolidate opinion in favour of the adoption of certain national objectives — such as social integration, reduction of poverty and of social isolation, the diffusion of modern medical, surgical and social-work skills to all sections of the population, the attainment of a modern standard of facilities in the home, and greater opportunity to participate in the life of the community, including leisure pursuits.

Priorities always have to be fixed by governments and at the present time there is of course very little room for manoeuvre *if* (a) we take account of the steady proportional increase in the number of dependants, the expansionist momentum that has been built up in higher education and the commitment to raise the school-leaving age; and *if* (b) we assume that the present tax system is inviolable.

But there is tremendous scope for manoeuvre if we remember that the British public tends to approve the extension of civil rights and is as willing to pay compulsory insurance contributions as it is unwilling to pay compulsory direct taxes. Proportional social security contributions within a national superannuation scheme could play a major part in the social strategy of the next ten years.

There is tremendous scope for manoeuvre if the two systems of recognizing dependency, public and fiscal, are rationalized. The value of tax allowances for children has increased by 174 per cent in the last ten years (to £630 million) while the cost of family allowances has increased by only 25 per cent (to £160 million). The possibility of switching much of the tax allowance cost into family allowances — and finding an additional smaller amount from tax-payers who do not have dependent children to add to the total paid in family allowances — would raise hundreds of thousands of families out of poverty by today's standards and would leave middle-income families with children no worse off. Other tax allowances, such as that on mortgage repayments could be reviewed.

There is also, to take a different example, considerable scope for manoeuvre if we were to put more fully into practice the objectives, to which lip service is often paid, of caring for old people at home rather than in institutions. We have done little or nothing in fact to reduce the much greater relative expenditure on institutional rather than on community services. For example, we spend £50 million to £60 million on chronic sick and geriatric hospitals and over £40 million a year on old people's homes, but only about half this final amount on home help, home nursing and meals services for the aged. With ingenuity and much more emphasis in each local community on small units of sheltered housing (which could be converted from existing property as well as newly built), it would be possible to greatly alter this maldistribution.

What is emerging now is a strategy governed by the application of universal principles to particular categories of need. There are fundamental arguments against the wider use of income tests or the introduction of measures such as negative income tax in social policy. Quite apart from its present technical impracticability, even a computerized income test would be a very crude instrument for identifying need and would merely reinforce some of the divisive features of British society.

For the chief existing means test reflects and sustains an elaborate system of public values. To live on the state is a matter for shame and derision. In all countries the receipt of public assistance implies inferior status. It signifies the lowest echelon of society, and people instinctively shy away from it. Even when historical improvements have been made in its administration, it is — by the very nature and purpose of the service according to today's standards — regarded with distaste or reluctance by potential applicants in the population. Many fail to come forward to claim benefits. There is considerable evidence therefore that most means tests are thoroughly inefficient.

The operation of a means test or an income test causes attention to be concentrated on problems of wilful concealment of resources and unwillingness to work instead of what are usually the underlying problems of disability, mental ill health, plural dependancy or adversity, and lack of opportunity for employment. Moreover, by resorting to arguments about income tests we fail to address ourselves to what may be the crucial problem of maldistribution of resources that hits people according to dependancy or adversity.

Should one section of the population that is fortunate enough to have employers who are willing to give them full pay for the first six months of sickness enjoy full security in sickness while another section first has to qualify through a contribution record for a sickness benefit of less than 'subsistence' standard and then have to seek supplementation to such a standard on test of means? Should not common principles of treatment be applied to the sick, even if the administering agency is sometimes State, sometimes employer?

Devaluation simply strengthens the case which already exists for action to reduce poverty — for much larger family allowances (financed partly by reduced children's tax allowances), pensions for the disabled, maintenance allowances for fatherless families and the rationalization of a chaotic variety of private and public pension schemes within a national superannuation scheme. A percentage disability pension could be of special value. Evidence is accumulating of the high proportion of disabled not only among the long-term unemployed, but also among the low-paid.

The introduction of a disability pension would almost certainly be more effective than the introduction of minimum wage legislation in reducing poverty. By virtue of being a sum of money which might be related to limitation of activity, it also offers means of supplementing the retirement pension without recourse to a means test and the exercise of discretion by officers of the Supplementary Benefits Commission. These are some of the measures which could serve national objectives.

5 Local Authority Plans for Social Services for Old People *

The health and welfare services, as at present constituted, have been operating for nearly fifteen years. The present Government has been in power for twelve years. Are the health and welfare needs of the elderly being met? In 1954 the Phillips Committee, in its report on the *Economic and Financial Problems of the Provision for Old Age,* concluded, 'At this stage of their development it is difficult to obtain a clear picture of the sort of services old people will need, or the scale on which they should be provided.' (2) The committee had not been very adventurous in instituting inquiries and devoted only half a dozen rather general pages of its report to the subject, as did the Guillebaud Committee in its report on the cost of the National Health Service. (3) Neither the Government nor the Opposition have displayed much interest in a social problem that is growing fast and no other committee or commission has been asked to investigate the care of the aged. In 1957 a semi-official report of a ministry survey of the services for the chronic sick and elderly, written by Dr C. A. Boucher, a Senior Medical Officer of the ministry, was published. (4) This contained some disturbing information which showed the need for administrative overhaul and for a general expansion of the domiciliary services but it did not lead to the general review of policy that the Guillebaud Committee, among others, had hoped for.

There are other examples from this era of a major social issue being pushed into the background, whether from conscious or subconscious motives. A National Advisory Council on the Employment of Old People was wound up peremptorily just when it had begun to tackle a large programme of work. This is not the place to give a detailed history. A clear picture from official sources of the services needed by old people has not been given. Considering the scale and severity of their problems, future historians are likely to regard this as a major indictment of British social policy. Has the situation now been remedied by the publication of the plans for the next ten years or so? Have we been presented in fact with a real plan for the development

---

* Address given to a Conference of the Association of Municipal Corporations, County Councils Association and London County Council at Morecambe on 23-4 April 1963. (1)

of health and welfare services for old people, or is it a tame projection of current trends in a number of fragmented and haphazard services?

That the Ministry of Health is now beginning to *plan* these kind of services is a most welcome fact. In any society seeking to justify itself as a democracy, anything is better than silence, or than that kind of haughty disdain for public inquiry and discussion which has for too long characterized the inner counsels of government. My anxiety is that the early planning will not get the ruthless criticism it deserves. I do not mean to imply that govermnent proposals which are even modestly constructive should always be met with destructive criticism. The best respect that can be paid to any review of social services or problems — and this applies to independent reviews as much as those prepared by government — is critical evaluation.

I cannot pretend to do this justice. I shall confine myself mainly to those services aimed primarily at the elderly and offer some thoughts on the problem of planning, using some of the research conclusions reached during a recent national survey of residential institutions and homes for old people in England and Wales. Some of what follows consists of first impressions of a publication still warm from the press.

Hospital Planning

At the start it is useful to remember that at the Ministry of Health during 1959-60 a new Permanent Secretary, new Chief Medical Officer, new Chief Architect and new Minister were appointed and also that the Minister has now been in office longer than all except two of his seven predecessors since the war. In 1961 Regional Hospital Boards were invited to submit plans for hospital development for the next ten years. After negotiation and discussion *A Hospital Plan for England and Wales* was published in January 1962. (5) The 146 local health and welfare authorities of England and Wales were then invited to submit corresponding plans for the development of their local services for the ten years up to 1972. The result was *Health and Welfare: The Development of Community Care.* (6)

The Hospital Plan contains some encouraging proposals but also depends on a number of vague and inconsistent assumptions. The need for geriatric beds, for example, is estimated to be 1.4 beds per 1,000 total population in 1975, on the basis of unspecified and unpublished studies by the ministry. This figure becomes 1.3 on p. 274 of the plan — a small inconsistency, perhaps, but one which nonetheless involves a few thousand beds. Between 1960 and 1975 it is planned to keep the same ratio of geriatric beds to total population but, of course, because the elderly population is increasing this means a relative reduction in the number of beds in chronic sick and geriatric hospitals. In 1960 there were 10.8 beds per 1,000 population aged 65 and over and in 1975 it is put at 9.4. (We might wonder in passing why it is put at 9.4 when the plan suggests that 'The necessary hospital provision is being achieved with about 10 hospital beds per 1,000 aged 65 and over.') The relative increase in the elderly population, particularly of the over 75s, seems to be ignored, yet they comprise most of the patients in such hospitals. Their numbers increased by 23 per cent in the last decade and, according to the Registrar General, they will increase by 15 per cent in the next decade, and by 23 per cent in the decade after that. We are left wondering how the ministry can justify the figures put forward in the plan. They are not necessarily too low, but the public is entitled to a more detailed explanation.

The Minister assumes that as more geriatric physicians are appointed and as greater emphasis is given to active treatment and rehabilitation, the number of patients will diminish. The assumption is the same for elderly patients in mental hospitals. Proportionate to the total elderly population, their numbers are expected to fall even more strikingly. Altogether, it is envisaged that by 1975 only 1.8 beds for mental illness per 1,000 population will be wanted, compared with 3.3 beds per 1,000 at present. (It should be noted, however, that a figure of 1.9 per 1,000 for 1975 is given in an appendix on p. 275.)

I believe it would be right to aim at gradually reducing long-stay accommodation in the next ten or twenty years, and this is the underlying theme of all I have to say, but only if alternative and re-organized services are built up swiftly. This qualification must be emphasized. Upon it turns the question of whether this plan really is a plan. A number of prickly questions might be asked. Is it not ir-responsible to assume that the flow out of hospital is good, without exploring rigorously whether it is and to what extent? There is little evidence of the Minister's anxiety to find out what is happening to elderly patients discharged from hospital and whether they really do receive adequate care and supervision. May we hope for a substantial and rigorous investigation?

In trying to estimate the number of different hospital beds that are needed it is necessary also to ask how many elderly patients in psychiatric hospitals might be in geriatric hospitals and vice versa. Elderly patients are admitted to one hospital rather than another some-times because it is the only one in the area with a vacant bed rather than because it supplies the appropriate treatment. Again, how many elderly people are there at home who should be in hospital? And how many patients are there in hospital who should be in hostels or residential homes? However difficult these questions may be to answer they seem to be obvious ones to ask. Yet they have not been considered in any depth in studies of the demand for hospital care. Until they are considered there is little prospect of adopting rational assumptions for policy. Sometimes clinical variables have been taken fitfully into account, but scarcely at all the relevant social and psychological variables. Without analysing the context within which different services function, as well as their interrelationships, a coherent policy cannot be developed. It is rather like building a superstructure without joints, cross-struts or even adequate foundations. We have never had a serious, official review of what would be a rational administration of social services for the elderly. The services have grown up piecemeal and without forethought.

There are other tests of good policies. In supporting a reduction in hospital beds for mental illness the Minister assumes that mental health hostels will be built as a part alternative. In addition to hostels for the elderly (the numbers of which are not separately identified in the plans), about 200 are to be built for other age-groups during the next ten years. Yet the ministry does not appear to have attempted to evaluate the success of hostels, particularly those for the confused aged, which have been open for five and in some instances ten years. Without this his plan has the suspicious marks of being an economy measure. Hostels are cheaper to build and to maintain. How far must old people be admitted to special hostels rather than to ordinary residential accommodation? Searching inquiries are vital if we are to weigh up humanely the alternative forms of care that should be provided in the coming years. The virtues of mental health hostels also deserve to be scrutinized. They could too easily become second-class hospitals remote from regular psychiatric supervision and care. And are they part of 'community' care? They are not necessarily more in the community than hospitals. They could be just as remote or more so. Much depends on where they are sited and how they might be run. You cannot regard the word 'community' as having magical properties which immediately transform reality every time it is used.

Planning for Community Care

To what extent has the publication of *Health and Welfare: The Development of Community Care* answered some at least of these questions? It is perhaps significant that the word 'plan', present in the publication which it is meant to complement, is missing from the title. The preface is similarly more diffident. What does the report reveal?

The preface states that 'an attempt is made to suggest the aims and standards which ought to govern' the development of the services. This is guarded language. To an outsider it seems surprising that the ministry did not advise local authorities on the submission of their plans, particularly on such matters as population projections. It did not give the kind of guidance which might be expected of any central organization with access to lines of communication, statistical personnel and funds. There seems to have been little encouragement, financial or otherwise, to strike out boldly in new directions and, moreover, no joint discussions were held. Evidence both of effective planning and of belief in the virtues of local government is lacking.

The Minister has been reluctant to adopt standards for the services even as distant targets. The command paper concludes regretfully that 'it is impracticable to suggest a ratio in such precise terms for the provision of residential accommodation by local authorities' as that for geriatric beds — though a possible range of 18 to 22 places for every 1,000 people aged 65 and over is put forward gingerly. Yet there is no more evidence for the geriatric ratio than there is for a residential homes ratio. After pointing out the average ratios for home nurses and home helps per 1,000 population which local authorities envisage by 1972 the Blue Book concludes that those who propose a smaller than average ratio 'will need to consider whether their assessment requires revision'. Not everyone will find this intoxicating language. The average ratio proposed for 1972 has already been reached by thirty-five local authorities.

Certainly there are reminders that the number of grouped dwellings for the elderly will 'need to be greatly expanded', that there is 'scope for much further expansion' in meals services and that for laundry services 'there is nothing to suggest that the limits of expansion are in sight'. But such remarks allow widely different interpretation. The cynic might be forgiven for noting that the smaller the size or the cost of the service being discussed, the more daring the minister's phraseology. Despite the admission of the need for expansion there is no corresponding financial commitment. Indeed, the Blue Book points out that for *all* the services the rate of increase in revenue expenditure for the next nine years 'is approximately the same as during the preceding *five* years.'

Conclusions can only be drawn with care from the published figures. Many councils would have wished, no doubt, to see notes published, explaining certain features of their own statistics which make comparison difficult. Indicators like staffing ratios, moreover, do not reveal everything about even the scope, still less the quality, of a service. Some councils have three and four times as much residential accommodation as others. Sometimes this is explained by the presence or absence of voluntary and private homes in the area, but not often. There is no evidence suggesting that the needs of the elderly vary so much and the ministry, in preparing its plans, should have initiated inquiries showing the extent to which hospital and residential accommodation for the elderly, when taken together, vary from area to area. Local councils have neither the information nor the resources to do this on their own. Yet if they are to be given the responsibility of deciding levels of need, this is part of the information they require.

There is little evidence that bigger residential services correspond with smaller domiciliary services or vice versa. Some of the councils providing most residential accommodation also have the best staffing ratios for home nursing and home help services. Among the dozen counties with the largest amount of residential accommodation are Montgomeryshire, Cardiganshire, Breconshire, Merionethshire and Carmarthenshire. They are also among the dozen or so counties with high staffing ratios for home nursing and home help and, moreover, remain among the top dozen or so in the plans projected for 1972. Again, however, it is important to remember that staffing ratios do not reveal everything. Home helps, for example, may be used thinly or intensively — visiting many old people just once a week in one area but few old people in another several times a week.

Inequality in Local Authority Services

How can the priorities in the local authority plans be described and discussed? After specifying the variations in the numbers of elderly people from area to area, Paragraph 46 states, 'It is therefore necessary that in each area the need for services for the elderly should be assessed not in relation to the total population but to the present and prospective numbers aged 65 and over.' Thus it is surprising that the numbers of home helps and district nurses in each authority are not given as a ratio of the population over 65, in view of the preponderance of their work for the elderly. However, it is possible to re-calculate the figures and an attempt is made in the accompanying table to bring out differences between authorities in their plans for the future. (7) Some of the county boroughs with around ten home helps per 1,000 people aged 65 and over, like Rotherham, Barnsley and Warrington, also have among the best home nurse ratios, and moreover, propose further expansion so that they will maintain their positions at the head of the league table. Other councils start with good, though not the highest, staffing ratios and propose big improvements. Oldham, Salford, West Hartlepool and Burton-on-Trent propose to double or treble the number of home helps relative to the elderly population within the next ten years. West Hartlepool and Salford also propose to double the number of home nurses.

The evidence from numerous surveys suggests that the expansion of domiciliary services for old people, even from the highest levels prevailing today, needs to be much greater. The average number of home helps per 1,000 population aged 65 and over, for example, might justifiably rise to 15 within ten years, and preferably to 20. Oldham is so far the only council to aim at achieving this figure, though Newcastle, Coventry, Rotherham, Warrington, Barnsley and Monmouthshire approach it.

Relative to the elderly population, the expansion in number of home helps envisaged by all councils is less than 24 per cent during the next ten years. There are 4½ home helps per 1,000 persons aged 65 and over, a figure which is expected to increase to only 5½ by 1972. There was a bigger expansion in the eight years 1953-61 — and these are generally regarded as lean years for the health and welfare services. Even more disturbing are the proposals for home nurses. Relative to the population of 65 and over, local councils propose increasing their numbers by less than 8 per cent. That is not very impressive over a period of ten years. Nor is it even easy to fulfil without special measures. There is a problem of recruitment and during the last five years there has been an absolute reduction in the number of visits paid by home nurses to old people. The command paper contains no reference to this.

Some councils possess from four to ten times as many home helps as others, relative to the population aged 65 and over. There are some at the bottom of the league which propose staying there. They include Cornwall, East Sussex, the Isle of Wight, Westmorland, Caernarvonshire, Eastbourne, Southampton, Tynemouth, Chester and Merthyr Tydfil. And from levels which are already below the national average there are councils responsible for large populations, like Birmingham, which are actually proposing to *reduce* the relative staffing ratio. The net cost of the home help service per 1,000 population varies from £10 to £450 (annual report for 1961, p.86) and the number of persons helped in a year (also per 1,000 population) from 1½ to 12.

Unification of Service

Unification of home services and not just their separate expansion is required. There is no focus of responsibility in each local area. Few older persons have just one particular need. Most have several needs simultaneously. When a person moves house, leaves hospital, or deteriorates or recovers in health it is difficult to ensure continuity of responsibility. No single authority or person can be named and told, 'You are responsible. You must see that the right things are done at the time.' Many relatives, doctors and social workers have experienced the frustration of having to phone several different local offices to arrange the care of an old person. If you are to achieve anything at all you have to harass them. They are short of workers; they often do not realize the essential fact of continuity. These are the precepts of the concerned outsider.

Consider elderly patients discharged from hospital. Who ensures that different services are laid on if they are needed? Who checks to find whether one service should in fact be supplemented by several others? It is really only an accident that meals and laundry services are administered separately from the home help service. Yet in many areas home helps already prepare meals and wash laundry for old people whom they visit. There is no reason why a single organization should not control and integrate these functions.

Sooner or later some kind of routine visiting to older people in their own homes will be an accepted duty of the public social services. Voluntary bodies do not possess the resources and are not really equipped to do the job fully. They can offer supplementary services but the elderly population is now far too large for voluntary organizations to cope on their own. Visiting should be linked with an expanded home help service or, as it might be called, a comprehensive family help service. Because it will take time to build up staff and strategies priority might be given to those aged 80 and over or those aged 75 and over.

In debating the virtues of routine visiting there are many who fear that individual freedom and privacy may be restricted by the over-zealous organization of welfare. They say that individual privacy should always be respected but so it can even when a simultaneous responsibility of offering help is acknowledged. People should, of course, retain the right to discourage callers. Initiatives can still be made. Much of the problem is in helping some people in the community as they grow older from becoming detached from the network of community contacts.

The domiciliary welfare services cannot be built up swiftly and effectively without administrative reform. Local services are fragmented and should be grouped together more logically. A unified or comprehensive family help service is therefore the first priority.

Sheltered Housing
Second in any list of priorities would be the expansion of special and sheltered housing for older people. More of the elderly than of other sections of the population occupy the worst kind of housing. Many are unable to continue as long as they might living independently in their own homes because of the poor condition of their homes. There is a strong case for more one-bedroom and two-bedroom accommodation. The Ministry of Housing does not understand or acknowledge the full

scale of the need. Several reasons for this might be given. For example, fewer elderly people have five or more married or unmarried children and more have only one or two. This change has unsuspected implications. If you have had a large family the youngest may have been born to you at forty. When you are sixty-five he or she might still not be married or, if married, may still be at home. He or she may not yet have had the two or three children to qualify for a council house. But old people with these family characteristics are becoming fewer. The generation having only one, two or three children in the 1920s is reaching old age. There will be a much smaller gap in age, on average, between them and their youngest children. The children are likely to be married and the grandchildren growing up long before the grandparents are drawing pensions. Therefore the need for accommodation just for married couples, or widows or widowers in their sixties or seventies, will have increased disproportionately. However, this is balanced in part by the widowed moving to rejoin their middle-aged children when they become very old and frail. This is just one reason why the demand for small housing, i.e. one or two-bedroom dwellings, has been rising faster than the population of pensionable age.

Current reports about sheltered or group dwelling schemes, with six, ten or twenty flatlets or bungalows with a housekeeper or warden on call in one house and some communal services, suggest that they are often successful. (8) They seem to be popular. Very few of the tenants find it necessary to enter residential accommodation subsequently. The Blue Book points out that only 3,400 had been provided by the end of 1962 (about one for every 1,700 old people) and suggests that there should be a big expansion. Study of various data suggests a minimum target figure of 50 per 1,000 persons aged 65 and over. In working out schemes the possibilities of modernization and conversion, especially of older but still solid buildings in the town centres, could be pursued. Too many councils think only of grouped dwellings outside the town or city, and forget the disadvantages of moving older people several miles. Small sites in urban centres can be used as well as the end of a row of terraced houses modernized. Many older people might thereby be saved the necessity of resorting to a home or even hospital.

Abandoning Institutions
Third in the list of priorities is the abandonment of outmoded institutions within ten if not five years. I have been told by staff that old buildings do not really matter so long as the staff in them are good and have reasonable facilities. The experience of visiting old institutions and new residential homes throughout the country contradicted these assurances. I learned of the subtle ways by which the severity of Poor

Law buildings is conveyed to both the staff and the residents. Anyone who studies the departure of staff and residents from the environment of an old institution into a small purpose-built or converted home will note an impressive change in behaviour and attitudes on both sides.

Yet some councils in the country are reluctant to close all the old institutions. When the report on residential Homes was published last November, (9) local press reports often followed a refrain. 'It is scandalous that these institutions are allowed to exist, but of course ours is not like all the others; we have improved it a lot.' It is not just that people become accustomed to deficiencies and what amount to cruel procedures. They console themselves with comparisons with the past when the comparisons should be with contemporary outside society. As a consequence people come to believe that the conditions are as good as the inmates deserve.

Rationalizations are made for practices people would not care to submit to themselves. One example is provision for married couples in residential Homes. When meeting chief welfare officers or wardens, say, it is natural to ask why a husband lives in one block and his wife in another. 'Well,' it is usually explained, 'some people who reach that age have had enough. They are really glad to see the back of each other. It gives them a bit of relief, in fact it is almost a pleasure. And,' as an afterthought, 'they can see each other for an hour every afternoon.' In our research we visited scores of institutions. We did not meet a married couple (though no doubt there may be a few) who did not want to live together.

The command paper does not show which councils have already abandoned former workhouses or propose doing so in the next few years. Apparently only 20,000 of the 34,000 places are to be closed by 1972. By comparing the results of the recent national survey with information in the report, however, it seems that among the forty-six authorities with more than 60 per cent of their accommodation in former workhouses in 1960 some, like Leicestershire, Wiltshire, the North Riding, Ipswich, Leicester, York and Barnsley, are replacing all or a lot; others, like London, Somerset, Worcestershire, Southend, Bristol and Glamorgan are making a modest but quite insufficient effort. Still others are proposing to do little or nothing. They include Derbyshire, Staffordshire, Birmingham, Doncaster, Gateshead, Middlesbrough and Worcester. To these might be added a number of councils with a smaller relative but large absolute amount of such accommodation who are not proposing to replace the greater part of it, including Surrey, Durham, Lancashire, Manchester and Liverpool. After his speech at Halesowen last September, the Minister will regard these as among the black sheep in his flock.

The Halesowen speech courageously sought the abandonment of old institutions and the present report is also emphatic on this point in interesting contrast to much else, though the poorer councils with a large inheritance of old buildings might reasonably have expected and deserved special Exchequer help. The alternatives require anxious thought and investigation. It is much easier to discard and to abandon than to be constructive. The Minister might have argued that in ten or twenty years time a prosperous society could consider abandoning long-stay residential homes just as he has been arguing that long-stay hospital accommodation might be greatly reduced. In the meantime Britain could set about the task of building up special housing and domiciliary services and so create the kind of society in which services could be taken to people instead of people being taken to institutions. Eventually it should be feasible to care for people in their own homes up to the point of them needing specialized hospital care — thereby being able to abandon intermediate institutions. (10)

Current evidence should encourage any council to be reluctant to add greatly to its residential accommodation. Sheltered housing would secure the same advantages of a measure of supervision and security and yet do more to meet the individual's need for independence and privacy and a greater measure of contact with former locality and family and friends. I sometimes wonder wistfully whether an unconventional council might try to dispense with residential homes by creating sheltered housing on a considerable scale and simultaneously expand the domiciliary services. This could be a major experiment with implications for other countries as well as the rest of Britain.

Finally, the need for more training must be added to this short list of priorities. Much attention has been given to the desirability of setting up university and Younghusband courses for welfare officers and social workers generally. One of the objects of providing these courses is to weed out those who do not possess a very humane attitude and who are temperamentally unsuited to welfare work of one kind or another. This is a neglected function of recruitment to social work courses but also means that there are some excellent people acting as social workers who have never received any training. We would be unwise to neglect the strong qualities of some untrained people, whether latent or expressed, by giving undue emphasis to long courses of higher education. There is the danger of forgetting the needs of people who have not had an advanced education, especially junior staff, in local authority departments and residential homes. It would be possible for local councils, in liaison with university departments, to run short courses for deputy matrons, nursing sisters and attendant staff, particularly senior attendant staff, far more widely than at present. Many staff are simply ignorant of some modern ideas about welfare that could be passed on easily. They are given an insufficient sense of their jobs being held in public respect. They feel they are treated with as few rights as domestic staff. One of the objects of short courses of training is to give staff greater commitment to their work and its quality. There is no doubt at all about the importance of expanding training and instruction courses of every kind. The training and refresher courses for matrons and assistant matrons held by the National Old People's Welfare Council do no more, in the words of the last annual report of the ministry, 'than touch the fringe of need'. A system of training for the vast majority, and not just a small élite, needs to be developed.

In summary, first, a comprehensive welfare or family help service is required. Secondly, there should be a great expansion in special and sheltered forms of housing for old people and the handicapped. Thirdly, old institutions must be closed and every effort made to reduce the need for residential Homes by introducing, among other things, schemes of rehabilitation which include short-stay provision. Finally, there must be a swift expansion in training courses, particularly short courses for junior welfare staff.

The Blue Book is indeed welcome as a first attempt to marshal the necessary intelligence, to which many people have contributed. But it is a limited start and not yet a plan in any respectworthy sense of that term. We are faced with an immense national problem. We are still awaiting an imaginative political lead from a government willing to commit itself to large-scale administrative reform and the kind of expansion in domiciliary services, special housing and training that the situation requires. This involves a deliberate decision to spend considerably more Exchequer money. In the health and welfare services you cannot achieve humanity through parsimony.

Inequality among Councils in plans for Welfare

Local authorities listed in order of provision of home helps per 1,000 population aged 65 and over in 1962	No. of home helps per 1,000 aged 65+		Councils according to rank order of provision as planned for 1972				
	1962 actual	1972 planned	Home helps per 1,000 aged 65+	Home nurses per 1,000 aged 65+	Places in homes per 1,000 aged 65+	Health visitors per 1,000 all ages	Social workers per 1,000 all ages
1. Rotherham	11.2	13.0	4	4	5	106	10
2. Monmouth	11.1	11.9	7	35	86	109	91
3. Newcastle	9.5	13.3	2	41	51	5	60
4. Barnsley	9.4	12.5	5	14	11	21	7
5. South Shields	8.7	8.4	23	61	21	45	53
6. Doncaster	8.4	9.1	15	98	32	90	29
7. Barrow	8.2	8.5	21	82	49	65	39
8. Warrington	8.1	12.4	6	5	22	72	52
8. *Breconshire*	8.1	8.2	27	38	64	86	145
10. Oldham	8.0	16.6	1	69	26	8	10
10. Kingston-on-Hull	8.0	10.2	10	47	13	76	27
12. Nottingham	7.9	8.6	20	30	110	8	74
12. Grimsby	7.9	9.0	17	70	62	51	14
14. *Nottinghamshire*	7.8	7.4	34	95	132	66	120
14. Sunderland	7.8	8.9	18	58	35	32	120
16. Coventry	7.5	13.1	3	20	25	58	136
17. *Northumberland*	7.4	7.4	34	45	129	64	136
18. *Durham*	7.2	9.9	12	88	140	45	128
18. Wigan	7.2	8.5	21	50	47	56	32
18. Newport	7.2	6.1	54	40	37	33	29

Cont'd . . . .

Local authorities listed in order of provision of home helps per 1,000 population aged 65 and over in 1962	No. of home helps per 1,000 aged 65+		Councils according to rank order of provision as planned for 1972				
	1962 actual	1972 planned	Home helps per 1,000 aged 65+	Home nurses per 1,000 aged 65+	Places in homes per 1,000 aged 65+	Health visitors per 1,000 all ages	Social workers per 1,000 all ages
21. Salford	6.9	11.5	8	16	23	3	3
22. Lancashire	6.8	8.0	29	22	115	102	99
22. Gloucestershire	6.8	6.9	43	82	104	49	133
24. London	6.7	7.7	32	93	45	42	37
25. Wakefield	6.5	7.4	34	16	30	14	21
25. Montgomery	6.5	8.2	27	16	5	109	43
27. Carmarthenshire	6.3	6.4	49	48	71	143	78
27. Bradford	6.3	8.3	24	127	64	8	48
29. West Bromwich	6.2	6.3	50	75	53	132	21
29. Leicester	6.2	7.0	42	85	10	3	105
31. Leicestershire	6.1	6.5	48	89	110	128	142
31. Smethwick	6.1	8.3	24	74	95	112	136
33. Reading	6.0	4.8	85	114	106	14	60
33. Huddersfield	6.0	9.6	13	6	4	19	55
35. Cardiganshire	5.9	7.4	34	6	34	130	134
35. Dewsbury	5.9	7.3	38	36	3	21	78
37. West Hartlepool	5.8	10.1	11	22	55	41	21
37. Cambridgeshire	5.8	7.2	39	105	123	80	111
37. East Ham	5.8	5.7	64	139	27	69	45
40. Carlisle	5.6	5.9	58	120	76	68	91
40. York	5.6	7.8	31	78	12	58	5
40. Staffordshire	5.6	9.1	15	125	117	57	111

Cont'd

Local authorities listed in order of provision of home helps per 1,000 population aged 65 and over in 1962	No. of home helps per 1,000 aged 65+		Councils according to rank order of provision as planned for 1972				
	1962 actual	1972 planned	Home helps per 1,000 aged 65+	Home nurses per 1,000 aged 65+	Places in homes per 1,000 aged 65+	Health visitors per 1,000 all ages	Social workers per 1,000 all ages
40. *Essex*	5.6	6.0	56	56	113	85	124
44. Bristol	5.5	8.0	29	54	116	20	48
44. Bolton	5.5	6.2	52	60	107	45	78
46. *Somerset*	5.4	6.2	52	77	135	98	102
46. West Ham	5.4	9.6	13	11	74	30	14
46. Sheffield	5.4	5.8	60	65	101	102	63
49. *Yorkshire/W.Riding*	5.1	5.3	69	103	110	137	69
49. Norwich	5.1	5.0	79	144	35	124	69
51. Gateshead	5.0	6.8	45	6	7	83	50
52. *Suffolk – West*	4.9	6.7	46	72	75	82	116
53. *Cumberland*	4.8	5.9	58	73	101	76	114
53. Ipswich	4.8	5.4	67	58	39	71	96
55. *Hampshire*	4.7	4.3	92	92	136	95	95
55. *Worcestershire*	4.7	5.6	66	44	140	124	136
57. Lincoln	4.6	8.7	19	67	67	80	109
57. *Hertfordshire*	4.6	4.7	88	51	130	115	142
57. Canterbury	4.6	5.1	77	97	138	55	132
57. Burton-on-Trent	4.6	11.4	9	20	32	8	4
57. Stoke-on-Trent	4.6	7.5	33	79	85	95	27
57. Gloucester	4.6	4.1	94	16	18	72	106
63. *Herefordshire*	4.4	8.3	24	71	88	90	60
64. Bury	4.3	4.5	90	132	8	70	21

Cont'd . . . .

Local authorities listed in order of provision of home helps per 1,000 population aged 65 and over in 1962	No of home helps per 1,000 aged 65+		Councils according to rank order of provision as planned for 1972				
	1962 actual	1972 planned	Home helps per 1,000 aged 65+	Home nurses per 1,000 aged 65+	Places in homes per 1,000 aged 65+	Health visitors per 1,000 all ages	Social workers per 1,000 all ages
65. Great Yarmouth	4.2	6.3	50	110	14	49	56
65. *Berkshire*	4.2	5.0	79	26	124	51	142
65. Birmingham	4.2	3.7	109	76	120	102	69
65. Burnley	4.2	5.2	73	94	30	27	45
65. St Helens	4.2	5.0	79	1	94	51	17
65. *Radnorshire*	4.2	5.1	77	6	23	2	17
71. *Lincoln-Lindsey*	4.1	5.2	73	117	126	44	87
71. Dudley	4.1	5.4	67	96	83	129	36
71. Preston	4.1	4.7	88	100	41	61	34
71. *Merioneth*	4.1	7.1	41	14	43	5	37
75. Cardiff	3.9	5.3	69	48	79	58	91
76. Brighton	3.8	4.1	94	34	39	54	7
77. Derbyshire	3.7	5.8	60	25	104	89	140
77. *Bedfordshire*	3.7	3.8	104	90	89	127	118
77. *Glamorgan*	3.7	7.2	39	6	56	122	9
80. Middlesborough	3.6	4.4	91	106	1	43	91
80. *Lincoln-Kesteven*	3.6	3.5	112	119	53	143	64
80. *Middlesex*	3.6	3.5	112	129	100	115	82
80. *Suffolk - East*	3.6	5.8	60	86	143	120	103
80. Oxford	3.6	3.9	101	101	15	74	83
85. Exeter	3.5	5.3	69	32	9	61	10
85. Walsall	3.5	5.3	69	115	120	24	54

Cont'd ....

Local authorities listed in order of provision of home helps per 1,000 population aged 65 and over in 1962	No. of home helps per 1,000 aged 65+		Councils according to rank order of provision as planned for 1972				
	1962 actual	1972 planned	Home helps per 1,000 aged 65+	Home nurses per 1,000 aged 65+	Places in homes per 1,000 aged 65+	Health visitors per 1,000 all ages	Social workers per 1,000 all ages
85. Rochdale	3.5	3.9	101	29	72	78	72
85. Wallasey	3.5	5.0	79	33	58	123	35
89. Leeds	3.4	4.0	97	43	2	36	74
89. Warwickshire	3.4	4.0	97	22	64	115	118
89. Worcester	3.4	4.2	93	145	29	36	66
89. Bootle	3.4	4.1	94	53	68	95	26
89. Anglesey	3.4	3.8	104	122	119	83	65
94. Yorkshire – E. Riding	3.3	3.5	112	63	134	141	129
94. Southend-on-Sea	3.3	3.8	104	139	77	142	129
94. Kent	3.3	3.3	119	139	128	114	140
94. Northamptonshire	3.3	4.0	97	87	98	118	89
94. Wiltshire	3.3	5.0	79	81	145	31	66
94. Stockport	3.3	5.2	73	46	45	39	77
100. Rutland	3.2	3.0	127	111	131	113	84
100. Croydon	3.2	3.5	112	123	43	134	33
100. Oxfordshire	3.2	3.1	124	55	19	109	120
100. Wolverhampton	3.2	3.8	104	108	87	67	106
100. Manchester	3.2	6.9	43	42	19	1	96
100. Swansea	3.2	3.5	112	68	101	98	87
100. Flintshire	3.2	3.3	119	107	114	140	29
107. Blackpool	3.0	6.6	47	84	144	87	41
108. Blackburn	3.0	3.8	104	52	16	145	1

Cont'd . . . . .

Local authorities listed in order of provision of home helps per 1,000 population aged 65 and over in 1962	No. of home helps per 1,000 aged 65+		Councils according to rank order of provision as planned for 1972				
	1962 actual	1972 planned	Home helps per 1,000 aged 65+	Home nurses per 1,000 aged 65+	Places in homes per 1,000 aged 65+	Health visitors per 1,000 all ages	Social workers per 1,000 all ages
109. Yorkshire – N. Riding	2.9	5.2	73	66	62	8	126
109. Peterborough	2.9	3.3	119	134	27	120	124
111. Halifax	2.8	5.7	64	1	70	14	10
112. Surrey	2.7	2.9	131	131	107	107	99
112. Dorset	2.7	4.9	84	143	109	133	117
112. Northampton	2.7	2.9	131	135	82	90	108
112. Pembroke	2.7	4.0	97	11	97	25	41
112. Denbighshire	2.7	3.0	127	3	127	118	50
117. Cheshire	2.6	3.0	127	136	117	138	129
117. Birkenhead	2.6	3.0	127	128	122	105	134
119. Norfolk	2.5	3.5	112	112	90	131	96
119. Sussex – East	2.5	2.8	134	130	90	78	66
119. Cornwall	2.5	2.4	140	113	93	98	56
119. Chester	2.5	2.3	141	138	38	124	74
123. Darlington	2.4	3.4	118	124	47	48	58
123. Southampton	2.4	2.9	131	126	79	98	78
123. Buckinghamshire	2.4	2.6	138	104	142	134	111
126. Derby	2.3	3.9	101	90	58	25	2
126. Tynemouth	2.3	2.8	134	132	79	107	73
126. Lincoln – Holland	2.3	2.2	142	115	51	61	17
126. Isle of Wight	2.3	2.6	138	37	124	33	84
126. Bath	2.3	6.0	56	99	58	23	5

Cont'd

85

Local authorities listed in order of provision of home helps per 1,000 population aged 65 and over in 1962	No. of home helps per 1,000 aged 65+		Councils according to rank order of provision as planned for 1972				
	1962 actual	1972 planned	Home helps per 1,000 aged 65+	Home nurses per 1,000 aged 65+	Places in homes per 1,000 aged 65+	Health visitors per 1,000 all ages	Social workers per 1,000 all ages
131. Shropshire	2.3	3.6	111	109	83	35	103
132. Devon	2.2	6.1	54	121	137	90	43
132. Southport	2.2	3.1	124	79	72	27	14
134. Westmorland	2.1	2.8	134	11	57	14	127
134. Sussex – West	2.1	3.2	123	57	139	138	109
136. Isle of Ely	2.0	3.1	124	102	16	134	89
137. Eastbourne	1.9	1.9	144	62	99	87	115
138. Huntingdonshire	1.8	3.7	109	118	54	90	99
138. Hastings	1.8	3.3	119	63	78	29	58
138. Portsmouth	1.8	4.8	85	137	95	5	17
138. Bournemouth	1.8	4.8	85	139	49	8	21
138. Liverpool	1.8	5.8	60	27	90	38	45
138. Caernarvonshire	1.8	2.7	137	39	68	14	40
144. Merthyr	1.7	2.2	142	28	42	74	120
145. Plymouth	0.6	0.8	145	31	132	40	84

Source: *Health and Welfare: The development of Community Care, Cmnd. 1973*, H.M.S.O., 1963
(County Councils in italics)

Notes

1. The Minister of Health, Mr Enoch Powell, had given the preceding address, in which he introduced the first of the ten-year plans on health and welfare drawn up by the local authorities, which was published in the same week. *(Health and Welfare: The Development of Community Care*, Cmnd. 1973, H.M.S.O., April 1963.) A version of this paper which included more detail about the local authority plans was published in *New Society*, 23 May 1963, and has been incorporated. Much of this special analysis was carried out by Miss Sheila Benson.

2. Para. 321, *Report of the Committee on the Economic and Financial Problems of the Provision for Old Age* (the Phillips Committee), Cmnd. 9333, H.M.S.O., 1954.

3. *Report of the Committee of Enquiry into the Cost of the National Health Service*, Cmnd. 9663, H.M.S.O., 1956.

4. Boucher, C., *Survey of Services Available to the Chronic Sick and Elderly in 1954-5*, Series of Reports on Public Health and Medical Subjects, no. 98, H.M.S.O., 1957.

5. *A Hospital Plan for England and Wales*, Cmnd. 1604, H.M.S.O., 1962.

6. *Health and Welfare: The Development of Community Care:* Plans for the Health and Welfare Services of the Local Authorities in England and Wales, Cmnd. 1973, H.M.S.O., 1963.

7. It is recognized that special factors explain some of the divergencies in the figures. Thus home help services in Plymouth are operated largely through voluntary effort supported by an annual council grant and the number of voluntary helpers are not included in the statistics. Again, Blackburn council is exceptional in treating health visitors as social workers and therefore the ratios for these two types of staff cannot properly be compared with those of other councils.

8. Ministry of Housing and Local Government, *Grouped Flatlets for Old People: A Sociological Study*, H.M.S.O., 1962.

9. Townsend, P., *The Last Refuge: A Survey of Residential Institutions and Homes for the Aged in England and Wales*, Routledge & Kegan Paul, 1962.

10. I have cut a summary of the reasons, because these are given in 'The Argument for Gradually Abandoning Communal Homes for the Aged', in my book, *The Social Minority*, Allen Lane, 1973.

6 Everyone His Own Home: Inequality in Housing and the Creation of a National Service *

In Britain, as in most countries, housing is not yet fully recognized as a social service. Thus, even in Government official statistics, net public expenditure on housing is sometimes amalgamated with that on health, education, welfare and social security and sometimes kept distinct.(1) It hovers awkwardly on the threshold of the status of a social service, partly because of the physical and technological emphasis with which town planning has been traditionally conceived, but partly because of the traditional role of property in the capitalist economy. If housing were no longer to be a secure element of the private market, where, it is rhetorically suggested, should we be? The Englishman's home is his castle and if that home were subject to social creativity and control England itself would be a changed place. Historically, therefore, there have been strong restraints even on treating housing as a social service for the working classes, still less on treating it as a national service concerned with urban and rural development as a whole. I shall argue that the problem of urban poverty and slums cannot be understood without knowledge of the housing market and the social allocation and use of all accommodation and land, and that the problems of slums, poverty and homelessness cannot be solved without making housing a national service. In contemporary terms this means, for example, redistribution to the poor of housing resources owned and used by the rich; a better balance between new housing and improvement and between new towns or estates and urban regeneration; the development, for poor and rich and tenants and owner-occupiers alike; of common principles about the use of land and accommodation; and flat-rate housing allowances as of right instead of means-tested allowances.

Measures of Need
Despite innovations introduced by successive Governments housing policy is still recognizably makeshift, fluctuating from a preference, under Labour, for housing as a social utility, to renewed emphasis, under the Tories, upon a free market.(2) The first step must be to obtain some understanding of housing needs. This can only be achieved

* First published in the *Royal Institute of British Architects' Journal*, January 1973.

by recognizing that conventional methods of defining and measuring them are biased and narrow. Needs are relative to society. This has to be digested and spelt out in relation to structures defined as slums, physical amenities, space, environment and community facilities. A distinction has to be made between a society's standards of need and objective standards. In its legislation and practice a society comes to define what it means by both good housing and minimally adequate housing. The standards tend to change with the passage of time. Thus the standards set by Octavia Hill and other reformers concerned with the housing of the working classes were that privies and a water tap could be shared by several households on the same landing and that it was justifiable for a family with one or two or even several children to live in a single room.(3) Today the Parker Morris Committee has defined a different and much more generous standard.(4) The official census definition of overcrowding has shifted from two or more persons per room around the turn of the century to 1½ or more persons per room in the 1950s and 1960s and is showing signs of changing again to one person or more per room or to an alternative standard. Similarly local authorities have come to be less stringent in their definitions of a slum. Changes in legislation, however, follow tardily in the wake of changes introduced in research or even in official measurement. Time is needed for different social groups and organizations and especially Governments to come to accept new standards.

Social perceptions of need therefore tend to change with the passage of time. To some extent their liability to change is affected by the search for objective or independent criteria of need. The correlations made by pioneers like Chadwick and Simon between insanitary dwellings and infectious disease led to the promulgation of Public Health Acts. Research into the relationship between overcrowding and, for example, tuberculosis has assisted the acceptance of more spacious units of accommodation for different sizes of family.(5)

Studies of the different effects of inequality of housing and environment can be put together and amount to a respectable line of inquiry. Hypothermia and the elderly,(6) the pollution of Billingham(7) and the uneven development of the community services of different authorities (8) provide three current examples. But certain general principles can be drawn from these examples. It is the duty of social scientists not merely to use the standards defined by society itself in its legislation and administrative regulations or implicit in its policy decisions, to find how far they are actually fulfilled, but also to develop new standards which help to reveal the effects of our policies and styles of living and suggest new insights into the human predicament. Of course the search for pure objectivity is illusory but not the search for vantage points from which to view the human predicament which are different from those erected by society itself. Just as society's standards can be demonstrated to change so any objective standards must relate to the conditions and needs in society at a particular time. The nature of the educational system and norms about child care help to shape the physical needs of the family for space and facilities. The extension of the school-leaving age, the lowering of the age of marriage and the changes in social relationships typified by the record player, the deep freeze and the cocktail cabinet are instances of the new obligations and inducements which are continuously shaping and re-shaping our needs. These needs are felt; or they are acknowledged socially or, finally, they can be demonstrated, against external criteria, to exist. There are therefore three clearly distinguishable approaches towards the measurement of need — identifying subjective, social and 'objective' need.

Why Housing Policies are Limited

Public discussion of housing tends to be dominated by society's percep-tions of housing needs, to the near exclusion of independent or alternative measurement of such needs. Housing problems have come to be defined in ways which are acceptable to ruling élites, particularly the Government, and are measured according to procedures devised by Government servants. The 'problems' of housing in Britain today are restrictedly defined in terms of minimal standards rather than of unequal distribution or inadequately controlled exploitation. They are measured in the Census and central departmental surveys and publicized by the press more in terms of physical appearance, amenities and layout than of social and economic allocation and use. Thus, little is known about the size of gardens or values of housing used by different social groups. Housing problems are seen by politicians as temporary aberrations which will either pass with increasing prosperity or in the streamlining of existing policies. They are not seen as an inevitable and continuing aspect of structural inequality. Their scale also tends to be underestimated by those with administrative responsibility for housing for the good reason that they are then seen as psychologically and financially more manageable.

This thesis, that social perception of the problem is unduly restricted, could be documented at length, but will only be illustrated briefly. The slum problem, for example, has been viewed repeatedly as a problem which can be solved in a matter of time with a moderate rebuilding programme. This mistake has been made time and again by Government ministers. In 1933, for example, a Ministry of Health Circular called upon all local authorities to estimate the number of their slums, on the basis of clearing them in five years. The Government have sounded the trumpet for a general attack upon slum evil . . . I am confident that this movement is going forwards with such force and conviction that nothing can stop it,' said the Minister of Health, Sir Hilton Young, in 1933. In the following year he added, 'Five years was not an unduly long time in which to cure an evil which had been growing for a hundred.'(9) In 1954 new estimates were called for. 'Many local authorities should be able to solve their housing problems in five year or so,' stated the Minister of Housing, Mr Harold Macmillan,(10) and in 1955 the Minister (now Mr Duncan Sandys) said, 'From now on we attack on all fronts . . . We think there may be about a million slum houses. If this figure proves correct, I suggest we should aim at breaking the back of the problem within ten years.'(11) In 1971 another Minister of Housing, Mr Julian Amery, renewed the call, 'What we have to do is to mount a final assault to clear the slums, end the overcrowding, improve the homes and give real help to the people in need . . . I can see no reason why local councils should not clear away all the existing slums by 1980.'(12) It seems that about once in every twenty years the Government of the day rediscovers that there are slums and takes over-optimistic action to abolish them, without realizing either that more slums are being manufactured all the time through its predecessors' and its own policies or that the definition of a slum will itself be changed as society becomes more prosperous.(13)

There are studies which throw considerable doubts on the numbers of dwellings estimated by administrative authorities to be unfit.(14) The local authority returns for 1954 and 1965, for example, have been exposed to devastating criticisms. Thus in 1954 more slums were registered in Aylesbury than the Rhondda, more in Tunbridge Wells than Llanelly, and more in Rickmansworth than Hackney; some towns like Cardiff and Newport were registered as having scarcely any slum housing at all,(15) and the figures often conflicted with the Census data about towns having large proportions of housing without basic amenities. One review concluded, 'As an assessment of the amount of unfit housing in this country . . . it is worthless.'(16) Similarly research carried out after the 1965 returns showed that these were of very little value. A Ministry of Housing survey carried out by public health inspectors showed that there were 1.8 million unfit dwellings and not 820,000, as counted by the local authorities.(17)

There are also difficulties in interpreting what appear to be strong statistical trends from one Census to the next even in matters as physically evident as the numbers of rooms. Thus when the 1966 definition of a room was adjusted to the 1961 definition the post-enumeration survey revealed a 39 per cent discrepancy for the count of rooms in the same household spaces in 1966, compared with 1961.(18) Sometimes this was because there was more than one household, sometimes because bathrooms or w.c.s were counted in error, or rooms divided by a curtain counted as two rooms. Some owner-occupiers and tenants believe there are advantages in withholding information about sub-tenants to escape tax or they believe the information is unnecessary. Little is known about the likely inaccuracy of Census findings but the extent of overcrowding is almost certainly underestimated, especially in city areas with high rates of household mobility.

The administrative information upon which policy decisions are taken is much weaker than is generally supposed. First, being open to administrative discretion or interpretation — like the local authority returns on slums — it tends to reflect collective or social perceptions rather than controlled measurement using external criteria. Secondly, it consists predominantly of information about the poorest housing, in a fixed, and usually dated, sense of that term, and therefore encourages misconceptions about social change and achievement. Thirdly, it is presented in rather static and physical terms and does not reflect the causal dynamics of community change and of the local economy.

The Relative Concept of the Slum

Attempts to quantify the population living below a conventionally defined minimum standard of housing — whether in 'slums', in 'overcrowded' conditions or among 'inadequate' amenities — are therefore insufficient and misleading. The definition of a slum or of poor housing cannot be treated as absolute. It is not absolute in practice, since mediocre or twilight housing can deteriorate at a rate faster than the clearance of an initial number of slums. Nor is it absolute in theory, since it is affected by changing social expectations of housing. I suspect that not many years will pass before, for example, many of the high blocks of flats erected in recent years in British cities, especially London, are classified as undesirable slums for early clearance.(19) We need better insights into the process by which structurally good housing is sometimes categorized as slums by the bureaucracy and replaced by housing having certain features which are regarded today as desirable but which may be structurally shoddy and not very durable. We are seduced into believing that the replacement of the run-down by the untried represents progress.

Instead, we should develop a concept of the slum, relative to the average standard, or the standard of the upper quartile in the distribution of all units of accommodation. The proportion of slums might then fluctuate independently of rate of economic growth. We might find that the existence of slums could be explained only in relation to the development of spacious and indeed extravagant or opulent accommodation.

It is therefore the inequality in housing which should concern us and it is this inequality which needs to be documented in all its subtle manifestations. For that is the point from which an explanation of the cause and proliferation of slums and of homelessness can begin to be developed. From the start we must be aware that measures of the physical quality of housing are very limited and official measures in the Census and elsewhere do not yet cover structural defects, obsolescence or environmental shortcomings. In particular housing directors, public health officers and planners need information about groups of dwellings in areas smaller than the enumeration districts. (20)

Inequality in Housing

Housing needs have to be understood more in terms of relative deprivation or inequality, therefore, than in terms of absolute minima. The decline of the percentage of the population living in accommodation of more than one person per room, lacking an indoor w.c., or living in privately rented accommodation, and the increase in the proportion of the population who are owner-occupiers is frequently interpreted as marking an undeniable advance in living standards. But in some respects the rich and prosperous are keeping more than one jump ahead, adding telephone extensions in every room, a second garage, press-button cooking and a holiday cottage.

Illustrations can be given of the method of approach to the documentation of inequality. The cost of housing to owner-occupiers and tenants in relation to the privileges that are bought, for example, is very unequal. Because his initial costs are high the owner-occupier is believed to pay much more for accommodation than, say, a council tenant. But this seems to be a myth which suits certain financial and political interest groups to maintain. One writer who calculated actual and expected housing costs of owner-occupiers and council tenants for the period 1970-76 found first that after paying, at the start, much more than double the amount for accommodation of the council tenant the owner-occupier was soon paying much less than double. Indeed, in even moderate conditions of inflation it seemed likely that he would be paying less absolutely before half the average mortgage term of twenty-five years was completed. Secondly, the calculations of their respective outgoings took no account of capital gains and of the fact that the average owner-occupier sells after six years. The asset appreciates faster than most other types of asset. This is not just a paper gain because money can be borrowed or a debt incurred on the strength of the asset, and capital gains will eventually be realized, if only by the heirs of the house-owner. And when the house is sold the profit generally helps to secure a bigger and better house, and increased appreciation, elsewhere. If the profits on resale are included in calculating the costs of owning, the owner-occupier pays, over a short span of even six or ten years, 'much less than the council tenant . . . the owner-occupier will pay less for housing than the council tenant in proportion to the extent that retail price inflation continues, and in proportion to the extent that house price inflation exceeds retail price inflation'.(21) This suggests why it is so important to compare the values, outgoings and capital appreciation of accommodation of different types, classifying the amounts, but also indices of the quality of accommodation, by the social characteristics of the occupants.

To turn to a different example, the distribution of housing resources could be ranked on different scales. Thus the percentage of households living more than 1½ persons per room diminished from 6.9 in 1951 to 3.8 in 1961 and diminished further to 1.6 in 1966, while the percentage having two or more rooms per person increased from 24.2 in 1961 to 33.9 in 1966.(22) The point of measuring trends in the relativity between different groups in the population can also be shown by changes in the housing stock. Between 1961 and 1966 the percentage of dwellings with six or more rooms in England and Wales increased from 16 to 21 per cent.(23) Another example would be to make use of the bedroom standard, which is a standard of overcrowding or under-occupancy designed to take account of the type as well as size of family occupying a dwelling. While 9.4 per cent of a national sample of households had one or more bedrooms too few, 52.8 per cent had one or more bedrooms in excess of the standard, including 17.1 per cent having *two* or more bedrooms in excess of the standard.(24) There are other ways of illustrating inequalities in the accommodation that is occupied. In 1966, for example, there were 100,000 people in England and Wales living, at one extreme, in just over 30,000 rooms, and there were 100,000 living, at the other extreme, in 750,000 rooms.(25)

Official and independent studies have attempted to develop sophisticated measures of housing defects. For example, there have been repeated attempts to devise a comprehensive housing index covering different features of structure and amenities.(26) More recently efforts have been made to add various environmental deficiencies to these scales, for example, offensive smells, air pollution, noise, absence of grass and trees, presence of litter and parked vehicles.(27) A tentative scale was used by the Ministry of Housing and Local Government in a study of the possibilities of improving old areas of a town, but Government departments have been shy both of adopting comprehensive methods of measurement and of discussing them publicly.(28) What is required is a concept of 'environmental poverty' which includes the lack of, or difficulty of access to, gardens, play spaces, parks, water, shopping facilities, health centres and so on, and exposure to noise and dirt.

The value assumptions upon which experimental indices of poor environmental conditions are based are usually neither expressed explicitly nor critically evaluated. As a consequence deficiencies short of some presumed social standard are listed without any very clear attempt to specify the mean or median or to show the kind of privileges enjoyed by those living in spacious and well-appointed amenities. Our standards, and therefore our data about poor housing conditions, are still too detached from any moorings. They lack reference points in a period of rapidly changing conditions.

To some extent the lack of objectivity is the result of a failure on the part of social scientists to examine and formulate in general terms the total effect now and in the past of loosely framed legislation, administrative control and guidance in the form of circulars, advisory pamphlets, grants and planning permission, local bye-laws and regulations and local administrative practices. Thus, concepts of *district* overcrowding and inadequacy of facilities are poorly defined, and information on a comparative basis can be compiled only in part. Control of environmental conditions has developed piecemeal. For example, different Royal Commissions and Government Committees have made recommendations about the heights of buildings in relation to open space, the space at the rear of the dwellings, and the powers that local authorities ought to have to control drainage and over-crowding and the replacement of dwellings.(29) Through its elected council each community has sought to superimpose its conception of minimum environmental decency upon the different physical manifestations of its predecessors' conceptions. There is a history of less assertive intervention by the Government in local housing policies than in, say, health and education. Control over developments has tended to remain in local hands, and has been subject, as a consequence, to greater influence from property-owners and local residents in general than would otherwise have been the case. By the 1950s there was still remarkably little central definition of environmental standards and, indeed, the emphasis was on physical rather than social standards. Thus the Ministry of Housing and Local Government was issuing guidelines to local authorities about the density of residential dwellings in the 1950s. These suggested, frequently, that the principal factors affecting density of houses were type of house, garden size, space for daylight and sunlight, space for privacy, space for access and space for trees and small green spaces.(30) The social needs of different types of population, households, families and work-groups were not formulated. Today what is required is some attempt to demonstrate inequalities between areas in the extent to which they satisfy the range of social needs of their inhabitants. Above all, the facilities enjoyed by the rich and well-to-do must be carefully measured.

Once better quantitative indices of inequality of housing costs, facilities and environment are developed there is a prospect of obtaining a more reliable evaluation of trends and policies. Thus, it may be possible to explain the paradox of poverty and plenty in housing, that despite conventional indices of 'progress' — like a diminution of households lacking bathrooms, a steady increase in the numbers of houses and flats, an extension of owner-occupation and a rise in real incomes — there are other indices of a worsening of housing problems. For example, official statistics show that the number of homeless persons in temporary accommodation in England and Wales, rose from 13,000 in 1966 to 21,000 in 1969 and 24,000 in 1970.(31) The number of people living in caravans, who certainly include some who find adequate housing beyond their means, increased from 95,000 in 1951 to 184,000 in 1961 and to an estimated 300,000 in 1965.(32) And although census data are difficult to interpret there was a marked increase in the proportion of households sharing dwellings in some London boroughs, for example, during the early 1960s.(33) The different parts of the total picture may be easier to fit together once we are able to describe and discuss housing within a distributional framework.

Regional and Area Inequality

Inequality in housing is also, of course, regional and not only national. The distribution regionally of housing values and quality follows a very consistent pattern. For example, the 1967 House Condition Survey demonstrated that while 12 per cent of the total stock of housing in England and Wales was unfit, the figure was only 6 per cent in the South-East, but 15 per cent in the Northern, Yorkshire and Humberside and North-West Regions.(34) Again, we learn from the Family Expenditure Survey for 1970 that while there was central heating in over 40 per cent of the homes in the South-East (outside London) the figure was only 26 per cent for Yorkshire and Humberside, the North-West and Scotland, 20 per cent for Wales and 13 per cent for Northern Ireland.(35) Despite the good intentions of successive Governments regional disparities have not responded to ameliorative policies. This cannot be attributed to chance or any 'natural' process of industrial or economic history. An explanation can only be sought in the assertion of social interests which are felt to be as superior as the economic power on which they rest.(36)

A Sociological Explanation for the Origins of Slums in Conditions of Social Inequality

Explanation of inequality has to take the form of sociological analysis as well as ecological and economic analyses. There are, for example, great differences in both the quality of housing and the social composition of areas within regions. Urban sociologists have attempted to identify particular zones in the city. Classically these efforts are associated with the names of Park, Burgess and Mackenzie.(37) They identified the lodging-house zone, the zones of working men's homes and middle-class areas and the commuters' suburbs. They showed that the use of space was related to socio-economic processes. For example, the lodging-house zone on the fringe of the business district was in part a creation of the expansion of the latter. British sociologists have recently attempted more detailed work. They have pointed out that the relationship and indeed interdependence of these zones has been insufficiently examined. Thus John Rex and Robert Moore point out that the different zones into which Birmingham can be divided might be the result of the continuing attempt by groups differentially placed according to their possession of property to protect their interests.(38) The groups develop rather different, though, I would add, overlapping styles of life. At later stages both municipal and private suburbia develop. The lower middle classes and skilled manual workers forsake the centre of cities, and indeed are helped and encouraged to do so by credit facilities, planning machinery and political institutions. Their deserted homes tend to be occupied by a mixture of social casualties and newcomers, occupying a zone of transition.(39) The communities and therefore the housing have to be understood in terms of continuous dynamic interaction and therefore changing status and composition. The changes are due in part to changes in land use brought about by the expansion and decline of industry but also developments in public transport, urban planning and national parks. Pahl has called attention to the possible multiplier effects of the expansion of offices and finance facilities upon the numbers of the low paid living in city centres (postmen, clerks, cleaners, workers in the catering trade).(40) Areas, and housing estates, have to be understood in relation to each other as social sub-systems as well as in relation to the different economic, political industrial and social service systems of which they are the physical expression. Just as the grammar school has to be understood partly by analogy with the public school, so the private and council housing estate has to be understood in the reflections of upper-middle and lower-class housing. The fact of movement and the possibility of movement help to explain the differentiated structure of society.

Just as some areas may rise and become fashionable, others may decay and lose population of relatively high social class. This can be illustrated from the history of any city and operates even among the poorest sub-communities. Around the outskirts of Paris, for example, there is a ring of shanty towns of discernibly different status.(41) When I visited La Campa, near Le Bourget airport, in 1967, it consisted predominantly of two categories of people. There were French unemployed, fatherless families, mentally handicapped individuals, the old and the disabled, who had descended into poverty and destitution, sometimes by a succession of steps through mediocre and poor housing. They were often abject and without hope. Then there were immigrants from Algeria, Spain, Portugal, Iran and elsewhere, many of them energetic and optimistic, experiencing deplorable housing conditions but beginning to earn incomes which compared very favourably with what they had known in their own countries. Comprising about 5,000 people, they were living in an assortment of huts four feet high, some of the walls consisting of loose concrete blocks and the rooms of corrugated iron, but also vans and cars without wheels, gipsy carts and even tents made of rough sacking. The only form of sanitation was by emptying slops in the canals.

This type of shanty town or slum is a recurring phenomenon in the world's literature.(42) Its scale and degree of deprivation in relation to the mean is a product of the social and economic system and not of the so-called culture of poverty. Its continuation depends more on external than upon internal mechanisms. As Rex and Moore argue, the inhabitants of the zones of transition were not just segregated communities but 'had their total situation defined by an urban value system in which they were at the back of a queue to move to the most desired style of life in the suburbs'.(43) Rex suggests that within the general zones into which a city can be divided there are loosely defined areas fitting within one or other of the housing classes, defined in terms of rights to property and security of tenure and forming an elaborate social hierarchy. There are:

1. The outright owners of large houses in desirable areas;
2. Mortgage payers who 'own' whole houses in desirable areas;
3. Council tenants in council-built houses;
4. Council tenants in slum houses awaiting demolition;
5. Tenants of private house-owners, usually in the inner ring;
6. House-owners who must take lodgers to meet loan repayments;
7. Lodgers in rooms. (44)

However, changes in land use and in industry, as well as changes of income, occupation and household composition during the course of the life-cycle, are continually diversifying this presumed structure. Some families move successfully through different types of housing without experiencing much change of income or occupation, and though there are good examples of council tenants and the tenants of private estates who act in a concerted way in groups or classes it is also true to say there are people with similar occupations, incomes and wealth who are in widely different types of housing. The concept of housing classes therefore needs to be used with qualification. Its strength is that it calls attention to the existence of a system with associated life-styles, resources and opportunities which take physical and spatial form. Access to types of housing is controlled by both a housing market and wider social control of the distribution of resources. To some extent, then, people's present housing situation has to be analysed more in terms of the 'means and criteria of access to desirable housing and the ability of different people to negotiate the rules of eligibility'. (45)

I would, therefore, argue that the release of fresh resources to the owner-occupier sector, for example, through improvement grants and the reduction of taxation or a rapid increase of property values will have the effect of consuming a disproportionately large share of building resources and put pressure on the poorer housing sectors, which may be reduced in physical numbers or, perhaps because of demographic changes, immigration or an increase in the population with very low incomes (as during conditions of unemployment) simply increase occupancy. Haddon, for example, shows how 'the relative confinement of West Indians to furnished accommodation is a product of discrimination elsewhere in the housing market.' (46)

Not only is either a shanty town or a more settled area of transition an element in social differentiation but it is itself differentiated. This does of course explain the relative submission of its population to national values.(47) Such differentiation has policy implications too, because poor housing conditions can be dealt with only by attacking the whole value structure and not by localized action.

The argument that the slum, or that housing deprivation, can be understood and explained only in relation to the full range of inequalities in housing seems to have two major advantages. First, it helps to bring coherence to the analysis of the problem. The discussion of housing tends to have been fragmented. Either the behaviour of the poor and the influences affecting their living conditions have been discussed independently of the behaviour of the rich and the influences affecting their living conditions; or housing has been divided artificially for purposes of analysis into three broad streams of owner-occupied, council and privately rented. The interconnections, and particularly the causal links between privilege and want, have been insufficiently explored.

Secondly, it provides a basis for unifying policy and planning. The needs, and the privileges as well as the rights, of both poor and rich can be looked at together. For example, it is important to be aware not just that there are some households with good wages who are paying a small proportion of their incomes in rent for council homes or rent-controlled private property, but some households with better salaries who are paying a minute proportion of their incomes in mortgage premiums and other housing costs for owner-occupied houses — just because they happened to start buying their homes before the rapid rise in values, and in earnings, during the last fifteen years. If it is right to ask whether prosperous tenants should obtain subsidies for rents it is right to ask whether prosperous owner-occupiers should obtain tax reliefs on mortgage interest, particularly when they are being helped to enjoy a rapidly appreciating capital asset.

Anomalous or inconsistent decisions in different tenure groups or areas are also more likely to be compared publicly. In the mid-1950s a large area of terraced housing in Bethnal Green (between Bethnal Green Road and the railway line) which I happened to know well was cleared as part of a slum-clearance scheme. Some of the houses were identical with those being jealously sought after, renovated and sold for extravagant sums in areas like Hampstead, Chelsea, Islington, and Notting Hill, occasionally to the self-same architects who were masterminding their replacement elsewhere. The curious alchemy by which the English define a dwelling sometimes as a slum and sometimes as an ancient monument worthy of having a preservation order slapped on it deserves a lot more scrutiny.

The concept of inequality as applied to housing also implies a continuum from bad to good housing and makes mutually exclusive and even contradictory policies less likely. A more rational balance between replacement and improvement of housing might be found. Just as there are far more people living on the margins of poverty than there are in severe destitution so, by almost any standards we care to devise, the amount of housing requiring slight or extensive repair dwarfs the amount requiring to be cleared and replaced. More sophisticated measures of inequality, and more consultation with occupiers, will help to inform the process by which a judgement of balance between the two is arrived at. Experts differ about the respective merits of slum clearance and improvement (48) and failure to apply the inequality standard means that slum clearance gets more support than it deserves. Thus, there is the psychological appeal to councillors of newness, of being able to demonstrate to the casual eye the distinguishable results of their political labours instead of results which merely merge with the urban scene. Architects often share this point of view and prefer to work with a large area for development. Yet just as they have begun to design buildings to preserve trees on the site, so wherever possible worthwhile established buildings and even walls or railings should also be preserved on urban sites. In recent years there has been welcome encouragement from the Department of the Environment for improvement schemes for old towns: Deeplish, Rochdale, 1966; Fulham, 1966; Bolton, 1966; Barnsbury, 1968; Skelmersdale, 1969; and Nelson and Rawtenstall, 1971.(49) But this development has still to be backed properly with resources and linked to general strategies of urban planning and renewal.

Some of the financial and political influences in favour of clearance are insidious. A diminution of the housing stock helps to maintain house prices elsewhere, particularly in areas with a declining population. For a local authority it can provide potential tenants for tower blocks which are not attracting sufficient applicants. There are pressures for change in land use and building use and for the removal of communities which are stigmatized as riddled with criminal propensities (50), so raising the tone, and hence property values, in the neighbourhood. But of course it is a mistake to suppose either that certain areas are socially homogeneous or that the housing of a district is necessarily as bad as the reputation of its community. Indeed, some of the efforts of housing authorities to establish a new way of life through the establishment of new housing estates seem to have resulted in a much stricter grading of populations by social status and even raised certain indices of social disorganization. The famous example of Easterhouse in Glasgow is a case in point.

Planning Against Poverty

The correlation between indices of poor housing conditions, such as overcrowding and poverty, has been attested since Charles Booth carried out his surveys in London towards the end of the nineteenth century.(51) Recent studies by the Government and independently have produced further evidence.(52) However, while there have been a large number of studies of housing conditions there have been very few which have also been able to collect reliable information about income and none, so far as I am aware, that have also obtained information about the income equivalence of industrial welfare and social service benefits, and of assets owned by the household. This makes generalization hazardous, but the correlation between poor housing and poverty, as distinct from low income, is not very high. For example, although some old people are poor, they can still afford to live in relatively good housing, because they have paid off mortgages, live in subsidized council property or rent-controlled private property, have their rents paid in full by the Supplementary Benefits Commission, or even live with relatives commanding a high income. What is indisputable is the chaotic relationship between expenditure on housing whether in absolute terms or proportionally, and the quality of, or need for, housing. The Milner Holland Committee has given an eloquent account of exhorbitant rents and other abuses in London,(53) and the Francis Committee of the enormous range in proportion of income paid in rent. For example, among tenants in unfurnished homes (unregistered tenancies) in Greater London, the West Midlands and South Wales, there were respectively 16 per cent, 4 per cent and 23 per cent paying more than 30 per cent of take-home pay as rent, but 15 per cent, 40 per cent and 23 per cent paying less than 10 per cent. (54)

The new Government policy announced in 1971 (55) seeks to bring order to this admitted chaos. 'We know', Mr Amery, the Minister of Housing, has said, 'that "A Fair Deal for Housing" is a sharp sword with which to slay the dragons of the slums, the overcrowding and the individual hardship which is still plaguing' our housing situation.' (56) While his is not, as we have seen the first British Government to assume the mantle of St George, the declared policy is a major one. It is likely to have wider repercussions than any housing measure of this century. It was debated angrily and at length in the House of Commons. The committee proceedings on the bill in the House of Commons occupied five months and the report fills four substantial volumes.(57) Even though the Government seems to have been forced by searching criticisms to modify its proposals for phased increases in rents (58) the main proposals have gone through relatively unscathed. In particular, there was little real criticism of the scheme for rebates and allowances.

The stated objectives of the policy are:

(i)   a decent home for every family at a price within their means;
(ii) a fairer choice between owing a home and renting one;
(iii) fairness between one citizen and another in giving and receiving help towards housing costs. (59)

Its chief proposals are to decontrol by stages from the beginning of

1973 1.3 million tenancies which are controlled as distinct from being regulated, to extend the system of 'fair' rents to local authority housing with the intention of raising rents substantially, and to introduce a national system, administered by local authorities, of rent allowances for private tenants of unfurnished accommodation and rebates for council tenants.

These proposals are unlikely to secure the Government's objectives. A 'decent home for every family' is, as I have suggested, a changing social conception which can only be defined justifiably in relation to the whole range of housing which is occupied, and the conditions in which it is occupied, in Britain. It cannot be assured for all by attending just to questions of price but also to questions of allocation, security and overcrowding — as the research on the homeless, for example, has abundantly testified. Nor can it be reasonably argued that the changes allow tenants to remain in their existing homes or move to new ones at 'a price within their means'. Even when the proposed rent allowances are taken into account net rents in some areas will rise to levels more than double the average proportion of household income which is assigned to housing. Must the market determine the price of housing or should society intervene? Rents will rise so steeply for some council tenants that they will be tempted to buy their own homes instead. House prices will rise. Some owner-occupiers will be able to sell their homes at a high price and will move into larger premises. Relatively more of the nation's building resources will be assigned to the middle-income groups and the dependent poor will have to compete for a shrinking share of rented housing. Again, there are likely to be many tenants who are poor or have low incomes but will not receive the allowances. There is plentiful evidence that all of the means tests being operated in Britain are inefficient.(60) Benefits do not reach substantial proportions of the families who are eligible for them. This seems to be particularly true of local authority rent rebates and the national rate rebate scheme.(61) By strenuous publicity the Government improved the take-up of certain free health and welfare benefits, free school meals and the Family Income Supplement during 1971-72, but to levels still far short of the estimated need. A system of means-tested allowances and rebates is therefore unlikely to work. The introduction of fair rents will raise housing costs disproportionately for low-income groups. But the introduction of a national scheme of rent allowances and rebates will not cover these increases for many people with low incomes, either because they do not pool household income in the way suggested by the Government in its rules for allowances, or because their rents will rise by an amount more than the allowances for which they become eligible.

The failure of the Government to achieve its third objective seems even more likely. 'Fairness between one citizen and another . . . in receiving help towards housing costs' will not be achieved by reducing subsidies for council housing while ignoring subsidies for owner-occupiers through tax relief on mortgage interest. As Professor Roy Parker has pointed out, some council tenants will not only lose rent subsidies and will be contributing, in the high rents that they will be paying, to the rent rebates and allowances of other council tenants and private tenants, but will be helping to reduce the cost to the Exchequer of its private sector subsidies. 'It is difficult to avoid the conclusion that some council tenants will, under this procedure, bear a disproportionately heavy tax burden.'(62)

What has to be recognized is that the Government is redistributing income in the wrong direction. Subsidized council housing developed in Britain so that working-class families would be able to occupy homes of better standard than would otherwise be the case. They would pay a rent lower than that which would normally be necessary to secure a home of the same standard on the private housing market. Housing was felt to be a necessity of life which should be distributed more equally than resources in general. The Government's Housing Finance policy will widen inequalities between owner-occupiers and tenants by raising rents disproportionately to general price levels and incomes, by reducing the relative amount of subsidies to tenants, and by extending financial help for owner-occupiers.(63) Through the new subsidy policy a wedge will also be driven between higher and lower income tenants, the former being expected to subsidize the latter through the rents paid. (64)

The Government does not propose to restrict the financial privileges of owner-occupiers. Among them, the higher the income, and the greater the initial purchase price of the property, the higher the tax concession. Thus, late in 1971 a Government spokesman estimated that tax relief for a standard rate income taxpayer on a normal twenty year mortgage would amount altogether, at 8 per cent rate of interest, to £2,009 on a mortgage costing £5,000, £4,019 on £10,000 and £8,038 on £20,000.(65) With the abolition of Schedule A tax in 1963 and the introduction of capital gains tax, from which the owner-occupier is exempt, and the extension of improvement grants, owner-occupation has become a very privileged form of investment. For 1967 it has been estimated, on a very approximate basis, that owner-occupiers enjoyed subsidies of £727 million (through not paying tax on imputed rental income or on capital gains) whereas council tenancies attracted subsidies amounting to £303 million.(66) During 1971 and 1972 the situation has been indefensible. Partly to catch up with the exceptional rise in earnings in 1970, house prices rose in 1971 by 21 per cent and rose by a further 18 per cent during the first six months of 1972. There are many instances of quick profits. In fashionable areas of London it is fairly common for houses to have gained £10,000 or more in value in the last four years.(67) In a village twenty miles from Oxford a cottage bought for £3,000 just over two years ago was renovated and rebuilt, partly with the help of a substantial improvement grant, sold for £11,000 a year ago and, after being lived in for six months, has just been sold for £18,500. The implications of all this are that the mere status of owner-occupation leads in many areas to very substantial financial advantage, directly when the house is sold, but also indirectly, because the real rate of mortgage repayment shrinks rapidly at a time of rapid increase of prices and earnings. The owner-occupier is often given an incentive to exchange his home for a larger or better one, to improve it to luxury standards, and to seek a second home as well, therefore using up building resources and even accommodation required for growing families in the low-income groups. Far more work needs to be done to reveal the comparative financial and social situation of owner-occupiers and council and private tenants, not only at the point of purchase or commencement of the tenancy, but at points ten or twenty years further on. Only then can 'fairness' *within* tenure groups and *between* tenure groups begin to be defined.(68)

Social Ownership and Investment

How, then, can the Government's objectives, (a 'decent home for all' and 'fairness' in housing costs between one citizen and another) be achieved? First, the worst housing is concentrated in the privately rented sector and the experience of different measures of decontrol, fair rents and improvement grants in the last ten years does not suggest that these types of measures will be any more successful in overcoming the problem in the future than they have been in the past.(69) The alternative which the nation must therefore consider is social ownership. The evidence suggests that less housing should be replaced and more repaired and renovated. Local authorities might be asked to draw up a community development programme which would include taking housing into social ownership, and improve both dwellings and area on the Deeplish and Nelson and Rawtenstall models. The worst housing would be taken over by stages and schemes for co-operative ownership and improvement could form part of the programme. Alternatively, community groups, like tenants' associations, could be encouraged to take over management from local authority housing departments after the initial programme of renovation. Schemes could also take the form of 'joint' ownership between councils and individual tenants, so that both shared in decisions about maintenance and improvement, transfers and new allocations of ownership, and even appreciating values of well-maintained homes. Some councils, especially in London, have already arranged for tenants' representatives to sit on committees of management (following some of the proposals of the Private Bill of Dick Leonard, M.P.). A commission appointed by Lambeth Council is studying further possibilities of management by tenants and cooperative ownership.

Social ownership implies management, and investment, if only temporarily, in the interests of communities and areas as a whole. It would be a rational rescue operation but also a positive assertion of the standards of housing in which citizens are entitled to be accommodated. But such a policy of housing investment would be inseparable from local community development. The urban aid, community development and educational priority area programmes which have been introduced in the last few years would need to be re-appraised and brought under stricter control. Relatively little has been spent on these programmes; sometimes the benefits have been spread too widely; sometimes funds have been used without any prospect that they would achieve their avowed objectives; and locally as well as nationally this new type of expenditure is being used to conceal or excuse the low growth of expenditure on long-established projects and services. For example, only about £20 million has been allocated to the Government's urban aid programme since 1968. Much of this sum has so far been allocated to building day nurseries and nursery schools and children's homes, although a few projects involve rehabilitation centres, playgrounds, adult education centres and a telephone answering system. Resources have been spread too widely and 'it is no longer possible to see the urban development programme as a supplement to compensate areas that have missed out in the past'.(70) The definition of environmental poverty would allow the specification of an environmental subsidy programme.

Social ownership poses major transitional and even permanent problems of management. How will tenancies in the poorest privately rented dwellings that have now been taken over be allocated? What risks are there of strengthening the tendencies in overworked housing departments to apply double standards, to give short shrift to, say, immigrants and fatherless families, and to blacklist particular families who have got behind with their rent, irritated other tenants and otherwise fallen foul of management rules? No one should underestimate the management problem and the need to preserve flexibility and standards of fairness. This is why diversification of management is so important.

Equalizing Privileges of Owner-Occupiers and Tenants

Secondly, the housing rights of all citizens would be more clearly defined. Fitness, crowding and environmental standards would be redefined regularly in relation to the range of actual housing conditions in various parts of the country. This would therefore include a statement about the accommodation requirements of families with different numbers of children compared with those of single people and married couples without children. But the definition would necessarily have to take account of, and reconcile, differences between tenants and owner-occupiers in security, freedom to have sub-tenants, keep animals, modernize, redecorate and so on. For example, the eviction of families with young children should be prohibited and other eviction procedures curtailed. This would be quite feasible if court proceedings to secure debts were reviewed and used. If owner-occupation is socially desirable, then its different desirable features should be identified and, where possible, conferred on tenants.(71) Inequality between tenants and owner-occupiers can be reduced by legislation and administrative regulation so that the privileges of the latter can be conferred on the former. For example, a long-standing tenancy might attract certain rights to a say in the disposal of that tenancy and to a lump sum when vacated. We have become accustomed to the principle of redundancy payments for workers and not only managers. A system of tenancy-termination payments might be one method of protecting the rights of tenants in relation to owner-occupiers. Similarly, some action would have to be taken to control the exploitation of building and accommodation resources. An experimental under-occupancy tax might be introduced for owner-occupiers. This could be applied immediately to some groups in the population, but to others, such as those in their sixties, only after considerable notice. Some groups, like the severely disabled or retirement pensioners aged seventy-five and over, might be exempt. The tax could be applied annually in arrears in conformity with the tax return. The ownership of second homes might have to be discouraged, and even made illegal under certain conditions in some areas. The miserable protection of tenants' rights has to be recognized as much as the privileges accorded to owner-occupiers under existing policies. The Government's 'fair' rents scheme, for example, is remarkable for the lack of appeal machinery. Again, the tenant has no right of access to Rent Scrutiny Committees.

A Flat-Rate Housing Allowance

Thirdly, the additional housing needs of families, the elderly and the disabled should be recognized through a national system of flat-rate housing allowances. Not only are means-tested rebates and allowances inefficient. Even in principle they fail to reach social categories who deserve help with their housing costs. There is the problem of inequity as well as the problem of poverty. Family dependants add to the accommodation needs of the household. Disability poses special accommodation needs which may be relatively costly to satisfy, adds to housing costs or poses extra problems of wear and tear. For both dependants and disabled a standard allowance (or credit) could justifiably be introduced. For example, £1 per week for each child under ten, £1.50 for each child over ten or adult dependant, and £1, £2, or £3 according to degree of disability, irrespective of age, might be paid. These amounts would help families with dependants or households in which there was a disabled person to obtain housing of the size and type that they need. Estimates of cost and possible savings in tax are set out in an Appendix. The proposed strategy would have the effect of redistributing subsidies in two ways — horizontally from people without dependants to those with dependants, and vertically, from people in owner-occupied property with high values and who have relatively high incomes to people in either rented or owner-occupied property with low incomes.

The point of beginning to define the cost of accommodation needed by certain types of family is that it breaks the circularity of present definitions of need. A major weakness of the social or Government measure of poverty is that it includes the actual cost of housing.(72) Three families of the same type might have identical incomes after paying rent and, if they had a net income below the supplementary benefit standard, would each be regarded as in poverty, and yet the first might be paying £1.50 rent per week for a rent-controlled slum flat, the second £3 for a small pre-war council flat and the third £8 per week as a mortgage repayment on a spacious owner-occupied house. The same point might be made in relation to statistical trends from year to year. If rents rise more sharply than the costs of other necessities, poverty would also tend to increase more sharply even if there were a disproportionate improvement at the same time in the quality of housing occupied by the population. The S.B.C. does not recognize the needs of a family receiving supplementary benefit to have a higher income for rent that it actually pays.

The Government's rent allowance proposals are not limited to a subsistence poverty standard.(73) Families with low incomes who are not in poverty will be eligible for allowances or rebates. This is an important departure from precedent. But payments will not be directly related to accommodation needs. They will depend only on level of income in relation to rents paid. This is a critical distinction. Whether the allowances that are paid will reflect accommodation needs is extremely doubtful. They will be 'variable and arbitrary'.(74) The Government might argue that in any area the rents of flats and houses will vary according to their size, and that a family with one more child than another family and occupying one more room may be paying after receiving rent allowance only about the same net amount in rent. It might also argue that overcrowded families on low incomes will have an incentive to move to larger and more costly accommodation once they know that their rent allowance will be larger. But there are many imponderables in the situation. One is that with incomes fluctuating from week to week as they do in many working-class homes, and with both incomes and prices changing constantly during current conditions of inflation, it will be virtually impossible for many families to predict the amount of the allowances to which they will be entitled if they decide to move. Another is that councils will have an incentive to steer large families to low-cost accommodation on relatively undesirable estates in order to reduce total council rebates and subsidies. Yet another is that in many areas accommodation with several rooms is hard to come by and, when it is, may be much more costly relative to accommodation with few rooms. Another is that in the next few years so-called fair rents will generally be higher rents. Many of the tenants with several children will lose on the swings what they gain on the roundabouts. Rent allowances or rebates will be balanced by rent increases. But some, especially those who live in sought-after housing, will find that the 'fair' rent rises so much that even when a rent allowance is taken into account they will be paying more per week than previously and will be forced to move to low-rent areas. Since relatively more tenants with several dependants than with few or none seem likely to be displaced from high-rent areas they may not all be able to find accommodation of the right size in low-rent areas. As a consequence the new Act may increase the extent of overcrowding and help to create more low-income ghettos.(75)

The Government's scheme is therefore inept not just because it cannot guarantee that all those eligible to receive rebates or allowances will get them, but because it does not guarantee that those with special needs for accommodation will get help in trying to meet them. There is an important principle at stake. If certain types of families have special needs for accommodation, whether because of size, composition or special problems, such as disability, then those needs should be acknowledged irrespective of the accommodation they actually occupy, (76) the rents they pay or the incomes they receive. Thus a family with a low income which is living in overcrowded conditions should not have to accept the costs and risks of moving to larger accommodation on a presumed calculation that they will be entitled to a larger rent allowance. That allowance should be theirs as of right beforehand and should be something on which they can always depend.

If society takes the view that above certain levels of income it does not wish to acknowledge the distinction between those who have and those who do not have special accommodation needs, then it would not be difficult to impose a tax, rather like the former Schedule A tax, which would progressively phase out the allowance. This is one of the possible savings in cost listed in the Appendix. There are many advantages to such a procedure, as compared with the alternative procedure, proposed by the Government, whereby those on low incomes will have to submit to a means test to qualify for a rent rebate or allowance. First and foremost, it ensures that all those who are eligible for the allowance will receive it. Secondly, it is cheaper and more convenient administratively. If applied only to high-income groups there are fewer people to whom the procedure has to be applied; it can be coordinated with annual tax assessments, would involve less expenditure on information services and lead to savings in time and costs of the social workers and others who will have to explain it to the public. Thirdly, this proposal is socially more acceptable. When rent allowances are known to vary locally the rules leading to such variation (covering number of dependants and disability, for example) are reasonably clear and uncontentious. If they were to depend on the level of household income, individual declarations of income, adjustments to keep pace with changes of income and allow for disregards, people would not understand the reasons for variation and would come to mistrust the system. This is the likely outcome of the Government's policy.

Some critics will argue that this proposal, for flat-rate housing allowances, does not meet the problems of low-income families paying very high rents in certain parts of the country, particularly London. Is it equitable to pay them flat-rate allowances of the same value as identically constituted families in low-rent areas? This problem cannot be met by paying part of the difference, say between the flat-rate allowances and their actual rent, on a means-tested basis, because a system of unequal rents would be perpetuated through subsidy. Moreover, families paying higher rents for accommodation with better facilities or in a privileged environment would be unfairly subsidized. It would be wrong for any Government to bolster the arbitrary privileges of the housing market. Instead, the principles according to which rents are fixed in the first place should be reviewed and new rates and controls introduced. The germ of a possible solution lies in Della Nevitt's suggestion for separating the rent of the dwelling from the rent of the land.(77) Rents of dwellings of similar size and with similar facilities would be more or less uniform across the country. These rents could be covered, as proposed, by the flat-rate allowances. And rents would vary widely according to site, environmental amenities, transport facilities and access, competition between different types of user and so on. In consultation with local councils and planning departments land rents for different types of user might be fixed for parts of the country by a Land Commission or the Department of the Environment. Alternatively, national land rents might be registered instead of being statutorily designated. Certain types of tenants (including families with children and the disabled) might be paid, say, 50 per cent of the land rent, which would be reclaimed by the Inland Revenue from those with high incomes. The purpose of the subsidy would be to maintain 'social balance' in the populations of certain areas.

Housing Values and Standards for Rents

An effective system of housing allowances and housing taxes cannot be developed without much better public valuation of all housing, in all tenure groups. Such a valuation should have publicly underwritten components, such as cubic footage of living accommodation, structural condition, amenities, density of local housing, garden space and environmental facilities. The dwellings element of the rent would be distinguished from the land element. This valuation should be subject to appeal by the occupant, or by any twenty, say, local residents. It could then form the basis of local rates and taxes paid by owner-occupiers, as well as provide a reference in rent assessments and rent appeals, quite apart from compensation awards. The defects of the 1963 revaluation (which increased aggregate values from £349,000 million to £967,000 million for England and Wales, for example), have been frequently exposed, not least in an Appendix to the Milner Holland Report. 'In any future revaluation it seems certain that the definition of gross value must be changed. It is a remarkable situation that current domestic valuations in the London Conurbation should be determined by the rents paid by such a small proportion of households renting such very untypical accommodation.' (78) No Government should allow the level of 'fair' rents for a large stock of council as well as private housing to be controlled by the vagaries of the private market, without any reference to the cost of owner-occupied housing.(79) Hard as it would be to claim 'objectivity' for any valuation of property based on a schedule about indoor and outdoor space, facilities and so on at least it would provide a national standard with which 'fair' as well as actual rents, rates, taxes and prices could be compared. The relative situations of tenants and owner-occupiers could more easily be compared and an equitable housing policy evolved. Without the definition of some such standard the second of the Government's three policy objectives, 'a fairer choice between owning a home and renting one', is a dead letter.

Summary

Inequality in the distribution, standard and cost of homes is the basic problem from which all housing problems spring. By failing to identify, measure or even properly discuss this problem, society must stumble from one *ad hoc* measure to the next in its attempts to deal with the casualties of slums, overcrowding, eviction, change of land use and environmental pollution. The Government's new housing proposals will fail to secure all three of its avowed housing objectives. They will make inequality much worse. An alternative strategy, which will reduce overcrowding, homelessness and slums and will greatly raise the standards of homes and areas occupied by low-income groups, must have three ingredients: (i) social ownership of rented housing; (ii) the extension to tenants of the rights and privileges of owner-occupiers, and (iii) the development of a system of flat-rate housing allowances for particular accommodation needs.

APPENDIX

Estimates of Costs of Flat-Rate Housing Allowance and Savings in Taxation

1.

Numbers of different types of dependants in the United Kingdom	
Number of children in the U.K. aged under 10	9.4 million
Number of children in the U.K. aged 10-14	4.1 million
Number of dependants aged 15+ †	5.0 million
Total	18.5 million

2.

Numbers of disabled in the United Kingdom ‡	
(i) Very seriously or severely handicapped	0.6 million
(ii) Appreciably handicapped	0.7 million
(iii) Impaired, but needing little or no support	2.2 million
Total	3.5 million

3.

Gross cost of housing allowances per annum	
(i) Child under 10: 9.4 m. at £1.00 per week	£489 million
(ii) Other dependants: 9.1 m. at £1.50 per week	£710 million
(iii) Disabled category I: 0.6 m. at £3.00 per week	£ 94 million
(iv) Disabled category II: 0.7 m. at £2.00 per week	£ 73 million
(v) Disabled category III: 2.2 m. at £1.00 per week	£114 million
	£1480 million

4.

	Possible savings in additional taxation per annum	
(a)	Capital gains tax on owner-occupied property (10 per cent on first £200 of annual appreciation and 20 per cent thereafter)	£350 million
(b)	Tax on imputed rental income (similar in principle to the reintroduction of Schedule A tax on basis of new property valuations)	£600 million
(c)	Withdrawal of tax relief on interest payments for that value of properties over £10,000 and on any value for tax-payers with annual gross income of £6,000 and over	£ 80 million
(d)	Withdrawal of tax relief from mortgage interest on all new housing loans.	£ 50 million
(e)	Housing allowances 'clawed back' progressively from tax-payers with high gross incomes (e.g. totally from people with £3,000 and one dependant and £3,500 and two dependants).	£150 million
(f)	In principle there would be savings too on any existing rent rebates. There would also be savings on supplementary benefit payments. The payment for the rent by the S.B.C. would be reduced by the value of the allowance. But if the allowance exceeded the rent any excess would be disregarded by the S.B.C. in calculating the rest of the allowance.	£100 million

† Provisional estimate. Excludes all economically active adults aged 15 and over, and all wives or husbands of employed persons. Includes wives of retired persons, and dependants other than wives or husbands of retired persons.

‡ Based on a survey by the Office of Population Censuses and Surveys, Harris, A., *Handicapped and Impaired in Great Britain*, H.M.S.O., 1971.

Adjustments have been made to include an estimate for the handicapped in Northern Ireland, and also to include handicapped children.

Notes

1. Compare, for example, the treatment of housing in the *Annual Abstract of Statistics* with that in *Social Trends, 1970 and 1971,* and in recent reports on future public expenditure (Cmnds. 4234, 4578). The fact that housing subsidies are included in the C.S.O. calculations of social service benefits published in *Economic Trends* should also be noted. See *Municipal Journal*, 5 November 1971 and 14 January 1972 for a discussion on housing as a social service.

2. For an introduction to changes in policy, see Rose, H., *The Housing Problem*, Heinemann, 1968, especially Chapters 1 and 2; Donnison, D., *Housing Policy Since the War*, Codicote Press, 1962; Greve, J., *The Housing Problem*, the Fabian Society, 1961; Cullingworth, J.B., *English Housing Trends*, Bell, 1965. 1965.

3. As late as 1883 Octavia Hill suggested that 'good-sized' single rooms should be built to meet the needs of (a) 'The small families of unskilled labourers', and (b) 'The larger families of unskilled labourers who have one or two children old enough to work, and who can afford to take a second or even a third room, but whose wages do not allow of their paying for the more elaborate appliances provided in tenements intended for artisans.' Hill, O., *Homes of the London Poor*, 2nd ed., Macmillan, 1883, pp. 14-15.

4. Ministry of Housing and Local Government, *Homes for Today and Tomorrow*, Report of a Sub-Committee of the Central Housing Advisory Committee, (The Parker Morris Report), H.M.S.O., 1961.

5. The general conclusion that can be drawn from a great variety of research studies is that the direct effect of bad housing conditions upon mortality is 'only demonstrable in infectious disease, especially tuberculosis'. Benjamin, B., *Social and Economic Factors Affecting Mortality*, Mouton, The Hague, 1965, p.42.

6. *Report of the Committee on Accidental Hypothermia*, Royal College of Physicians, 1966. See also the report of research now being carried out at the Centre for Environmental Studies (Annual Report, 1971).

7. Gregory, P., *Polluted Homes*, Bell, 1965.

8. Davies, B., *et al.*, *Variations in Services for the Aged*, Bell, 1970.

9. *Manchester Guardian*, 1933, and *The Times*, 8 March 1934. Quoted in an impressive review of slum clearance and other housing policies by Samuel, R., Kincaid, J. and Slater, E., "But Nothing Happens", *New Left Review*, 1962, pp.39-40.

10. Ministry press release for annual conference, Urban District Councils Association, 25 June 1954.

11. *Manchester Guardian*, 12 January 1955.

12. *Conservative Party Annual Conference 1971, Verbatim Report* (5th Session, 15 October), pp.91-3.

13. For an attempt to measure the rate of obsolescence see the account of the Tayside study in Duncan, T.L.C., *Measuring Housing Quality: A Study of Methods*, Occasional Paper, no. 20, Centre for Urban and Regional Studies, University of Birmingham, 1971, pp.11-15.

14. Officially the term slum is 'variously applied to houses unfit for human habitation, unfit houses beyond repair at reasonable cost and houses in clearance areas'. (Minister of Housing, in a parliamentary written answer in February 1971.) The criteria are set out in Section 4 of the Housing Act of 1957, as amended by Section 71 of the Housing Act of 1969. 'In determining . . . whether a house is unfit for human habitation, regard shall be had to . . . (a) repair, (b) stability, (c) freedom from damp, (d) natural lighting, (e) venti-

lation, (f) water-supply, (g) drainage and sanitary conveniences, (h) facilities for . . . preparation and cooking of food and for the disposal of waste water (plus internal arrangements of dwelling, added by the 1969 Act) and the house shall be deemed unfit for human habitation if and only if it is so far defective in one or more of the said matters that it is not reasonably suitable for occupation in that condition.' It is evident that the term 'not reasonably suitable' is very flexible in interpretation. The 1969 Act incorporated some of the recommendations of the Denington Committee which suggested a minimum fitness standard 'close to the present one', which would involve the collection and reporting of data on all housing. *Our Older Homes: A Call for Action*, H.M.S.O., 1966.

15. *Slum Clearance (England and Wales)*, Cmnd. 9593, H.M.S.O., 1955.

16. Samuel, R., Kincaid, J., and Slater, E., op. cit., p.51.

17. 'House Conditions Survey, England and Wales, 1967', *Economic Trends*, no. 175, H.M.S.O., 1968. See also the discussion in Dennis, N., *People and Planning: The Sociology of Housing in Sunderland*, Faber, 1970, pp. 120-28. Similarly the returns of local authorities in Scotland suggested there were 100,000 unfit dwellings in 1964 but an official report came to the conclusion, on the basis of information about sanitary facilities, that 200,000 would be a more accurate minimum estimate. *Scotland's Older Houses* (the Cullingworth Report), Edinburgh, H.M.S.O., 1967. Although policy objectives are based on estimates of numbers of slums there is little information on the varying definitions of unfitness actually used by local authorities and the extent to which slums are scattered among fit property. See, for example, Burnett, F., and Scott, S., 'A Survey of Housing Conditions in the Urban Areas of England and Wales, 1960', *Sociological Review*, 10, 1962.

18. *Social Trends*, no. 2, 1971, p.183. 'Of the 3,950 households in buildings which existed in 1961 and where the living space was apparently comparable with that in 1966, as many as 39 per cent were assigned a different number of rooms in 1961 to what we believe to be the true position in 1966 . . . Social survey experience has shown that to determine a household's rooms according to the Census definition requires a whole battery of questions.' Gray, P., and Gee, F.G., *A Quality Check on the 1966 Ten Per Cent Sample Census of England and Wales*, H.M.S.O., 1972, p.48.

19. See an excellent review of the evidence, 'Life at the Top', in *Lancet*, 25 March 1972.

20. Tentative measures like the House Condition Index described above are intermediate to detailed quantity estimations for individual dwellings and the categorization of large areas.

21. Hare, P.H., 'Comparing the Costs of Owning and Renting in Scotland', *Housing Review*, April 1973.

22. *Social Trends*, no. 1, 1970, p.138.

23. General Register Office, *Sample Census 1966, England and Wales, Housing Tables, Part I*, H.M.S.O., 1968, p.1.

24. Woolf, M., *The Housing Survey in England and Wales, 1964*, Government Social Survey, 1967.

25. Calculated from General Register Office, *Sample Census 1966, England and Wales, Housing Tables, Part I,* op. cit., p.9.

26. See, for example, Chapman, D., *The Home and Social Status,* Routledge & Kegan Paul, 1955; Duncan, T.L.C., op. cit., especially pp. 38-43.

27. For example, Medhurst, F., and Lewis, J.P., *Urban Decay: An Analysis and a Policy,* Macmillan, 1969.

28. Ministry of Housing and Local Government, *The Deeplish Study: Improvement Possibilities in a District of Rochdale,* H.M.S.O., 1966. The 'house condition index' used in that report is not, however, described in detail and discussed. See also Duncan, T.L.C., op. cit., pp.46-58. Recommendations for more comprehensive measures to be adopted will be found for example in Ministry of Housing and Local Government, Central Housing Advisory Committee, *Our Older Homes — A Call for Action,* H.M.S.O., 1966, and Scottish Development Department, Scottish Housing Advisory Committee, *Scotland's Older Houses,* Edinburgh, H.M.S.O., 1967. The latter describes a Housing Defects Index in an Appendix. This covers services and sanitation, deterioration and access.

29. For example, the 1885 Commissioners recommend, '1. That upon the lines of existing enactments in the Acts of 1862 and 1878 rules of more general application be framed to control the height of buildings in relation to the open space which should be required to be provided in front of the buildings, either in the form of land exclusively belonging to each building and kept free from erections, or in the form of an adjoining street. 2. That in the rear of every new dwelling-house or other building to be controlled by rules ordinarily applicable to dwelling-houses, and whether in old or in new streets, there be provided a proportionate extent of space exclusively belonging to the dwelling-house or building; that this space be free from erections from the ground level upwards, that it extend laterally throughout the entire width of the dwelling-house or building; that for the distance across the space from the building to the boundary of adjoining premises a minimum be prescribed; and that this minimum increase with the height of the dwelling-house or building.' 'The First Report ... Housing of the Working Classes', op. cit., pp. 32-3.

30. Ministry of Housing and Local Government, *The Density of Residential Areas,* H.M.S.O., 1952, p.6.

31. *Social Trends,* no. 2, 1971, H.M.S.O., 1972, p.127. See also the detailed discussion in Greve, J., Page, D., and Greve, S., *Homelessness in London,* Scottish Academic Press, 1971.

32. Ministry of Housing and Local Government, *Caravans as Houses,* Cmnd. 872, H.M.S.O., 1959. See also Spencer, K., 'Housing and Socially Deprived Families', in Holman, R. (ed.), *Socially Deprived Families in Britain,* The Bedford Square Press, 1970, pp.104-7.

33. Greve, J., Page, D. and Greve, S., op. cit., pp.11-21, and pp.247-51.

34. *Social Trends,* no. 2, 1971, p.126.

35. Department of Employment, *Family Expenditure Survey, Report for 1970,* H.M.S.O., 1971, p.114.

36. 'What puts this region in a special category is the fact that it has a great deal of

bad housing *plus* an economy and infrastructure greatly weakened by decades of decline in its traditional industries', Northern Economic Planning Council, *Report of the Working Group on Housing Needs in the Northern Region,* August 1971, p.20.

37. Park, R., Burgess, E., and Mackenzie, R., *The City,* Chicago University Press, 1925. The article 'The Growth of the City' by E.W. Burgess was originally published in *Proceedings of the American Sociological Society,* vol. XVIII, 1923.

38. Rex, J., and Moore, R., *Race Community and Conflict: A Study of Sparkbrook,* Oxford University Press, 1967, pp.8-9.

39. 'Their deserted homes then pass to a motley population consisting on the one hand of the city's social rejects and on the other of newcomers who lack the defensive communal institutions of the working class, but who defend themselves and seek security within some sort of colony structure.' Rex, J., and Moore, R., op. cit., pp.8-9.

40. Pahl, R.E., 'Poverty and the Urban System', in Chisholm, M. and Manners, G. (eds.), *Spatial Policy Problems of the British Economy,* Cambridge University Press, 1972.

41. See, for example, Labbens, J., *La Condition Sous-Proletarienne,* Bureau de Recherchés Sociales, Paris, 1965.

42. Abrams, C., *Housing in the Modern World,* Faber & Faber, 1964, Chapter 2; Clinard, M.B., *Slums and Community Development,* The Free Press, New York, 1966, pp.47-54.

43. Rex, J. and Moore, R., op. cit., p.9.

44. Rex, J.A., 'The Sociology of a Zone of Transition', in Pahl, R.E. (ed.), *Readings in Urban Sociology,* Pergamon Press, 1968, p. 215.

45. Haddon, R.F., 'A Minority in a Welfare State Society: The Location of West Indians in the London Housing Market', *New Atlantis,* 1972, esp. pp.124-33.

46. Haddon, R.F., loc. cit. p.113.

47. 'The movement of the few, in other words, is conditional upon the marginality of the rest. But while the majority remain in a situation of relative instability and poverty, the mobility of the minority constitutes a source of legitimacy for differentiation and hence also of relative deprivation.' MacEwen, A., 'Differentiation Amongst the Urban Poor: An Argentine Study', paper presented to the annual conference of the British Sociological Association, University of York, 11-14 April, 1972.

48. Dennis, N., *People and Planning: The Sociology of Housing in Sunderland,* Faber & Faber, 1970, pp.119-20. See also, Jones, C., 'The Renewal of Areas of Twilight Housing', R.I.B.A. Conference, *Living in Britain,* July 1967.

49. See, for example, Matthew, R., *et al., New Life in Old Towns,* H.M.S.O., 1971; and Pepper, S., *Housing Improvement: Goals and Strategies,* Lund Humphries, 1971.

50. One example was the decision by Islington Borough Council in 1968 to clear the Westbourne Road area because it was 'socially undesirable'. Power, A., 'Homes and Squatters', *New Society,* 6 July 1972.

51. See, for example, Booth, C., *Life and Labour of the People in London,* final volume, Macmillan, 1902, pp. 3-15.

52. *Circumstances of Families,* H.M.S.O., 1967; Coates, K., and Silburn, R., *St Anns: Poverty, Deprivation and Morale in a Nottingham Community,* Nottingham University Adult Education Department, 1967, incorporated also in their later publication, *Poverty: The Forgotten Englishmen,* Penguin, 1970; *The Characteristics of London's Homeless,* G.L.C. Report no. 5, August 1970.

53. *Report of the Committee on Housing in Greater London* (The Milner Holland Committee), Cmnd. 2605, H.M.S.O., 1965.

54. *Report of the Committee on the Rent Acts* (The Francis Committee), Cmnd. 4609, H.M.S.O., 1971, pp.254. The wide variation in proportions of income paid in rent is not a new phenomenon. The Commissioners reporting in 1885 on the housing of the working classes quoted an investigation of 1,000 dwellings randomly surveyed in poor parts of London which showed that 46 per cent paid from one quarter to one half of their incomes and 12 per cent less than a fifth. *First Report of Her Majesty's Commissioners for Inquiring into the Housing of the Working Classes,* Eyre & Spottiswoode, 1885, p.17.

55. *Fair Deal for Housing,* Cmnd. 4728, H.M.S.O., July 1971.

56. Conservative Party Annual Conference, 15 October 1971.

57. *Official Report of the Standing Committee E on the Housing Finance Bill,* H.M.S.O., vols. 1-4, 1972.

58. See, for example, 'Mr Crosland's speech on the Third Reading of the Housing Finance Bill, *Hansard,* 8 May 1972, cols. 939-49.

59. *Fair Deal for Housing,* op. cit., p.1.

60. See, for example, Field, F., in *Poverty,* winter 1971-2; Meacher, M., 'Means-Tests' (publication forthcoming): Townsend, P., 'The Scope and Limitations of Means-Tested Social Services in Britain', paper presented to Manchester Statistical Society, February 1972.

61. For example, in 1968 Birmingham Corporation took powers through a Private Act of Parliament to pay rent allowances similar to those now proposed by the Government. Though 6,000 families were believed to be eligible, only 1,000 applications were made and only 250 were granted. Cocks, F., 'Housing Allowances for Private Tenants – Birmingham's Experience', *The Housing Review,* February 1972. The annual reports of the numbers of recipients of rate rebates show that disproportionately large numbers of eligible persons who are pensioners and who are owner-occupiers obtain rebates. Thus the numbers of claimants in Clacton and Morecambe is relatively eight or nine times higher than in Tower Hamlets and Islington. *Rate Rebates in England and Wales,* 1971. See also Nevitt, A.A., 'How Fair are Rate Rebates', *New Society,* 10 June 1971, and Meacher, M., *Rate Rebates: A Study of the Effectiveness of Means Tests,* Child Poverty Action Group, November 1972.

62. Parker, R.A., 'The Housing Finance Bill and Council Tenants, *Poverty Pamphlet,* no. 9, Child Poverty Action Group, 1972.

63. 'According to the latest figures, the central Government's housing subsidies, plus rate fund contribution and supplementary benefit rent payments, amounted

in 1970-71, to £465m. By 1975-6, when the fair rent system is operational, the best available figures suggest that rent rebate and rent allowance subsidies, plus supplementary benefit rent payment, will amount to only £240m. . . . what it means for the local authorities and the private tenants . . . is a cut in subsidy from £63 to £33 a year . . . By contrast, over exactly the same period the total of mortgage interest tax relief to owner-occupiers will rise from £300m. to about £400m., representing an average rise for the owner-occupier of from about £62 a year to about £68. It is this shift from the poorer half of the nation in favour of the better-off other half, that lies at the heart of the Bill', Meacher, M., *Hansard*, 8 May 1972, col. 1020.

64. See the comprehensive and rightly polemical guides issued by the Association of London Housing Estates.

65. Written answer to a parliamentary question, *Hansard*, 16 November 1971, col. 83.

66. Crouch, C., and Woolf, M., 'Inequality in Housing', in Townsend, P., and Bosanquet, N., *Labour and Inequality*, Fabian Society, 1972, pp.34-5 (estimates based on Woolf, M., *Government Housing Policy*, unpublished B. Phil. thesis, University of Oxford, 1971).

67. Insight Consumer Unit, 'The Great British Housing Crisis', *Sunday Times Magazine*, 16 April 1972.

68. It is interesting to find that the Royal Commissioners inquiring into the housing of the working classes in 1885 were also rather sceptical of the concept of 'fairness' as applied in market conditions. In discussing compensation they stated, 'The Artizans Dwellings Act of 1875 provided that the estimated value of the premises within the unhealthy area shall be based upon the fair market value as estimated at the time of the valuation being made and of the several interests in the premises, due regard being had to the nature and the then condition of the property, to the probable duration of the buildings in their existing state, and the state or repair thereof, and of all circumstances affecting such value, without any additional allowance for compulsory purchase. *So far as the intention of the Act goes, it appears manifest that the object of the authors and the object of Parliament was that the owners of this property should only obtain a fair value and nothing more; but, as a matter of fact, and in practice, they have succeeded in spite of the Act in obtaining a great deal more.'* The First Report . . . Housing of the Working Classes, op.cit. p.45 (my emphasis).

69. 'Improvement grants, although highly successful in improving the housing stock, also operate regressively. They are overwhelmingly taken up by better-off owner-occupiers and speculative property developers, who receive not only the amount of the grant but also an appreciation in the capital value of the house.' Crosland, A., 'Housing and Inequality', *Guardian*, 15 June 1972.

70. 'Inequalities remain too large; and current research and activity in these areas is more likely to give prominence to these and new forms of inequality than to show any closing of the gap. A programme the size of urban aid can only patch — as first aid.' Smith, T., and G., 'Urban First Aid', *New Society*, 30 December 1971.

71. Much the same strategy is advocated by Nevitt, A.A., *Fair Deal for House-*

holders, Fabian Research Series, no. 297, 1971, in which, for example, she advocates a system of seven, fourteen and twenty-one year leases for council tenants, and specifies a form of communal tenant ownership, in which the tenant shares ownership with the council.

72. Department of Health and Social Security, *Two-Parent Families: A Study of their Resources and Needs in 1968, 1969, and 1970,* Statistical Report Series, no.14, H.M.S.O., 1971.

73. 'To be fair the rent subsidy must not only be available to tenants whose income is at or below the minimum level judged to be tolerable for such purposes as Supplementary Benefit. It must also be available to tenants with incomes above this level, if the rent of their home would otherwise impose an unfair burden on their family budget.' *Fair Deal for Housing,* op.cit., p.12.

74. 'It is fraudulent to pretend that the rent rebate policy will be in any sense "national" in its application. On the contrary, it will be highly localized, will treat similar families in different ways, and will ensure that the value of the needs allowance will be least to families with the highest housing costs.' Jessup, C., 'A Fair Allowance?', *New Society,* 30 March 1972.

75. In a detailed comparison of housing in Britain and in the United States one scholar concluded that the economic stratification of metropolitan populations was much more marked in the U.S. and mixed residential patterns more marked in Britain. He suggested that a principal explanatory factor was the greater Government support in the U.S. for the private market, Schorr, A.L., *Slums and Social Insecurity,* Nelson, 1964, Chapter 6.

76. Other writers have called for 'the introduction of one system of subsidies which is equitable as between different tenure groups. All families should be treated alike regardless of whether they are council tenants, owner-occupiers or the tenants of private landlords.' Nevitt, A.A., *Housing, Taxation and Subsidies,* Nelson, 1966, p.151.

77. Nevitt, A.A., 'A Tax on Land as Rent', in *Towards a National Rent Policy,* The Land Institute, April 1968.

78. Gray, P.G., and Todd, J., 'Privately Rented Accommodation in London', A Report on inquiries made in December 1963 and June 1964 for the Committee on Housing in Greater London, Appendix 5, in *Report of the Committee on Housing in Greater London* (the Milner Holland Report), Cmnd. 2605, H.M.S.O., 1965, p.350.

79. As the National Board for Prices and Incomes also pointed out, 'it would seem anomalous to relate the rents of the growing [public sector] to those of the declining private sector; and this anomaly would increase with the years, so that as a long term principle the concept is likely to lose its validity.' National Board for Prices and Incomes, Report no. 62, *Increases in Rents of Local Authority Housing,* Cmnd., 3604, H.M.S.O., 1968, p.22.

7 Selectivity: A Nation Divided?*

Early in 1968 the Fabian Society called a conference to discuss a fundamental disagreement about the development of social policy which appeared to exist among leading spokesmen of the Labour Government and the Labour Party. Leading Ministers and ex-Ministers, such as Mr Ray Gunter, Mr Douglas Houghton and Mr Patrick Gordon-Walker, and M.P.s such as Mr Brian Walden (1) have been presenting arguments in favour of greater 'selectivity'. Other Ministers, such as Mr Richard Crossman, Mr Kenneth Robinson and Mrs Judith Hart (and before Mrs Hart as Minister of Social Security, Miss Margaret Herbison) have vehemently opposed any extension of 'the means test'.(2) Many of those who are most deeply informed about social policy, whether as strategists and social scientists, like Richard Titmuss, or as administrators, like Sir John Walley, the ex-Deputy Secretary of the Ministry of Social Security, counsel caution and point out the general and particular difficulties that exist, preferring the emphasis in policy to be given to 'universalistic' measures, like family allowances.(3) But there remains a lot of public confusion about the arguments, and a failure to isolate the key issues. What is at stake is not just the most technically efficient or cheapest means of reaching an agreed end. It is the kind and quality of the society we wish to achieve in Britain.

The starting point must be the recent history of government strategy. A few years ago the universalistic emphases in the Labour Party's policies were quite clear. They were to extend and not restrict national insurance, curtail means tests and income tests in the social services (one result of which was to be the scaling down of the National Assistance Board to the dimensions of a residual service), abolish prescription charges, extend educational opportunity through the reorganization of secondary schools, develop and expand community services, and integrate immigrant groups, partly through strong legislation against racial discrimination. The theme of *equal rights* or social equality could be said to have been the dominant domestic theme of the party manifesto for both the elections of 1964 and 1966.

What has brought about the rapid change that has occurred in the

* First published in *Social Services for All?*, Eleven Fabian Essays, the Fabian Society, 1968.

climate of opinion since then? This is an intriguing question which future historians will want to try to answer at length, but which, in our bafflement, requires some provisional explanation. Here it is possible only to give a personal interpretation. First, there has been a subordination of social to economic objectives and strategies. The nation's economic difficulties have seemed so great that they have been used as an excuse for inaction in spheres which they did not seriously affect. Not only was there less money in 1964 and again in 1966 than had been hoped for housing, schools and hospitals, but it was believed that there was insufficient money too for social security reforms. The Government did not consider it could press through a strong redistributionist policy in the face of public opinion at home and financial opinion abroad. And instead of treating social policy as a major instrument in overcoming economic difficulties − for example, by developing at a disproportionate speed those sectors of the educational system which could produce scarce technical and scientific skills or, more generally, by creating the sense of social vitality from which might spring new attitudes to productivity − social policy was made subservient to traditional economic doctrine. This might be illustrated by the National Plan of 1965, by the statements made by the Chancellor, the Prime Minister and others in July 1966, and by the White Paper of February 1968 on the cuts that had been made in public expenditure.

Lately the Treasury's desire to evaluate social service developments through cost-benefit analysis and not other types of analysis as well is another indication of the subordination of social to economic policy. To concentrate attention on the alternative ways of most cheaply achieving a certain end is not only to divert attention from alternative ends. It is to divert attention from alternative *social* means which are difficult or impossible to cost. The institutional processes have been complex and subtle. They have included pressures from the City, the United States and financial centres in Europe. But, by and large, the concerns of the market have gained ascendancy over the essentially social concerns with which the Government took office in 1964.

Secondly, there has been a marked shift of emphasis away from social equality as a national objective. The White Paper on *Immigration from the Commonwealth* in 1965 (together with the latest failure to promote integration) can now be perceived as representing a major retreat from universalistic values which inevitably sapped the moral authority of the Government in other social spheres and affected the whole delicate structure of community services. A sociologist is acutely aware of the interdependence of institutions and values and accepts the fact that changes in one part of the social structure are bound to affect other parts of that structure. The restrictive policies reflected by the White Paper and by measures, like the Commonwealth Immigrants Act, were bound to make racial equality harder to achieve. But they make social equality harder to achieve too.

Irrational expressions of the prejudice and extreme forms of discrimination cannot be confined to one social group. White persons who live in the same slums and attend the same employment exchanges and housing offices as coloured persons are likely also to be victims of aggressive superiority. In the United States racial discrimination in many ways coincides with class discrimination, and the development of the former in Britain is likely to widen the social distance between classes.

The tone of recent articles and letters in the press about unemployed men alleged, against all the evidence, to be avoiding work at the nation's expense, and about unsupported women who are imagined to be neglecting their children, are disturbing examples. After the White Paper of 1965, it became difficult for members of the Labour Party to use the term 'equality' unselfconsciously. Much more important, the concept could no longer lend coherence and simplicity to the Government's long-term objectives.

Thirdly, large-scale planning has given way to piecemeal improvisation. Understandable as it was at the time, the decision to strengthen the existing national insurance scheme in March 1965 rather than to replace it, say, a year afterwards, and to introduce social security reforms in instalments, beginning with redundancy payments and wage-related unemployment and sickness benefits, has postponed comprehensive reform along the lines of the national superannuation scheme proposed earlier. Attention has been diverted away from strategic planning to the achievement of limited objectives of different kinds.

The Meaning of Selectivity

For such reasons as these, then, the issues posed by 'selectivity' have recently become real to many people. But what does the term *mean*? Here it is important to exclude two interpretations: choosing priorities, and defining groups in the population with particular social or physical characteristics. These two have been the source of a lot of misunderstanding — when confused with the third and narrower interpretation. No one seriously doubts that at any single time there must be some kind of rationale according to which the Government has to distribute limited resources as between education and health services, for example, or has to distribute them within any particular service, as between primary, secondary and tertiary education. Selection of priorities is a necessary and continuous process.

How they can be identified is an interesting and serious question which is discussed far too little in relation to national objectives. In the United States, despite a similar subordination of social to economic goals, more strenuous attempts at self-analysis are going on, through the Planning Programming Budgeting System introduced into each agency of his Cabinet by President Johnson in 1965.

Again, a section of the population might be selected according to some social, physical or educational criterion in order that they might receive certain benefits or services. Thus, fatherless families, the blind, the disabled, people aged eighty and over, educationally subnormal children, *irrespective of their incomes,* might qualify for benefits. But again, the appropriateness of this strategy, at least in principle, is not seriously questioned. It is selectivity in a third and narrower meaning of the term which is in dispute. A test of means or of income is applied to the population in general, or indeed even to a particular category of the population, like fatherless families, the blind and the disabled, to decide who is poor enough to be provided with cash benefits, or free services, to be excused charges or pay lower charges. Current examples in Britain, taken at random, are supplementary benefits, free school meals, free milk for young children, rate rebates and, in many areas, free home help services.

Two Objections to Selectivity

Every selective measure, whether actually in operation or merely proposed, is designed to meet highly specific problems. To some extent therefore each measure requires separate discussion. But there are at least two common problems. First, substantial proportions of the people who are in theory eligible for benefits under income-test schemes do not apply for them. Secondly, administratively they are difficult to fit to circumstances. Proposals to extend income-test schemes by modifying methods of tax assessment, for example, by paying allowances to those below the tax paying level, cannot be speedily implemented and cannot be made wholly equitable, both because the administrative and technical machinery which would be required in Britain could not be developed for several years at least (some Cabinet Ministers say eight years at the earliest), and because a huge proportion of those who should qualify could not be fitted into any 'automatic' scheme. These would be people with different sources of income and insecure employment — most likely to be numbered among the poor. They would also be people living in households in which the wife or adolescent children have some earnings. We still do not know, because there exists no empirical study, whether the number of those dependent on earnings who actually live in poverty and who could be fitted even in principle into a computerized automatic scheme of, say, negative income tax is as high as, say, 40 per cent.

There are thus two powerful objections to the extension of income-tested services. One is inefficiency (in terms of not reaching many of the people they are supposed to reach). The other is impracticality. To meet the complicated circumstances of different families the rules themselves would have to be complicated. But then they would be difficult to operate or comprehend and would discourage applicants. But these objections are not fatal. Proponents argue that they could be more efficient. They say public attitudes to income tests are changing, that income tests can be applied in a more tactful style, that campaigns can be mounted to persuade eligible persons to apply for benefits, and that a modern form of combined tax and social security assessment could, with imagination and government support, be introduced more quickly than civil servants pessimistically suppose — at least for some of those who are poor. But are public attitudes really changing? I am sceptical of this assertion. At least we require better evidence than that so far provided. Although the Government has, for example, changed the name of means-tested allowances from 'national assistance' to 'supplementary benefit' and has improved certain administrative procedures, similar changes have been made previously (for example, from 'public' to 'national' assistance).

Again, the number of retirement pensioners coming forward for supplementary benefit has certainly increased since the implementation in 1966 of the Social Security Act. But how many of these new beneficiaries have come forward because benefit levels have been raised, because income and capital disregards have been made more generous, or only because the ministry has at last got through to those who were too proud or uninformed to apply?

Changes in attitudes to national assistance require substantial changes in social structure, in attitudes towards the working class and particularly towards the poor, and in the bureaucratic institutions which are concerned with the poor, by the replacement of offices, the introduction of new forms of training and staff recruitment and the improvement of pay, all of which are bound to take time. Yet limited progress, of course, is not impossible. While arguing the case for, and awaiting the opportunity to introduce, a totally different scheme, there is much to be said in favour of making existing forms of selectivity less objectionable and by exposing their deficiencies. The efforts of the Supplementary Benefits Commission to modify the harsher rules affecting the wage-stop are a good example. So also are the large advertisements now placed by the Minister of Housing in the *Daily Mirror* and other newspapers to persuade those who are eligible for rate rebates to apply for them. In encouraging the Government to modernize its reception and treatment of the poor, pressure groups like the Child Poverty Action Group, Shelter and the Disablement Income Group, are playing a useful role. They are emphasizing rights and publicizing unequal treatment which was formerly hidden. But in a rapidly developing society this may be no more than moving a little faster to maintain the same relative place of the poor in the nation's hierarchy of status, treatment and regard. Piecemeal reform of the procedures and institutions for the poor may look like progress by the standards of history, but not by the standards of structural inequality.

The Third Objection to Selectivity

There is a final question to bear in mind. Would a major extension of the principle of selectivity in the social services make society more or less unequal? My own answer to this question might be expressed in the following general terms. The fatal objection to a policy of extending selectivity is that it misconceives the nature of poverty and reinforces the condition it is supposed to alleviate. The policy assumes that poverty is an absolute condition, a lack of a minimum subsistence cash income, which requires little more than the diversion of a minute proportion of national income in an efficient manner to alleviate it. It fosters hierarchical relationships of superiority and inferiority in society, diminishes rather than enhances the status of the poor, and has the effect of widening rather than of reducing social inequalities. Far from sensitively discriminating different kinds of need it lumps the unemployed, sick, widowed, aged and others into one undifferentiated and inevitably stigmatized category. It distracts attention from the problems of improving the quality of public services and of expanding the resources available for the general welfare of the community. It also assumes that the circumstances of the poor can be greatly improved without changing major social institutions and severely limiting the opportunity of the prosperous sections of the population to accumulate more privileges.

Instead, poverty has to be regarded as a relative condition, as a lack of the physical assets, housing standards and environmental and occupational facilities as well as the cash incomes which are needed to allow people to participate in activities and customs, including the dietary customs, which are normal in that society. For it to be alleviated there has to be a complex reconstruction of the systems of reward in society, as between those at work and those who are not at work, those with and without dependants, and those who live in depressed and prosperous regions.

Primary in this reconstruction would be the reform of the tax and social security systems, but much would also depend on the gradual recasting of the housing, education and employment systems, including income differentials as well as workers' participation in management. The strengthening of individual rights, through new forms of political representation and better legal information and aid, the revision of the law would be crucial. Only by recognizing that our social structure is a rather rigid network with very distinct class 'levels' (typified even within 'selectivity' itself by the more generous system of means-tested university student grants than of school educational maintenance allowances) can we begin to discern the scale of the reconstruction required to abolish poverty.

Perhaps these conclusions are strongly expressed. Certainly their force would vary according to any particular example of selectivity that might be brought up for discussion. But in terms of the diagnosis of the problem, the methods of remedying it and achieving a better society, I submit that 'selectivity' represents an extremely limited and inadequate social philosophy. For when applied in policy this philosophy would have the effect of reinforcing the divisive structural characteristics of society instead of bridging them in the interests of equal rights and individual freedom.

Notes

1. See, for example, reports in the *Sunday Times* of a speech made by Mr Ray Gunter, 19 August 1967; Douglas Houghton, *Hansard*, 9 June 1967 and also *Paying for the Social Services*, Occasional Paper no. 16, Institute of Economic Affairs, 1967; and Brian Walden, 'Means-Test Justice', *Sunday Times*, 25 June 1967.

2. See, for example, reports in the press of speeches made by Kenneth Robinson (16 September 1967) and Mrs Judith Hart (25 September 1967).

3. Titmuss, R.M., 'Universal or Selective: the practical Case Against the Means-Test State', *New Statesman*, 15 September 1967; Walley, Sir John, 'New Approach to Abolishing Child Poverty', *The Times*, 11 December 1967.

8 The Difficulties of Negative Income Tax*

A negative income tax scheme, especially as applied to families with children, has been proposed in Britain by, among others, Dennis Lees, ('Poor Families and Fiscal Reform', *Lloyds Bank Review,* 1967) and in the United States by Milton Friedman (*Capitalism and Freedom,* 1963), James Tobin ('Improving the Economic Status of the Negro', *Daedalus,* 1965), and Robert Lampman (see the discussion in W. A. Klein, 'Some Problems of Negative Income Taxation', *Wisconsin Law Review,* 1966). Just as families with substantial incomes are credited with allowances for children when the amount of tax they should pay is assessed, so poor families would be paid part or all of the difference between their actual incomes and the total allowances credited to them by virtue of their family size and other factors. For example, if a family with three children have an income of £300 below their total of personal exemptions and minimum standard deductions under income tax law, this 'unused' allowance could be called their negative taxable income. A tax rate of, say, 50 per cent, could be applied to this allowance and the family would receive special payments during the year amounting to £150.

It should be noted that there are three governing elements in the scheme: (i) the definition of the minimum income for families of different composition that is to be treated as adequate or desirable — perhaps we could call this *'the basic income'*; (ii) the *'rate'* (or rates, for there could be a sliding scale) of negative tax, which would apply to the amount by which actual income fell short of the basic income; and (iii) the minimum 'subsistence' income which is guaranteed to different families by the scheme. We could call this *'the guaranteed income'*. Any two of these elements determine the third.

Thus in an example given by Professor Lees, (i) *the basic income* is defined as consisting of current personal and child tax allowances plus two ninths of earned income. For a family with three children under the age of eleven and an earned income of £400 the basic income would therefore consist of £685 (personal allowance for man and wife of £340 plus £115 for each child) plus £88, amounting to a total of £773. He

* First published in Townsend, P. *et al, Social Services for All?* Eleven Fabian Essays, the Fabian Society, 1968.

defines (ii) *the rate of negative tax* arbitrarily at 50 per cent, and therefore (iii) *the guaranteed income* becomes the earned income of £400 plus 50 per cent of the difference between the £400 and the basic income of £773, or £186.50, amounting in total to £586.50.

Critical Questions

Many awkward questions can be asked about this kind of proposal. The three elements have received very little critical scrutiny. Why should an allowance of two ninths of earned incomes be built into the conception of both 'basic' and 'guaranteed' income? Suppose two poor families, each with three children, have an income of less than the basic income; one husband earns £400 and the other £600. The former would receive a welfare payment of £142.50, and the latter £42.50, by virtue of their composition. But Professor Lees proposes to add to the income of the former £44 and yet to the income of the latter £67 *by virtue of their level of earnings.* To define the need for income even partly in terms of actual earnings seems difficult to justify whether in terms of current social values or traditional practice.

How are different income units within the same household to be treated? Suppose that the third 'child' in the example given above of the family with £400 earned income was in fact a boy aged sixteen (though the other two children were still aged under eleven). If he were at school the family would receive a total welfare payment under the scheme of £199. But if he were at work, and earning, say, £220 a year, the family would still receive £129, even though its total earned income was already more (£620) than the earned income plus welfare payment (£599) in the previous case. Many other problems affecting income units in relation to household composition, of wives in employment, retirement pensioners and children in higher education, could be raised. The proponents of negative income tax have not begun to explain how the conception of the income unit under income tax law can be reconciled equitably with that of the household under social security legislation.

How can a scheme based on the slight rearrangement of regular cash incomes be appropriate for abolishing poverty in a society in which standards of living are increasingly determined by other kinds of personal resources (assets, fringe benefits, social services) and by occasional or irregular income (occasional fees, weekend jobs, bonuses, periodic overtime earnings, deferred pay)? There are problems about the value of owner-occupied homes, the value of homes rented far more cheaply in some than in other regions of the country, the value of food grown on farms for the farm family, and the canteen meals subsidized by the firm. Present income-tax law would have to be drastically changed to accommodate more explicit welfare objectives in relation to a new definition of income. More important still, *any* scheme based on the *readjustment* of regular cash incomes might be peripheral to the problems of those who do in fact have the lowest incomes. For good budgeting they must have the security of foreknowledge of a regular and reliable source of income. It may be impossible to apply a scheme based on fairly simple rules to people with fluctuating incomes. Most schemes that have been devised are clumsily crude. Or, in adopting simple rules for a means-tested scheme, a government may dangerously flout its avowed aim of tailoring subsidy to need. Instead, policies based on income allowances granted as of right in fulfilment of specific conditions, and policies based on the conferment of benefits other than cash (housing, other assets, services), will do much more than any combination of means-tested schemes to reduce real poverty.

Incentives to Work

Why do the proponents suggest that the rate of negative tax should be less than 100 per cent, or, to express the same point rather differently, why should the subsistence income that is to be guaranteed by the State be less than the basic income which is regarded as adequate? Without attempting to relate the proposal to the real circumstances of families or to collect evidence some economists *assume* that a figure of 50 per cent would be approximately right to preserve a sufficient element of incentive to earn more. In an accompanying Fabian paper *(Social Services for All?)* Mr Kaim-Caudle draws attention to the fact that even in present conditions a rate as low as 50 per cent represents a very high marginal rate of tax for persons with low earnings and that the introduction of more income-tested welfare payments could have ludicrous implications for the usual economic assumptions about monetary incentives.

The emphasis on preserving money incentives to earn more at the lower levels is misplaced. It distracts attention from methods of augmenting earnings in some kinds of family because of the needs created by adult disability, redundant skills, handicap among children or presence of only one parent, and misleads the public into believing that welfare payments must fall substantially short of desirable or necessary levels.

Moreover, the controls over work are in fact much more social than economic. The structure of society exerts powerful constraints on men both to work and to adjust to different types and earning-levels of work. A man works to preserve the respect of his wife, children, friends and neighbours, to fulfil the psychological needs induced by the customs and expectations of a lifetime and to occupy time fruitfully and replenish the stock of information, cautionary tales and anecdotes which he requires to maintain his participation in the web of social relations. The level at which he is paid is of course important to him but is frequently used as the symbol rather than the real source of any dissatisfaction he may have. Arguments about wage-levels are often arguments about status and dignity and the behaviour expected of management. At low levels of earnings the situation is further complicated by questions of age, loss of status, redundant skills, loss of strength, ill-organized unions, regional poverty, and, above all, disability. The valuable compendium of regional statistics prepared by Edwin Hammond shows how absurd it is to pretend that the wage-stop (the rule applied by the Ministry of Social Security to reduce a man's entitlement to supplementary benefit to a figure below his last earnings) helps to preserve incentives to work. It is a rule which tends to operate only in some regions of the country. It is time we divested ourselves of the idea that the incentive level of earnings, at least for the low paid, is more than one of a dozen elements in the problem of devising an appropriate system of income-support for those in poverty. The problem of the incentive level of earnings has been exaggerated out of proportion to its importance.

As far as I am aware none of the proposals for negative income tax have been made with direct reference to the *actual* circumstances of a cross-section of even ten or twenty households in poverty and with reference to different numbers and kinds of income recipients in the household. The proposals therefore invite the charge that they are abstract and are indeed vague economic exercises. Even if they were viable in the long term they do not meet certain obvious transitional problems and do not meet most of the objections which might be put by the practical politician. The scheme put forward by Professor Lees for replacing family allowances by a negative income tax scheme would involve a net financial loss to many families who are just above the poverty line but who have very modest incomes. A family with an earned income of £20 per week and three children aged 5-10 would have a net financial loss of 30s. per week and even one with the same income but five children (three aged 5-10 and the others under 5) would have a net loss of £2 per week.

The Problem of Equity

The problem of equity, whether as between that part of the population below and that part above a poverty line, between households with only one earner and households with two or more earners, or among households comprising persons with very different kinds of need (age, marital status, physical capacity, skill), is not notably one that has been explored by proponents of negative income tax. Nor have they given much sign of recognizing the problems of any transitional period — of reconciling the benefits of an ideal future scheme of income redistribution with the benefits of an existing scheme. Failing to perceive the relative nature of poverty they fail also to perceive the necessity of applying in policy the principle of equity. Professor Lees thinks that it is 'muddled' and 'mischievous' to mix up the principle with the problem of abolishing poverty and he goes on to suggest that far from equalizing living standards of households all we need to do to overcome family poverty is replace family allowances with negative income tax at no extra cost and possibly with a net saving. This is a sad misunderstanding of the problem and a grave underestimate of the measures that are required to remedy it.

Negative income tax may make more sense for the United States than for Britain. In that country there is an extraordinarily diverse 'system' of public assistance. Benefits and coverage in some states, especially in the south, are extremely poor. Negative income tax could be regarded as a slightly better scheme which would help those of the poor in America who are a long way below government standards of adequacy. However, even in America it is doubtful whether more than a minority of the poor could be helped appreciably.

For both the United States and Britain it can be argued that if any negative income tax scheme is to be viable it would have to embody some of the principles and practices of existing means-tests. It would have to be a compromise scheme rather than a 'new' scheme. There are many households among the poor in which persons frequently change employers, are casually employed or self-employed, earn widely fluctuating amounts from week to week, cannot master the income-tax forms, are periodically sick, are disabled, cannot speak English and where the number of earners and even of persons may change fairly often. The initiative for taking action to supplement their incomes will have to rest with them or with the Supplementary Benefits Commission rather than with their employers acting on behalf of a transformed Board of Inland Revenue. In no real sense can benefit be 'automatic' and 'impersonal'. Moreover, even those families who might in theory receive supplementation automatically week by week will often have to be kept under surveillance. Desertion, for example, will need to be defined and verified. Checks will have to be made on casual earnings and wives' and children's earnings. It will be difficult to avoid official intervention and supervision and those who favour negative income tax because it does not entail a personal declaration of poverty will have to demonstrate their case better. How will the scheme be administered?

Abuse

Another argument against negative income tax is that it would not discourage certain widespread misconceptions about poor families abusing the services of the State. It would not provide the right framework for raising public standards of tolerance and reducing social prejudice. The belief that many unemployed persons are deliberately living on existing State services is widespread but is a myth and is contradicted by the available evidence. Insufficient jobs are available in some local areas; the majority of the long-term unemployed are, by the reckoning of both the Ministry of Labour and the former National Assistance Board, physically or mentally handicapped. In any event, the policing system of the Supplementary Benefits Commission is already stringent — too stringent according to some critics for the sufficient respect of individual freedom and privacy.

But a section of the public, and many of the officials who staff the system, still believe that a large number of people are cheating or are trying to cheat. They think that the poor consist predominantly of people who will not do an honest day's work, who are pretending to be sick, and who have too many children. They want strict conditions for receiving benefit to be applied. They want men to be forced wherever possible to work longer to free the State from the obligation to supplement their incomes, and they want the unemployed to be prevented from receiving as high an income as the employed.

It is not surprising that the system of supplementation and assistance reflects these attitudes, despite efforts continuously made by enlightened senior civil servants to catch up on the standards of modern industry and commerce. The system cannot escape from the structural necessity of having relatively inferior offices, inferior waiting rooms, ill-paid and ill-treated staff and a discouraging style. The extent of poverty and the current methods of treating the poor are inescapably linked to the prosperity and expectations of other sections of society. One is a correlate of the other. The way we treat the poor is *one* way by which our society controls how much work the rest of us do. People who have to plead poverty are obliged to fit at the bottom of a hierarchy governed by an elaborate system of rewards and of status. The standards by which their treatment and their incomes are judged will inevitably tend to be inferior to those by which the treatment and incomes of the majority of persons who experience different kinds of adversity are judged. It is not surprising that they *feel* stigmatized because to a large extent they *are* stigmatized.

The Problem of Collective Stigma

Our object then is to rescue as many of the poor as possible from collective stigma. People in need are not just those who do not have an income which the rest of society thinks adequate. They are the unemployed, sick, deserted, old, bereaved and unskilled. The incomes they should receive (and the way they should be treated) should be determined therefore according to common principles which are developed to meet each category of adversity or need, whether unemployment, sickness, desertion, disability, old age, or dependency. And the only way we can proceed is (i) by comparing the circumstances of each category of persons with their counterparts in the population, the unemployed with the employed, the sick with the well, the old with the young, and so on; and (ii) by comparing rich and poor *within* each category, prosperous unemployed with poor unemployed and prosperous elderly with poor elderly. Let us consider carefully the terms under which redundant or unemployed managers, sick businessmen or teachers, deserted actresses, aged civil servants and doctors and the widows of colonels and major-generals are treated. Let us ask whether these terms might be extended to poor persons within the same categories and to other groups and whether the gradual adoption of common principles might remove thousands of individuals from the lists of the poor and make British society a little less divided. The arguments against means-tested housing allowances and means-tested hospital and school fees would have to be developed rather differently but bear many basic similarities.

Our greatest error is in thinking we can meet poverty by considering the poor alone and just developing policies to give them modest additions to cash income. The introduction of a minimum wage is thought likely by some critics to lead only to a temporary improvement in the relative standard of living of low-paid employees. Before long old differentials would be re-established. It might be argued that an increase in income through the introduction of some form of negative income tax would lead to similar repercussions. The social and economic structure could not be changed except through a more drastic and sophisticated strategy.

In summary, I have raised a number of critical questions about the definition and application of proposals for negative income tax. Generally I have tried to argue that these proposals misconceive the nature of poverty; exaggerate the problems of the incentive level of earnings; overlook political, legal and moral principles of equity; ignore the diverse circumstances and needs of poor families, and fail to provide the kind of framework which will promote that greater social tolerance and respect of minorities which, fundamentally, is necessary for any major reduction in the amount of poverty.

The great majority of countries in the world have public assistance programmes. In the early 1960s at least forty-three of the sixty-one nations for which data about social security was assembled by the International Labour Office then incurred expenditure on such programmes. The exceptions were principally to be found among the poorest developing societies and the Communist industrial countries, though in both instances there were exceptions. For example, Nicaragua but not Colombia, Kenya but not Ghana, and Rumania but not Bulgaria were listed as having programmes.(1)

Present-day developments in the poorest countries and the history of industrialized countries suggest that in the early stages of the establishment of centralized and localized bureaucracy the introduction of means-tested services is common. Resources are scarce; administration is fragmentary and some forms of deviance pose a threat to the maintenance of social order. As a consequence means-tested schemes are convenient. Countrywide rights need not be enforced. Expenditures can be watched and kept to proportions regarded by the Government as manageable. Conditions for the receipt of benefit can be laid down and the system kept within fairly tight administrative control. And yet the system can be responsive to community concern about those who are destitute.

Directly or indirectly many societies have followed the model which was established in England under the Elizabethan Poor Law. From varied schemes of parish relief more integrated schemes of public assistance have been evolved. The question is whether in modern conditions it is desirable to move into a third phase and extend the selective principles and procedures of public assistance programmes to a wide area of social policy. This paper will examine the extension of means-tested services under successive governments in the United Kingdom and review the strategy now being adopted by the Conservative administration. Its conclusion is that there are good reasons to abandon this strategy and to adopt an alternative strategy which will, in a series of steps, reduce 'selective' social services to an

* Paper given to the Manchester Statistical Society, 29 February 1972.

inconsequential if not proscribed element in the total operation of social policy.

Selective and Universalistic Principles

There is some confusion about the meaning that should be given to 'selectivity'. There is no dispute that groups have to be selected from the population to receive special benefits. Thus, there are reasonable grounds for making certain services available only to the aged, or children or the handicapped. Again, there is no dispute that priorities have to be selected in allocating resources to, say, health services rather than education, or one area of the country rather than another, or community care rather than institutional care. While there can be considerable disagreement about the criteria according to which either of these types of decision are handled no one seriously questions that they are taken, however implicitly, and in the future might be seen to be taken more explicitly and rationally.

What is in dispute is whether a test of means should be applied in any of these circumstances or even to the population as a whole to determine who should obtain help. The selective principle that benefits should be allocated according to means has to be judged in relationship to its possible and likely applications. Those invoking it tend to assume that universal benefits would be withdrawn or would not be introduced and that the aggregate resources redistributed through the public sector would be reduced. Public expenditure on benefits would be smaller because families with average and high incomes would not be entitled to receive them, and sums collected in taxes, particularly progressive taxes, would be smaller. They also assume that only the poor and marginally poor would apply for benefits and that therefore a separate service would be administered specifically for these groups, with the consequence that reviews of the needs and treatment of the poor would tend to be divorced from the definition of the needs and mode of treatment in adversity of the rest of the population. Finally, they assume that such administration would possess strong control functions: benefit would become conditional on a body of rather opaque administrative rules and conventions governing behaviour, including, for example, job-seeking behaviour and cohabitation between men and women, and not only on financial entitlement to benefit. In principle 'selectivity' does not necessarily have these consequences but they tend to arise in practice or are implicit in proposed developments in social policy. And it is in its actual implementation and therefore its social meaning that selectivity might more usefully be discussed.

Its meaning can also be made clearer by identifying its obverse.

'Universality' in social policy is the principle of allocating services or benefits to the population or a group in the population irrespective of income. Those invoking it tend to assume that its application would involve redistributing substantial resources through the public sector. Taxes would be collected according to means but benefits allocated equally. The rights of the citizen would be further defined in law and regulation. There would be a reduction of separate services and institutions for rich and poor and greater unity of administration. Finally, such unity would represent an important form of social integration.

Approaches to the Explanation of Historical Trends in Social Policy

It might be reasonably argued that in the course of this century there were in Britain at least two periods when universalistic principles were pursued relatively strongly in social policy, namely during 1905-11 and 1942-48, and at least one period when selective principles have tended to be more in the ascendant, namely 1966-72.(2)

These social trends are by no means simply attributable to different policy choices on the part of governments. They are attributable to deep-seated changes in society. For example, the reforms introduced by the Liberal administration in the early years of the century owed a great deal to widening inequalities and the perception that inequalities and poverty threatened the legitimacy of the social order; the growing power of the enfranchised working class, trade unions and Labour Party; the observation of external examples of civil war; and the coincidence of interests of working class and rich élites economically and militarily. Britain's lead in industrial development was being threatened, and army recruitment in the Boer War had revealed the physical inadequacies of a disturbingly large proportion of the adult male population. There was general agreement about the importance of quickly developing educational, nutritional and health services for the working class as a whole and not just for the fraction who were very poor.

Similarly, during and immediately after the Second World War there was an unprecedented social upheaval and a fundamental re-alignment of interest groups. The population united against an external enemy. There was common service in the armed forces, community organization against air raids and invasion, and general acceptance of high rates of taxation and of rationing. The rights of the citizen, fair shares, equality, the collective good — all these values were stressed. Moreover, wartime improvisations, such as the emergency medical scheme, involved forms of public organization and administration which were difficult to unscramble after several years, and which carried implications for formal and permanent consolidation. There was too an unusual concentration of public opinion on social aims, which involved the nation in choosing to make a radical departure from what was characterized as the poverty, unemployment, slums and ill-health of the 1930s. Given the circumstances of the time it is not difficult to understand why Lord Beveridge could write as he did in 1942 and why steps to implement universalistic principles in education, family allowances, national insurance and the National Health Service were taken. People were concerned about their fellows and and there was massive support for social reconstruction. The spartan conditions of the immediate post-war years together with the retention of food subsidies, rationing and high taxation by the Attlee and even for a time by the Churchill administration may have helped to maintain these values.

By contrast the growing attraction of the Government to selectivist policies in the 1960s and now the early 1970s had its origins in the economic conditions of the mid and late 1950s, the reaction of the middle classes to what was thought to be a loss of income relativities, a property boom which introduced more inequality of wealth, the demand for immigrant labour, and the drift of public values towards styles of 'conspicuous consumption'. The priority accorded to productivity and economic growth, and therefore to economic policies, as defined in the narrow sense, diminished the consciousness of social objectives and policies and had certain negative effects. Managerial, professional and technocratic élites began to expect higher rewards at the same time as their numbers were growing. This was one source of strain in the social structure. Another was the disproportionate growth of the dependent sections of the population, especially of the elderly and children, which automatically led to disproportionate increases in public expenditure on social security, health and welfare. This too was a source of strain. Indeed, the failure of those monitoring the growth of social expenditure in Government and the universities to explain the momentum in all industrial societies towards higher public expenditure on the social services, especially because of the fast-growing costs of education and medical care, was itself a source of political and administrative confusion. To the pressures upon successive governments to put a ceiling on public expenditure and cut tax rates was added the pressures of inescapably growing costs. By citing Government plans and Public Expenditure White Papers a good case could be made for the 'incomprehension' of planning in Britain, because the sum effect of social trends has not been traced or projected. This is perhaps the major underlying factor in the fragmented evolution of means-tested services.

But in the 1960s there seems to have been some increase in social divisiveness and in discriminatory practices against certain minorities, including separated wives and unmarried mothers bringing up children alone, and particularly coloured immigrants and the unemployed. Pressures to restrict the scope of certain services, and to make them conditional on various forms of good behaviour, tended to reinforce the selective rather than the universal social services. Paradoxically, the growth of the numbers of the unemployed in the late 1960s led to greater coverage in the press, radio and television about the so-called 'workshy' and 'scroungers'. The failure of governments to strike a sufficiently strong moral stance on race relations and on behalf of the vulnerable unemployed has contributed to this breaking-up of community relationships and consciousness. The control functions of selective services have been emphasized in consequence.

The Structure and Development of Selective Services
In 1972 there exist at least forty-five different types of benefit or services which are provided on test of means, some of them administered by local offices of central departments, such as the Department of Health and Social Security and Department of Employment and Productivity, and others by local authorities. Some of the principal schemes are listed in Table 1. (3) In addition there are higher education awards; schemes for exemption from prescription charges, dental charges and optical charges; local charges for residential accommodation for the elderly and handicapped and homeless; local charges for home help, meals, day nursery, chiropody, convalescent and family planning services; school uniform and clothing grants and maintenance allowances. Different local authorities operate different kinds of means tests, for the same services. This has led to anomalies at local as well as national level.(4)

The selective system has grown quite rapidly in recent years. First the supplementary benefits scheme, which is by far the most costly of the means-tested services, has increased in scope, partly but not only because of an increase in unemployment during the late 1960s. Thus, the number of people in households receiving supplementary benefits (known as national assistance before 1966) grew from 2,841,000 in December 1965 to 4,166,000 in November 1970. Secondly, successive governments have raised charges for certain health and welfare benefits and simultaneously raised the maximum levels of income up to which families could qualify for benefit by amounts larger than would be strictly necessary to keep pace either with prices or earnings. From April 1971, for example, a man and wife with three children and between £22 and £24 per week could normally qualify for one or more of free school meals, free prescriptions, free milk and welfare

Table 1 Cost and numbers receiving and eligible for selected means-tested benefits

Type of Scheme	Number of people in receipt annually or at any time	Total expenditure or cost to the Exchequer or local authorities per annum	Estimated 'take-up' among those eligible (4) per cent
Supplementary benefits	4,166,000	£570 m.	60-70
Free school meals	805,000	£ 28 m.	under 70
Local authority rent rebates	425,000	£ 18 m.	Not known
Rate rebates	795,000(1)	£ 15 m.	30-40
Legal aid and advice (civil)	227,000	£ 14 m.	Not known
Free welfare milk and foods	220,000(2)	£ 7 m.	50-55
Family income supplement	68,000(3)	£ 7 m.	40-50

Notes: (1) England and Wales only.
(2) Excluding people also in receipt of supplementary benefits.
(3) Working families only.
(4) These are rough estimates based on information drawn from different surveys.

Sources: Department of Health and Social Security, *Annual Report for 1970*, Cmnd. 4714, 1971; *Rate Rebates in England and Wales*, 1971; *Hansard*, 3 August, 5 August, 3 December, 9 December 1971.

foods and free optical and dental treatment. Thirdly, some universal benefits have been restricted. Thus the Labour Government abolished free school milk for all in secondary schools, and the Conservative Government abolished free school milk for children in primary schools over the age of seven. The Conservative Government also restricted unemployment benefits in the Social Security Act of 1971. Finally, new benefits have been and are being introduced. Thus, the Labour Government introduced rate rebates in 1966, encouraged local authority rent rebate schemes, replaced national assistance by supplementary benefits, also in 1966, and reintroduced prescription charges, for which there could be exemption on test of means. Since taking office the Conservative administration has introduced the Family Income Supplements scheme for families with low pay who are not eligible for supplementary benefits. It is proposing to introduce a rent allowance and rebate scheme up to comparatively high levels of income at the same time as withdrawing other forms of housing subsidy and allowing rents to rise quite sharply to the level of so-called 'fair rents'.

There has been, and remains, pressure in some quarters both for the modification of universal health and education services and national insurance, and the introduction of a scheme of negative income tax. Proposals for introducing charges for stays in hospital and other health services,(5) education vouchers as a means of encouraging private schools (6) have been made, sometimes by people who since putting them forward have become prominent members of the Government.(7) There are possibilities, then, of the erosion of universal services. However, this has to be placed in perspective. There has been a disproportionate growth in expenditure upon health and education services in recent years, partly because of population trends but also the growth of the numbers staying on at school and entering higher education, a recognition of low standards in long-stay hospitals and developments in medical technology. An extension of certain universal services has therefore occurred at the same time as there has been a contraction of others and while further selective services have been added.

The universal element in the social security scheme is also threatened by advocates on right and left of a negative income tax scheme.(8) Too few people appreciate that it is bound to involve in implementation the reincarnation of many of the practices of public assistance. In the abstract the principles of such a scheme are often believed to be appealing. Some people are attracted by novelty, even when enthusiastically espoused by such figures as Senator Goldwater (during his presidential campaign) and his senior economic adviser, Professor Milton Friedman.(9) Something different, however ambiguous and uncertain, is preferred over well-tried and even successful methods of redistribution. But for Britain no scheme has been worked out and presented in operational detail, which satisfactorily answers pertinent questions about the precise definition of income; how comprehensive information on income for the whole household is to be provided; how assets are to be treated; how the incomes of different income units as well as wives and children in the household are to be aggregated; what income, including work expenses, might be disregarded; how household members who are not present continuously are to be treated; whether reduced, as well as full, national insurance benefits are to be made up uniformly; whether the incomes of households which fluctuate enormously are to be averaged over five weeks, 13 weeks or 52 weeks and then made up to a prescribed amount, or whether they are to be made up in any single week when they fall below the prescribed' amount. The problems of equity which would arise in the short run from some families obtaining disproportionately large increases of income while others, some of whom, like war pensioners and the blind and tubercular, might be felt to be particularly 'deserving', obtain very small increases or no increases at all, are left unexamined.

In the United States attempts have at least been made, if unpersuasively, to suggest how such a scheme might be introduced and how certain administrative problems might be overcome.(10) In Britain those who have begun to recognize how difficult the scheme is to implement have admitted that in operation it would have to resemble the existing supplementary benefits system.(11) The advocates of such schemes differ profoundly among themselves in the scale, design and presentation of their schemes.(12) All seem to suffer from an inability to relate their ideas to existing services. History bequeathes a very limited range of political possibilities. The constraints have to be investigated patiently and revealed. If this task is shirked there are endless delays in getting any scheme to the point of being politically viable. Pressure to introduce immediate social reforms by well-tried methods may be fatally compromised or weakened. Or the new methods may turn out to be very different from what they are supposed to be. When finally stripped to realities negative income taxation is usually a scheme to restrict public expenditure on social security by confining redistributive payments to those only having less than a particular level of income. Proponents excuse this by claiming that benefits are not wasted on those who do not need them and that those at the foot of the income scale obtain a particularly high rate of benefit. However, the relatively poor as well as the very poor may deserve help; even prosperous families may need financial aid through social security which would not otherwise be available to them, and many of the very poor may not be reached by this type of scheme or may not find it acceptable.

Four Problems of Means-Tested Schemes

At least four general criticisms of means-tested schemes can be advanced. Two have been generally conceded — even by proponents. First, these schemes involve relatively high indirect as well as direct costs in administrative overheads and manpower. The administrative costs of national insurance were 3.5 per cent of total benefits plus administrative costs in 1969-70. The comparable figure for supplementary benefits seems to be 8 to 9 per cent. In 1965 the comparable figure for the National Assistance Board was 7.4 per cent. But there are other indirect costs — such as the time given up by social workers, local government officials and others to the task of informing themselves and others about the schemes.

Secondly, the schemes are felt to reduce incentives to work or to

earn more, and so offend certain basic social values. For the low paid
the effective marginal rate of tax experienced by those who actually
apply for, and receive, several of the benefits for which they are eligible,
is now reaching absurd levels. In 1972 a man earning £20 per week
with a wife and two children, and therefore entitled to an extra
90p as a family allowance, was subject to the following deductions if he
earned an additional £1:

Loss of Family Income Supplement	50p
Loss of free school meal for one child	60p
Income tax	10p
Loss of rent rebate (under Housing Finance Act)	8p
Loss of rate rebate	14p
Increased National Insurance contribution	4p
Total	£1.46

If he had been claiming other means-tested benefits, such as school
clothing grants, the loss would have been greater.

Although the Chancellor of the Exchequer is likely to raise personal
allowances and possibly take action in other ways in April 1972 to
reduce the tax obligations of the very low paid this embarrassing
structure, which indeed does not take account of all means-tested
schemes, will remain. The lack of co-ordination between taxation and
social security and the existence of very high rates of marginal tax,
identified as the 'poverty trap', are now recognized to be real
problems.(13) On the other hand, empirical substantiation of disincentive effects is sparse. Few families actually receive more than two
means-tested benefits. Those who do are understandably vague about
the exact relationship between rise of earnings and loss of benefits —
partly because net earnings and benefits in cash or kind are paid from
a variety of sources, partly because incomes from these sources tend to
fluctuate anyway and partly because different benefits are assessed
according to means over different periods. The limited social
experiments in New Jersey and elsewhere in the United States with
schemes of income maintenance using different tax 'rates' suggest that
the disincentive effects are small. But, as Morgan points out, it is
difficult to draw conclusions from a small sample who do not themselves interact.(14) The 'snowball' effect of the diffusion of knowledge
and the reactive behaviour of large numbers of people instead of just
a few remains highly uncertain. All that might be said of conditions in
Britain is that it is difficult to reconcile the theoretical effects of a
combination of means-tested schemes upon rising incomes either with
the work-ethic of society or the widespread beliefs among economists

and politicians about the factors which influence incentives to earn or produce, at least among the high paid.

The Inefficiency of Means-Tested Services

The other criticisms are more contentious. Third is the question of under-use. During the 1950s and early 1960s a series of research studies gradually led to the realization that large numbers of people were eligible for benefits but did not claim them. The evidence was concerned primarily with old people.(15) Government spokesmen were at first openly critical of such research, then sceptical of the findings, but finally convinced by research carried out by the Ministry of Pensions and National Insurance itself. A national survey showed that nearly a million retirement pensioners were entitled to national assistance but were not receiving assistance. Even when allowance was made for misreported income the ministry estimated that the figure was 850,000.(16) This figure was equivalent to rather more than half those actually receiving assistance at the time.

The design of the supplementary benefit scheme, which was introduced by the Government in late 1966 to replace National Assistance, was partly influenced by this research. The Ministry hoped to improve uptake by eliminating 'three features of the existing scheme which are misunderstood or disliked, while preserving the humanity and efficiency of its administration'.(17) People satisfying the conditions laid down in the Social Security Act and its regulations now had a specific entitlement to benefit, the procedure for claiming benefits was simplified, national insurance and assistance were linked more closely in administration, and a new long-term addition to payments was introduced. The ministry also undertook an advertising campaign. Several hundred thousand people applied within a few weeks and Government ministers were quick to claim a remarkable success.(18)

However, the extent of the success was debatable. Rates of benefit had been raised and more generous disregards for income and savings had been introduced at the same time. Careful estimates were made on the basis of information published in the Government's own report on the incomes of the retired which showed that even ignoring the more generous disregards the increase in numbers of retirement pensioners receiving supplements between December 1965 and November 1968 'not explained by the higher assistance scale amounts to only some 100,000-200,000'.(19) No field survey was carried out subsequently by Government departments to confirm or reject these estimates, and the secondary analyses of Family Expenditure Survey data undertaken by the Department of Health and Social Security have not so far included reports on uptake among pensioners.(20) It would seem that the number of retirement pensioners eligible for supplementary benefit but not receiving it must still be considerably in excess of half a million. Certainly the data produced in the 1965 national survey shows that large numbers of pensioners had incomes of only up to £1 more than the supplementary benefit scale rates. This is shown in Table 2. A relatively modest relaxation of the qualifying conditions (as occurred in 1966) must lead to a big increase in applications – even if only half or two thirds of newly eligible people actually come forward.

Table 2 Incomes of families and pensioners in relation to supplementary benefit levels

Amount in £s above or below basic supplementary benefit level	Families with two or more children. No. of people in families (1966)	Retirement Pensioners	
		Married couples (1965)	Single or widowed (1965)
£5 or more above	9,580,000	201,000	146,000
£2-5 above	1,868,000	243,000	240,000
£1-2 above	336,000	175,000	250,000
Under £1 above	377,000	377,000	1,401,000
Under £1 below	158,000	162,000	614,000
£1-2 below	93,000	30,000	93,000
£2 or more below	108,000	6,000	14,000
	12,520,000	1,194,000	2,758,000

Sources: Circumstances of Families, H.M.S.O., 1967; The Financial and Other Circumstances of Retirement Pensioners, H.M.S.O., 1966. Some categories in the second and third columns include estimates based on data given in the report.

Research among groups other than pensioners has not been so extensive. There had been scattered evidence of reluctance to apply for benefits.(21) A secondary analysis of the Family Expenditure Surveys for 1953-4 and 1960 concluded cautiously that over 3 per cent of people in the sample, representing about 1½ million in the total population, were living at a level 'which, prima facie, might have allowed them to qualify for supplementary help from the National Assistance Board'. They included about a million people dependent primarily on pensions and half a million on other State benefits.(22) A survey in 1966 by the Ministry of Social Security of families with two or more children found that about two fifths of those in which the father was sick or unemployed were eligible for assistance but were not receiving it. They represented about 34,000 families (including 209,000 people). In the case of the sick, however, relatively fewer of those who had been off work for three months or more than of the short-term sick were not receiving assistance. Only a small number of fatherless families with two or more children (about 8,000, including about 32,000 people) were not receiving assistance.(23)

The authors of the report on this Government survey also concluded that only just over 60 per cent of those children having school meals who were eligible to receive them free did so. The comparable figure among the children of men in full-time work was only 34 per cent.(24) The data on free welfare milk were not easy to analyse but 'very few families with fathers in full-time work were receiving free welfare milk'.(25) The rebate scheme had been operating only for a few months when the survey was carried out and as few as 10 per cent of the poorest families had even applied for a rebate, though the great majority were eligible. 'Uptake' increased in late 1966 and early 1967 but a minority of eligible households now receive rebates. The annual reports on numbers of recipients in different areas of England and Wales shows that disproportionately large numbers of eligible persons who are pensioners and who are owner-occupiers obtain rebates. There are relatively eight or nine times as many claimants in holiday resorts such as Clacton or Morecambe as there are in city areas such as Tower Hamlets and Islington.(26)

In view of the Government's introduction of legislation for a national scheme of rent rebates and allowances for poorer private and council tenants, scattered evidence of uptake in areas where schemes are already operating is of great interest. In 1968 Birmingham Corporation took powers through a private Act of Parliament to pay allowances similar to those now proposed by the Government. Though 6,000 families were believed to be eligible, only 1,000 applications were made and only 250 were granted.(27)

Although there is far too little statistical data made available by the Government and the local authorities about eligibility and uptake, two general conclusions can be drawn. First, uptake varies according to type of scheme and, for different households and individuals, within each type of scheme. A study of the combination of different factors would help to predict variation and improve our understanding of the functions, and effects, of such schemes. In undertaking a recent study of entitlement to free school meals, B. Davies and M. Reddin have attempted to distribute factors into three groups: the stigma that attaches to applying for and receiving free school meals; the lack of

information about the service; and the difficulties in using the service.
(28) No doubt the study of factors which predict variation for any
particular service can be extended to predict variation between different
services. Groups in the population to whom it is difficult to convey
information may not be the same groups who are sensitive to stigma
or who can easily use the services.

Secondly, successive governments have demonstrated that very low
uptakes at least can be improved. Thus in 1966 and 1967 Government
ministers were prompted by the Child Poverty Action Group and
others to publicize rate rebates and free school meals. As a consequence
there were increases in the numbers of claimants.(29) The Education
Minister, for example, was persuaded to send a circular letter to all
parents of schoolchildren, describing the income limits and reminding
them of the possibility of claiming free school meals. This helped to
raise the numbers of claimants and was repeated, though less effectively,
in May 1970. Table 3 shows the results. The Minister of Social
Security announced an 'entitlement campaign' for a wide selection of
means-tested benefits in March 1968, but publicity in fact fell far
short of what appeared to have been promised in the announcement
and was also delayed. Moreover, the announcement of new punitive
measures against the 'workshy' in the same summer probably neutral-
ized much of the potential effects of the entitlement campaign and
certainly attracted more counter-publicity.(30)

The Conservative administration has made efforts to improve
information about means-tests. Circular letters have been sent to many
thousands of social workers and others and advertisements taken in
the press and on television. Substantial increases in the numbers of
applicants for exemption from optical, dental and prescription charges,
for free welfare milk and foods and for Family Income Supplements
(introduced in August 1971) were registered in 1971. In some cases the
increases were built on an extraordinarily low application rate. Thus
although exemptions from dental charges increased dramatically
between the start of the advertising campaign in April 1971 and
October 1971, the increase expressed as a proportion of those
estimated to be eligible was only 6 per cent to 15 per cent.

No doubt more might be done with a coherent strategy to smooth
out anomalies between many different means-tests, extend the 'pass-
port' to several benefits and hence improve uptake. But this might be
at the expense of making clearer to politicians and public the disincentive
implications of excessive marginal tax rates, increasing stigma and
creating a more identifiable section of 'the poor', who might be
treated with greater suspicion, distrust or derision by many others
among the population.

During the attempts by the Government to make means-tests work it has been difficult to forgive the failure to explore the nature, and scale, of the problem. It is evident to most students of poverty that there is a distinction to be made between temporary and permanent poverty, and that during a period of, say, five years, a very large

Table 3   Number and percentage of school meals which are free

Year	Free meals (thousands)	Per cent of total meals
1964	282	6.9
1965	308	7.1
1966	330	7.1
1967	404	8.3
1968*	841	16.8
1969	594	11.5
1970	627	12.2
1971	763	18.3
1972	805	17.3

* including free meal to fourth and subsequent children in family, irrespective of family income.

Source: *Hansard*, 3 December 1971, col. 181.

section of the population may have some experience of poverty. Similarly there is a distinction to be made between partial and total poverty, such that problems in the distribution of assets, including housing and its amenities, the quality of the environment and of conditions at work, as well as the distribution and quality of different social services, including schools, have to be considered, and not simply problems in the distribution of cash incomes. Finally, no attempt has been made to re-appraise the official Government definition of a poverty standard, namely the supplementary benefit scale rates. The rates have been raised more or less in line with earnings since the early post-war years. But in terms of examining their justification in relation to independent criteria of deprivation, or examining the justification of the rates for different types of individual or family, no effort has been made by successive governments.

The importance of this is illustrated by Table 2. A very small lifting of the poverty 'line' would greatly increase the numbers adjudged to be in poverty. Moreover, better understanding of temporary and permanent poverty and of partial and total poverty would make clearer the 'efficiency' of present methods of meeting poverty. One of the problems about estimating uptake is the dependence of social scientists upon Government data, which are highly restricted in their availability. For example, the public has been dependent on statements in Parliament by Sir Keith Joseph for estimates of the numbers who are believed to be eligible for the Family Income Supplement. But there are at least three difficulties about accepting Government estimates of uptake. First, simplifications have been made in the definition of income and the award of benefit such that families go on receiving benefit throughout a period of twenty-six weeks even if their circumstances improve. This is only one possible way in which the number of those receiving the supplement may be inflated unduly in relation to the number who are judged to be eligible for it at any time.(31) Information is required in detail about the circumstances of recipients. Secondly, estimates of the numbers who are eligible for the supplement are not given on the basis of hard evidence which is open to public scrutiny. In January 1972 Sir Keith Joseph stated that the number was smaller than he had previously estimated. Yet in the intervening period there was no evidence that the earnings of the low paid had improved and the Government had actually increased the prescribed amounts in the scheme by amounts greater than would have been strictly necessary according to movements in earnings. A glance at Table 2 or at statistical tables giving the dispersion of earnings by number and amount is bound to strain credulity.

What can be concluded from this analysis is that even allowing for energetic publicity means-tested schemes do not reach all those in poverty who are stated to be eligible for them. This must remain one of the strongest grounds for doubting the value of their extension, or even retention.

Social Divisiveness

There is a fourth criticism. Low uptakes are often explained loosely in terms not only of stigma but administrative and social separation of the poor from the rest of society. Polarization of attitudes, behaviour and administrative practices is believed to take place after the introduction of means-tested schemes. However, the sociologist has still to present systematically the complexities of this process and provide supporting evidence in detail.(32) He can start historically and contemporaneously with some analysis of the major functions of means-tested schemes. Perhaps the basic distinction is between the formal welfare function of meeting need and the implicit function of social control.

The 1834 report on the Poor Laws remarks that, 'The great object of our early pauper legislation seems to have been the restraint of vagrancy'.(33) Thus the legislation of the fifteenth century required beggars who were unable to work to go to the hundred where they last lived and not beg outside that hundred. Legislation passed in the sixteenth century introduced compulsory charity but the motive for its establishment was the desire to 'repress vagrancy'. The 1834 report also adopted a restrictive approach and sought to liquidate outdoor relief and subject the able-bodied to the workhouse test. At various stages the desire to control deviance and spur the poor into un-questioning conformity with economic and social values has dominated the development of public assistance policies. Today in the United States, for example, public assistance is believed to be a degrading process in which 'various forms of coercion may be used to impose conditions on recipients of aid. Recipients may be harassed by investigators, and their private lives may be exposed to governmental scrutiny seldom found in an open society'.(34)

Some of the objectives or goals of public assistance and other means-tested programmes can be inferred from their operation. After examining American public assistance programmes one social scientist concluded that they sought (i) to relieve a segment of the deserving very poor at a minimal level of subsistence, and for as short a time per case as possible; (ii) to prevent the 'undeserving' poor from gaining access to the system; (iii) to minimize the impact of the system on the tax-payer, because other public expenditures are preferred that show tangible gain to the tax-payers. More positively the programmes sought (i) to provide support for those who, for good and identifiable reasons, cannot now support themselves; and (ii) to increase the labour force participation rate of 'employables'. (35) This helps to bring out the very mixed objectives of the system.

Piven and Cloward put forward a broader thesis. 'Historical evidence suggests', they write, 'that relief arrangements are initiated or expanded during the occasional outbreaks of civil disorder produced by mass unemployment, and are then abolished or contracted when political stability is restored. . . Expansive relief policies are designed to mute civil disorder, and restrictive ones to reinforce work norms. In other words, relief policies are cyclical-liberal or restrictive depending on the problems of regulation in the larger society with which government must contend. . . This view clearly belies the popular supposition that government social policies, including relief policies, are becoming progressively more responsible, humane and generous'.(36) Their book is one antidote to the superficial view that welfare policies are progressively beneficent. It properly calls attention to the control functions of welfare. Yet it oversimplifies the mechanisms of social policies. The authors implicitly regard welfare expenditure as uniformly good. But expenditure and the pattern of services can have uneven or inconsistent functions and these can of course change over a period of years. Depending on the areas in which it takes place expansion of expenditure can *increase*, or fail to affect, the likelihood of disorder, because it can actually increase, or fail to decrease, certain forms of inequality. And far from spending more on the unemployed as the unemployment rate increases and disorder threatens, society often adopts restrictive measures so as to comfort itself that mass unemployment is attributable more to undeserving men than an inadequate industrial and economic system. It is in such terms that certain divisive effects of public assistance programmes have to be analysed. Divisiveness of administration is a necessary element of coercive control.

In British conditions how would the combination of functions of welfare and control, which are in some respects contradictory, be analysed to show how they are reconciled? There are a number of possibilities. First, legal entitlement to benefit can be examined in relation to different types of beneficiary. Thus, unlike supplementary pensioners and the sick, the unemployed do not qualify immediately or after two years for the long-term addition. Secondly, differences in treatment of different types of beneficiary can be examined. Thus, account might be taken of which types of beneficiary are visited in their own homes rather than expected to queue up in offices, how long allowances are paid before review, what area differences there are in discretionary allowances, and, more elaborately, how the allowances actually made are related to different criteria of need. Table 4 gives a preliminary illustration of the methods of approach. It registers a a number of inconsistencies which seem to demand deeper exploration. For example, fewer of the sick and disabled without than with national insurance benefits, who have been receiving benefits for two or more years, receive the long-term addition. And fewer receive exceptional circumstances additions, though more of them have been sick or disabled for lengthy periods (and more lack any form of capital assets). Again, the proportions of women with dependent children and of unemployed with and without national insurance benefits who receive either a long term addition or an exceptional circumstances addition are relatively small, especially when the numbers of long-term recipients in the last two columns of the table, are taken into account. Although further information about the circumstances of these different types of beneficiary is required it seems difficult, on the face of it, to suggest that the variations are explicable in terms of variations in need rather than of variations in status of beneficiary.

Table 4   Per cent of different types of beneficiary receiving long-term additions and exceptional circumstances additions to their supplementary benefits November 1970.

Type of Beneficiary	% Receiving long-term addition	% Receiving exceptional circum-stances addition	% Receiving benefits	
			for 3 months or more	for 2 years or more
1. Retirement pensioners and N.I. widows over 60 years	99	18	96	78
2. Others over pension age	88	13	98	88
3. Sick and disabled without N.I. benefits	60	9	90	69
4. N.I. widows under 60	53	15	89	52
5. Sick and disabled with N.I. benefits	45	30	82	44
6. Women with dependent children	42	7	87	41
7. Miscellaneous	35	24	84	45
8. Unemployed with N.I. benefits	0.3 3	6	37	1
9. Unemployed without N.I. benefits	0.2 2	7	41	24

Source: *Annual Report of the D.H.S.S. for 1970,* Cmnd. 4714, H.M.S.O., 1971, pp. 343 and 348.

Thirdly, levels of allowances, and particularly levels of discretionary allowances, as well as frequency and amounts of discretionary grants, can be compared with other incomes and examined for internal consistency. Only 16 per cent of recipients had exceptional circumstances additions in 1970 (compared with 23 per cent in 1967). The average addition was 37p (compared with 31p in 1967). During the year there were 560,000 payments for exceptional needs, averaging rather less than £7 each (compared with 470,000 in 1967). As a proportion of average industrial earnings supplementary benefit scale rates fell slightly in the late 1960s from the levels reached in 1966-7. Thus in October 1967 the rate for a single person was 20.1 per cent of the average industrial earnings of male manual workers aged twenty-one and over, and in November 1970 18.3 per cent. In 1965, 16 per cent of those whose unemployment insurance benefits were supplemented by the National Assistance Board received discretionary additions but by 1969 the number had dropped to 7 per cent and, as Table 4 shows, was 6 per cent in 1970. These are just a few of the indicators which can be used to assess the formal objectives of meeting needs and adjusting payments flexibly to need.

These standards also show the changes in income levels of means-tested schemes in relation to other incomes. Restrictions in the scope of certain benefits (as by the standardization of the four-week rule in 1968), the qualifying conditions and levels of benefit (as in the Social Security Act of 1971) and relative decreases in the incomes of recipients might all be given as examples of a worsening of living conditions among the poor. The expansion and introduction of means-tested schemes may actually defeat the expressed aims of abolishing poverty. Differences in outcome for individual households and administrative complexity tend to create public confusion and uneasiness. Attention may be called to the social control rather than the welfare functions of the system. After all, the Government set up the Fisher Committee to inquire into abuse of social security benefits, but no committee to inquire into tax evasion or tax avoidance. There are pressures to increase the severity of the operation of the system at the same time as political arguments are being deployed to enlarge its scope. Administrative procedures are developed which may have the effect of reducing the proportion of eligible persons who make applications for aid. Public criticism of excessive use of manpower in the civil service and of extravagant use of tax-payers' money may result in a slower expansion of staff than of applicants or of recipients. The system develops quite independently of other systems meeting the financial needs of more prosperous sections of society when *they* experience comparable situations of sickness, disability, loss of spouse, retirement, redundancy or unemployment. The result may be that the public becomes less ready to finance benefit scales at previous levels.

The process is complex and only some of the steps have been indicated. But selection of potential recipients on grounds of income may lead inevitably to divisions of attitude as well as of population and administration.

An Alternative Strategy

What alternative strategy to reduce and eliminate poverty is there to that adopted by the Conservative administration in the last two years? There are three components. First, the true scale and complexity of the problem has to be officially recognized, admitted and fully revealed. Thus, the Government should appoint a Royal Commission or Committee to review the rates payable by the Supplementary Benefits Commission and the D.H.S.S. in relation to various criteria of deprivation. These should include standards of accommodation, environmental amenities, access to health and welfare services, working conditions, and social and leisure-time opportunities as well as standards of nutrition.

There has been no independent, wide-ranging study commissioned by the Government of the nation's definition of poverty for over thirty years. Conditions have changed and there are many families and individuals who experience deprivation in different forms and who nonetheless have incomes which are higher than those paid by the Commission. At the same time independent national research should be sponsored to document in greater detail the numbers and kinds of people living below, or on the margins of, the Commission's and other, more objective, standards. Analysis of the different sources, and regularity, of their incomes will help to show more clearly than has been possible hitherto how the different systems of distribution and redistribution of income can be modified.

But action need not be postponed on this account, merely developed with greater precision at a second stage. The Government has sufficient published and unpublished information in its possession to describe and summarize the gravity of the situation and deploy an effective strategy. In doing so it will have to show the implications for other needs and objectives. The preceding discussion of the disadvantages of a selectivist strategy suggests that a universalistic strategy would have as its by-products certain advantages, such as the reduction of social conflict, the greater integration of certain social minorities, and a strengthening of the earning incentives of low-income households, quite apart from any strengthening of social morale as a basis for a more productive economy.

Secondly, the strategy would place emphasis on universal rights, allowances, benefits and guarantees. Thus, a disability pension awarded as of right and assessed as a percentage of an allowance of, say, £10 per week for a totally disabled person (independent of any attendance allowance) might be paid to the elderly as well as younger adults. A 20 per cent pension would be £2, and would be payable in addition to any earnings or retirement pension. A parallel allowance might be paid to the family on behalf of any handicapped child under the age of sixteen. The attendance allowance for a severely disabled person could be generously extended and converted into a two-tier allowance of, say, £8 per week for the very severely disabled and £4 for the severely disabled. Unemployment flat-rate and earnings-related insurance benefits could be reviewed and their coverage and duration of payment extended. An allowance made payable by judgement of a Family Court to the adult in a one-parent family, on the basis solely of evidence of absence of financial support, provides a further example (a fatherless family allowance is another possibility). Finally, the transformation of the present system of family allowances (which are meagre by the standards of most European societies) into a system which consists of tax-free cash allowances varying only according to age and about double the present average amount per child (balanced, by implication, by the withdrawal of child tax allowances) would automatically lift out of 'official' poverty most families of people who are unemployed, sick, disabled and separated from their husbands or wives, as well as most families of the low paid. In fact the introduction of disability pensions and better family allowances would together substantially improve the living standards of the great majority of low-paid men, and most low-paid women, over the age of twenty-five. By these measures I estimate that more than three million of the present 4¼ million would be 'floated off' supplementary benefits, at a net national cost which could be kept to under £300 million per annum.

A series of supporting measures would include reintroducing free milk in schools for all children; introducing free school meals for all children (as in some other countries) and energetically setting about improving the quality of the service; and creating a national legal aid and advice service, with centres in each locality. Finally, instead of the rent rebates and allowances proposed in the Housing Finance Bill on test of means, universal allowances would be paid as of right on behalf of every dependent person in the household of non-working age, and to every person having slight, moderate or severe disability. Thus, £1 per week might be paid for each dependant and £1, £2, or £3, according to degree of disability, towards the accommodation needs of the household. The problem of unduly high rents in some areas might be met by a supplementary flat-rate area allowance.(37) By these means the rate rebate, local rent rebate and Family Income Supplement schemes would be gradually phased out of existence.

Thirdly, 'compensatory' social security would be insufficient alone. Income security schemes developed by the Government should not be treated as a kind of safety net for the casualties of the labour market. Positive steps have to be taken in incomes, wealth, employment and fiscal policies to promote different public attitudes, fairer differentials and a fairer distribution of employment. Existing Wages Council machinery could be strengthened preparatory to the introduction of minimum earnings legislation. Schedule A tax at a higher level should be reintroduced for owner-occupiers. Higher rates of tax should be introduced for earnings above £3,000 and different tax allowances should be abolished or curtailed. If the public considered that some of the rich should not benefit from universal cash allowances then special types of taxes, at 50 per cent, 75 per cent or 100 per cent rates, to 'clawback' these benefits, could be considered.

Detailed work has been done on many of the elements of this outlined strategy in the last few years and could form the basis of an immediate policy. Universal cash allowances strengthen earning incentives as between those in work and those out of work and between the lowest paid and lower paid. Universal cash allowances reach *all* the poor and not only some of them and in this way are more efficient. Universal cash allowances have to be based on principles and paid by methods which have to be scrutinized and approved by the educated middle class, for they are among the recipients; the payment of these allowances is less likely to become part of a second-class service. Finally, universal cash allowances need not be 'squandered' on the rich; for the well-tried tax system can ensure either that they are balanced by deductions from their monthly payments of salary or that they pay an appropriate rebate at the end of each year.

Notes

1. See International Labour Office, *The Cost of Social Security*, Geneva, 1967, pp. 316-22.

2. Even in these three periods exceptions should be noted, such as means-tested old age pensions in 1908 and universal earnings-related supplements to unemployment and sickness benefits in 1966.

3. For an up-to-date outline, see Meacher, M., 'Means Tests', February, 1972.

4. Reddin, M., 'Local Authority Means-Tested Services', in *Social Services for All?*, the Fabian Society, 1968.

5. See, for example, Lees, D.S., *Health Through Choice*, Institute of Economic Affairs. 1961; Houghton, D., *Paying for the Social Services*, Occasional Paper no.16, Institute of Economic Affairs, 1967; and the discussion of such schemes by Richard Titmuss in his *Commitment to Welfare*, Allen & Unwin, 1968, Chapter XXI and postscript.

6. Peacock, A.T., and Wiseman, J., *Education for Democrats*, Institute for Economic Affairs, Hobart Paper 25, 1964; West, E.G., *Education and the State*, Institute for Economic Affairs, 1965; Blaug, M., 'Selectivity in Education', in

Social Services for All?, the Fabian Society, 1968. For discussion of the problems see Hughes, H.D., 'How far is Selectivity Really Necessary in Education?', in *Social Services for All?;* Robinson, G., 'The Voucher System of Education Finance and Independence in Education', *Social and Economic Administration,* January 1968; and Horobin, G.W., *et al.,* Vouchers for Education: Reply and Counter-Reply', in Blaug, M. (ed.), *Economics of Education,* 2, Penguin, 1969.

7. Howe, G., 'Reform of the Social Services', in Beaton, L., *et al., Principles in Practice,* Conservative Political Centre, 1961.

8. The Government Green Paper on *Proposals for a Tax-Credit System* (Cmnd. 5116) was published after this paper was written. The proposals must not be confused with negative income tax. They accommodate both universalistic and selective features and several crucial elements are left to further public discussion. Thus, if credits for children are paid in cash through the Post Office (and therefore are available to the parents of *all* children, including the self-employed, the unemployed and the extremely low paid) this will be similar in all but name to an extension of 'universalistic' family allowances. But if they are simply included in the tax adjustment of the husband's wage they would not be 'paid' automatically in all instances. Thus, automatic weekly tax adjustments could not be made for the self-employed and for people between jobs and, it seems, for the lowest paid workers; and since special arrangements have to be made to pay equivalent allowances to the sick and the unemployed there may be delays of more than seven days in payment by social security offices, as well as an administrative need for confirmation of entitlement. In some instances credits for children might obtain the stigmatizing properties of means-tested benefits and certainly those receiving supplementary benefits would tend to be more dependent on that source of income, since the equivalent of any family allowances would now be included in the total payment of supplementary benefits. For these and other reasons, and especially since its social objectives are plainly subservient to its objectives to simplify taxation and shift some of the administration of tax back from the Board of Inland Revenue to employers, the scheme has to be treated with scepticism.

9. Friedman, M., *Capital and Freedom,* University of Chicago Press, Chicago, 1962.

10. Two brief quotations from one review might be given to illustrate the point that the meaning, and therefore the viability, of negative income tax remains at issue. 'The problem of defining a household to take account of economies of scale and pooling of resources is the most difficult problem in designing a Negative Income Tax' (p.404). 'The Supreme Court has now ruled that cohabitation is an insufficient criterion for household membership under the Social Security Law' (p.406). Popkin, W.D., 'Administration of a Negative Income Tax', *The Yale Law Journal,* vol. 78, no.3, January 1969. See also the very detailed work by Speth, J.G., *et al.,* 'A Model Negative Income Tax Statute', *The Yale Law Journal,* vol. 78, no.2, 1968, and by Klein, W.A., 'Familial Relationships and Economic Well-Being: Rules for a Negative Income Tax', *Harvard Journal on Legislation,* March 1971. Under the auspices of the Institute for Research on Poverty, the University of Wisconsin, three negative income-tax experiments were introduced, covering 1,250 families, in five urban areas of New Jersey and Pennsylvania in 1968, and covering 825 families in two rural areas of North Carolina and Iowa in 1969. See Orcutt, G.H. and

Orcutt, A.G., 'Incentive Experimentation for Income Maintenance Policy Purposes', *American Economic Review,* September 1968; Watts, H.W., 'Graduated Work Incentives: An Experiment in Negative Taxation', *American Economic Review,* May 1969; and Bairden, D.L., 'Income Maintenance and the Rural Poor: An Experimental Approach', *American Journal of Agricultural Economics,* August 1970. See also the series of papers by H.W. Watts, and others, and particularly the discussion paper by James N. Morgan in *The American Economic Review,* May 1971.

11. One group of authors recommending a Minimum Income Guarantee (a negative income tax at 100 per cent rate of tax) admit that there is some 'justified' criticism of administrative proposals in such schemes. They agree that there are the problems of the tax machinery being organized around individuals rather than families, of fluctuating income and of the need for very frequent assessment, but do not offer solutions. They concede that 'the agency administering a Reverse Income Tax may have to use separate procedures for assessment of means from those now used for income tax', and go on to point out how well the Supplementary Benefits Commission does this job. Christopher, R., Polanyi, G., Seldon, A., and Shenfield, B., *Policy for Poverty,* I.E.A., 1970. pp. 83-5.

12. For example, the gross costs of the scheme outlined by D.S. Lees for families with children ('Poor Families and Fiscal Reform', *Lloyds Bank Review,* October 1967) was estimated to be between £75 million and £118 million for 1967. Assuming the simultaneous abolition of family allowances Lees envisaged a *net saving.* The scheme put forward by Christopher and others (ibid.) envisaged an annual cost of £925 million, but much of the existing social security scheme was assumed to be swept away, together with half the cost of the National Health Service. There would be savings per annum of £1,800 million. Finally, the scheme proposed by C.V. Brown and D.A. Dawson *(Personal Taxation, Incentives and Tax Reform,* Political and Economic Planning, Broadsheet 506, January 1969) provides a guaranteed income for all and has a gross cost of over £9,000 million per annum, though part of this would replace existing grants, pensions and allowances. Although the authors present this as a form of negative income taxation, it might more reasonably be distinguished as a type of Social Dividend Scheme, which is in principle a universal allowance system.

13. See, for example, Piachaud, D., 'Poverty and Taxation', *Political Quarterly,* January-March 1971. Prest, A.R., *Social Benefits and Tax Rates,* Institute of Economic Affairs, Research Monograph 22, 1970; Lynes, T., 'How to Pay Surtax while Living on the Breadline', *Oxford Mail,* 3 March 1971; Bradshaw, J. and Wakeman, I., 'The Poverty Trap Updated', *Political Quarterly,* October–December 1972.

14. He argues against negative income-tax experiments in limited localities and believes they are a mistake. Morgan, J.N., 'Current Status of Income Maintenance Experiments: Discussion', *American Economic Review,* May 1971, p.39.

15. Cole Wedderburn, D., with Utting, J., *The Economic Circumstances of Old People,* Codicote Press, 1962; Townsend, P., *The Family Life of Old People,* Routledge & Kegan Paul, 1957; Townsend, P., and Wedderburn, D., *The Aged in the Welfare State,* Bell, 1965; *Report of the Committee of Inquiry into the Impact of Rates on Households* (The Allen Report), Cmnd.

2582, H.M.S.O., 1965, p.117.

16. Ministry of Pensions and National Insurance, *Financial and Other Circumstances of Retirement Pensioners*, H.M.S.O., 1966, Tables III.2 and III.4, pp.20 and 83-4.

17. Ministry of Pensions and National Insurance, *Ministry of Social Security Bill 1966*, H.M.S.O., 1966, p.1.

18. See, for example, Houghton, D., *Paying for the Social Services*, Institute of Economic Affairs, 1967, p.12; *Annual Report of the Ministry of Social Security for 1966*, H.M.S.O., 1967, p.53; and Department of Health and Social Security, *National Superannuation and Social Insurance*, H.M.S.O., January 1967, p.7.

19. Atkinson, A.B., *Poverty in Britain and the Reform of Social Security*, Cambridge University Press, 1969, pp.75-6.

20. The Minister of Social Security announced in 1968 that secondary analysis of the extent of poverty had been launched. A report in July 1971 on two-parent families stated 'Further studies will report on analyses of F.E.S. data covering the circumstances of families without children, one-parent families and pensioners.' Department of Health and Social Security, *Two-Parent Families: A Study of their Resources and Needs in 1968, 1969, and 1970*, Statistical Report Series, no.14, H.M.S.O., 1971, p.1.

21. Marris, P., *Widows and Their Families*, Routledge & Kegan Paul, 1958; Shaw, L.A., and Bowerbank, M., 'Living on a State-Maintained Income', I and II, *Case Conference*, March and April 1958; Marsden, D., *Mothers Alone*, Penguin, 1973.

22. Abel-Smith, B., and Townsend, P., *The Poor and the Poorest*, Bell, 1965, p.48.

23. Ministry of Social Security, *Circumstances of Families*, H.M.S.O., 1967, estimated from Table A.1., p.133.

24. *Circumstances of Families*, op.cit., calculated on the basis of Table III.10, p.29.

25. ibid., p.28.

26. *Rate Rebates in England and Wales*, 1971. The tendency 'for retired owners to make most use of the scheme' is discussed by Nevitt, A.A., 'How Fair are Rate Rebates?', *New Society*, 10 June 1971. A secondary analysis carried out by Dr C.F. Legg of Brunel University (publication forthcoming) finds, however, that in both 1966-7 and 1969-70 'uptake' was only around two fifths for eligible pensioners, though it was higher for owner-occupiers than for tenants.

27. Cocks, F., 'Housing Allowances for Private Tenants — Birmingham's Experience', *The Housing Review*, Journal of the Housing Centre Trust, January—February 1972.

28. For 1967 they had estimated that perhaps 40 per cent who were eligible were not getting them. Davies, B., and Reddin, M., 'School Meals and Plowden', *New Society*, May 1967. See also Davies, B., and Williamson, V., 'School Meals — Short Fall and Poverty', *Social and Economic Administration*, January 1968.

29. See the account given by T. Lynes, 'The Failure of Selectivity', in Bull, D. (ed.), *Family Poverty*, Duckworth, 1971.

30. Lynes, T., 'The Failure of Selectivity', op.cit., pp.25-6.

31. This aspect of the inefficiency of means tests has been remarked in other research. Davies and Williamson (op.cit.) point out that estimated uptake of free school meals may be too high because 'some free meals appear to be consumed by those not eligible for them.' The Government's claim that more than 80 per cent eligible for free school meals receive them cannot be accepted for at least two reasons. First, children who do not have school meals at all, some of whom go home or take sandwiches, either because their parents think they have to pay for them and cannot afford it or because they do not want to be picked out as children receiving 'free dinners', are not included in the base. Secondly, those receiving free meals include a substantial proportion, possibly a third, where the local authority assessment was made six months or more beforehand, since when parental income has increased and the family is no longer below the eligible income limits. Administrative statistics cannot be directly compared with survey estimates of the numbers of families below certain levels of income at a particular time.

32. Recent work has begun to demonstrate the possibilities. See, for example; Marsden, D., *Mothers Alone,* Penguin, 1973; Hill, M.J., 'The Exercise of Discretion in the National Assistance Board', *Public Administration,* 1968; Hill, M.J., *The Sociology of Public Administration,* Weidenfeld & Nicolson, 1972. Perhaps the best recent example for the United States is Piven, F.F., and Cloward, R.A., *Regulating the Poor: The Functions of Public Welfare,* Tavistock, 1972.

33. *Report from His Majesty's Commissioners for Inquiry into the Administration and Practical Operation of the Poor Laws,* B. Fellowes, 1834, p.6.

34. President's Commission on Income Maintenance Programs, *Poverty and Plenty,* Washington, Government Printing Office, 1969, p.50.

35. Stein, B., *On Relief: The Economics of Poverty and Public Welfare,* Basic Books, New York, 1971, pp.23-29.

36. Piven, F.F., and Cloward, R.A., *Regulating the Poor,* op.cit., p.xiii.

37. See Chapter 6.

Social Planning for the Mentally Handicapped [*]

Do we need totally to revise our conceptions of mental handicap and therefore transform our methods of treating it? This is the fundamental question which the research carried out by Dr Pauline Morris and her colleagues obliges us to pose. Until now we have lacked information of a kind and range sufficient to challenge in detail the system not just of services but of thought and belief about handicap which has developed over the years. Valuable work has been undertaken recently on the meaning and prevalence of handicap (by, among others, Kushlick, Castell and Mittler), the effects upon handicapped children of care in small residential units rather than in large hospitals (Tizard) and the response even of the severely handicapped to industrial and social training schemes (A. and A.B.D. Clarke, O'Connor and Tizard). But research into mental illness and handicap has always been starved of resources, by comparison with research into physical illness and certain forms of physical handicap. Kenneth Robinson, the Minister of Health from 1964 to 1968, pointed out in 1958 that only 6d. in every £1 spent by the Medical Research Council went towards research on mental illness and handicap. (1) The Mental Health Research Fund has difficulty in raising more than modest sums from voluntary and private sources.

In the absence of comprehensive data about their physical and mental capacities plainly it is impossible to obtain an intelligent understanding of the needs of the handicapped, the conditions in which they live, the educational, social and occupational facilities afforded to them and the kind of skilled treatment they receive. And since the nature of the problem, especially of needs, has not previously been documented for the country as a whole, it is not surprising that the most imaginative and enlightened proposals for change, put forward by pressure-groups of parents (2) as well as individual specialists, (3) have lacked the persuasive force they may have deserved.

Too much must not be claimed for the research carried out by Dr Pauline Morris. She has not attempted to explore the origins, development and prevalence of handicap, nor the problems of the handicapped who live at home with family or friends. She carefully states the

* First published as the Foreword to Morris, P., *Put Away: A Sociological Study of Institutions for the Mentally Retarded,* Routledge & Kegan Paul, 1969.

limitations. Detailed studies require to be undertaken on, for example, committal procedures, diet, relations between parents and children, effectiveness of different forms of industrial training and social therapy, methods of recruitment and training of hospital staff, and the social structure of both the hospital and the hostel. This research survey has concentrated upon institutional services and much of the evidence has been drawn from staff rather than from interviews with patients and their families.

Yet, when these and other reservations are expressed, the coverage of the study is still extremely wide. For the first time it is possible to comprehend the size, organization, staffing and operation of a national system of hospitals and residential services for the subnormal. For the first time it is possible for reliable estimates to be given of the scale and severity of certain problems. The basis has been laid for an evaluation of the effectiveness of hospitals for the subnormal. The basis has also been laid for rational planning of services for the subnormal, hitherto missing from the Hospital Plan of 1962 and the subsequent revision of 1966 (4) as well as from the complementary local authority plans for community care. (5) All this has been made possible by a generous grant from the National Society for Mentally Handicapped Children to the Department of Sociology in the University of Essex upon the foundation of the university. Of course, a great deal of further research remains to be done but a preliminary network of information is now available to all those deeply concerned about the handicapped.

The study was conceived as the third in a series of national surveys of institutions (6) and although other comparative research on institutions has been done in this country and overseas, little or none of it has yet been national in range and representation. (7) This kind of research offers special advantages. Knowledge about institutionalized minorities puts knowledge about non-institutionalized majorities in a new light. The connexions between organizations and social structure, and between organizations and national policy, tend to be revealed. And programmes of further research can be devised more rationally and alternative policies discussed more realistically than in terms just of the information which is available in administrative reports.

In this introduction I shall try to review our conceptions and methods of treating mental handicap in the light of Dr Morris's findings and also other recent work. I shall argue, first, that the accumulating evidence of social influences upon intelligence has weakened if not destroyed the eugenic case for social segregation; secondly that the evidence of the present survey, together with evidence from other countries, notably the Soviet Union, throws grave doubt on the hospital as the right environment for the care of the subnormal; and finally that the social, occupational and emotional needs of the great majority of the subnormal might be met better within various forms of sheltered family or community care than in existing hospitals and hostels. I shall then attempt to suggest how a phased programme of changes in policy might be introduced.

Social Structure and Mental Handicap: (1) Subnormal Intelligence

In classifying someone as mentally retarded, defective or subnormal most societies refer, though not in so many words, to subnormal intelligence, personal incapacity and deviant behaviour. I want to consider each of these conceptions in turn, for I believe that this is essential in defining needs and finding whether they are met. From early in this century subnormal intelligence has come to dominate scientific conceptions of mental handicap, and the implications for the care of the handicapped should be considered at some length. (8) Societies find that individuals vary along a continuum according to verbal, numerical, spatial and other aptitudes. Below a certain level it is found that they make little progress at school and cannot hold any one of a range of ordinary occupations. They seem to require special schooling and occupation. But in families and neighbourhood groups in Britain, many young children who would obtain very low scores in an intelligence test are not denied an ordinary upbringing or singled out for special treatment. A distinction has to be made between real and perceived ability. This suggests that the *identification* of those with low ability may depend considerably on culture.

In psychology some of the pioneering attempts to measure intelligence tried to identify mental handicap. Early in this century Alfred Binet was asked to help the Paris education authorities to produce a scale for picking out retarded children. Later, in Britain, Cyril Burt and others worked on the mentally deficient and then seized on intelligence testing to show how poor but bright children might be selected to be given an academic type of education. It is ironic in present circumstances to recall that intelligence tests were originally regarded as a means of bringing about radical social reform and of establishing equality of educational opportunity. At first the results of intelligence testing were interpreted too strictly. Educationists and psychologists believed that with few exceptions individual abilities were more or less constant from early childhood. They also assumed too readily that intelligence tests measured intelligence. The separation of mildly subnormal children from ordinary schools and communities and the creation of the tripartite education system was unjustly legitimated.

In recent years society has become very conscious of the limitations of such tests. First, although tests of varying scope have been devised they tend to measure a limited number and combination of individual abilities. They rarely reflect qualities of perseverance, creativity, and judgement, for example. And we now know that many children and adults who are classified as mentally subnormal have astonishing powers of perseverance. (9)

Secondly, the tests are only crudely approximate for individual persons. Results obtained from pre-school tests are extremely unreliable. Results for some children may vary by up to ten points or more even when similar tests are carried out within a short space of time. Over a period of two or three years between tests some children's performance differs by up to 25 or 30 points. (10) It is also difficult to measure intelligence when physical handicaps like deafness intrude.

Thirdly, performance in intelligence tests often improves with practice and coaching. Simply by taking one previous test an average score can be raised five points. McIntosh found an average gain of 7.2 points among eleven-year-olds at the second trial. (11) When eleven-year-olds are given two complete practice tests and a few hours of interspersed coaching the average gain is about nine points. A significant minority of children gain from 15 to 25 or more points. (12) The implications are important. If this is what can be done by familiarity and concentrated practice for a few hours or weeks, how much more important may be the years of 'coaching' in a privileged social setting?

Perhaps the most important fact about intelligence tests is that they are not culture-free. Psychologists admit the great difficulties in comparing different races and ethnic groups. Some sociologists have gone on to argue, in effect, that the same difficulty arises in applying the same tests to different social classes and different sub-cultures. Middle-class children may have an unfair advantage, in the sense that the tests are usually drawn up from the vantage point of the kind of intellectual qualities shown by those in middle-class occupations and those who have had the kind of education typified by the grammar and independent schools.

The recent discussion of intelligence testing has acknowledged the many subtle ways in which society and not just environment (for that is a static concept), shapes individual ability. The impact of this idea upon education has been huge and the repercussions are still being felt. Streaming at young ages in schools and selection for secondary schooling at eleven on the basis of intelligence tests are now discouraged. Comprehensive schools are slowly being introduced and the school system is changing. Authoritative surveys, by the Crowther and Robbins committees, for example, have called attention to the wastage of ability. Few people still believe in a limited 'pool' of ability. It is possible, for example, that before long 40 or 50 per cent of each age-group in

Britain will be eligible to enter higher education. (13) Any wide-ranging analysis of recent evidence must conclude that human excellence is a social product as well as an individual quality. The kind and degree of ability may not only be shaped by the structure and organization of family, peer-group, social class and community, but also of the school and the firm as social organizations. The resources available to individuals within these settings, such as books, T.V., and facilities for play, are important, as are also the type of relationships and the complicated interplay of speech, gesture and emotional expression.

The identification of mental handicap and the development of special services for handicap now have to be looked at in this new context. There seems to be wastage of ability in hospitals for the subnormal as well as in ordinary schools. Before the Mental Health Act of 1959 was passed there was keen controversy about the extent to which the classification of a person as 'subnormal' would have to depend on him being demonstrably subnormal in intelligence. Many argued that 'social competence' and 'emotional maturity' should continue to be crucial criteria. The British Psychological Society and others contended that these social and emotional criteria were imprecise and if they continued to be used it was possible for people to be treated wrongly as mentally defective instead of being treated for various forms of neurosis. (14) The eventual Act adopted a clause including subnormality of intelligence within mental subnormality.

But former practice has been maintained and there is evidence that a substantial number of people are classified either as 'subnormal' or 'severely subnormal' when their intelligence test scores considerably exceed the limits normally accepted for purposes of definition by psychologists. (15) Dr Morris was unable to trace the scores for large numbers of a random sample of patients. For over a quarter of all patients no evidence existed that tests had been carried out, and another substantial proportion was said to be untestable. Even among those for whom scores could be given about two thirds had not been tested for at least two years, most of them not for more than five years. Ignorance and inertia in obtaining scientific information about ability seem to be poor foundations for a service which owes its legal justification to a definition of subnormality which includes subnormality of intelligence.

There is evidence too that severely subnormal persons improve in intelligence test scores and in other ways when given training elsewhere than in an institution. The best known example is the work of Tizard. He took a group of severely subnormal children from a large and overcrowded hospital and arranged for them to be looked after in a small, family-type unit like a children's home. This was the Brooklands experiment. He compared their progress with that made by a matched group of children who remained in the hospital. The children in the home made significantly greater advances than those in hospital in verbal and social development. (16) There are a range of supporting research studies, though most of them refer to children of higher grades of intelligence. (17) In a study in 1965 Stein and Stores found an intellectual improvement up to the school-leaving age among a large proportion of subnormal children, sufficient in a few cases to 'lift the children well into the range of intellectual normality'. (18) In general there is more evidence of improvement in test scores for mildly than for severely subnormal people and a distinction needs to be made between the two. For the latter there are not many data on improvement in scores — except verbal I.Q. — but perhaps this is partly because of the difficulties of devising and applying suitable tests.

Finally, there is evidence from general studies of the distribution of intelligence in the population as well as from special studies of the prevalence of mental subnormality that there are many subnormal and even severely subnormal persons who are not known to the services supposed to be dealing with them. The most carefully devised recent study is that of Kushlick. He found a peak for the age 15-19 of 3.65 severely subnormal persons per 1,000 population in the Wessex region of England who were known to the local authorities, hospitals, and nursing and residential Homes. As in other studies the prevalence rates for both severe and mild subnormality were found to rise after infancy and during adolescence, as shown in Table 1. This phenomenon is very important and illustrates the strong social element in the identification of handicap. At the age of compulsory schooling, and then again after the end of compulsory schooling, the administrative prevalence of subnormality rises. The step to a new social milieu is one which some individuals cannot take or are prevented from taking.

Kushlick and those who have studied the 'administrative' or perceived prevalence of subnormality consider that the rates for the mildly subnormal cannot be used to make estimates of the 'real' prevalence in the population. By the late teens there may be substantial numbers of people at work who have completed a school career and who have not been identified as requiring special education or other services and who may yet score only 50-70 in a carefully applied intelligence test. The great majority of them are integrated into the community and the crucial question is why some are placed in hospitals and hostels. But by ages 15-19 most of the severely subnormal are believed to have been notified to the appropriate authorities. Kushlick uses the rates for this age-group to show how many children below this age remain undetected. For every 100,000 people in Wessex he estimates that as many as 45 of a total of 96 severely subnormal children aged fifteen and under are not known to the local authority. This gives one measure of the desirable expansion in services. (19)

Table 1 Subnormal persons per thousand population identified in the Wessex region.

Age	Severely Subnormal	Mildly Subnormal	All Subnormal
0 –	0.52	0.18	0.72
5 –	2.52	0.60	3.16
10 –	3.01	0.56	3.59
15 –	3.65	3.17	6.84
20 –	2.91	2.98	5.91
30 –	2.19	1.83	4.05
40 –	1.87	1.76	3.66
50 –	1.27	1.38	2.66
60 +	0.52	0.63	1.11
All Ages	1.87	1.46	3.35

Source: Kushlick, A. and Cox, G., 'The Ascertained Prevalence of Mental Subnormality in the Wessex Region on 1 July, 1963', Proceedings of the First Congress of the International Association for the Scientific Study of Mental Deficiency, Montpellier, September 1967.

I have tried to establish first in general terms and then with specific reference to the handicapped how the concept of intelligence is much more elastic and much more open to social influences than we have hitherto supposed. A test of intelligence must not be treated as a sufficient criterion therefore of mental handicap or of admission to an institution. By this I do not mean to deny that it has a valuable function as a diagnostic device. It is particularly useful in planning, to distinguish between the mildly and the severely subnormal and elucidate the numbers of the latter. However, we might heed the terms in which a member of the Eugenics Society resigned from the society. After working for six years among the handicapped and experiencing doubts about the utility of the criterion of intelligence, the ex-member observed that the handicapped 'showed such a great variety of other virtues — generosity, goodwill, altruism, sweet temper — that I began to think a world peopled by mental defectives might be an improvement on the present one'. (20)

Social Structure and Mental Handicap: (2) Personal Incapacity

A second means of understanding mental handicap in relation to the social structure is through the concept of personal incapacity. (21) Legislation in Britain and in other countries has included references to people 'incapable of leading an independent life'. Intellectual ability overlaps with behavioural capacity but a population can be ranked according to individual incapacity to manage personal functions and undertake a range of common personal and household tasks, such as walking, running, climbing stairs, tying string, washing and dressing. Some of Dr Morris's most striking data refer to the low extent of physical incapacity among a large proportion of patients. It would be wrong, of course, not to emphasize the dependent state of substantial numbers of patients who are bedfast, doubly incontinent and grossly disabled. But it is important to note that 83 per cent are fully ambulant; 66 per cent can both feed and dress themselves, and another 17 per cent can feed although not dress themselves; 74 per cent of the adult patients are continent (and half the remaining adults only moderately incontinent); rather less than a third of all patients are said by staff to have one, two or more physical handicaps or to suffer from severe mental illness (though Dr Morris points out that this may have been an underestimate).

Dr Kushlick recently found in his Wessex survey that no less than 56 per cent of the severely (and 88 per cent of the mildly) subnormal adults in institutions could feed, wash and dress themselves. Nearly all of these were also continent, ambulant and free of severe behaviour disorders. He showed that over two fifths of the severely and three fifths of the mildly subnormal, some of them with severe incapacity, were living at home under the supervision of the local health authority. (22)

In another recent study 1,652 patients in thirteen hospitals for the subnormal in the Birmingham region were assessed by a hospital doctor and a charge-nurse. Only seven patients required investigation or active medical treatment of a kind which would make it necessary for them to be in hospital. About half were considered to require no medical treatment of any kind. Forty per cent were believed to need mental nursing with or without basic nursing and about 13 per cent required only basic nursing. (23) These data certainly pose the awkward question whether large numbers of patients require nursing and medical treatment in hospital. The real extent of personal incapacity in a population is determined to some extent by the demands placed upon individuals by the culture. The level of incapacity accepted for special attention and care depends on the perceptions and tolerance of families, peer groups, the community and the bureaucratic institutions.

Social Structure and Mental Handicap: (3) Deviance

There is a third means of understanding mental handicap in relation to the social structure. Sociology can help to teach that some persons are classified as mentally handicapped not so much because they are of subnormal intelligence or are incapacitated but because they are deviant. A population can be ranked according to its conformity with social norms. Norms are not minute regulations which are precisely formulated. They are standards of conduct to which people are expected to approximate in their daily activities. Again we must make a distinction between 'real' and 'perceived' behaviour. There are no distinct categories of behaviour. Just as physical restraint shades off into violence, so gossip by degrees becomes slander, or seduction becomes rape. Moreover, the exact points on this continuum at which norms are offended are difficult to locate and they tend to vary from place to place, class to class or society to society. Thus a loving family may not recognize a child's backward behaviour for several years until it is pointed out to them in the child's first year at school. Alternatively, an agricultural community with small need, say, for the symbols of literacy may not find it necessary to take notice of the backward behaviour of an adult man other than to express mild reproofs, to the effect that he is 'a bit simple'. It follows, therefore, that a 'censure-line', if it may be called such, may be drawn at one level within a sub-community of society, but at another level elsewhere. A compromise tends to be struck by the different groups in society. The norms for society as a whole may be more loosely interpreted. Difficult cases may be determined through the formal procedure of the courts which apply the more stringent rules of law.

If a person behaves to others invariably with trusting obedience, makes gestures or noises inappropriate to the context, repeats statements or instructions, touches and embraces others with embarrassing familiarity or affection, he is liable to be assigned to a social category of 'simple fool' and perhaps soon of 'imbecile', 'moron', or 'mentally subnormal'. He runs the risk of becoming a deviant with inferior status. As Dr Morris reminds us, strong views are held even among psychiatric and nursing staff as well as the public about the supposed inability of many mentally handicapped people to observe social norms. In particular there are fears and prejudices about violence and promiscuity, which are as difficult as racial fears and prejudices to allay. (24) On the one hand we must ask coolly for statistical evidence of assault and violence, and of promiscuity, to compare with that for comparable age-groups in the ordinary community. It is difficult to obtain suitable evidence, but certain data are on the whole reassuring. For example, Kushlick finds only about 14 per cent of severely subnormal and only 5 per cent of mildly subnormal persons in Wessex with behavioural disorders, though an additional small percentage have mild disorders. (25) On the other hand, one has to investigate carefully the ways in which the organizational communities within which handicapped persons live oblige them, as much as any other persons who might be placed in such conditions, to react stridently. A bleak and overcrowded environment, together with the denial of certain physical and occupational outlets, seems likely to induce occasional frustrated behaviour of extreme forms. So we need to introduce the idea that organizational form may reinforce if not actually cause 'handicapped' behaviour. A person tends to adopt the role expected of him. Some families impose handicapped roles upon their members. And in their structure and operation hospitals may steer individuals into performing more exaggerated versions, including more limited versions, of the handicapped roles they have played in outside society. Behaviour adapts, in short, to social form, and is causally connected.

There is a tendency for society to separate people into strictly distinct categories of deviant and non-deviant, incapacitated and non-incapacitated, subnormal and normal, irrespective of the graded differences of degree revealed in any objective study of behaviour. In one psychiatric study a research team found that although a majority of people in a community could accept a proposition that mental illness could be cured they found it hard to stomach a proposition that abnormality and normality were not distinct but shaded into one another.(26) It seems that people are prepared to ignore mental illness as far as possible and tolerate a wide range of behaviour. But once this tolerance is exhausted and illness recognized people at once wish a patient to be segregated and sent off to hospital. A potential danger to the community is removed, and a sick person is symbolically identified as different, going through all kinds of 'stripping' or 'degradation' procedures, and being deprived of common rights and resources. If people admit that abnormality is just one end of a continuum then they might have to admit that a sick or handicapped person might not be different from themselves, and segregation might not be the obvious solution. We have to be aware that different beliefs are linked in a system of belief.

Explaining Variations in the Prevalence of Mental Handicap

There are a number of implications of this approach for the study of mental handicap. One is that a society may go through a cycle of identifying relatively large and relatively small numbers of mentally handicapped persons, even though the prevalence of handicap, when measured according to objective criteria of subnormal intelligence, personal incapacity and behavioural deviance, may remain constant. Or again, its mode of treating them may depend on the relative weight attached socially to each of these three criteria. The development in the late nineteenth century of a national school system brought to light those who could not be accommodated, or accommodated only with difficulty, in that system. So occurred an expansion in the proportion in society who were identified as mentally handicapped and this was reinforced by the rigid and punitive trends in the moral code of society during the Victorian period. Custodial values were extolled by eugenicists who claimed that the subnormal would reproduce their kind disproportionately and contribute to a decline in national intelligence. (27)

Although from the fourteenth century a legal distinction was drawn between 'lunatics' and 'idiots' most persons with mental disorders were in practice housed indiscriminately in workhouses and, later, asylums. It was only in the middle of the nineteenth century that the first 'idiot asylum' was opened by a voluntary society, and later still before such asylums added the term 'institution for the feeble-minded' to their title. (28) I am therefore arguing that as time went on the demands of the educational system, together with the imposition of a stricter moral code, increased the proportion of persons with mildly subnormal intelligence or mildly deviant behaviour who were institutionalized. It was the incursion of many 'feeble-minded' persons without personal incapacity but with supposedly fixed low intelligence which caused institutions independent of asylums to be set up. The system of mental deficiency hospitals evolved. More recently there has been a tendency for the rates to diminish, partly because intelligence is now seen to be more complicated and adaptable than formerly supposed, and partly because punitive control of individual departures from moral conformity is thought to be less necessary.

It is within some such framework that the prevalence of mental handicap in different societies, and the division between institutional and community care, has to be explained. In appreciating what the imprecise criteria of subnormal intelligence, personal incapacity and deviance contribute to our concept of mental handicap we can perhaps see the need to revise our standards of humanity and justice. For the significance of this analysis is much more than semantic. It implies that there may be persons who are deprived of full civic rights and responsibilities and even in some cases of their personal freedom because their ability to read and write has not yet been perceived, their relatively adequate intelligence has not been measured (or not measured efficiently), their behaviour is found to be morally distasteful or they are an embarrassment in school. It also implies that *any* physical segregation, even of people of extreme handicap, may be improper.

The Unsuitability of Hospitals

To what extent are hospitals for the subnormal the right setting for the patients in them? What sort of facilities do they provide? Theoretically the needs of the patients can be explored first in relation to the formal or agreed purposes of the hospitals; we can show how far clinical, nursing, occupational and welfare purposes are actually fulfilled. Secondly, we can compare the patients with the population outside (or with patients in other hospitals or in hostels); we can show the space they occupy, the resources they command, the diets they consume and the number of close friends and relatives to whom they have access, and we can go on to apply objective criteria of deprivation, such as the prevalence of infectious disease correlating with degree of overcrowding. The first is primarily organizational and the second comparative in method. Sometimes standards of comparison may be indirect rather than direct.

The quality of any hospital service varies and Dr Morris studiously avoids laying undue emphasis on either end of the continuum. She pays tribute to the nursing staff and goes to considerable lengths to place data which might be interpreted as critical of individuals in a context which makes us aware that it is the organization that is at fault. Since her report follows hard on the heels of the report of an inquiry into a Welsh hospital (29), which has provoked public anxiety, this approach is most important, for it helps us to concentrate attention on the fundamental issues rather than embark on a self-righteous search for scapegoats.

A depressing picture emerges from the national survey. There is considerable personal, environmental, occupational and social deprivation among the hospital population, and no good purpose can be served by concealing this fact. This can be shown either by reference to a memorandum circulated to all hospitals by the Ministry of Health in 1965 (30) or to what is known about facilities and resources enjoyed by individuals in the outside community. I shall select just a few indicators. Sixty-one per cent of patients are in hospital complexes of more than 1,000 beds each, and a third are in annexes which are often isolated from the main buildings, themselves sometimes remote from urban and shopping centres. Only 1 per cent of patients are in single rooms; 38 per cent are in wards with 60 beds or more. The Ministry of Health recommends, 'A ward should not normally accommodate more than 30 adult patients or 20 children'. Sixty-nine per cent are in dormitories with only two feet or less space between the beds. Nearly 60 per cent are in dormitories with only one or two amenities or none at all among a list including lockers, bedside chairs, bedside mats, pictures and ornaments. Nearly 60 per cent are in dormitories where no personal possessions are displayed on beds, tables or windowsills and many of the others are in dormitories where personal possessions of only *some* patients are found. The Ministry states, 'Each patient requires a measure of privacy and at least a locker in which to keep his private possessions and, in the case of a child, his toys'. Only 21 per cent have their own toothbrushes, shaving kit or hairbrushes. Most of the clothing is communal in the sense that it is not retained by the individual after being laundered. And brassieres and corsets, for example, are not generally supplied to women. In 1966-7 the average cost of food and drink per patient per week was only £1 19s. 10d. compared with £2 4s. 6d. in mental illness hospitals, £2 10s. 4d. in chronic sick hospitals and much larger amounts in general hospitals. There is insufficient variety in meals and there is doubt, because of the patience and time required to feed some of them, whether all are fed adequately.

The great majority of children either have no toys or the toys tend to remain shut up in cupboards. The Ministry recommends:

Each child needs to have toys and possessions of his own. There should also be a large stock of playthings which can be used by all the children on the ward. Simple, solid, play equipment of a semi-permanent or permanent nature should be provided, e.g. swings, climbing frames, chutes, roundabouts, and toy trucks and push carts in which children can sit.

All these provide some measure of the barren conditions in which many patients live and of the meagre resources available to them.

Large proportions of the patients have little to occupy them in the day and few social relationships. Just over a tenth of patients are of school age. Approximately 43 per cent of them attend the hospital schools, though measured intelligence seems to have only a little bearing upon whether or not a child attends school, and there are children who could attend school who do not. Facilities for part-time adult schooling exist for only a third of the patients in hospitals and only 12 per cent of them actually attend classes. The proportion of adult patients attending for occupational therapy or industrial training fluctuates from about 3 per cent in some hospital units to over 60 per cent in others. The average in any particular week appears to be about 22 per cent, though a further 24 per cent work in the hospital or its grounds and a small percentage outside the hospital on daily licence. However, nearly half the patients either have no occupation or only domestic work or occupational therapy on their own ward.

Contacts with family and community are relatively few. Dr Morris points out that the failure to look upon admission as being of concern to the family as a whole sets the seal upon the patients' isolation. The staff assume parental roles without actually fulfilling them. Forty-three per cent of patients are not visited in the course of a year and only a third as often as once a month. Seventy-five per cent have never gone home. Forty-two per cent are confined to the ward in which they live, even though this figure far exceeds the proportion limited in mobility by physical handicap. Wards are locked for 14 per cent of patients. (The worst and very exceptional instance was a hospital in which 41 per cent of the patients were in locked wards. Many adults and children were netted into their cots, a practice which has disappeared from most parts of Britain.) Altogether, 18 per cent are allowed to go unaccompanied outside the hospital. Few patients go on holiday for as much as a week, whether organized by the hospital, relatives or voluntary associations. In most hospitals the figure varies between 10 and 25 per cent. Though there are many institutionalized relationships with voluntary associations, raising funds, holding religious services, celebrating Christmas and birthdays and so on, the fostering of personal relations — through invitations to visit clubs or houses in the community, or call regularly on particular patients — is not highly developed. They are better developed in medium-sized hospital units than in those with 1,000 beds or more. Some of the biggest hospitals have no Parents' Association.

Perhaps the most serious findings of all for policy are those which show that medical treatment and skilled nursing are not the predominant functions of the hospitals. Medical staff are in practice concerned with the supervision of hospital organization, the introduction of occupational therapy, the provision of a sheltered environment and the treatment of those temporary illnesses and disabilities such as colds and minor injuries which afflict any population. Only with a relatively small proportion of patients suffering from illness, including mental illness, are they immersed in questions of specialist medical care. Some medical staff have launched positive programmes of rehabilitation. They are concerned constantly to improve the specialized facilities of the hospital and they run extremely efficient, and sometimes modern, units. Yet few of these leadership activities are specifically medical in content. And at the other extreme there are medical staff who seem to avoid medical involvement in the hospital and become engrossed with solely administrative duties and outside conferences. Significantly, few medical staff are involved in research. Some of the hospital annexes are rarely visited.

Nursing roles tend to be confined to dressing, washing and feeding patients, supervising occupations on the ward and accompanying patients outside the ward. It must be remembered that 83 per cent of patients are fully ambulant and only 9 per cent bedfast. The high proportion of domestic work tends to reduce morale, particularly among nurses who are trained. Some say they are not nurses but glorified domestic workers or, alternatively, jailers.

Yet, because these institutions are hospitals, with medical and nursing staff in charge, the expansion of specialized services needed by subnormal persons is discouraged. The services are felt by medical and nursing staff to be a threat to their interests. Dr Morris calls attention to the conflict between medical and nursing staff, on the one hand, and specialized staff, on the other. Only 2 per cent of the patients receive physiotherapy and many more than an average of 12 per cent could receive occupational therapy. Only a quarter of the hospitals employ a speech therapist, inadequately in most even of these. Only half the hospitals employ social workers, and of these most are untrained. There is insufficient provision for psychopaths, epileptics, spastics, and autistic and psychotic children. There is, in short, a gross lack of basic professional services of various kinds.

Future Policy

Even when every account is taken of the immense variety of need and of quality of service, and the devoted efforts on behalf of subnormal patients made by many of the staff, the disturbing conclusion has to be faced that the wrong system of care has been developed over the years for this minority of the population. What can now be done to remedy the system? Drawing upon the evidence so far available, the long-term purposes or objectives must first be defined, and the strategy to achieve those purposes then devised.

Useful lessons can be learned from some other countries. In the Soviet Union, for example, there seem to be only about a third as many mentally handicapped persons in hospitals and welfare institutions as in Britain and the United States, proportionate to population. That group of severely subnormal children who are 'imbecile' rather than 'idiot' fall under the administrative care of the Ministry of Education. Craft states, 'it seems that far more imbecile children are both afforded a chance of state schooling in the U.S.S.R., and are persisted with, than in the U.K.' They are taught by special teachers, with high status and extra pay, in day or boarding schools. These schools lay emphasis on self-help rather than adult protection but by Western standards are generously staffed. After school all are expected to work in the home district. (31)

Britain may now be cautiously embarking on this path. In November 1968, following various pressures, (32) the Government announced that legislation would be introduced transferring responsibility for education of all subnormal children from health (whether hospital or local authorities) to education. Until now relatively fewer children in Britain than in the United States, though more than in the Soviet Union, have been a responsibility of health authorities. (33) Compared with many areas of the United States, hospitals for the subnormal are more advanced in

Britain. Services are more plentiful and ward organization more varied and idiosyncratic — in keeping with the rather piecemeal accumulation of different buildings over the decades. In most of them standards of care seem to be higher than in certain other industrial societies — than those, for example, in Austria and Hungary, which I visited recently. Yet the care is not only deficient. It is inappropriate. The problem is not simply one of finding more money and more staff, putting up new buildings and introducing comprehensive training schemes. It is one of reconstructing the system.

The evidence collected by Dr Morris, and by others, such as Dr Kushlick and Professor Tizard, justifies a much more dramatic shift from custodial or institutional to community care than has so far been proposed. (34) And the evidence on mental nursing and residential homes (or hostels) does not really suggest that, at least in their present form, they are a suitable stopping-point. Dr Morris shows that they provide a much more homely environment and are less isolated from the community. For example, proportionately more of the residents go home, or go on holiday for a week or more, than do patients in hospital. But by the criteria of occupation and social relations those who live in them are not dramatically better off than persons in hospital. Few are employed in the community and though many are engaged on domestic work few have occupational therapy. As many as 27 per cent (compared with 42 per cent in hospital) are not visited at all in the course of a year and only 18 per cent (the same figure as in hospital) are allowed out, despite fewer being severely subnormal. Few of these halfway institutions have Parents' Associations and they can be very isolated from a range of psychiatric and other professional services. (35)

The long-term aim should be to allow the great majority of people with the same handicaps as those now in hospitals for the subnormal to live in sheltered housing or small family homes in the community — when they can no longer be cared for by their families. Sheltered housing is being provided on an increasing scale for old people and the disabled, and could be planned to accommodate the subnormal. There might be family homes for the severely subnormal run in the same way as small group homes for 6 or 10 children, with housemothers and housefathers. Private housing for groups of 6, 10 or 15 less severely subnormal adults could be provided in clusters of bungalows, ground-floor flatlets or even converted flatlets in ordinary houses in all localities. Subnormal persons with really severe psychiatric illnesses or multiple disabilities who require constant nursing and medical treatment would be cared for in units attached to district general hospitals.

The tenants of this sheltered housing would be able to take advantage of certain communal facilities, and there would usually be a resident housekeeper in one of the flatlets, or an adjoining house. In the day children would attend the local school, and adults would go to ordinary employment, sheltered workshops, day hospitals or day centres. In each local authority area Community Boards would be set up to manage a number of sheltered housing units, appoint staff and safeguard the tenants' welfare. These Boards would consist of three equal groups of people: lay representatives of the local community, representatives of parents or other relatives, and specialists, such as doctors, social workers, physiotherapists and occupational therapists. Associations of parents and of local residents would have specific functions. For example, they might staff a person-to-person visiting service for subnormal persons lacking relatives, organized by a full-time social worker. They might organize regular outings to shops and holidays. The social integration of the handicapped depends on two principles — the continuity of relationships with family and locality and the supervision and organization (under the Community Boards) of all community services by full-time paid specialist staff. A network of professional services — medicine, nursing, physiotherapy, occupational therapy, speech therapy and the rest — has to be provided in health centres, day hospitals and day centres, rather than in long-stay institutions. Consultants might be appointed to serve groups of health centres. A strong independent inspectorate covering community services as well as hospitals should also be created. Minimum standards of care and education should be laid down nationally.

Work in sheltered workshops and in ordinary employment would be a necessary part of this plan. The derisory and degrading system of 'rewards' for those in hospital would be replaced by a wage-structure worked out nationally. People with an intelligence quotient of between 25 and 50 have been shown not only to respond to training but to become so enthusiastic that in one case, for example, they broke into their workshop on Sundays for the entire day to do extra work. (36) The best known workshop is one at Slough, first run by the National Society for Mentally Handicapped Children and then by Buckinghamshire County Council, which has shown in practice the possibilities of industrial training even for the severely subnormal. The employment services provided by the Department of Employment for all kinds of handicapped people need to be overhauled. In particular, strong placement services and properly conducted schemes for workshop instructors need to be introduced.

This entire pattern would require new legislation, together with a deliberate and massive redirection of resources, in money and manpower, from hospitals to community care. In 1966-7 about £128 million was spent on hospitals for the mentally ill and subnormal, compared with only about £17 million on all local authority mental health services. (37) The actual distribution of resources should be explored further but these figures give a rough indication of the relative value we actually place on institutional care as compared with community care. Only when this ratio is reversed will the distribution of services begin to represent the distribution of need, as revealed by the evidence. All this is conditional too on a drastic change in public attitudes.

What can be done in the meantime? While preparing legislation the Secretary of State for Social Services should invite local authorities and Parents' Associations, in conjunction with Hospital Management Committees to set up *ad hoc* Community Boards of the kind outlined. He should urge local authorities to review their plans for sheltered housing, training centres and mental health workers, in advance of legislation which introduces special government subsidies and perhaps percentage grants to expand facilities for community care. He should at the same time give them guidance about the assumptions on which planning might be based and also bring the Hospital Plan of 1962 up to date.

As sheltered housing and other services expand it will be possible to divert persons who would formerly have been admitted to hospital to the community. Some long-stay patients might also be encouraged to live in group homes. Some of the smaller hospital annexes could be transferred to the local authorities for use temporarily as residential hostels, and overcrowding in the large hospitals could be reduced. Dr Morris pays particular attention to the problem of the physical and professional isolation of many of the hospital units and argues that as well as turning some of them into hostels other units should progressively be staffed by autonomous groups of training staff and social workers. She also stresses the desirability of patients going out to schools, workshops and centres in the day and of living in mixed units in the hospital. She rightly perceives that improvements in the quality of care depend on changes in social and professional structures.

Throughout this period staff should be encouraged to recognize that they are participating in a planned reform of benefit to the subnormal. Some of them might take part in training programmes for mental health workers or welfare assistants in the community services and be transferred at the appropriate time. Others might prefer to transfer eventually to other parts of the hospital service, and should be given the opportunity of having spells of duty at general hospitals.

From the start, Regional Hospital Boards should be committed to finding the resources so that the environment and facilities of the hospitals can be improved immediately. A few million pounds a year represents a tiny fraction of expenditure on the National Health Service and yet if devoted to furniture, carpeting, clothing, toilet requisites, toys, partitions and so on could transform the wards and raise the morale of both patients and staff. With the help of social workers attached to the local authority, associations representing parents and local residents should be made responsible for organizing person-to-person visiting services, play groups, shopping expeditions, hair-styling, holidays and so on. A local authority social worker should be temporarily attached to each hospital for this purpose. Meetings should be encouraged between groups of parents, local residents and staff on wards to discuss measures that might be adopted. Patients themselves should be persuaded to play a part in improving and furnishing the wards.

The general direction taken by these proposals is not original. The Royal Commission on the Law Relating to Mental Illness and Mental Deficiency of 1954-7 foresaw that the admission to hospital at least of the subnormal rather than of the severely subnormal would become unnecessary in the future. The Hospital Plan of 1962 tried to suggest dividing the subnormal from the severely subnormal, so that the former would be cared for in smaller units of not more than 200 beds — a proposal which has shown no signs of coming into being — and recognized that community care services would continue to expand. A memorandum issued by the Ministry of Health in 1965 stated,

> In the absence of complicating conditions, such as severe physical disability or disturbed behaviour, the severely subnormal patient who has been adequately investigated and treated ought not to be primarily the responsibility of the hospital service for long-term care. Ultimately, when facilities outside hospitals are fully developed, continued hospital care will be necessary only for patients who require special or continuous nursing and for those who, because of unstable behaviour, need the kind of supervision and control provided by a hospital.(38)

And independent specialists have sometimes elaborated the compelling arguments for a transfer of resources to the community services. (39)

There are grounds, then, for believing that the Government would not be opposed to changing policy so as to favour community care. But whether it could be persuaded to move far enough and fast enough is another thing. The difficulties of achieving a dramatic change should not be underrated. A much more serious approach to planning is required. Expressions of good intent in ministers' speeches and exhortations in Government circulars, though perhaps necessary, do not penetrate very far into the system. What is lacking is a leadership strategy, worked out in fine detail with the co-operation of the hospital management committees, local authorities, staff and parents. Reform does not consist just in releasing more government money for staff and new buildings, important as these additional resources are. Nor does it consist in sitting tight and acting only when public attitudes soften. A structural change must be started which will ramify the length and breadth of society. There must be a complete reorganization of services — so that the subnormal are no longer isolated in hospitals remote from the community and can be accepted into ordinary schooling and employment. They should have access as easily to family or locality and as easily to the professional services of physiotherapists, occupational therapists, psychotherapists and social workers as to the professional services of hospital doctors and nurses. For it is in a different structure of relations that the best hope lies of protecting their rights. The interests of parents, community and professions can be given a new, and more balanced, representation.

It is only in this different structure of relations that the punitive attitudes of some sections of the public and, indeed, of some professional staff can be modified. The present system of hospitals for the subnormal has been created very largely, I have tried to show, by social conceptions of low intelligence, personal incapacity and deviant behaviour. The isolation, cruelty and deprivation of the hospital organization, as it must be seen to be, is of our own making.

Disturbing accounts of conditions at individual hospitals have recently been described in the press (40) and in a Blue Book presented to Parliament. It would be wrong in such instances to assume that all we must do is apportion blame among individuals, discipline those who are narrowly responsible, and set up an inspectorate. The Committee inquiring into irregularities at the Ely Hospital, Cardiff, were not to know that the overcrowding and many of the deprivations, such as the shortage of toothbrushes and dentures, did not apply just to that hospital but to many other hospitals in Britain, as Dr Morris now shows. The Committee concluded, 'the trouble has arisen not from any lack of [staff] goodwill . . . but, more than anything else, from a lack of awareness of how far Ely has lagged behind what ought to have been, and can be, achieved'. (41) This conclusion could be applied more generally. Because almost everyone — hospital management committees, staff and public — regards the poor conditions of these hospitals with comparative equanimity and because almost everyone adopts an attitude of untutored pessimism about the possibilities of educating and occupying the handicapped, unjustifiably low standards of care are tolerated. The hospitals have been gripped with a kind of creeping organizational sickness, within which the handicapped have little chance either to fulfil themselves or enjoy the rights available to other citizens. This is the tragic problem we must try to understand and solve.

Notes

1. *Policy for Mental Health,* Fabian Research Series, no.200, 1958.

2. For an account of the activities of groups of parents, see *Parents Voice,* Journal of the National Society for Mentally Handicapped Children.

3. For example, Tizard, J., *Community Services for the Mentally Handicapped,* Oxford University Press, 1964.

4. *A Hospital Plan for England and Wales,* Cmnd. 1604, H.M.S.O., 1962; The Hospital Building Programme: *A Revision of the Hospital Plan for England and Wales,* Cmnd. 3000, H.M.S.O., 1966.

5. Ministry of Health, *Health and Welfare: The Development of Community Care,* Cmnd. 1973, H.M.S.O., 1963; and revisions under the same title published in 1964 and 1966. The latter (Cmnd. 3022) took the plans for the health and welfare services of the local authorities in England and Wales to 1976.

6. The other two studies were: Townsend, P., *The Last Refuge: A Survey of Residential Institutions and Homes for the Aged in England and Wales,* Routledge & Kegan Paul, 1962; and a survey of old people in hospital reported in part in Townsend, P., 'The Needs of the Elderly and the Planning of Hospitals', in Cavin, R.W. and Pearson, N.G. (eds.), *The Needs of the Elderly,* University of Exeter, 1972.

7. There have been a number of comparative studies of institutions and of institutional conditions both in this country and overseas. See, for example, Wing, J.K., and Brown, G.W., 'Social Treatment of Chronic Schizophrenia: A Comparative Survey of Three Mental Hospitals,' *Journal of Mental Science,* 107, 1961; Jones, K., and Sidebotham, R., *Mental Hospitals at Work,* Routledge & Kegan Paul, 1963. For the United States, see Ullmann, L.P., *Institutions and Outcome: A Comparative Study of Psychiatric Hospitals,* Pergamon Press, 1968.

8. For a particularly discerning and astringent discussion of the criteria of handicap, see Wootton, B., *Social Science and Social Pathology,* Allen & Unwin, 1959, pp.254-67.

9. Tizard, J., *Survey and Experiment in Special Education,* Harrap, 1967, p.13.

10. Professor Vernon, an acknowledged expert on intelligence tests, is one of those whose accounts of the scope of such tests have become properly more cautious over the years. For example, 'One should never think of a child's I.Q. (or other test result) as accurate to 1 per cent. Rather an I.Q. of, say, 95 should be thought of as a kind of region or general level. For a few weeks or months to come there are even chances that it falls between 92 and 98; and the odds are about 10 to 1 that his I.Q. lies within the range of 88 to 102. But the possibilities of much larger discrepancies should not be forgotten. Over several years, say from 6 to 10 or from 11 to 15, the most we can say is that there is fair certainty (i.e. 10 to 1) of its lying between 80 and 110.' Vernon, P.E., *Intelligence and Attainment Tests,* University of London Press, 1960, p.114.

11. McIntosh, D.M., 'The Effect of Practice in Intelligence Test Results', *British Journal of Educational Psychology,* 14, 1944.

12. Vernon, P.E., op.cit., p.131.

13. The Robbins Committee was unable to specify an upper limit, and although the percentage of each age-group in England and Wales with entry qualifications was likely to grow from 6.9 in 1961 to 14.5 in 1985 untapped ability was 'most unlikely to be fully mobilized within the next twenty years'. Half of each age-group in California already enters higher education, though to correspond roughly with British university entry qualifications the figure would probably be reduced to between 25 and 30 per cent. The United States Office of Education accepts an estimate that a figure of 50 per cent of each age-group entering higher education will be reached for the United States as a whole in 1970. In Oslo the number passing the university entrance test has reached 40 per cent. See, for example, Halsey, A.H. (ed.), *Ability and Educational Opportunity*, Paris, O.E.C.D., 1961.

14. See, for example, British Psychological Society, Working Party on the Report of the Royal Commission, *Bulletin of the British Psychological Society*, vol.35, 1958, pp. 1-26.

15. Thus, while psychologists generally regard an I.Q. of 70 (on a Wechsler-type test with a mean of 100 and a standard deviation of 15 points) as the upper limit of subnormality, a quarter of a sample of adult admissions who were studied in 1961 had scores of over 80. And while they regard an I.Q. of 55 as indicating the upper limit of *severe* subnormality, half the sample of patients actually classified as severely subnormal had I.Q.s of over 60. Mittler, P., 'The Contribution of Intelligence Testing to Classification', *Journal of Mental Subnormality*, vol. XI, Part 1, December 1964.

16. Tizard, J., *Community Services for the Mentally Handicapped*, Oxford University Press, 1964, pp.85-137.

17. See a review by Kirk, S.A., *Early Education of the Mentally Retarded*, Urbana, United States, 1958.

18. Stein, Z.A., and Stores, G., 'I.Q. Changes in Educationally Subnormal Children at Special School', *British Journal of Educational Psychology*, vol.35, Part 3, November 1965.

19. Kushlick, A., 'A Method of Evaluating the Effectiveness of a Community Health Service', *Social and Economic Administration*, vol. 1, no.4, October 1967.

20. *Eugenics Review*, October 1946, p.115. Quoted by Wootton, B., op.cit., p.264.

21. See, for example, Townsend, P., *The Last Refuge*, especially Chapter 10 and Appendix 2; Shanas, E., *et al.*, *Old People in Three Industrial Societies*, Routledge & Kegan Paul and Atherton, New York, 1968, especially Chapter 2.

22. Kushlick, A., and Cox, G., op.cit.

23. Leck, I., Gordon, W.L., and McKeown, T., 'Medical and Social Needs of Patients in Hospitals for the Mentally Subnormal', *British Journal of Preventive and Social Medicine*, vol. 21, 1967.

24. Under former legislation there was a category of moral defective, in addition to the categories of idiot, imbecile and feeble-minded. In 1960, 73 moral defectives were admitted to hospitals for the subnormal in England and Wales, all but a few to two hospitals in the Sheffield region. Although this category is now in disrepute, social deviance is undoubtedly an important influence in

determining admissions and, indeed, the pattern of hospital management. General Register Office, *Registrar General's Statistical Review of England and Wales for the Year 1960, Supplement on Mental Health*, H.M.S.O., 1964, p.37.

25. Kushlick, A., and Cox, G., op.cit.

26. Cumming, J., and Cumming, E., 'Mental Health Education in a Canadian Community', in Paul, B. (ed.), *Health, Culture and Community*, New York, 1955.

27. These claims were confounded by measures taken over time in the distribution of national intelligence and by studies of the handicapped. Penrose, for example, found that over 90 per cent of the mildly subnormal in his hospital survey had parents of normal or dull average intelligence. Penrose, L.S., *A Clinical and Genetic Study of 1280 Cases of Mental Defect*, H.M.S.O., 1938.

28. *Report of the Royal Commission on the Law Relating to Mental Illness and Mental Deficiency*, 1954-7, Cmnd. 169, H.M.S.O., 1957.

29. *Report of the Committee of Inquiry into Allegations of Ill-Treatment of Patients and Other Irregularities at the Ely Hospital, Cardiff*, Cmnd. 3975, H.M.S.O., 1969.

30. Ministry of Health, *Improving the Effectiveness of the Hospital Service for the Mentally Subnormal*, H.M. (65) 104.

31. It is difficult to be sure how well the system works throughout the U.S.S.R., and how many gaps there are, but the major difference in the stress on education seems genuine enough. Craft, M., 'A Comparative Study of Facilities for the Retarded in the Soviet Union, United States and United Kingdom', in Freeman, H., and Farndale, J. (eds.), *New Aspects of the Mental Health Services*, Pergamon Press, 1967.

32. The Seebohm Committee has recommended that 'the local education authority should become responsible for the education and training of all subnormal children and take over the junior training centres'. *Report of the Committee on Local Authority and Allied Personal Social Services*, H.M.S.O., 1968, p.116.

33. Kety, S.S. (Chairman), *Report of the Mission to the U.S.S.R.*, President's Panel on Mental Retardation, Washington, United States Department of Health, Education and Welfare, 1962.

34. By community care I mean living in a private household, not a hospital or a residential home, and receiving a range of medical, social and occupational services, which may include attending a day school or a day hospital.

35. See also Apte, R.Z., *Halfway Houses: A New Dilemma in Institutional Care*, Occasional Papers on Social Administration, no. 27, Bell, 1968. Mittler points out that 'Small hostels are not necessarily superior to hospitals: there is always the danger that, unless well run, they may be unstimulating and remote places in which too little is done for the children educationally or socially.' Mittler, P., *The Mental Health Services*, Fabian Research Series, no.252, 1966, p.23.

36. For example, Clarke, A., and Clarke, A.D.B., *Mental Deficiency: The Changing Outlook*, Methuen, 1966.

37. *Annual Report of the Ministry of Health for the Year 1967*, Cmnd. 3702, H.M.S.O., 1968, p.147 and estimate of costs of psychiatric hospitals made on

basis of weekly costs and numbers of patients on pp.189 and 201.

38.*Improving the Effectiveness of the Hospital Service for the Mentally Subnormal.*

39.In particular, Tizard, J., *Community Services for the Handicapped;* Kushlick, A., 'A Community Service for the Mentally Subnormal', *Social Psychiatry,* vol. 1, no.2, 1966; and Mittler, P., *The Mental Health Services.*

40.See, for example, Shearer, A., 'Dirty Children in a Locked Room: A Mental Hospital on a Bad Day', *Guardian,* 28 March 1968 (and subsequent correspondence).

41.*The Howe Report,* p.115.

1 Needs and Leadership Strategies in the Mental Health Services*

If ever there was a year for bold and decisive government action in social policy then that year would seem to have been reached. The Government's review of social security has been rumbling on for four years and although, with the publication in January 1969 of the White Paper on Social Security, it has begun to gather momentum, proposals to raise the living standards of most sections of the population who are in poverty have still to be worked out. For example, the introduction of a pensions scheme for the handicapped and disabled, including those in institutions, is awaited. The Ministries of Health and Social Security have been joined together in name but not yet in consummated matrimony. And although a number of authoritative reports have been completed they clamour for central decision. The Seebohm Report on the local authority social services, the Government's Green Paper on the administrative structure of the National Health Service, the Royal Commission report on medical education, and the prospective Royal Commission report on the structure of local government are attempts to take stock of and put right the deficiencies in the regional and local network of services that have been increasingly acknowledged in recent years.

What can we reasonably expect of the Government, especially in developing services for the mentally ill and handicapped? Have the various problems been properly investigated and described? Have the objectives of policy been properly formulated? And is authority observing the conditions necessary for a reformist strategy? I shall briefly review what has been done to describe trends in the services and to identify objectives, needs and strategies as a basis for planning. My theme will be the lack of a planning framework and the lack too of a constructive leadership response to criticisms in contemplating dramatic reform. I shall argue that planning for major reform requires not only a wider and a deeper understanding of needs but a different style of leadership or management which is far less defensive and self-righteous than that displayed by many Government ministers, chairmen of Regional Boards and chief officers of local authorities.

* Paper given to the annual conference of the National Association for Mental Health, 20 February 1969.

Trends in the System of Services

The demand for change in the mental health services has deep-seated sources. Methods of treatment and attitudes to treatment in psychiatric hospitals began to change in the early 1950s. The emphasis began to shift from custodial confinement to active therapy and rehabilitation. The ideas of a small group of physician superintendents were widely publicized.(1) New drugs such as reserpine and chlorpromazine were introduced. Experiments in occupational and industrial therapy were eagerly discussed. The idea of a therapeutic community seemed to be applicable even to long-stay patients. Locked wards began to be unlocked and an 'open-doors' policy began to be adopted by physician superintendents. The number of long-stay patients, and the proportion of the population who were in mental illness hospitals, began to decline. Many qualifications have to be made to this description of change. Drug therapy may dull or atrophy some patients' senses and may allow them to live merely a limited existence in hospital or at home. Frequent readmission to hospital can be socially unsettling for individual, family and hospital community. A reduction in the population of hospital patients may not mean that a reduction has taken place in the real prevalence of illness. Again, the reduction in the population of patients may succeed a long period in which the rate of recruitment to long-stay status has actually declined and in which most hospitals have become more overcrowded than intended.(2) But it is fair to say that in industrial societies a revolution in attitudes to the treatment of mental illness began to develop in the 1950s, with certain hospitals and staffs in Britain very much in the van. The possibility that this revolution represented in some ways no more than a return to some of the humane attitudes and practices which prevailed in early nineteenth-century Britain does not minimize its importance.

What has to be pointed out, I believe, is that the change is attributable to a growing awareness of the social aspects of illness and of therapy. Yet the impact of sociology upon the mental health services has still to be felt. Physicians, psychiatrists and nurses have tended to lead the way in calling attention to the connection between illness and social isolation or between illness and membership of abnormal social groups. Some have also described the disadvantages of custodial treatment and the advantages of rehabilitation and have discussed how social relations as well as the environmental poverty within hospitals may act as obstacles to recovery. But the sociologist might argue that all this represents a very provisional and disconnected, if inspired, formulation of the relationship between mental illness or handicap and society and of the means whereby certain kinds of deviant behaviour can be treated or accommodated. There is a further stage in which knowledge can be sought systematically in three spheres. One is the social origin or causation of mental illness. There can be a weak or a strong version of sociological theory: either social variables may constitute a few but by no means all of the explanatory variables in mental illness or they may constitute all of the variables. A second sphere of knowledge is the relationship between scientific (whether medical, psychiatric or sociological) and social definition of illness or handicap. Between two dates in history the proportion of people categorized as mentally ill and hospitalized or otherwise listed for treatment may be doubled. Yet according to certain scientific criteria the real prevalence of illness may remain the same. Alternatively, within certain cultures only extreme forms of mental illness may be recognized or acknowledged in any formal way. And the third sphere of knowledge is the social aspects of treatment and recovery: for example, the relationship between patient and family or patient and psychiatrist: the structure and social relations of mental institutions; and the network of social relations and services for mentally ill or handicapped persons in the community.

In each of these spheres knowledge is being and will be obtained which will have direct implications for policy. What we lack at present is a planning framework within which findings can be put to immediate use and research priorities determined. I am thinking in particular of a central planning office or department as a kind of brain of the major social service departments, including housing and education as well as welfare, health, and social security.(3) The case for this can be illustrated in the history of mental health planning in Britain from the mid-1950s. The first explicit commitment to mental health planning in Britain was based, however crudely, on a systems-management type of theory rather than upon an analysis of needs or of purposes. The influential paper in 1961 by Tooth and Brooke showed that places occupied in mental hospitals in England and Wales had reached a peak in 1954 and were declining steadily.(4) The Ministry of Health published a Hospital Plan in 1962 which simply projected this trend.(5) It suggested that between 1960 and 1975 there would be a reduction in the number of mental illness beds from 3.3 to 1.8 per 1,000 population or from 152,000 to 92,000. This last figure was stated to be probably too high rather than too low since it took no account of the 'expansion of community mental health services or . . . further advances in medical treatment'. The assumptions were by no means fully spelt out and the ministry's reasoning was open to heavy criticism. There was no discussion of the relationship between places in psychiatric hospitals, chronic sick hospitals and residential homes, especially for long-stay elderly patients or residents. No allowance seems to have been made for the possibility that in the later as compared with the earlier years after an administrative change in discharge policy, the hospitals would be left not with a representative cross-section of long-stay patients but those whom it was particularly difficult to place in the outside community. Most of all the policy depended, despite the disclaimers, on the expansion and effectiveness of a system of community care, in which there would be out-patient facilities, day centres, social work guidance and the support of welfare services, but for which the evidence was uncertain. The statistical basis of the projection was also criticized.(6) Rather embarrassingly for the ministry, the run-down policy for mental hospitals was not accepted by the Scottish Home and Health Department.(7) Indeed, the phenomenon everywhere of an increase in re-admissions was regarded there as compensating for the beds left vacant by the small diminution in the number of long-stay patients.(8)

There were those too who argued that the run-down of the mental hospitals was undesirable as well as unrealistic. They thought that some of the claims for the psychotropic drugs were grandiose, and they were merely palliatives, that there were large numbers of long-stay patients who did not have the capacities to be rehabilitated, that the effectiveness of community as compared with hospital services was over-rated, and that the early discharge policy was placing an unfair burden on many families. Better, they felt, to improve hospital services but allow for broadly the same numbers of patients.(9)

The ministry's tentative excursion into planning in 1962 seems to have been regarded as too daring by ministry officials and subsequent ministers. When one hoped for intelligent development of the general ideas expressed in 1962 and for the rational discussion of each of the issues debated in the medical and social science journals, there was only an embarrassed silence. Astonishingly little has been added in the past four years by the present Government. No elaboration of the 1962 plan has appeared. In 1965 Hospital Boards were asked to review their building programmes and a summary was published in 1966.(10) But virtually no change was made to the principles tentatively adopted and inadequately discussed in 1962, and since 1965 no further work of a comprehensive kind, especially work taking in the evolution of the community services, appears to have been completed. There has been disturbingly little reference to psychiatric provision within the plan. First, low priority was and is given to psychiatric accommodation. A careful examination of the original plan shows that mental illness and subnormality hospitals, along with chronic sick hospitals, did not feature prominently in building proposals. A study of five regional plans showed that the capital allocation per bed over a ten-year period varied from £95 to £176 for mental illness in three regions and was £368 and £604 respectively in a further two regions, compared with figures varying between £2,198 and £3,817 for general hospitals in the five regions.(11) Although the Plan aimed to provide an additional 7,400 beds for mental illness in general hospitals only about 2,000 were listed in the Plan or in reports of schemes in progress. Building notes published subsequently by the Ministry did not adequately pursue the possibility, moreover, that psychiatric might be very different from other hospital accommodation.

There seemed to be some chance that the imbalance in spending between psychiatric and other hospitals would be put right with the return of the Labour Government and the appointment of Mr Kenneth Robinson as Minister of Health. Mr Robinson was well known for his support for the mental health services. In a pamphlet called *Policy for Mental Health*, which was published in 1958, for example, (12) he repeatedly called attention to the problem of giving higher priority to mental health services. He pointed out that only sixpence in every £1 spent by the Medical Research Council went towards research into mental illness. He showed that whereas expenditure per patient per week in the Maudsley teaching hospital was nearly as high as in the other London teaching hospitals, the figure in mental illness hospitals generally was only 30 per cent of that in acute general hospitals. And he condemned the great majority of the buildings in which the mentally ill were treated, saying that they must be replaced as fast as possible, preferably by units in general hospitals.

Perhaps individual ministers can only ride a momentum generated by large-scale structural changes in society. Or perhaps they might do better to lead a public campaign on these issues to rally support in many different organizations and groups than rely on back-room diplomacy. There are many rueful lessons which I am sure we can learn from the disappointments in power of men who appear beforehand to have the right qualifications. The fact is that the weekly in-patient cost in 1964-5 of mental illness hospitals was 31 per cent of that of acute general hospitals and in 1966-7 still 31 per cent — despite the shrinking proportion of long-stay patients who are presumably less urgently in need of treatment.(13) In 1965 Mr Robinson had asked Hospital Boards to review building programmes to 'ensure that the geriatric and psychiatric services should receive not only a due share of the resources likely to be available, but an early share'.(14) There is no hard information about the effects of this exhortation. All that one can extract is that among the seventy-eight major building schemes each costing £1 million or more and listed in the last annual report of the Ministry of Health as having been completed in the year 1966-7, or as having been completed or started subsequently, only two are said to include a psychiatric unit, only two are subnormality hospitals and only one is a geriatric hospital. Of the total cost for all seventy-eight schemes of £215 million these five schemes account for £7 million.(15) I conclude that there is no evidence of relatively higher priority being given to the psychiatric services in hospital; if anything, rather the reverse.

Secondly, events since 1962 indicate that the Hospital Plan underestimated the problem of replacement. The population of psychiatric patients may not fall quite as sharply as predicted. The number of patients in mental illness beds has been declining at the rate of about 2,300 a year in recent years, or around 2 per cent, and if this trend continues there would be just over 100,000 of them in 1975. Making allowances for previous calculations of numbers of beds rather than of numbers of patients, changes in population forecasts and the redesignation of accommodation in terms of types of beds than of types of hospital, it looks as if the ministry's estimate of the beds required for mental illness in 1975 may have been about 10-15 per cent too low. It would be nearer the predicted figure than some critics have suggested but higher than assumed by those drawing up the building programmes. Moreover, the number of chronic sick and geriatric patients has increased slightly, against the ministry's expectation, and the number of elderly residents in welfare homes has increased strikingly. The failure to study the interrelations between the three types of institutional accommodation, psychiatric, chronic sick or geriatric and welfare, and the implications of such study for the planning and organization of district general hospitals is perhaps the greatest single lapse so far in hospital planning.

Needs and Purposes

To consider hospital planning in terms of a conception of system-management, however, is too limited. It is rather as if we take for granted the objectives and organization of the system and suppose that it is meeting the needs of those who are ill. There is the danger that statistical extrapolations of trends become self-fulfilling prophecies and that we mistake the conventional wisdom for planning. We have to be forced into the realization that trends in admissions and discharges are not just governed by the interconnexions between rates of illness and success of therapy. They are governed by the capital and current resources being made available by government but, more fundamentally, by changes in the norms of behaviour and values held about mental illness by different groups of hospital staff and, ultimately, outside society. This is why planning must involve, first, a search for the objectives inherent in if not made explicit in current treatment, followed by rational discussion of what the objectives should be; and secondly, objectives are partly defined through perceptions of need. Much of the real task of planning involves, on the one hand, the explication of objectives, and on the other, the measurement and publication of need.

Planning therefore has to be conceived within a wide comparative context. This might be illustrated both in terms of psychiatric hospitals and the proposals in the Seebohm Report. Conditions of patients and methods of treatment in different psychiatric hospitals can be compared. Examples are the work of Wing and Brown; (16) Jones and Sidebotham; (17) Townsend; (18) and the survey of subnormality hospitals by Pauline Morris. (19) All this inevitably calls into question standards of amenities, overcrowding, clothing, privacy, comfort and occupation compared with what is expected in the ordinary home conditions of modern society. Despite gallant attempts in some hospitals to introduce modern furniture and decoration, conditions are still wretched in many places. Particularly useful comparisons can be made with general hospitals or private nursing Homes. But though standards of clinical and nursing practice can be compared profitably among different hospitals (sometimes in different countries) it is likely that some of the most useful future work will be to compare the situation of psychiatric patients in the community with that of those in hospital, especially on the basis of area registers such as that established by Wing and others in Camberwell. (20)

Had the Seebohm Committee fully set out the evidence about need and paid more attention to a measured presentation of the objectives of a local social services department, I believe they would have reached a much more forceful and cogent conclusion. They were right to suggest the amalgamation of different services into a single local department and right at this stage to recommend that it should be independent of health departments, but presented it too much as a case for tidy and efficient administration instead of an exciting case for a major new service to meet social need. The objectives might have been expressed in terms which would have defined community care and captured public imagination, so easing the political problem of finding extra resources to finance the service. Instead the committee was cautious and pessimistic. 'It would be naive to think that any massive additional resources will be made available in the near future, not only on account of the present economic situation, but also because of the inevitable time lag in planning, recruitment, training and the construction of buildings. The pace at which our recommendations are implemented must be a matter for political decision'. (21)

Social need might also have been described in ways which allowed the clearer definition of priorities. The committee took the view that they could not sponsor research, or consumer reaction to the services, although their work occupied two and a half years — a year and a half longer than it took to prepare the Beveridge Report. Neither did they systematically examine evidence of need in relation to each of the services under review. To express the point most simply, it would be reasonable to suppose that not all of the services which the committee propose to amalgamate have reached the same stage of development in relation to community need. The children's service expanded early after the last war, with the local mental health services being late on the scene. On the basis of a scrutiny of research data it might be possible to conclude that the children's service has reached 70 per cent, say, of its potential development to meet need, but that the home help service has only reached 40 per cent and the local mental health service only 30 per cent. There would be corresponding estimates of 'shortfall' in terms of both expenditure and types of skilled manpower. Of course there are serious gaps in our knowledge, but the committee did not fully exploit the evidence that exists in order to describe a rational strategy of priorities and of expansion so as to achieve the long-term objectives of a balanced service. Instead, they stated that the various services were 'inadequate' or in 'urgent need of development'. The reiteration of phrases such as these is a poor substitute for estimates of the extra expenditure and manpower and new types of organization required. As a consequence I believe the committee seriously underestimated the importance of home helps, material aids for handicap, visiting services for the elderly and disabled, sheltered housing, a system of housing transfers and the organization of community self-help as a counterpart to skilled casework advisory services.

The pages in the committee's report which deal with the local mental health services contain some important recommendations — for example, that the local education authority should take over the junior training centres and that the other services should become the responsibility of the social services department. But the true needs of the mentally ill and subnormal in relation to the purposes of community care and in relation to the all-important distinction between community and hospital care are not spelt out. Total local authority expenditure in England and Wales rose from about £4 million in 1959-60 to £17 million in 1966-7, but in the latter year this compared with about £128 million on hospitals for the mentally ill and subnormal. On the evidence we have about the numbers of mentally handicapped persons living outside hospital, the strain and privations borne by parents of handicapped children, the need of families and individuals for home help, laundry and occupational services, and the need of mental welfare officers for short-courses of training and for ancillary help, this ratio is entirely wrong. The sum spent on community care must be rapidly accelerated. The accumulation of data about need can only reinforce this conclusion.

The conclusion becomes irresistible if the purposes of community care can be clearly stated. These must be primarily social rather than medical and this is what justifies both the Department of Health and

Social Security's 'run-down' policy for the huge, out-dated psychiatric hospitals and the Seebohm Committee's recommendation that the community mental health services should be managed by social rather than by health officers. The periods of the day in which the great majority of mentally ill and handicapped people require skilled nursing and medical treatment are short or non-existent. Their needs are primarily social, educational, occupational and emotional. It would be strange to banish them to artificial or quasi-communities, far from ordinary urban society, in which they are expected to lead restricted lives with persons usually of similar age and sex and with similar handicaps. Is it rational that they should take up the entire working time of scarce nurses and doctors, or that the latter should have entire control over the management of their lives? Is it rational, even, that they should occupy half-way hostels uneasily on the fringes of ordinary society, unless these hostels can be fully integrated with family, neighbourhood and local workforce? (22) Although there are many subtle overtones the central social purpose of community care can be expressed simply. It is to integrate individuals into the community and not segregate them from the community. The term community care is treated ambiguously. The Department of Health tends to include care in residential institutions. Sometimes the concept is extended further to include hospitals that adopt particular strategies. More properly it should be confined to measures concerned with maintaining individuals in home, family and neighbourhood.

If there could be a dramatic increase in domiciliary services and of special housing to match such an analysis of needs and objectives it would be possible to reduce long-stay accommodation in hospitals and residential homes. Eventually — not overnight or even in five years time, but eventually — it would be possible and desirable to abandon the residential home as an instrument of policy and reorganize the hospital service with a wider range of facilities for treatment. Fundamentally the hospital needs to develop more privacy and informality for the individual patient, and more links with the work and life of the community outside to foster his speedy rehabilitation. The proposals in the Green Paper might help to contribute the right administrative framework, though in the long run there should be a bipartite rather than tripartite administrative structure based on hospitals, on the one hand, and community health centres or group practices on the other.

Leadership Strategy

Finally, planning must take more account of strategy. This is generally neglected. It is not enough to make a case for dramatic reform. How is reform to be introduced democratically? The assumption is made too frequently in Britain that the accession to power of a political party is enough to guarantee that reform will be introduced. I should like to call attention to the problem of leadership strategy and use as an example Mr Kenneth Robinson's handling of the AEGIS affair. An association called Aid for the Elderly in Government Institutions became interested in certain privations said to be experienced by old people in hospitals, especially psychiatric hospitals. A book containing a number of testimonies by ex-staff of these hospitals was published in 1967.(23) There was widespread public concern and eventually Mr Robinson, as Minister of Health, set up committees of inquiry for each of the hospitals involved to look into the complaints of cruelty to elderly patients.

The Council on Tribunals has since rebuked the Minister for not setting up a statutory inquiry. At one inquiry the chairman allowed the hospital but not the complainants to have legal representation; and on three of the six committees the so-called lay members were or had been members of hospital boards. The reports of the committees, published in July 1968, varied in length from 1½ pages to 32 pages. Certain allegations seemed to be convincingly denied and doubt was thrown on the reliability of a few of the testimonies in *Sans Everything*. The book was not as carefully marshalled and presented as it might have been. But one committee accepted that an elderly man who was incontinent was 'dragged from his bed by the charge nurse and shaken like a rabbit, while he dangled about a foot from the ground, before being thrown with great force on the floor'. It went on to conclude that 'other incidents of ill-treatment of patients may well have taken place'. Other committees referred to staff who had been dismissed for handling patients roughly and pointed out how difficult it was to inquire into the truth of allegations years afterwards when some patients had died and staff had left the hospitals. The committee concerned with Friern Hospital, Barnet, agreed with the criticism that it was 'a dump for geriatrics' and went into detail about poor conditions and overcrowding in many wards and the shortage of clothing, facilities and staff. Yet the Minister reported to Parliament that the allegations in *Sans Everything* were found by the committees of inquiry to be 'totally unfounded or grossly exaggerated . . . I deeply regret the anxieties which have been caused to patients and their relatives, to hospital staff and to the public generally by the publication, which I believe the whole House will deplore, of so many allegations which are now authoritatively discredited'. (24) He went on television to say this comprehensively and flatly, and stuck loyally to the entire staffs of the hospitals.

I may not be alone in believing that by this interpretation of his role the Minister deferred the possibility of major reform of these hospitals and their staffing structure. He applied the doctrine of ministerial responsibility, taking the view that patients and staff would be frightened away or lose morale if he conceded any substantial criticisms at all. He seemed to be ignoring much of the authoritative work on conditions in hospitals for long-stay patients — by Barton, Sheldon, Wing and Brown, Roth, Jones, Mills and others. He even seemed to be denying what he himself had formerly argued.(25) The dividing line between deprivation and cruelty is difficult to draw, and there is no doubt that facilities are meagre, wards are overcrowded and staff are overworked in many institutions. While the work of many staff is unstinting and noble are we so sure that in the situation of many hospitals for long-stay patients the behaviour of a small minority is not sometimes reprehensible? Conditions in most British psychiatric hospitals are better than those in many comparable institutions in the United States and Europe, but they can still be greatly improved, by better pay, more training (especially short courses) and a relaxation of social relations (allowing outsiders, including relatives and friends, to come and go more easily). The Minister might have gently asserted the interests of patients as well as staff and perhaps embarked on a campaign to raise staffing standards. I suspect he could have enlisted the support of the public as well as the nursing and medical professions. Steps might also have been taken to appoint a Parliamentary Commissioner for hospitals and create an independent inspectorate.

It is all very well, with the benefits of hindsight, to offer these comments. But those who are responsible for running organizations and professions need to come to terms with these complaints and criticisms. Otherwise it may be impossible to accommodate major reforms, whether of their own or other's choosing. The handling of the AEGIS affair raises a general question. Can reformers who are appointed to high office reconcile their desire for change with their duty to represent the merits of their organization to the consumer and to the outside world — without them admitting substantial criticism of that organization? The structural contradiction between reformist ideology and stable management is not just the dilemma of left-wing parties when they achieve power. The question applies as much to the chairman of a company, the chief officer of a local social service, the chairman of the Supplementary Benefits Commission and the head of a university department as to a government minister. Can criticism be accepted of procedures and not staffing as well? I doubt it, if the social services are involved. And is a self-critical *style* of management possible without a different structure of management? May it not be time for patients to be consulted, if not participate, in the management of hospitals, and more of those in the community organize and administer their own community care? In the last analysis good social planning promotes the ends of democracy.

Notes

1. See 'In the Mental Hospital' – eleven articles printed in *Lancet* in 1955 and 1956.

2. See, for example, Oram, E.G., and Knowles, M.C., 'The Chronically Mentally Ill – Movements in a Rural Area: 1900-1961', in McLachlan, G. (ed.), *Problems and Progress in Medical Care*, Oxford University Press, 1964.

3. See also Townsend, P., 'The Need for a Social Plan', *New Society*, 14 December 1967.

4. Tooth, G., and Brooke, E., 'Trends in the Mental Hospital Population and their Effect on Future Planning', *Lancet*, 1 April 1961, p.710.

5. A Hospital Plan for England and Wales, Cmnd. 1604, H.M.S.O., 1962.

6. See, for example, Lindsay, J.S.B., *Lancet*, 1962 (i), p.354; Norton, A., *The Lancet*, 1961 (i), p.884; Political and Economic Planning, *Psychiatric Services in 1975*, 1963.

7. *Hospital Plan for Scotland*, Cmnd. 2877, Edinburgh, H.M.S.O., 1966.

8. Baldwin, H.A., 'The Growth of Mental Hospitalization: the S-shaped Curve', in Freeman, H., and Farndale, J., *New Aspects of the Mental Health Services*, Pergamon Press, 1967.

9. Jones, K., 'Too Few Psychiatric Beds', *New Society*, 10 September 1964; Gore, C.P., Jones, K., Taylor, W., and Ward, B., 'Needs and Beds – A Regional Census of Psychiatric Hospital Patients', *Lancet*, 29 August 1964, p.457; Jones, K., 'The Role and Function of the Mental Hospital', in Freeman, H., and Farndale, J., *Trends in the Mental Health Services*, Pergamon Press, 1963.

10. *The Hospital Building Programme: A Revision of the Hospital Plan for England and Wales*, Cmnd. 3000, H.M.S.O., 1966.

11. MacFarlane, G., *Capital Allocation in the Hospital Plan*, Department of Social Administration, L.S.E., 1963, (unpublished).

12. Fabian Research Series, no. 200, the Fabian Society, 1958.

13. *Annual Report for the Ministry of Health for 1966*, Cmnd. 3326, H.M.S.O., 1967, p.183, and *Annual Report for the Ministry of Health for 1967*, Cmnd. 3702, H.M.S.O., p.189.

14. *Annual Report of the Ministry of Health for 1965*, Cmnd. 3039, H.M.S.O., p.37.

15. *Annual Report of the Ministry of Health for 1967*, loc. cit., pp.184-5. There is no information available on the number of psychiatric beds covered by all building schemes.

16. For example, Wing, J.K., and Brown, G.W., 'Social Treatment of Chronic Schizophrenia: A Comparative Survey of Three Mental Hospitals', *Journal of Mental Science*, 1961, 107, p.847.

17. Jones, K., and Sidebotham, R., *Mental Hospitals at Work*, Routledge & Kegan Paul, 1962.

18. Townsend, P., 'Old People in Psychiatric and Geriatric Hospitals, Nursing Homes and Residential Homes', Freeman, H. (ed.), *Psychiatric Hospital Care*, Pergamon Press, 1966.

19. Morris, P., *Put Away: A Sociological Study of Hospitals for the Mentally Retarded*, Routledge & Kegan Paul, 1969.

20. Wing, L., and Wing, J.K., *The Camberwell Psychiatric Diseases Register* (unpublished), 1965; Wing, J.K., 'The Modern Management of Schizophrenia', in Freeman, H., and Farndale, J., *New Aspects of the Mental Health Services*, op.cit.

21. *Report of the Committee on Local Authority and Allied Personal Social Services* (The Seebohm Report), H.M.S.O., 1968, p.15.

22. Apte, R.Z., *Halfway Houses: A New Dilemma in Institutional Care*, Occasional Papers on Social Administration, no. 27, Bell, 1968.

23. Robb, B., (ed.), *Sans Everything*, Nelson, 1967.

24. *Hansard*, 9 July 1968, col. 214.

25. For example, 'The unpleasant conditions in which mental nurses have to train and work in so many of our out-of-date and over-crowded hospitals must act as a strong disincentive to recruitment. It goes without saying that an increase in the number of recruits coming forward would make possible a more careful selection of student nurses. This, in turn, would [eliminate] unsuitable candidates who might today be enrolled through sheer desperation . . .' *Policy for Mental Health*, op.cit., p.12.

12 The Argument for Comprehensive Schools *

Much of the evidence collected in recent years by sociologists, social psychologists and educationists about ability in relation to schooling and educational achievement suggests that Britain should abandon the tripartite structure of secondary schooling and develop comprehensive schools. The existing structure rests on three broad assumptions: that levels of ability remain roughly constant, at least from the age of ten or eleven; that only a small proportion of children, say a fifth or a quarter, are capable of benefiting from an 'academic' type of secondary education; and that it is possible to teach children to higher educational standards only when they are separated into different types of school according to their ability. Few social scientists would now accept any of these assumptions and I shall discuss them in turn.

First, a constant level of ability. The results of intelligence tests and other tests of ability are treated with more caution and scepticism than formerly. The I.Q. reflects verbal and arithmetical skills rather than qualities of creativity, industriousness and good judgement. Test scores have been found to be only crudely approximate because some children vary from test to test by ten points or more even when they have had previous practice. Over a period of two or three years some children vary by up to 25–30 points. Vernon concludes: 'One should never think of a child's I.Q. (or other test result) as accurate to 1 per cent. Rather, an I.Q. of say, 95 should be thought of as a kind of region or general level. Over several years, say from 6 to 10 or from 11 to 15, the most we can say is that there is a fair certainty (i.e. 10 to 1) of its lying between 80 and 110.' It is disturbing to compare this kind of statement by an expert with the comparative rigidity of streaming in primary schools and the low rates of transfer between different types of secondary school.

Secondly, the small 'academic' minority. Many more children than has been supposed are capable of benefiting from an academic type of education. The reports of the Crowther and Robbins committees both showed that there were huge reserves of ability in the population. In 1961 the number obtaining university entry qualifications was just under

*Paper given at a meeting called to announce the formation of the Comprehensive Schools Committee and first published in the *Guardian*, 30 September 1965.

7 per cent for both sexes, and was just under 9 per cent for boys only.

The Crowther Report indicates, on the basis of a survey of army recruits, that the figure of 9 per cent could be raised to 16 per cent if the same fraction of able working-class as of upper-middle-class children were successful. The committee quoted careful Swedish calculations which suggested that at least 28 per cent of young people could gain the equivalent of British university entry qualifications. Half of each age-group in California already enter higher education. The figure would probably come down to 25 to 30 per cent to represent the numbers obtaining the equivalent of British university entry qualifications. Persson gives a figure of 40 per cent passing the university entrance test in Oslo.

The Robbins committee was unable to 'specify an upper limit' for this country. The committee said only that the percentage of each age-group in England and Wales with entry qualifications was likely to grow from 6.9 in 1961 to 10.8 in 1973 and 14.5 in 1985. On present trends untapped ability was 'most unlikely to be fully mobilized within the next 20 years'. There is no reason why we should doubt that 40 per cent of our children have the capacity to take a university course and perhaps another 20 or 30 per cent at least five subjects in the G.C.E. at 'O' level.

I say this because good teaching over a number of years may not only help to raise children's mental and arithmetical ability and thus their I.Q., but allow them to reach unexpectedly high educational standards. A recent study of 1,000 boys who did not succeed at the 11-plus examination but went to public schools showed that 75 per cent passed the G.C.E. at 'O' level in five or more subjects (compared with 56 per cent of all grammar school leavers) and about a third of them passed two subjects at 'A' level. Between a fifth and a quarter went to university. These successes may be brought about by social and cultural influences at home, however, as well as by good teaching in the classroom.

Bernstein and others have begun to show that middle-class children not only have the well-known advantages of parental encouragement and more opportunity for quiet study. They are also introduced to conceptual frameworks through the 'formal' language as well as the public language that is used in the home environment. If we could overcome the handicaps of poverty, bad housing and lack of certain kinds of cultural stimulus, far more working-class children of 'lesser ability' could be given an academic secondary education.

Many of our ideas about the pattern of individual ability are derived unconsciously from the social structure. The belief that only 20 per cent of an age-group are capable of a grammar school type of education reflects the fact that only 20 per cent have had such an education. The streaming of children in primary schools into three groups — upper, middle and lower — reflects the division into social classes among the population at large. As Brian Jackson found, even when the school is large enough to have nine classes in each group, there are not nine streams but three streams with three classes in each stream.

The third mistaken assumption is that separate schools suit separate abilities. The division into three broad types of secondary school from the age of eleven, and streaming even before eleven, can be criticized severely. The Stockholm experiments provided the first really strong evidence in favour of the comprehensive system. Broadly they showed that in comprehensive schools children of higher academic ability perform at least as well as, and the children of lower ability rather better than, they do in segregated schools. Studies so far carried out in Britain point to the same conclusion — though among those of lower ability improvements are not uniform. In some comprehensive schools very high proportions of children are taking examinations at 'O' level and are entering sixth forms. The evidence in favour of unstreamed classes in primary schools also suggests it is wrong to suppose that bright children are 'held back' and dull children inhibited from trying in each other's presence.

Segregation into physically distinct schools at eleven is still advocated by some local authorities but it can no longer be justified — except as a temporary expedient. When parents of children who are admitted to secondary-modern schools begin to understand the shortcomings of selection at eleven and have more knowledge of the educational process the corridors of Town Hall power will really begin to hum.

The minimum arguments for comprehensive schools are therefore that the majority of children can profit from an academic type of education until at least sixteen; that since children's performance varies so uncertainly from year to year decisions about those qualifying for sixth-form work and higher education should be postponed to as late a stage as possible; and that the educational standards of the brightest children can be maintained but those of the academically weaker children significantly improved.

To these I would add a number of social arguments, which are really educational arguments in the widest sense. More children not only have access to a wide range of skills — from turning a lathe to learning Russian. They have access to a wide cross-section of children, who have different cultural backgrounds and different kinds of talent. Children will be better equipped to communicate with individuals at all social levels and, perhaps, a shade more comprehending of society and its problems than otherwise they might have been.

But, finally, we need to recognize that in applying the comprehensive principle to the school system we are doing no more than breaking with the past so that we can make a fresh start. This break does not mean we are solving all our educational problems, only adopting a framework which will make the task easier. There are rigidly separate streams in some comprehensive schools with little movement between one stream and another. Curricular and extra-curricular activities are devised so that there is a minimum of social interaction. There is scope for sharp argument and experiment about the forms of comprehensive schooling. But at least there will be a minimum fulfilment of the principle of equality of educational opportunity and a corporate social unity which may even spill over into adult life.

13 Seebohm and Family Welfare*

The Seebohm Committee's conclusion that the local social services must be unified is undoubtedly right. But the report does not make out an unremitting and unambiguous case for a major new service to take its place alongside health, education and social security, thus enhancing the quality of British society. Much of it gives the impression of recommending only a modest operation to tidy up anomalies and overlap without incurring greatly increased cost. The committee may have persuaded itself that this was politically expedient but if through lack of public enthusiasm the recommendations are watered down or shelved the committee will have only itself to blame. For it does not properly describe the extent of social need, nor does it set targets and priorities in the allocation of future resources or spell out all the uncomfortable implications for central and local authorities and social workers that a new philosophy of community care would really involve.

All thinking about the organization of services must start with the problems of the people whom they are expected to serve. This is the first step in planning. The committee did not undertake consumer or community research or systematically compare conditions in England and Wales with those in other countries. Its references to needs, though forceful, are secondary to a discussion of administration and are by no means as fully documented as recent evidence would allow (on the lines, say, of a recent report, *Health and Welfare Services in Britain in 1975,* by Deborah Paige and Kit Jones, Cambridge, 1966). If the case for a new service is to be fully made out the deprivations which affect large minorities of the population have to be laid bare for all to see. Statements such as 'the present services for children are falling far short of meeting the extent of the need for them', 'services for the physically handicapped are in urgent need of development', and 'the widespread belief that we have "community care" of the mentally disordered is, for many parts of the country, still a sad illusion and judging by published plans will remain so for years ahead', are all correct but do not go far enough. The range, scale and nature of the component problems must

* First published in *New Society,* 1 August 1968, as a review of the Seebohm Report *(Report of the Committee on Local Authority and Allied Personal Social Services).*

be made known. Otherwise it is difficult to judge what should be the size and emphases of any future service.

In particular three types of information are necessary. First, estimates have to be made of the numbers who are in general conditions of need. Among these conditions are poverty, handicap, illness, isolation, lack of parental care and difficulty in providing supportive care. For example, a substantial minority of the population, by the Government's as well as by independent reckoning, are living in poverty. Moreover, their numbers appear to have been growing, because the aged, disabled, members of large families and unemployed have been increasing relative to the total population and family allowances and some wage rates have been lagging.

Secondly, estimates have to be made of the needs unmet by particular services. For example, research in Denmark, the United States and Sweden and in local areas of England suggests that the registers of the physically handicapped in this country cover rather less than a third of the severely handicapped even below pensionable age. Again, different national surveys of the aged suggest that, quite apart from frequency. type and quality of service, the numbers receiving the home help and meals services are less than a third of what they ought to be.

Thirdly, estimates have to be made of needs unmet by particular local authorities. In an appendix to its report the committee gives some evidence of variation between authorities but does not link the data sufficiently to its argument in the text. Relative to population some authorities have home help, social work, handicapped persons' and sheltered housing services which are less than a quarter or a fifth as large as others. There is no evidence to justify these variations. Sometimes services are not provided at all. In 1965 as many as 32 of the 173 authorities had no adult training centres for the subnormal and 11 had no junior training centres. One question not yet answered is how the Government can prevent certain services in areas from falling far behind the national average. This is possibly more important than the scheduling of special areas of community development.

Thus in various ways it can be shown how desperately inadequate local community services are. There are too many people living in poverty, neglect and isolation and far too few, especially among the aged and disabled, receiving the local services for which it can be shown they are eligible. This is deplorable and must be put right. This is the case for dramatic expansion which underlies the case for the introduction of a unified service.

The committee is aware of many of these shortcomings but because it does not properly measure them it cannot easily determine priorities and say what should be the balance of functions of the new department.

Current evidence, when taken with population forecasts, suggests giving priority to the aged and handicapped (including the mentally subnormal), with these two groups accounting for a very large part indeed of the eventual expenditure and activity of the department.

But what kind of help should be given? Although the committee rightly stresses that administrators should have professional social work qualifications it would be wrong if the impression were given that casework was the *raison d'être* of the new department. The object of a service based on the principles of continuity of care and of preserving the family unit must be to substitute for the family when the individual has no family, and support it when its resources are inadequate. Home help services have to be greatly expanded in range and must include shopping, laundry, night attendance, evening relief and private excursions, as well as meals and domestic help. Wheelchairs, electric blankets, fireguards, bed linen, modern forms of heating, and many other aids and amenities have to be supplied in much greater quantities. Many more of the disabled have to be helped to transfer to more suitable housing without steps or stairs (much their biggest housing 'need'). Contrary to the committee's recommendation, the new department should control sheltered housing schemes. The tenants in these schemes require a variety of home services and the department would be better equipped than the housing department to decide who should be admitted to them rather than to residential institutions.

An essential part of the organization of help is to contact people needing help. Keeping the isolated and handicapped in touch with the social services is too big a problem to be left to chance contacts and the committee should have recommended such a service. Only on the basis of routine visiting will authorities become convinced of the extent of their responsibilities. A start might be made with those aged seventy-five and over, later to be extended to all the elderly and disabled. In particular, social workers could check during visits that people were receiving all the benefits from social security and other services for which they qualified.

Casework versus the provision of physical resources is one important issue; community versus institutional care is another — which the committee does not manage to resolve. It just isn't good enough to pretend that 'community' care includes residential care in communal institutions — which might be old workhouses for 200 people or modern buildings for 50 or 60. The lives of these people are fundamentally different from those living in private households in ordinary neighbourhoods. As much as £33 million was spent on residential institutions for the elderly and disabled in 1965, but only £12 million on home help services. This ratio is wrong and should be reversed as quickly as possible. Communal institutions mid-way between private household and hospital should eventually be abandoned. As society becomes more prosperous, and housing, particularly sheltered housing, more plentiful, and as domiciliary services themselves become more effective, people can be maintained in ordinary households right up to the point of requiring admission to hospital.

A policy of community care as an alternative to institutional care would be consistent with the practice of at least one of the component services. For many years the object of the children's service has been to keep children with their parents in their own homes and, when that has been impossible, to place them in a foster-home or a 'residential' unit very much like an ordinary household. Yet because in the past it has lacked the means, the welfare service has practised a rather different policy for the aged and handicapped. Now there is the chance to integrate the two policies. This is why it is important for the new department to have control of sheltered housing.

There is also evidence that large numbers of people in institutions are capable of living in the community and, when presented with a realistic choice, would wish to do so. Resources would be released for home services and it would be possible in time to place the remaining institutions, which by then would be composed of residents hardly distinguishable from long-term hospital patients, under the area health boards envisaged in the Minister of Health's new Green Paper.

Most of the committee's proposals for administrative reorganization are sound. The arguments for the amalgamation of children's and welfare departments and for the transfer, following the White Paper, *Children in Trouble,* of functions and staff from the probation service to the new department are convincing. Its decision not to amalgamate the social care and health departments (while transferring some of the major functions of the latter to the former) is justified less for the reasons adduced than for the lack of suitable training and experience on the part of medical officers and the need to develop elsewhere preventive medicine and the medical care of the chronic sick. But those mental health staff concerned in the community with the short-term as distinct from the long-term mentally ill might be attached to health centres or group practices rather than to the new department. The general practitioner's willingness to care for the mentally ill badly requires encouragement.

The Government should accept the argument for administrative unification and set up, in consequence, a Ministry of Family Welfare, distinct from the Ministries of Health and Social Security. Whether the three ministries might then be linked under a senior secretary of state having a social planning office at his command is another matter. Since health and education are also social services, the new local department might be best relabelled 'Family Welfare' or 'Family Help'.

The different problems of training become urgent. There is an immediate crisis of leadership. Few of the contenders for the post of principal officer of the new department have all the right qualifications. They might attend specially arranged courses, like one beginning in October, which deal not so much with social work as social planning. For the conception of social work must now change. The provision of physical services and resources and the representation of the individual and the family in the struggle to obtain resources from other departments, and not the practice of individual casework, becomes paramount. The concern should be with the quality of life and the integration and development of the local community.

Contrary to what the committee proposes, this means making the training council independent of government. It means strengthening professional ethics at the expense of employee loyalties. It involves rejecting the ill-conceived Williams Committee proposals for separate training for residential care. It also involves giving far more emphasis to short courses and sandwich courses than full-time one-year and two-year courses for junior staff and short refresher courses for existing field and administrative staff. Many are middle-aged but will be working in the service for another twenty years and the Seebohm Committee, like other bodies, tends to neglect their training needs.

The democratization of the service should not be forgotten. The committee writes sympathetically about consumer and citizen participation but does not come forward with strong recommendations. Representatives of those who receive services should be on every appropriate committee. The elderly and disabled should be members of the committees of management of homes. There should be a strong central welfare board set up independently by government not only to assist voluntary associations with such things as training and relief staff but also to act as a clearing house for new ideas and experiments and review the progress and inspect the standards of local services on behalf of the public. The concept of civil rights should inspire every government action and committee.

A unified local family welfare service could help to breathe new life into the darkest recesses of industrial society. But the ideal of community care and the extent of deprivation must be presented more powerfully if the service is to capture the support and enthusiasm of the public, and so attract the greatly increased resources it badly requires.

The Objectives of the New Social Service *

All planning must involve the formulation of objectives. The Seebohm Committee was appointed on 20 December 1965 to 'review the organization and responsibilities of the local authority personal social services in England and Wales, and to consider what changes are desirable to secure an effective family service'. The committee decided that these terms of reference allowed them to consider the needs of individuals and married couples as well as families and to inquire into the whole of the work of children's and welfare departments and those elements of the work of health, education and housing departments which were concerned with social work. The scope of the inquiry could therefore be widely drawn. Events in Scotland had moved more swiftly. The Kilbrandon Report in 1964 (Scottish Home and Health Department, *Children and Young Persons* (Scotland), Cmnd. 2306, London, H.M.S.O. 1964) led to a working group being set up which reported on reorganization of services in 1966 (*Social Work and the Community: Proposals for Reorganizing Local Authority Services in Scotland*, Cmnd. 3605, London, H.M.S.O. 1966). This resulted quickly in legislation.

How should the Seebohm Committee have set about the job of defining policy objectives? There are a number of awkward choices. First, subjective opinions can be collected from both consumers and suppliers of services about the quality of existing services, how they might be improved in the future and what new services might be added. The comments of those with direct current experience of particular services can be illuminating but the comments of others may be largely meaningless. The opinions of individuals offer little guidance to the policy-maker unless they are founded on information and experience. Even then it is difficult to evaluate them without a knowledge of the social circumstances and situation of those expressing them. The same is true of subjective expressions of need. The individual may feel deprived even if others consider he has no cause and even if there appear to be no objective criteria to justify his feeling. Equally, he may deny any need whatsoever and yet be destitute, ill or live in squalor. Subjective deprivation is subtle and hard to ascertain, because there are social rules and situations which govern whether or not and when it will be

* First published in *The Fifth Social Service*, the Fabian Society, May 1970.

expressed, and yet this information is not superfluous. It is one bit of vital information in planning.

Secondly, there are conventional or social 'views' or definitions of needs and standards of service. These too can be identified and collected. There are social norms about the upbringing of children, the care of the ill and the handicapped and the help that should be given to families who are poor. These are often implicit in behaviour, organization and opinion rather than consciously formulated, and have to be analysed. Sometimes they form the basis of law and regulation. For example, government and local authority regulations embody social views about decent standards of housing and the point at which houses or flats are treated as overcrowded. Different societies (and indeed different sections of any single society) may define these standards differently but in principle the social scientist can measure the extent to which they are or are not met. He can help a society to understand how practice may differ from precept. How many in the population fall below the poverty line as defined socially by public assistance scales? How many are living in conditions treated by society as unsanitary or overcrowded? How many are in need of hospital care, residential care, sheltered housing, rehabilitation, special schooling, domiciliary service and so on, according to criteria implicit or explicit in laws and regulations and government policy statements? In examining social or normative definitions of need the social scientist can help to bring them into the open, reveal contradictions and loose ends and show the different functions played by law, regulation, policy and custom. He can even show the degrees of efficiency with which different standards are being met and therefore suggest what might be gained with alternative emphases in policy.

This gives a rough outline of a two-stage procedure or model that might be followed in planning. Certainly we would have a basis for comparing subjective with collectively acknowledged need, and policy aims with policy achievements. We could pursue the connections between the rise of subjective deprivation in particular groups and professions, change in society's definition of need and change in society's services and practices.

But this would be insufficient as a basis for planning. Social policy would be viewed too much from within, psychologically and institutionally. Services would be judged too much in terms of objectives already defined than of those which have yet to be defined, too much in terms of needs already recognized, subjectively and socially, than of those which have still to be recognized. Standards and needs have to be judged also from some external standpoint. While ultimately it may be difficult to substantiate a true objectivity, nonetheless this goal is worth striving for. Needs can be shown to exist, independent of the feelings engendered within a particular society and independent of those which are recognized by society's institutions. Just as there is subjective deprivation and socially acknowledged deprivation, so there is objective deprivation. A man may not feel deprived and he may not even meet society's rules defining someone who is deprived, and yet he may be shown to be deprived. He lacks what his fellows can be demonstrated to to have and suffers in some tangible and measurable way as a consequence.

This would complete a three-part model for the analysis of social policy and the production of policy objectives. But how could need be defined objectively? How could standards be evolved, independent of those that have been developed historically and which society recognizes? The interconnections between the concepts of inequality and deprivation provide the best answer. Inequality has two aspects. There is inequality of resources: individuals and families fall into horizontal strata, according to their cash incomes, assets, fringe benefits received from employers, and benefits in kind received from the public social services. Through rigorous comparison between regions and communities as well as individuals and families the inequalities in the distribution of resources can be revealed in elaborate detail, including, for example, inequalities of space at home, working conditions and school facilities. There is also inequality of social integration: individuals, families and ethnic communities fall into vertical categories according to the degree of isolation or segregation from society. People vary in the density and range of their household, family, community and social networks; and some populations of hospitals and other institutions are extraordinarily isolated. There are inequalities of social support in illness, infirmity, disability and bereavement. While planning cannot make good private loss it can provide substitute and compensating services. Visiting services can be developed for the isolated elderly and home help services for the infirm and disabled. Services like teaching in English and information and legal aid services can also be developed as integrating mechanisms and protection against exploitation for immigrant communities.

Complementing these two measures of inequality would be measures of deprivation. In descending the scale of income or of other resources, such as assets, there is a point at which the individual's or the family's participation in the ordinary activities, customs and pleasures of the community is likely to fall off more sharply than the reduction of income. His opportunities to share in the pursuits and meet the needs enjoined by the culture become grossly restricted. As a consequence he may be malnourished, inadequately housed, disadvantaged in schooling, unable to use public services like buses and trains, and restricted to impoverished sectors of the social services. If he belongs to an ethnic group which feels itself to be cold-shouldered by external society and which responds by turning in upon its own improvised resources, he runs the risk of being by-passed by new scientific and cultural developments, excluded from the ordinary range of information and communication media, ignorant of legal and welfare rights and left with the housing, the land and the commodities least desired by outsiders. If he is someone isolated from the community because he has not married, has been bereaved, has lost contemporaries during the ageing process, has become separated from family and friends because of work or migration, is disabled or lives in a sparsely populated area, or is affected by a number of these factors, he may not be put in touch with health and welfare services at necessary times, may remain unaware of social developments (for example, rent rebate schemes, a change to decimal coinage, reading and hearing aids) and *become* deprived and perhaps liable to exploitation even if not deprived beforehand. The interaction of the two kinds of inequality – poverty of resources and isolation – can have devastating consequences for some sections of the population during periods of rapid technological and institutional change.

Subjective Opinion as a Basis for Planning

Such is a possible framework of thought and analysis. How did the Seebohm Committee proceed? First, subjective opinion. Through memoranda presented as evidence and through various consultations the committee learned the views of suppliers of services. The opinions of 'all those concerned with the services' were felt to be important but the opinions of those utilizing the services were not collected. 'We were, regrettably, unable to sound consumer reaction to the services in any systematic fashion' (p.21). This decision was taken, the committee says, because a research programme would have delayed publication by a year or two. But the committee took 2½ years to report, and the Government took a further twenty months to react to the report. Much research of value could have been launched, even if some of it could not have reached fruition until the months following the publication of the report. The gross lack of information about the nature and functions of the services covered by the committee, and about consumer opinion, could hardly have gone unnoticed. The Younghusband Committee on local authority social workers had toiled for 3½ years in the late 1950s and had dared to conclude, 'We should like to have undertaken a complementary inquiry into the reactions of those using the services. An investigation of this nature would, however, have prolonged our own inquiries unduly'. And they went on, 'We were struck . . . by the lack of any systematic study of the part played by social workers in meeting needs within the framework of the social services. Such information could have had an important bearing on our own inquiry.

We should like to draw attention to the desirability of such study. We think much of the confusion in regard to the functions of social workers in the health and welfare services, as elsewhere, is due to lack of analyses of this kind'. (*Report of the Working Party on Social Workers in the Local Authority Health and Welfare Services*, H.M.S.O., 1959, pp. 2-3.)

But the Seebohm Committee appear to have ignored this recommendation and failed to clear up the confusion. Other committees have instigated and brought to a successful culmination very large research inquiries within a similar time span. The Robbins Committee on higher education, for example, had launched a very ambitious research programme and yet had reported within 2½ years.

The implications of failing to find out consumer opinion run deep. Some far-reaching criticisms of professional activity may be either undetected or underestimated. Some needs which are felt by individuals or groups may be ignored. Most important, some of the rights of the consumer to a voice in planning and administration may be unrecognized.

Social Standards

The Seebohm Committee did in fact go some way towards fulfilling the second and third parts of our planning model. They attempted to present conventional views on needs and standards of service. They also attempted to collate statistics giving objective measures of need. However, such secondary analysis as was carried out was neither complete nor consistent.

For example, insufficient effort was made to define the criteria by which people are helped by the existing services and to subject these to searching examination. A rather haphazard collection of over a hundred pages of appendices attached to the committee's report contain chiefly an account of administrative structure and statistics, and the data are not digested and integrated with the argument in the body of the text. What are existing standards of service? Which children are taken into care and why? How are homeless families defined in practice, and is it logical to exclude single persons and married couples from services? Which disabled people are placed on registers and how does this vary among the different areas of the country? These are the kinds of question which have to be answered in detail if the standards of service which prevail at present are to be delineated.

Again, the attempts to measure objectively the extent of unmet need were very clumsy. Such attempts can determine the conclusions which may be reached not only about the *structure* but also the *scale* and *scope* of a future service. Thus it is vital to ask whether there are any important needs which are totally unmet at present and for which new social services might be developed. In terms of possible contribution to social integration there might be a public radio-telephone service and a transport service for certain disabled or elderly persons and their relatives and friends; an architect and design service for do-it-yourself enthusiasts; a mobile national housing repairs and improvement squad; neighbourhood and home tuition in speaking and writing English for immigrant families and handicapped pupils; and a shopping and sightseeing touring service for the hospitalized and infirm. Only by systematic study of social inequalities, comparing the circumstances of different families and individuals and comparing the real functions of the social services with implicit as well as explicit social objectives can these lacunae be revealed. The Seebohm Committee did not produce guidelines for fresh developments in social policy as a result of analysing social conditions and policies.

However, it did not measure possible developments in existing services either. Chapters on services for children, old people, the physically handicapped, the mentally ill and subnormal, other local health services and housing seem to have been allocated to different authors. This must partly explain their uneven quality. Some of these neglect valuable sources of information. For example, there is no analysis of trends in the development of services in relation to previous and prospective changes in population structure (as in Paige, D. and Jones, K., *Health and Welfare Services in Britain in 1975*, Cambridge University Press, 1966). Some chapters, like that on old people, mix the trivial with the crucial as if they were of equal importance. Present shortcomings are, however, emphasized. But they are emphasized without corresponding documentation and therefore lose thrust and power. A refrain runs through a number of the chapters. The services for children are 'sadly inadequate' (p. 53); for old people 'underdeveloped, limited and patchy' (p. 90); housing for old people 'quite inadequate' (p. 92); services for the physically handicapped 'in urgent need of development' (p. 101); for the chronic sick 'seriously inadequate' (p. 118); and community care for the mentally disordered 'still a sad illusion and judging by published plans will remain so for years ahead' (p. 107). Yet the committee failed to bring these indictments together in a major challenge to the Government and public to find massive new resources for the creation of a major new service. Consider the weak advocacy in the introductory pages for a single department and in particular the incomprehensible surrender of judgements about social need to judgements about what is politically expedient in the statement that 'it would be naïve to think that any massive additional resources will be made available in the near future' (p. 15). Even if the committee believed this to be true why did they have to withhold an argument which might have captured the imagination of the public and induced a readiness to provide more resources?

By failing to document the extent to which services also fell short of needs the committee made it difficult for priorities and the eventual structure of the service to be defined. The nearest it came in fact to specifying requirements on the basis of evidence was in the first few paragraphs of its discussion of services for children. The committee accepted an estimate from Appendix Q that '*at least* one child in ten in the population will need special educational, psychiatric or social help before it reaches the age of 18 but at present *at most* one child in twenty-two is receiving such help' (p. 53). This is a deceptively exact statement. What does it mean? The estimate of need includes children who are in poverty, have a whole range of physical handicaps, including asthma and speech defects, are subnormal and have psychiatric disorders, are in homeless and fatherless families, as well as children who are taken into care and delinquent boys 'with at least three court appearances'. Quite a variety of trouble. And the reader who attempts to find which needs are least well met will emerge utterly baffled after studying Appendix Q. One table includes statistics of the number of children experiencing a condition at a particular time (poverty) and a condition at any time during the first seventeen years of life (admitted to care). There is no discussion of the extent to which the local authority children's service fails to meet need. All that can safely be concluded is that the bulk of unmet needs are those — for special education and training, psychiatric supervision, health services, housing, home help, and financial help — which lie outside the scope of the children's service, as formerly administered. But in discussing the new social services department the consequences for its structure and functions are not drawn by the committee.

Yet this matter is crucial if we are to decide what should be the character and function of the future service. If material aid is to be dominant then casework may have to be minimal. If the children's part of the social work services is reasonably well developed then the fastest growing parts may need to be those for the elderly and disabled. This too will be crucial in determining the direction which the new service takes and the kind of staff required. In Appendix L the committee lists 90,000 staff working in 1966 in services proposed for inclusion in the new Seebohm department. Only 7,700 of them were child care officers and other social workers. There may be a greater need for a small number of highly trained planners and managerial staff and for a large number of ancillary workers, like home helps and visitors who receive short spells of training, than for a much larger middle tier of field-workers with a fairly lengthy training.

The Resulting Aims of the New Service

The relationship between research or the collection of evidence and the identification of need is therefore critical. And it is the identification of need on the basis of demonstrable inequality of resources and of social integration that can justify the choice of objectives and the specification of those objectives. It was because the Seebohm Committee did not properly establish needs that it did not properly formulate the aims of the new service. If the reader combs the report he will not find a full and unambiguous statement of the aims of the service. This criticism should not be misunderstood. There are numerous statements about the possible aims of the new service, but these are mostly 'second-order' aims. Thus, amalgamation is said to give the service more power to speak up for a rightful share of resources within local administration and help to make the service more adequate (pp. 30, 32-3 and 46-7). It is said to break down artificial boundaries between services, reduce divided responsibility and lead to better coordination and continuity (pp. 31, 34-5 and 44-5). It is said to allow the development of more emphasis on preventive as compared with casualty services for social distress (pp. 136-41). A number of specific aims are also expressed in the chapters on particular services.

Perhaps the best approximation to a general statement is the first paragraph of Chapter 7 of the report:

> We are convinced that if local authorities are to provide an effective family service they must assume wider responsibilities than they have at present for the prevention, treatment and relief of social problems. The evidence we have received, the visits we have undertaken, and our own experience leave us in no doubt that the resources at present allocated to these tasks are quite inadequate. Much more ought to be done, for example, for the very old and the under fives, for physically and mentally handicapped people in the community, for disturbed adolescents and for the neglected flotsam and jetsam of society. Moreover, the ways in which existing resources are organized and deployed are inefficient. Much more ought to be done in the fields of prevention, community involvement, the guidance of voluntary workers and in making fuller use of voluntary organizations. We believe that the best way of achieving these ends is by setting up a unified social service department which will include the present children's and welfare services together with some of the social service functions of health, education and housing departments. (p. 44)

An impression is given of inchoate, multiple aims and loose reasoning. Is the primary purpose to provide family services for those who lack a family or whose family resources are meagre? If so, there would be profound implications for the organization of residential homes and

hostels for children, the elderly and the mentally and physically handicapped. Either the residential homes would all have to be organized on
a 'family' basis, which is an aim that would require detailed exposition,
or a policy of closing them down and integrating their occupants in
different types of private households would have to be followed. There
would be profound implications also for professional social work roles,
staffing and training. The system would have to be recast to a very
considerable extent.

In opening the debate on the second reading of the bill in the House
of Commons the Secretary of State for Social Services, Mr Crossman,
plainly felt the need for a statement of aims. He said:

> The primary objective of the personal social services we can best
> describe as strengthening the capacity of the family to care for its
> members and to supply, as it were, the family's place where necessary;
> that is, to provide as far as may be social support or if necessary a
> home for people who cannot look after themselves or be adequately
> looked after in their family. This is not the only objective of the
> personal social services. They have an important role to play in com-
> munity development, for example. But it has been the idea of forming
> a 'family' service that has inspired the call for a review of the organi-
> zation of the services with which the Bill is concerned. (*Hansard*,
> 26 February 1970, Col. 1407)

He did not attempt to spell out what this view would imply for the
reorganization of services. Had he attempted to do so, or had the Seebohm Committee done so beforehand, there might not have been such
a friendly welcome to the bill from all political quarters in Parliament.

For the really important issues have been ducked in securing a precarious consensus. What kind of family relationships should the State
support and in what circumstances? How far must residential institutions
be abandoned in favour of true community care? Is professional independence and the opportunity for the expression of public dissent
threatened by monolithic bureaucratic conformity? Is the social worker
an agent of social control or an articulate representative of minority
interests and views? Should community development include a network
of information and legal services, a policy of racial integration and an
extension of democracy by means of local pressure-groups and protest
groups?

A Policy for Seebohm Departments

A radical statement of objectives would have to start by revealing the
extent of inequality of resources and of social isolation and separation.
Community development would be seen in terms of the equalization of

resources, the reduction of isolation, family support and community integration. I will describe these in turn.

1. *Equalization of resources.* Although national social services, such as social insurance, family allowances and taxation, would be primarily concerned with the redistribution of resources, local social services have a major part to play in equalizing amenities, providing special kinds of housing, supplementing transport services for the elderly and disabled, supplying aids in the home for the handicapped, delivering meals, undertaking housing repairs and improvement, and restocking houses which have become denuded because of debts, drug addiction, alcoholism or a husband's desertion. The identification and mobilization of resource needs would be a major part of the work of the social worker. The Seebohm department should take the initiative locally in equalizing facilities between different sub-areas of the authority and identifying and meeting the special needs of particular communities. For this there must be an area resource plan.

2. *The reduction of isolation.* One important means of reducing isolation is by organizing routine visiting services. The Seebohm Committee lamentably failed to understand the importance of these, particularly as a means of prevention and developing comprehensive services. Once routine visiting and assessment is started many sceptics will finally become convinced of the need to expand services. A start could be made with services for people of advanced age, later extending to all the elderly and to the handicapped, including families with handicapped children. One valuable feature of such a service is that social workers could check systematically whether people were receiving the various local and national benefits for which they were eligible. Isolation can also be greatly reduced by means of day clubs and centres, group holidays and improved methods of communication (including telephones). By extension to ethnic groups the same principles can be applied.

3. *Support for the family.* We have to remind ourselves that any policy aimed at replacing the family is inconceivable in present or prospective conditions. The Seebohm Committee did not consider the evidence that exists of the functions played by the family, and its strengths and shortcomings, as a means of obtaining insights into policy. Certainly the 'welfare' work of the family for children, the handicapped and the aged, dwarfs that of the officially established social services. And certainly family relationships help to keep people in touch with the feelings and problems of all age-groups, and also help them achieve a sense of individual identity and integrate them with a variety of social groups. Those with slender family resources are those who most commonly receive and need the help of welfare services. (See, for example, Shanas, E., *et al.*, *Old People in Three Industrial Societies,* Routledge, 1968,

Chapters 5 and 14.) Home help services can include shopping, laundry, night attendance, evening relief and accompanied outings, as well as the preparation of meals and domestic cleaning. Several research reports have shown that they need to be expanded rapidly. A recent official survey found that the home help service could be doubled or tripled. (Government Social Survey, *The Home Help Service*, H.M.S.O., 1970.) Adoption and foster-care in approved conditions are extensions of the same principles.

4. This merges with the fourth aim, of *community integration*. Any logical development of a policy of family support must lead to a policy of community as against institutional care. The Seebohm Committee equivocated between the two and did not call attention to the fact, for example, that nearly three times as much is spent by local authorities on residential institutions as on home help services for the elderly and disabled. It also failed to anticipate and resolve a possible conflict between the personnel from children's and welfare departments. The aim of the former has been broadly to keep children with their parents in their own homes and when that cannot be done to place them in foster homes or residential units similar in structure and operation to the family household. I believe that this policy should be applied consistently to handicapped adults and the elderly as well, and that the subjective and objective evidence so far collected supports it. Yet because in the past the local authority welfare department has lacked the means it has practised a rather different policy, of swelling the number of small residential institutions.

The Seebohm Committee recommended that the home help service should be transferred to the new department but did not also see the importance of placing the provision and management of sheltered housing under the same auspices. If at the time of admission to residential institutions the handicapped and the elderly (and their relatives) had a genuine choice of either sheltered housing in the community (with home services if necessary) or a residential institution the vast majority would opt for the former and be capable of living there up to the time of requiring admission to hospital. Demand for residential institutions would decline. The new Seebohm departments could not of course start shutting down residential institutions overnight but they could adopt bold but feasible plans giving priority to sheltered housing and home services and gradually reducing residential accommodation. Residential institutions for the elderly and infirm could be transferred gradually to the new area health authorities and placed under the charge of geriatricians and others concerned with the nursing and medical care of the incapacitated. They would concentrate the attentions of the new Seebohm-type departments upon community care.

There are other arguments for reducing the emphasis on long-term institutional care, as shown in the anxious discussion going on recently about hospitals for the mentally handicapped. There is evidence in many cases of loss of contacts with relatives and friends without the substitution of social relations with fellow residents. There is the restriction of occupational activity and evidence of loneliness and apathy — by comparison with people of comparable age and physical condition outside. And quite apart from the deplorably low standards of amenities there is also the organizational rigidity of institutional life, which inevitably creates severe problems of adjustment and integration for residents from diverse backgrounds. Many old people are dismayed at the interruption of a lifetime's routine, loss of contact with locality and family and reduction of privacy and identity. The closer a residential institution approximates to the scale, privacy and freedom of the private household the greater the qualified expression of contentment. The promise in policy to protect people from admission to institutions except in extreme ill-health could attract public enthusiasm for the new service. In the 1950s and 1960s 'community care' has been interpreted variously and because of this is regarded with a measure of cynicism by some students, doctors and social workers. Even the term 'community' has no settled meaning in the social sciences (see, for example, Stacey, M. 'The Myth of Community Studies', *British Journal of Sociology,* June 1969). But if presented along the lines outlined here, of the equalization of resources, support of the family, and support for the individual to maintain a private household and an 'ordinary' pattern of local relations as opposed to entering a communal institution community care can become a meaningful objective.

Community integration means more, however, than community care. It means the promotion of citizen rights and of certain kinds of group activity. Tony Lynes puts the problem succinctly: 'The poor, as such, are in a weak bargaining position. The circumstances which make them poor also tend to make them powerless. Short of violent protest, just how are the homeless and the slum-dwellers, the disabled and the fatherless, to become a force on their own behalf?' (See *The Fifth Social Service, op. cit.* p. 120.) The Seebohm department can foster this self-assertiveness but only if its relationship with local democracy is carefully worked out, its professional semi-independence of local bureaucracy emphasized and the nature of and training for social work re-stated. This is a tall order. Perhaps the best chapter in the Seebohm Report is on community development.

The term 'community development' is used primarily to denote work with neighbourhood groups. Community development in this country is seen as a process whereby local groups are assisted to clarify and express their needs and objectives and to take collective action to attempt to meet them. It emphasizes the involvement of the people themselves in determining and meeting their own needs. The role of the community worker is that of a source of information and expertise, a stimulator, a catalyst and an encourager. (p. 148)

This view was cautiously presented, however, as adding to existing conceptions of social work rather than replacing them. Extra appointments and experiments were recommended. Certainly the conception of group work is beginning to be worked out in more detail. In 1969 an Association for Groupwork was proposed (McNay, M., *The Concept of Groupwork in the Field of Social Work,* Association for Groupwork, 21a Kingsland High Street, London E.8). Much can be done in organizing tenants' associations, groups of mental hospital out-patients and of drug addicts, the homeless and so on. But group work can only be developed effectively if there are swift improvements in information services, legal services and political machinery.

Local political machinery has not been examined carefully in relation to community development and the evolution of the local social services. The Redcliffe-Maud Commission did not devote very much attention to this question and the opportunity was not taken up in the government's White Paper on local government reform (Cmnd. 4276). There is a haphazard mushrooming of new procedures. The proposals of the Skeffington Report for a community forum and community development officers (*People and Planning,* H.M.S.O., 1969) and of the Green Paper on the Health Service need to be linked with the work of the Community Relations Council and Race Relations Board, the Home Office experiments in community development, Ministry of Housing experiments in urban aid and the Seebohm proposals for the participation of the public in the local social services. Much more coherent systems of public involvement in the management of the social services (schools, residential homes, hospitals, day centres and so on), complaints procedures, and accountability of those administering services need to be worked out. At every level the traditional British assumption of the appropriateness of a hierarchical 'class' structure, needs to be questioned. The consumer should have a much stronger voice in many different and even modest contexts. There is no reason, for example, why old people in residential homes should not have a representative committee which advises on a diary of events, the menu, the operating rules of management and other relevant matters.

The Seebohm departments should offer information shops in shopping centres. But the main national network of information services should be administered independently of local government. While there are a large number of Citizen's Advice Bureaux throughout the country, they are not to be found in many areas and are run on a shoe-string in others.

From aiding and abetting the individual and the family by providing information in a digestible form, it is a logical next step to offer better legal services and to relate the two. In recent years there has been a growth of interest in the social responsibilities of the legal profession (Abel-Smith, B. and Stevens, R., *In Search of Justice*, Allen Lane, 1968; Whitaker, B., *Participation and Poverty*, Fabian Research Series 272, 1968; Zander, M., *Lawyers and the Public Interest*, 1968; Lester, A., *Democracy and Individual Rights*, Fabian Tract 390, 1969). Legal aid for poor families is grossly restricted and is mainly taken up with aid for matrimonial proceedings. There is a strong argument for a two-stage development in information and legal centres. Experimental schemes to increase the amount and quality of legal aid and advice should be financed by the Government and an incentive scheme introduced to encourage a better distribution of lawyers and persuade more of them to work in poor areas. At a second stage, a National Citizens' Rights Council should be established with members appointed by the Crown on the advice of the Lord Chancellor (Brooke, R., Field, F., and Townsend, P., *A Policy to Establish the Legal Rights of Low Income Families*, Poverty Pamphlet 1, Child Poverty Action Group, 1969; and Abel-Smith, B., and Stevens, R., op. cit., p. 271). The Government's record in reforming and extending legal services has been dismal and there is as yet little realization of what can be done to buttress and accelerate community development and the extension of democracy through legal and information services. In the meantime the Child Poverty Action Group established in April 1970 an experimental Citizen's Rights Office, including both legal and information services under its director, Mrs Audrey Harvey. Some other experiments are being tried elsewhere, for example, in Notting Hill, London, (*Freedom and Choice: A. Community Planning Project for Notting Hill*, Notting Hill Housing Service and Research Group, June 1969). Inevitably such experimental offices will need to have very close relations with the new Seebohm departments, and can do much to offer short courses of training in welfare rights to social workers.

The repercussions for the type of work undertaken by Seebohm-type departments would be considerable. There would be greater stress on the provision of information, the exploration and notification of need for financial, material and domestic aid, the initiation of contacts between families in need and appropriate pressure-groups as well as appropriate social and occupational groups, and, finally, representation of the needs and problems of families to authority — housing and education departments, supplementary benefit offices, the new lower tier local councils proposed by the Redcliffe-Maud Commission and the district committees proposed by the Green Paper on the Health Service, as well as the new main councils and the central departments of government. All this demands a large measure of professional autonomy on the part of senior staff. It also has ramifications for the training and ideology of social workers.

What is at stake is the quality of family and community life and the whole direction of community development. Is the new Seebohm service to be a poorly financed, meagre department which takes the edge off the distress and deprivation arising in modern society and which, in effect, reinforces the assumptions of an increasingly inegalitarian society? Or is it to be the fifth major social service, on a scale equivalent, eventually, in manpower and expenditure to the health, education, housing and social security services, which has a deliberate commitment to the reduction of inequalities of resources and of social isolation, whether of individuals or groups? A force for conformity to hierarchical society, or a force for non-conformity in an equal one?

The Seebohm Committee did not undertake the research or adequately assess the evidence that is available so as to establish community needs. As a consequence it did not express clearly the objectives of the service, its priorities and its future organization, structure and functions. The case for doubling or tripling material and domestic services, implementing community care through the rapid development, for example, of visiting services and sheltered housing and involving the public more effectively in the management of services was not made, or not made forcefully. Although the committee recommended a variety of reforms, the one given greatest attention was expressed in terms of administrative unification of local social services or a tidying-up operation believed to pave the way for greater co-ordination of service. Conflicting elements in the proposed department — such as casework and group work, material aid and advisory services, and differences of aim between children's and welfare officers — were not identified or raised for discussion. However, the problems which might arise as a consequence of extending the power of officials over a larger area, creating a monopoly of certain kinds of service, weakening some citizens' power to seek redress for maladministration and neglect through alternative organizations, and emphasizing the professional power of social work, were not examined critically enough. With minor changes, except for a failure to provide for effective central direction, the Government has incorporated the main recommendations in the Local Authority Social Services Bill.

In short, a great opportunity has been missed. It is an opportunity to launch a major new Family or Community Welfare Service (for that would be a more accurate term) and information services and legal services in a costly programme of community development. Such a programme is badly needed. The isolation and deprivation of the elderly and disabled, the poverty of environment of some local authority areas, such as their lack of play facilities, the difficulties in adversity of ordinary families with children, the problems of looking after elderly and handi-capped dependants and the fear of losing one's home and having to enter an institution, are problems which are widely recognized and should be of central concern to the new service. They are seen to diminish the quality of life itself. The formal aims of a programme of community development, which arise from an analysis of different kinds of inequal-ity, should be fourfold: (i) the equalization of resources locally; (ii) the reduction of isolation; (iii) family support; and (iv) community integra-tion.

The first Annual General Meeting of the British Association of Social Workers is bound to be a rather heady occasion, especially as it takes place only a few months after the passing of an Act of Parliament to reorganize and amalgamate the personal social services. Vital decisions by the Government, the local authorities and the profession itself have still to be taken, in defining policies, preparing programmes, determining an administrative structure, making senior appointments, deciding priorities, allocating resources and reviewing the consequences of all this for training, research and information. It would be wrong, of course, to suggest that either an Act of Parliament or the formal consolidation of a profession represents in itself a significant social change. Neither of these events necessarily leads to an upsurge of spending or a marked change in activity overnight. Indeed, the Seebohm Committee and the last Labour Government both went out of their way to emphasize the increased efficiency to be gained from reorganization rather than from increased spending and manpower.(1)

Still, expectations have been raised and if, instead of being diverted into professional rivalries, energies can be employed shrewdly to persuade or compel the Government into more generous planning then this period of administrative and professional flux could be historic indeed. The fifth social service could yet be properly established in this decade rather than inched forward in a piecemeal fashion during the next fifty years. But how do we inform ourselves better about the scale or nature of the effort that is required? There have to be elaborate measures of need and of performance. There is evidence in support of a dramatic expansion of the local welfare services, and this has to be pressed long and remorselessly upon the Government. The evidence arises from official sources, such as studies carried out by government departments and the Government Social Survey, as well as independent research. Even without any redefinition of scope or function and any improvement in standard of service it is evident that the home help and meals services should be doubled or more than doubled, (2) sheltered housing and sheltered workshops for the physically disabled, mentally handicapped

* Address to the first annual general meeting of the British Association of Social Workers, University of Aston, Birmingham, 13 February 1971.

and elderly built up from their present small beginnings, (3) and a whole range of preventive and hospital after-care services — visiting, chiropody, district nursing, laundry, bathing attendance, night-sitters, holiday relief, aids to disability — greatly increased in scale. (4) Expansion is required not just for people who are in need of services but not yet receiving them. Many people actually receiving one or more services are not getting all those to which they would be entitled.

One method of demonstrating the shortcomings and the want of central direction and control is to compare the performance of different areas. Some councils have three and four times more district nurses and home helps per 1,000 people aged 65 and over than others.(5) There are, for example, nearly four times as many home helps in Warrington (10.8 per 1,000 population aged 65 and over) as in Halifax (2.8); over four times as many in Durham (10.2) as in Kent (2.2) and over five times as many in Hackney (14.2) as in Brent (2.6). (6) Some councils spend ten or twelve times as much upon every registered disabled person as others and there are huge differences in the numbers registered per 1,000 population. (7) If all county councils and all county boroughs spent as much as the top five in each category then expenditure on the personal social services would be approximately trebled.

One by-product of a recent study by Miss E. Matilda Goldberg to test the effectiveness of social casework was its demonstration of unmet practical needs among a group of old people, 72 per cent of whom were already receiving at least one domiciliary service. The assessors uncovered 946 additional needs among the 299 people interviewed. Altogether 791 of the total needs were for housing, home help, chiropody, clubs, holidays and material aid, such as the supply of bed linen, and the other 155 for casework with clients or relatives. Miss Goldberg conceded that much of the greater effectiveness of the specially recruited social workers who worked solely with half of the people in the random sample was attributable to the smaller caseload. She concluded that about a third of the sample did not need the help of a skilled social worker but only of welfare assistants. (8) An estimate might also be made of the amount of help that could be given and proportion of visits paid by welfare assistants and not fully trained social workers among the other two thirds. Both measures are important in predicting the staffing needs of local departments in the future.

There are two further methods of putting overall needs into perspective. One is to compare performance with previous national plans. It is deplorable that the ten-year forward plans for community health and welfare in England and Wales ceased to appear after three of them had been published between 1963 and 1966. When they were produced social scientists and social workers complained that too little guidance had been given to local authorities in drawing up their plans. As a result they were over-modest and of course bore no relation to either the growth or the possible reallocation of national resources. There were 174 local plans that had been aggregated. Everyone hoped that this would in time be remedied and a central strategy evolved. The plans are not being fulfilled in the time allotted. In 1969 the number of places for the mentally handicapped in junior training centres was 11 per cent and in adult training centres 5 per cent below the figures planned as lately as 1964. Among the other services which fell short by a small or a large margin are: places in hostels, for the mentally ill, 27 per cent; places in hostels and other accommodation for the mentally handicapped, 7 per cent for children and 10 per cent for adults; district nurses, 3 per cent; health visitors, 23 per cent, and home helps, 11 per cent. (9) Even figures such as these can be misleading, since the expansion which was planned was in some instances small. Only 700 of the modest addition of 1,000 home nurses between 1964 and 1968 were found; only 200 of the additional 1,900 health visitors, and less than 3,000 of the additional 7,000 home helps. Most serious of all during the period from 1967 to 1969 has been not just the reduction, during a time of economic difficulties, in capital spending, but the slight absolute fall in numbers of home helps in two successive years, when a rapid increase is required both to keep abreast with population and make good the gaps in scope and frequency of service. (10)

Another important measure of performance is expenditure relative to national income and other services. Estimates can be made for the years since the war of current and capital spending on services covered by the Local Authority Social Services Act of 1970.(11) In 1951 total expenditure was approximately £39 million or 0.3 per cent of G.N.P. and in 1969 £224 million, a little less than 0.6 per cent of G.N.P.(12) Between 1959 and 1969 the rate of growth of expenditure at constant prices has been approximately 7 per cent. However, the rate of growth of all social services has been 5.2 per cent per annum (or 4.5 per cent if social security payments and other transfer incomes are excluded). The new service accounts for less than 2½ per cent of spending on all social services — the other four services being social security (£3,562m.), education (£2,328m.), health (£1,752m.) and housing (£1,118m.). Moreover, the bulk of this expenditure, approximately £130m. or 58 per cent of the total in 1969 of £224m., is absorbed by residential services. We can thus conclude that according to the three separate criteria of (a) satisfaction of measured need, (b) fulfilment of local authority plans and (c) rate of growth of expenditure, compared with other social services, there is no evidence of a rapid rate of expansion or a 'take-off' of expenditure to herald a new era of social development.

This fact stands perhaps as an affront and certainly as a challenge to British values. The nation has a touching faith in the powers of sweet reason and compassion, once aroused, to influence events. The rational case for expansion and strong public concern for the elderly and the handicapped have been much in evidence during the last ten years. But the effect has been astonishingly small. Let me list just a few examples from recent history. There was the general momentum behind community care fostered in the early 1960s by the hospital plan as well as the local authority plans. There was the build-up too of acknowledgement of the urgent needs of the community as a whole at the time of the appointment of the Seebohm Committee and in anticipation of their report. Then there were specific pressures in favour of expansion. From the mid-1950s the number of patients in mental illness hospitals has been diminishing steadily at the rate of about 2 per cent per annum;(13) and although treatment in hospital has been more positive, much more has been expected of the community mental health services. Since the mid-1950s again, there has been a stream of research reports calling for better domiciliary services for the elderly and for more community involvement in the standards of care in hospital.(14) Finally there have been the campaigns in the mid and late 1960s on behalf of the disabled in general and the mentally handicapped in particular. Both of these deserve more sustained analysis than I could give here. There have been many press photographs of ministers benignly receiving deputations in Whitehall and at the House of Commons, and many television documentaries on the difficulties of the disabled at home and the plight of the mentally handicapped in hospital. Mr Crossman took a wholly admirable initiative early in 1969 in publishing the Howe Report on the Ely Hospital, (15) appointing a working group on policy and stalking the country making speeches about the crisis of the mentally handicapped. But the effort has largely disappeared into the sands of time. In December 1969 a miserable £3 million was added, as a temporary measure, to hospital expenditure. The extent to which a British Government is prepared to spend money to resolve a welfare crisis or deal with poverty does not yet bear comparison with its willingness to help industry out of bankruptcy. When the Labour Government left office in June 1970, so it has been reported, a White Paper was about to be published. Even by then there had been delay in evolving policy. The new Government was bound to take a few months sizing up its problems but the further delay is tragic and inexcusable. It is now almost two years since the Howe Report was published.

The failure to act substantially on behalf of the disabled is even more puzzling. They were included in the major review of social security upon which the Labour Government embarked when it came to office in 1964.

Miss Margaret Herbison and Mrs Judith Hart, as successive Ministers of Social Security, acknowledged the severity and urgency of the problem. The really major requirement is a comprehensive disability pension scheme and an allowance for families with handicapped children, supported by other big developments in special housing, home services and sheltered employment. Instead, measures were enacted which although valuable were peripheral. These are the attendance allowance and the Chronically Sick and Disabled Persons Act.

What are the lessons to be drawn from all this? I have concentrated so far on the case for expansion of the community care services and their failure to grow as fast even as the local authorities cautiously estimated they should. I have not discussed the questions of priorities and the function of such bodies as the B.A.S.W. in any new strategy. We can reasonably infer from recent history that initiatives in social planning which are taken by Government can quickly lose momentum; that a strong case for reform can be transmitted repeatedly by the mass media and even espoused by ministers without being translated into positive action; that good research studies can have next to no effect on policy; that pressure-group activity can attract a lot of notice without affecting practice or behaviour and that public approval or at least tacit acceptance of reform does not necessarily mean that it will take place. I suggest that the *structural connectedness* of reform has neither been fully recognized and implemented in policy nor accidentally achieved in practice. Much social change is a terribly slow process of imperceptible adjustment of institutions and social sub-systems to the influence of a thousand developments in social structure — in population, household organization, family structure, commercial and industrial organization, education and culture. The social scientist can use models of structural differentiation to try to make sense of these changes or general concepts of cultural lag, erosion or evolution. But just as conflict after a long period of discontent and hostility or the coincidence of several different events can sometimes achieve swifter change or even a transformation of society, so the sociologist of welfare must strive to go beyond the conception of slow accretions of change to develop models of dramatic development of the welfare system.

Policy changes have to be pressed more resolutely through to their logical conclusions than we have appreciated hitherto. It is more than a question of introducing some new factor into the situation which, it is optimistically supposed, will trigger off a succession of changes right through the system. Thus, recommendations for policy have to be worked out in detail, programmed and costed. They have to be considered in relation to likely effects not just on different sections of the public but upon professional and other staff and on other services and social institutions. Manpower has to be used a lot more efficiently. Opinion has to be tapped at different levels; methods of conveying information to the public considered and new patterns of recruitment, work organization and training developed. In short, a concerted policy is required.

Either through the Government's new Central Policy Review Unit or the enlarged Department of Health and Social Security, there is the possibility of producing a more concerted policy. General objectives such as the equalization of resources within a community, the reduction of isolation, the achievement of a family service, care in the community as a viable alternative to care in institutions, or community integration, could each be spelt out operationally as different parts of a programme of community development. I think it is unfortunate that the community development projects sponsored by the Home Office have been regarded as small-scale, innovatory exercises in a few areas, instead of being linked to a national plan for the expansion of community services and involvement of local populations. (16) They should form part of the whole programme of work of the new social services departments. The definition operationally of the objectives I have specified would help to show the relationship to each other of the different parts of the welfare service and arrive at priorities. For example, although the See-bohm Committee argued for an effective family service nowhere did they discuss the implications of a consistent fulfilment of that principle. Does it mean providing family services for those who lack a family or whose family resources are meagre? Does it mean setting up quasi-private households for small groups of the disabled and old people like the family-unit Homes in the children's service, in place of residential hostels? Does it mean re-casting the methods of training those formerly recruited for residential work?

Again, to take a different example, Sir Keith Joseph is beginning to place a lot of emphasis on community care. The latest Government White Paper on public expenditure, that very austere document which is carefully controlled by the Treasury, contains a significant commitment. After stating the proportions of expenditure being devoted to hospital, family practitioner and community health and welfare services the White Paper goes on, 'it is envisaged that these proportions will gradually change in favour of the community health and welfare services as the policy develops of providing care in the community where this is more appropriate than hospital care.' In case the commitment may have been overlooked the authors repeat it, for good measure, three paragraphs later, adding, 'It is proposed to give particular emphasis to meeting the needs of the mentally handicapped, the mentally ill and the elderly.'(17) We shall see. I have listened to several of Sir Keith's predecessors, both Conservative and Labour, making the same sort of commitment. There are obstacles in the administrative division between hospitals and local authorities, the system of local authority finance, the weak control over local decision-making, the vested interests of hospital superintendents and staffs, and the powerful representation of hospital interests in medical politics and in the Department of Health itself. It is also tempting, as Mr Crossman discovered, to surrender resources for temporary buildings and units on grounds that this will reduce overcrowding and placate medical and nursing staff. But such resources can easily dwarf resources released to the community, and can be swallowed up without trace in the costly hospital system or end, paradoxically, by reinforcing the very system one aims to run down and replace. It will take far more ingenuity, drive and sheer obstinacy to achieve a substantial result than this or any previous Government has demonstrated itself capable of mounting. Sir Keith Joseph needs to have a strong administrative wing and research unit in the Department of Health, and a programme worked out jointly with the hospitals and local authorities, which is carefully phased and related to manpower changes; he needs to prohibit the development of what would amount to a second-class hospital system by the local authorities, and continuously publicize and encourage the domiciliary services and sheltered housing. The management of sheltered housing indeed should become a responsibility of the new social services departments, perhaps by delegation by housing departments.

If, in a programme of community development, the objectives of equalization of resources, reduction of isolation, family support and community integration are to be adopted there are implications for the organization, practice and teaching of social work. More staff will be needed for home help, washing and dressing, cooking and serving meals, shopping, ferrying the disabled in cars and mini-buses, organizing holidays and entertainment, producing and issuing aids to disability and fetching prescriptions. The Seebohm Committee listed the numbers of staff employed in the services recommended for reorganization. (18) At the end of 1966 only 7,000 of the total of nearly 90,000 staff in England and Wales were social workers, and only 1,500 of these in the children's, mental health and welfare services had professional qualifications. Yet there has been little discussion about the training, future requirement, recruitment and disposition of different kinds of staff. The model of future organization of the welfare services which seems to be accepted almost without question is that of the familiar hierarchy — though in some areas the director is trying to shorten it. The pay of a chief officer has been raised to that of a captain of, if not of private, then of public, industry. Instead of his department being organized functionally around the conceptions of family service or community care, it is beginning to reflect some of the administrative sub-divisions of big organizations.

The situation is still fluid in many areas but under the director and his deputy are usually field-work, residential, training and administrative divisions and within the field-work division a number of large area offices, often with fifteen or twenty staff. (19) Historically this may have been predictable, and it will make much easier the preservation of the status quo, but it is not obligatory. I mean that existing divisions of responsibility between domiciliary and institutional services, and number and type of staff, are likely to be maintained, instead of recast with immediate priority for home helps and home aid for the disabled. Reorganization will add a few layers to the status and career hierarchy and, when combined with professionalization, this implies that a greater share of future expenditure will be devoted to filling and maintaining senior positions.

Let me try to present realistically, if perhaps brutally, the kind of choice that is being made. Reorganization is a way of manipulating the development of services to obtain respect for welfare. By joining the league of big organizations and paying salaries at the top which are commensurate with bigness it is assumed that welfare will attract better staff and a rising proportion of national resources. But this could be illusory. Suppose, for example, that the additional expenditure were devoted to producing 5,000 more social workers, say, with two or more years of professional training who work haphazardly and perhaps uneconomically in relation to all the other staff. Instead, the same investment of resources to training could recruit, say, 1,000 more social workers, but 8,000 welfare assistants and 20,000 other workers who have had some exposure to short courses of training.

There are alternative models of organization to correspond with alternative methods of allocating resources. One is group practice. Three or four general social workers would work from an office in each of a number of localities in the area of a county council or county borough. They would have some scope for specialization. Welfare assistants and volunteer workers of different kinds would be attached to the group and would serve the locality, visiting the old and disabled, checking queries about supplementary benefits, putting families in touch with information offices and legal aid and so on. At headquarters would be certain specialist and consultant staff, including transport staff and those in charge of sheltered employment and residential services.

This would be a front-line type of organization with less dependence on hierarchical and centralized supervision of field staff. By developing a work-group to include welfare assistants and maybe even volunteers it would be arguably more economical and more effective. It would also represent an intelligent form of control over the growth of public expenditure. I appreciate that there would be a variety of problems, for example, of monopoly of local service and communication of information about changes in central policy. But no alternative is free of objections.

The conception of social work would be enlarged. Although personal service and case-work would be included other objectives and methods would be stressed. In practice, social work may be very different from what its critics assume. In 1959 Barbara Wootton made a devastating analysis of the pretensions and limitations of case-work, (20) and since then social workers have become more aware of wider and specifically practical responsibilities. Research into the reactions of working-class families has speeded that process. (21) The change can be traced in the writings of leading exponents of social work like Dame Eileen Young-husband. For example, references were made in the Younghusband Report of 1959 on social workers to practical assistance, the supply of information, and the representation of clients but these topics were not considered with anything like the same attention as guidance on prob-lems of personal adjustment. However, in a recent paper Dame Eileen agrees that there is a danger that social workers can be used as 'agents of conformity, as people who have the professional ability to manipulate from within powerful administrative structures to fulfil the policies and thus implement the values of their employing agencies, or to practise the latest fashionable theory in social work'. She goes on to warn, 'Social Work as a profession will thus have an even greater obligation than in the past to be sensitive to unmet or ill-met need, and as a profession to campaign for more resources, better administration, a wider range of provision, the right of clients to protest and constant fact finding, analy-sis, evaluation and research.' (22) Increasingly sociology is likely to contribute to theories of social work — in particular, to theories of inequalities in the distribution of resources, integration of racial and other minorities, reduction of isolation, substitution of or support for the family and the organization of residential groups. As a consequence the intellectual basis for group work and community work will be strengthened and the roles of staff more clearly defined.

This will strengthen alternative forms of organization. Front-line group practice would make it easier than specialized divisions of labour within a centralized department to be semi-independent of the local authority, gain the confidence of families, represent community needs and anxieties and protest on its behalf. The problems of 'scientific benevolence' (23) and remote bureaucracy would be lessened.

The British Association of Social Workers is in the formative stage of its existence, and it can influence the type of organization of welfare services and the scale of resources which the Government and local councils release and the effectiveness with which they are used. The challenge is very great. The histories of most professions make somewhat depressing reading because preoccupation with pay, status and security has often obstructed, although sometimes very indirectly, the expansion of service to the community. (24) The strengths of social work rest at present in its diversity despite its limited educational ethic and its first-hand contacts with families and communities. But professional training could too quickly become a licence just to administer.

The association could choose to play a major function in pressing for swift expansion of services, by issuing a stream of authoritative reports on the extent of unmet needs and negotiating at branch level with social service committees and councils. It could help to ensure better training for welfare assistants and short courses for many different kinds of staff who lack professional qualifications. Experimental proposals for the involvement of the disabled and elderly, parents of mentally handicapped children and patients discharged from mental illness hospitals in the decisions of management could be put forward. The Government could be pressed to extend legal aid and advice and establish a national network of information offices.

Established professions, like other trades, include some licence to deviate from ordinary modes of behaviour. This can amount to a broad moral and intellectual as well as legal mandate. It includes licence to express as professional values what would in other contexts be regarded as highly political views on specific topics. The new recruit to the profession is therefore encouraged to adopt the demeanour and trappings of someone with an historic inheritance, who can speak with authority on certain aspects of social life. This can have very mixed results. A professional code of conduct, for instance, can be a splendid source of dignity and corporate identity but also a means of strengthening monopoly powers.

Inevitably a profession will come to reflect the structure, the values and the inequalities of society as a whole. But it will also help to shape them. It has its own conception of the good life and of what is right for society. At this moment in time, there are great opportunities of campaigning for an accelerated expansion of community services. I hope the profession can listen long and hard to the poor, keep in touch with them and represent their interests before its own. (25) That would be a fine principle to honour.

Notes
1. The final paragraph of the Seebohm Committee's Report begins, 'The first responsibility of the new departments will be to deploy existing resources more effectively, but additional resources will be needed. Measured in manpower, buildings, training, intelligence and research these will not be large in relation to total local authority budgets . . .' *Report of the Committee on*

Local Authority and Allied Personal Social Services, Cmnd. 3703, H.M.S.O., 1968, p.218.

2. Hunt, A., *The Home Help Service in England and Wales*, a survey carried out in 1967 by the Government Social Survey for the Ministry of Health, H.M.S.O., 1970; Williamson, J., *et al.*, 'Old People at Home: Their Unreported Needs', *Lancet*, 1967, vol. 1, p. 1117.

3. For example, 29 authorities had not provided any special housing for the elderly, 123 no adult hostels and 32 no places in adult training centres for the mentally subnormal. *Report of the Committee on Local Authority and Allied Personal Social Services*, op.cit., pp.314-15. See also, *Health and Welfare: The Development of Community Care*, Cmnd. 3022, H.M.S.O., 1966, pp.17-18.

4. Skeet, M., *Home from Hospital*, the Dan Mason Nursing Research Committee, 1970.

5. *Report of the Committee on Local Authority and Allied Personal Social Services*, op.cit., pp.314-15.

6. Information kindly provided to the author for 1969 by the Department of Health and Social Security.

7. Sainsbury, S., *Registered as Disabled*, Bell, 1970, pp.201-5. A survey in Tower Hamlets produced an estimate that there were over four times as many physically disabled people in the borough as were registered in 1967; Skinner, F.W., *Physical Disability and Community Care*, Bedford Square Press, 1969, p.90.

8. Goldberg, E.M., *Helping the Aged: A Field Experiment in Social Work*, Allen & Unwin, 1970, pp.74-8, and 199.

9. Ministry of Health, *Health and Welfare: The Development of Community Care, Revision to 1973-4 of Plans for the Health and Welfare Services of the Local Authorities in England and Wales*, H.M.S.O., pp.324-7. *Annual Reports of the Department of Health and Social Security for 1968 and 1969*, Cmnds. 4100 and 4462, pp.128-9, and pp.194-5 respectively. The figures of places are for England only, and those for staff are as in the plan, for 31 December 1964 and 31 December 1968.

10. There was a fall from 29,900 to 29,500 in England between 1967 and 1969. *Annual Report of the Department of Health and Social Security for 1969*, op. cit., p.190.

11. Some but only partial guidance is given in Appendix J of the Seebohm Committee's Report.

12. To the costs of child care and local welfare services I have added the costs of local authority home help and mental health services, as given, both current and capital, in annual Government reports. The estimates are for the U.K. as a whole and are based partly on *National Income and Expenditure*, H.M.S.O., 1970. Perhaps it should be noted that the Department of Health does not consider it is possible to give official estimates of the cost in recent years of the services now covered by the Local Authority Social Services Act of 1970. It is felt that the necessary financial statistics cannot be broken down and reassembled in the appropriate form.

13. Department of Health and Social Security, *Digest of Health Statistics for*

England and Wales, 1969, H.M.S.O., 1969.

14. Culminating in the campaign by AEGIS to persuade Mr Kenneth Robinson, the Minister of Health, to improve hospital conditions and after-care services, and appoint a Hospital Commissioner. Robb, B., *et al., Sans Everything,* Nelson, 1967.

15. *Report of the Committee of Inquiry into Allegations of Ill-Treatment of Patients and other Irregularities at the Ely Hospital, Cardiff,* Cmnd. 3975, H.M.S.O., March 1969.

16. See, for example, Bennington, J., 'Community Development Project', *Social Work Today,* August 1970.

17. *Public Expenditure 1969-70 and 1974-5,* Cmnd. 4578, H.M.S.O., January 1971, p.38.

18. *Report of the Committee on Local Authority and Allied Personal Social Services,* H.M.S.O., 1968, pp. 329-37.

19. See, for example, Foren, R., and Brown, M.J., *Planning for Service: An Examination of the Organisation and Administration of Local Authority Social Services Departments,* Knight, 1971.

20. Wootton, B., 'Contemporary Attitudes in Social Work', in her *Social Science and Social Pathology,* Allen & Unwin, 1959.

21. '. . . Clients in search of material assistance . . . were consumed with worry over debts, the possibility of an eviction, the cutting-off of their electricity, and it is absurd to expect that the urgency of their needs could be met by a non-material approach . . .' Mayer, J.E. and Timms, N., *The Client Speaks: Working-Class Impressions of Casework,* Routledge & Kegan Paul, 1970.

22. Younghusband, E., 'Social Work and Social Values', *Social Work Today,* September 1970.

23. The allusion is to the approving quotation of the aim 'to make benevolence scientific is the great problem of the present day', by Dame Eileen Younghusband in Morris, C. (ed.), *Social Case-Work in Great Britain.* The organization of social work has become controversial. For example, 'The most vocal and dynamic of the new recruits to social work are anti-professionalism with its built-in paternalism and inequalities. They do not see themselves as skilled experts dispensing therapy to social misfits, but as community workers where the client is no longer the sick person but the sick society.' Rankin, G., 'Professional Social Work and the Campaign against Poverty', *Social Work Today,* January 1971, p.20.

24. See, for example, Eckstein, H., *Pressure Group Politics: The Case of the B.M.A.,* Allen & Unwin, 1960; Abel-Smith, B. and Stevens, R., *In Search of Justice,* Allen Lane, 1968 (especially Chapter 9).

25. As the former Chairman of the Standing Conference of Organizations of Social Workers has said, 'A Profession is . . . concerned to protect the interests of its members but this cannot be its first aim.' McDougall, K., 'Obligations of a Profession', *Social Work Today,* September 1970, p.18.

The Government is about to introduce a major new pensions bill. Will it remove the principal structural defect of the scheme described in the White Paper of January 1969? This defect is crucial to any conception of need and affects people who will become retirement pensioners later in this century as well as the pensioners who are alive today.

In preparing its plans the Government has been faced with a dual problem. First, there is a huge gap in living standards between the vast majority of the aged and the working population. A number of research studies, including a report by the former Ministry of Pensions, have shown that around 2½ million people are living at or below the old national assistance or new supplementary benefit rates, and another 2½ million have an income of only up to £1 or £2 more. Throughout the years since the war this problem of inequality has not changed very much, despite the increase from 4 to 7 million in the number of retirement pensioners. To give one illustration, the retirement pension for a single person, expressed as a percentage of average earnings, was 19 in 1948, 19 in 1958 and 20 in 1968. Dorothy Wedderburn, Amelia Harris, Jeremy Tunstall and others have testified in their work that the problem is not just one of low incomes but few assets, poor housing and inadequate aids and services for infirmity. This is structural inequality with a vengeance.

The gap in living standards is unlikely to close. There seems to be a growing problem of redundancy, disability and low pay in late middle age. The savings and other assets of many people are likely to be reduced even before retirement. And the contribution of occupational pension schemes will be a lot smaller than is sometimes supposed. The rate of increase in number of people covered by such schemes has been falling off and a figure of only about half of employed persons (though about two thirds of men) has been reached. A very substantial section of the population is not covered and in the foreseeable future is not likely to be covered by these schemes. Moreover, the occupational pensions expected by many people, especially those now in their forties and fifties, are very small. Between a third and a half can expect to get under £3. Nor should it be forgotten that the value of occupational pensions tends to

* First published in *Tribune*, 7 November 1969.

fall behind wages and often prices too as time goes on. Again, widows can rarely inherit even part of a husband's pension. Those who speak of the Life Offices as if they were distributing loaves and fishes to the grateful multitudes are not speaking the language of socialism.

Secondly, there is the problem of two nations in old age. The vast majority of the elderly are living around the subsistence level and many can only make their incomes up to a subsistence level by submitting themselves to a means test. But a minority of old people enjoy conditions of prosperity. Some former salaried employees have both the State pension and a substantial occupational pension. This is based on principles which are very different from the State scheme: pension at sixty, possibility of taking another job afterwards without reduction of earnings, substantial lump sum (frequently £1,000 or more) and a pension of around two thirds of previous earnings — partly paid for by the general tax-payer but also indirectly by those who lose pension rights by changes from one employer to another. The existence of the national and the occupational schemes may indeed correspond in some ways to the two systems of salaries and wages in working life, with associated fringe benefits. This is a two-tier system of rewards. Even those who support the existence of substantial differentials in earning life find it difficult to justify wide differentials in living standards throughout old age.

In 1957 the Labour Party attempted to deal with this dual problem in its national superannuation plan — a document of 120 pages presented in that year to the party conference by Dick Crossman. Any scheme for income security is bound to be complicated but the central argument of the plan was simple. It aimed to raise the standard of living of existing pensioners swiftly and reduce or eliminate the inequality between the principles of the State scheme and of the occupational schemes. The party argued that the population would be willing to contribute much larger sums than at present for social security providing they could expect larger pensions. By introducing proportional contributions, more revenue could be collected and bigger pensions financed immediately. The increase in the basic pension proposed in the 1957 plan was substantial by any standards. Moreover, as the scheme grew to maturity, those who had paid higher contributions could expect increased pensions. While keeping control over the lower and upper limits of pensions, a structure with much narrower differentials than the earnings structure could gradually take the place of the two-tier structure which was rightly castigated as unjust in a modern society. Relative to the rest of the population the standard of living of pensioners would be raised. The great majority would find their incomes increased above the national assistance or supplementary benefit level. The means test would be given a deserved knock. And a minority of people would find that the occupational pension schemes which provided them with excessively generous benefits would be brought under tighter control. Excessive tax-free lump sums would not be approved and pension rights would be fully transferable.

This was the basic strategy of the 1957 plan. The White Paper of January 1969 differs substantially in that an immediate increase in the real level of pension is not an integral part of the proposals but left to the Government to decide when the scheme begins to function. But the difference cuts much deeper. The removal of that part of the plan which proposed to raise the real living standards of existing pensioners greatly accentuates the advantages conferred on younger, married pensioners as the scheme matures. In 1972 a man retiring at 65 will be receiving the same pension as a man of 85. But by 1992 he will be receiving, on average, more than twice as much. A married couple who have both been earning about average in paid employment and who retire at 65 will be receiving three times as much as a married couple of 85. Those earning above average will be even better off, in relative terms. And these illustrations depend on a further assumption which has not been guaranteed in the scheme — that pension levels keep pace with earnings. The Government has not had the courage to insist that what has been practised for twenty years should now become law.

Already in industrial societies the phenomenon of 'double' deprivation in advanced old age is common. By this I mean not just living standards which are low by comparison with the working population but low by comparison with younger retired people in their sixties and early seventies. The 'young' elderly who have retired more recently are more likely than their elders to live in homes which reflect the rising prosperity of the post-war years. Some will have earned higher pensions by postponing retirement. Others will have wives young enough to gain supplementary earnings or themselves will have a modest occupational pension. In a cross-national study of old people in the early 1960s, Dorothy Wedderburn showed that 'double' deprivation was more marked in Britain than in Denmark, although not as marked as in the United States. The Government now proposes to devote the greater part of new revenue to accentuating an inequality which already exists instead of devoting a large part of such revenue to reducing it. Since 1957 considerable evidence has been collected of the needs, and especially the disabilities, of those of advanced age. There is plainly a fourth generation in substantial numbers, as well as a third generation, in British society and Dick Crossman is in danger of legislating not for the present but for the future third generation only. Once there is a shift of emphasis in the distribution of income, that shift will in all political likelihood be perpetuated — whatever the present Government may say about the eventual maturity of its scheme in the second decade of the next century.

What can be done? The Parliamentary Labour Party and other organizations concerned with the special interests of the elderly cannot let this matter rest. While recognizing novel and constructive features in the proposals, and recognizing that over a period of twenty years many more people in their late sixties and seventies will earn a higher pension, an attempt must be made to restore a guaranteed substantial real increase in the level of pension to be paid, and to add disability and age-supplements to the bill. The level of individual infirmity might be assessed by a general practitioner, with a check by a regional team. The pensioner should receive a supplement of 10s., 20s. or 40s. (according to degree of infirmity) automatically. A similar supplement could be paid to those of seventy-five and over. I estimate that both these measures could be introduced while yet leaving a substantial surplus on current account in the early years of the scheme.

The structure of the new scheme is unbalanced, partly because it does not attempt to deal with the problems of the disabled of all ages and with the other current problems of poverty. It is not as truly comprehensive as, say, the Beveridge Report of 1942. Douglas Houghton, Peggy Herbison, Patrick Gordon-Walker and Judith Hart have in turn proclaimed the 'long-term review' of social security during the last five years. Despite a number of modest reforms the Government has yet to take positive and substantial action on the major problems of the poverty of fatherless families, the disabled and low-paid wage-earners and their families as well as the aged. After four years' 'review' the Government announced in its White Paper last January, for example, that research would be undertaken and a committee set up on fatherless families. Ten months afterwards even the composition of the committee has not been announced. Research on disability is being completed but there is no sign that the principles of alternative pension schemes for disability are being seriously examined and discussed. If they had been, perhaps the problems of the aged who are disabled or of advanced age would have been brought more fully into notice. The Beveridge Report was prepared from start to finish in seventeen months — and practically all of it in ten months.

After five years the Government has still to tackle the really big problems of poverty and inequality today. Its new pensions bill promises half a loaf for tomorrow.

It is not easy to fit single, married and widowed women into an equitable pension scheme. The main difficulty arises over the responsibilities of motherhood. A single or childless woman often has nothing to prevent her taking paid employment; she is therefore able to provide for her old age. A married woman usually spends some twenty years of her life rearing her children; for these years at least she is unable to provide for her old age. Should these years of motherhood be allowed for in some way in assessing her pension and, if so, to what extent?

In discussing this question and others, two broad assumptions are made. The first is that it is, and will continue to be, Labour's policy to provide equal pay for equal work, to promote employment in different areas which is suitable for married and unmarried women, and to abolish those restrictive practices which prevent women entering or playing a full part in certain occupations. The second is that the attitude implied by the use of the word 'dependant' for a married woman is not defensible and must be opposed. The housewife *supports* her husband so that he can go to work. Her services are unpaid but are as vital to the well-being of the nation as services that are paid. In the last twenty or thirty years the number of domestic servants has greatly decreased and presumably many housewives have taken over their work; yet is it sense to call the latter 'dependants' and the former not? Husbands and wives reciprocate services and are equally dependent on each other.

Married Women in the Present Scheme
Under the national insurance scheme a married woman can choose whether or not to contribute towards a pension in her own right. The employer's contribution has to be paid whatever her decision. Actuarially

---

* This paper comprises the two earliest of a series of memoranda on women and social security which I submitted in October and December 1956 to the Labour Party's Social Policy Advisory Committee, when plans for a national superannuation scheme were being prepared. They are included in this volume partly for historical reasons but also because there has been much keener public discussion of the inequality of women in recent years — for example during 1972-3 in response to the Government's tax-credit proposals. The proposal to introduce an attendance allowance, presented briefly on pp. 246–7, was later revived by the Labour Government in 1969 and enacted by the Conservative Government in 1971.

it does not pay the younger woman to contribute, and in fact nearly 2 million of the 3¼ million married women who were at work in 1954 had chosen not to contribute. A young woman who married after July 1948 will not qualify even for a *reduced* pension unless she has either paid contributions or received credits for at least half the weeks between the date of her marriage and her sixtieth birthday; to qualify for 40s. (or 15s. more than the 25s. she would receive under her husband's insurance) she must have an average of fifty contributions a year from her last entry into insurance, which must be at least ten years preceding pensionable age. A married woman who remains at work all her life can, if she has contributed, qualify for a pension increment of 15s., or 37½ per cent of the single woman's 40s. Even for a flat-rate scheme this seems to be rather unjust: the reason more has not been heard of this anomaly is probably due to the fact that this is a 'transitional' period (in which, under the 1948 Act, some women qualify after ten and others after five years' insurance). Married women who choose to contribute for most of their lives would, by the age of sixty, have a strong grievance over the amount of their pension. A major criticism of the present scheme is that it discriminates against married women at work by giving them no opportunity to earn an adequate pension and by giving a poor return for money; moreover, by discouraging contributions, it does not spread evenly over the earning population the load of contributions and, indeed, neglects a useful source of revenue.

Although these criticisms may not be fully met in any alternative scheme there is little doubt that some improvements can be made. Recent changes in the working population have made such improvements doubly necessary. Many more married women are taking paid employment. In 1931 1.4 million, or 23 per cent, of the 6.2 million women aged 35-54 were gainfully occupied; in 1951 2.5 million, or 34 per cent of the 7.3 million women in the same age group, were so occupied. Nearly all the million extra women of that age in the labour force were married. Not much is known about the causes of this trend but there is no strong reason to suppose that it will not continue. If it is true that full employment, earlier marriage, smaller families, the changing status of women and the increase in the number of grandmothers available to look after grandchildren have all contributed to this trend, then there is every likelihood it will continue. If more married women maintain, or return to, employment in middle age the numbers staying in employment at older ages are likely to increase. In 1951 6.2 million women, or 31 per cent, were in full-time employment and 6.9 million, or 35 per cent, in full- and part-time employment. The total comprised about 3¾ million single, 2½ million married and ½ million widowed women.

The New Scheme

In determining pension rights it would be unwise to think of women falling into separate categories — such as the unmarried, the married without dependent children, the married with dependent children, and the widowed. Most women pass through most of these phases during their lifetime: they are single, they marry, they have children, their children grow up and their husbands die. But in fitting women into a pension scheme it is perhaps right to discuss first the position of those whose marital and employment status does not change during active life. From such straightforward, if more extreme, cases it may be easier to move to the commoner problems of women whose status frequently changes.

Single Women Remaining at Work

Under the proposed national superannuation scheme all employees pay 3 per cent, all employers 5 per cent. A single man earning £12 a week (roughly the present average industrial earnings) qualifies for a pension of £7 a week at sixty-five (providing he has worked, or is credited, for forty years). There seems to be no justification for denying a single woman of sixty-five the same pension rights if she has worked all her life. Earning £6 (roughly the present average industrial earnings), she qualifies for £5 — basic pension of £3, plus a third of average earnings, like the man. It should be remembered, however, that if rough equality between men and women is to be sought then the question whether women should draw pensions at the same age as men becomes important (discussed below). A woman of sixty-five has an expectation of life of over 20 per cent longer than a man of the same age, 14½ years compared with 12, and for this reason it could be argued that her contributions should be correspondingly bigger or paid over a longer period, or that the pension should be correspondingly smaller. (1) On the whole this argument does not carry weight, largely because it seems unjust to expect women to pay higher contributions or receive a smaller pension when their earnings tend to be low.

Childless Married Women Remaining at Work

In principle, however, it seems right to treat, for the purposes of pension, a single woman in the same way as a single man when both have been at work all their lives. Now let us consider the case of the childless woman of sixty-five, who like the single woman has worked all her life. Should she be entitled to the same pension? Under the national insurance scheme she qualifies for very meagre benefits if she maintains contributions — a mere 15s. However just or unjust this is, there is little doubt that it is more defensible in a flat-rate than in an earnings-related type of scheme. One can hardly expect a working married woman to contribute three per cent, whatever her earnings, and receive 15s. at sixty-five. Leaving the choice to her whether to contribute or not does not make it easier to offer such poor terms.

One possibility for this married woman is that she should be able to earn a pension amounting to a third of her average earnings, in addition to a basic pension of 25s. Her total pension would differ from a single woman's only in that her basic pension would be 25s. (the present rate) instead of £3. The following examples show the difference between single and married women who have contributed for forty years in the pension payable.

Average earnings per week	Single Woman's pension	Married Woman's pension
£ 5	£4 13s. 4d.	£2 18s. 4d.
£ 7	£5 6s. 8d.	£3 11s. 8d.
£10	£6 6s. 8d.	£4 11s. 8d.
£20	£9 13s. 4d.	£7 18s. 4d.

One reason for allowing her to qualify for a smaller basic pension would be that two mouths in one home cost less to feed than two mouths in separate homes. Under the new scheme a married woman will generally have a husband who has, on the basis of his own past earnings, an adequate pension. Moreover, unlike the single woman, she will have had widow's cover on her husband's insurance. There are three additional advantages: it makes it easier to fit widows into the scheme; it has the merit of making the adjustment from the old to the new scheme a smooth one (because the 25s. benefit already exists); and in the early years at least it will cost little.

The second possibility is that such a married woman would be entitled to the same basic pension as a single woman or a man on the basis of years of contribution. If this were implemented retrospectively it would have the effect of raising the pension levels of many married couples relative to those of single and widowed people, cause a great deal of resentment and be enormously expensive. If it were introduced gradually, as the scheme matured, and if other steps were taken to improve the incomes of the single and widowed, it would be a step towards more general equity for women.

Married Women Working Part of their Lives

We can now discuss the situation of the married woman who does not work late in life. The first thing to emphasize is that a very high proportion of married and widowed women reaching sixty-five must have at least ten or twenty years' full- or part-time paid employment behind them. About 66 per cent of women aged 20-24, 35 per cent aged 35-44 and 34 per cent aged 45-54 are in paid employment. Little is known about the employment history of women over their lifetime, as distinct from the proportions of women of different age in different occupations, but the following may be conjectured. Most women work for about ten years before marriage, many work for a further two or three years after marriage and, apart from the 20 per cent of women who are single or childless and who go on working in middle life, it seems probable that a further 20-30 per cent work for from five to ten years after having children. Of all women reaching sixty-five in future

15-20 per cent may have been in paid employment 40 years or more;
5-10 per cent may have been in paid employment 20 to 39 years;
30-40 per cent may have been in paid employment 10 to 19 years;
10-25 per cent may have been in paid employment 5 to 9 years;
10-20 per cent may have been in paid employment under 5 years.

These figures are no more than guesses, yet it would be useful to try to produce reliable estimates. Without fuller information on these lines it is not easy to decide the exact terms on which married women could have a pension of their own. Thus, the scheme could be so arranged as to give nearly all married women, even if they work for only a few years in adult life, a small pension of their own; or it could be so arranged as to give no more than a small proportion the chance of adding to their 25s. — by making the qualifying conditions stringent (e.g. ten years' contributions in the last twenty before retirement) and eliminating the early years of contribution by, for example, paying on marriage, or childbirth, a lump sum for previous contributions.

On balance, we believe it is correct to keep as close as possible to the principle of counting each year of working life as 1/120 of average earnings in assessing the earnings-related part of the pension. The alternatives would be hard to justify. Suppose, for example, a grant were payable upon marriage to women on the grounds that they required compensation for previous contributions and that this was one of the most helpful ways of benefiting new marriages and avoiding the complications at age sixty-five of taking account of contributions made forty or fifty years sooner. Should this marriage grant be payable on marriage or only when women gave up work? If the former what would be done with the contributions of women working for two or three years after marriage but, after starting a family, not again in life? How could those marrying in their forties and fifties be fitted into the scheme without the State being involved in charges of elderly spinsters buying husbands or of men marrying elderly women for their State dowries? The difficulties of introducing such a scheme, *as part of a national superannuation scheme,* are too large and there is less justification at a time when the number of married women taking paid employment seems to be increasing. If a grant to newly married couples is desirable then it should be considered separately.

We recommend, therefore, that from the appointed day account is taken of each year of working life in assessing pension rights, for women as well as men. If this were effected it would be easier either to encourage or compel married women to contribute. For those women who work only in early adult life the pensions payable are likely to be very small indeed.

Married Women with Children

The central question may now be posed. If some such scheme were adopted, should credits be given for years of motherhood? One possibility we considered was to allow a shilling additional to the 25s. pension for each year a woman had a dependent child at home. There are two major objections to such a proposal. One is the difficulty of defining a principle by which credits of such a kind would be allowed. Suppose it were, 'A woman should be allowed credits for each year she is prevented from taking gainful employment by having the care of young children'. But at what point does this start? Thirteen weeks before childbirth? And at what point should it end? When the last child starts school, or leaves school? Surely a woman with an only child is not going to be tied to her home once that child goes to school, especially when he or she is likely to have a midday meal there, and especially if the child is a capable teenage girl. What about women with *other* dependants, and not children, at home? What of the period of home-making immediately after marriage, when there might be some justification for a young housewife being credited with a period of 'settling in'? What about the grandmother in her fifties and early sixties who does so much for her grandchildren and adult children? How would it be possible to limit the period within which credits may be given, especially when it is remembered most mothers would get about twenty years of credit? (Second child born three years after first means 3 + 15 years at least of motherhood.)

There is no easy rule whereby women who are unable to take paid employment because of the needs of their families can be separated from others. The child-rearing system of credits might be rather unfair for the single or childless woman who takes on other jobs in the family — such as looking after aged parents, a sick brother, a sister's children and so on. Recent research has shown that single and childless people often act, or want to act, as universal aunts and take on the most varied family jobs. This means some might not build up credits for retirement when not at work. There is also the important evidence of the single and childless being the most likely people to be in desperate poverty and need of help. Whatever happens, those with children will always get all kinds of supplementary help and comfort — gifts of money from their children, presents, and holidays, for example. Those without children *may* get some help and company from brothers and sisters and nephews and nieces but some may not have such relatives and, in any case, the bonds are usually less close than with children. Moreover, those with children will have had the benefits of less taxation, family allowances and welfare foods during the child-rearing phase. This is when they most require help from the State, which properly has the task of redistributing income from those who have no dependent children to those who have them. During retirement the arguments for continuing such re-distribution are far weaker, particularly because the same children, far from being dependent, generally contribute something to the parents' standard of life.

The other objection to 'child-rearing' credits is a financial one. If it is true, as suggested, that most women have completed over ten, and many over twenty, years' paid work by the time that they reach the age of sixty-five, and if it is true, as also suggested, that most have spent some twenty years of their lives bringing up infants or children of school age, then it may well be true that many married women would qualify for a pension of a third earnings as well as the basic 25s. The cost might be prohibitive. The average married woman would be entitled to an extra 20s. on account of child-rearing credits as well as her differential pension and the basic 25s. Three hypothetical examples make the problem clear. In each case the woman is married, aged sixty-five, with a husband qualifying for a pension of £7 because of average earnings of £12 and a work-span of forty years. In each case too the woman has averaged £6 earnings when at work. (See table, p.246).

In effect the pension of B and C is close to five sixths of their income immediately before retirement. To achieve such a pension, contributions would have to be much higher than 3 per cent and 5 per cent.

For these reasons it is not easy to justify subsidizing in old age those who have had children. It is obviously right to waive normal contributions during a person's sickness or unemployment and to credit him for the spell off work. In assessing his pension, his work-span should not be reduced by these periods off work. Such periods in a person's life are periods of adversity, which he *avoids* if given a choice. The years of motherhood are plainly not comparable. Few women choose to avoid them. The State can be expected to compensate people for time off work only when what is clearly an adversity is imposed on them against their wishes.

	A	B	C
Husband	£3+4	£3+4	£3+4
Wife's basic pension	25s.	25s.	25s.
Wife's differential	£2 (40 yrs' work)	15s. (15 yrs)	5s. (5 yrs)
Total	£10 5s. 0d.	£9 0s. 0d.	£8 10s. 0d.
Wife's child-rearing credits	0 (no children)	18s. (18 yrs' child-rearing)	£1 8s. 0d. (28 yrs)
Total	£10 5s. 0d.	£9 18s. 0d.	£9 18s. 0d.
Personal income immediately preceding retirement	£18 0s. 0d.	£12 0s. 0d.	£12 0s. 0d.

Attendance Allowance

Such a rule of thumb, or principle, does however supply justification for one supplementary proposal, for 'personal attendance' credits. This must be explained. 'Constant Attendance Allowances' are available to war and disablement pensioners receiving pensions at the 100 per cent rate who, because of their disablement, require regular personal attendance. (Some 11,000 are in payment.) It is clear that many old people are prevented from becoming a charge on the National Health Services by children or other relatives who nurse them at home. Some old people getting national assistance get a discretionary addition of a few shillings for laundry or special diet but generally the State provides little or no help either for infirm old people or their relatives. More in particular should be done for relatives, who bear so many of the strains of nursing. It should be possible for pensioners to apply for a 'constant attendance allowance' when they require personal attendance. This could be a flat rate of, say, 10s. a week, paid by the Exchequer, combined possibly

with raising the minimum pension to a new 'personal attendance' minimum pension. In addition, any relative or other person not being paid
for performing a service of this kind to an old person and who shows
that he or she would normally be in paid employment is credited for
the period when the time comes to assess the pension. The same system
might be extended to the care of people other than the old. It is
unlikely it would be abused, for people would be unlikely to bother to
claim for short illnesses or they could be discouraged by administrative
measures from doing so. The suggestion is different from the mother-
care or child-rearing system of credits mainly because a person's inability
to go to work because of the infirmity or illness of a close relative is
generally regarded as a disaster which would be avoided if possible,
rather like one's own unemployment or sickness. Having the care of
children is not generally regarded as a disaster.

Conclusion

We recommend that single and married women be treated in the same
way as men in the proposed pension scheme. Therefore both employees'
and employers' contributions would be payable. Employers' contributions would have to be paid in any event because otherwise employers
would engage married women rather than other workers. All would
contribute. Women, like men, would qualify for pension at sixty-five
(see below). At that age women should be entitled to the same rate of
pension as men (i.e. £3 basic pension plus differential pension of 1/120
of average earnings for each year of employment) subject to a percentage
maximum of earnings. No dependants' benefits under the new pension
scheme are proposed. Additional 'constant attendance allowances', paid
by the Exchequer at a flat rate of 10s. a week, would be payable to
pensioners who are bedfast or who are so infirm they require regular
personal attendance. Combined with this a 'credit' would be allowed to
a relative or other person attending the pensioner who would otherwise
be in paid employment, so that he or she is under no penalty when his
pension rights come to be assessed.

Raising the Pension Age for Women from 60 to 65

Non-contributory old age pensions payable from the age of seventy
were introduced in 1908; contributory pensions payable from the age of
sixty-five followed in 1925. The pensionable age for women was reduced
to sixty in 1940 and was not altered by the National Insurance Act of
1946. Under the new scheme now proposed the question of restoration
of parity between pension ages for the two sexes obviously arises. It is
worth noting that in the United States, New Zealand, Switzerland,
Sweden, Norway and Canada, for example, the pensionable age is the

same for both men and women.

The whole emphasis in our proposals has been in the direction of treating women in the same way as men in any national superannuation scheme. One of the main justifications for giving pensions to women between the ages of 60-64 has been that many women of that age would in any case get benefits on the insurance of husbands aged sixty-five and over. If, under the proposed scheme, wives are not to be treated as dependants but as individuals qualifying for a pension in their own right, in exactly the same way as other women, then there is no special reason why they should gain a pension at sixty.

In general it is difficult to argue that women should receive a pension five years earlier than men when they have an expectation of life, at sixty-five, 2½ years longer than men. This is particularly true of a wage-related scheme in which both sexes are given broadly the same terms. One problem is, however, whether men and women have the same opportunity to get work in later life. If women received a pension at sixty, it would be hard to resist the argument that their contributions in working life should be relatively bigger or their pensions relatively smaller. In view of the fact that women's earnings are generally small it is not desirable that they should pay higher contributions or receive smaller pensions.

However, the consequences need to be studied. In 1951 1.3 million or 20 per cent of all men and women of pensionable age, were aged 60-64. We shall consider the single, widowed and married in turn. Sixteen per cent were spinsters. Of these nearly two thirds were not at work. How far they were unable to take paid employment is unknown, and deserves special inquiry. Undoubtedly some provision must be made for the single woman who is obliged by disability or infirmity to give up work before sixty-five. It is possible that for a transitional period she should receive a pension at the present rate. Alternatively, such a woman should be able, from the age of sixty, to claim a pension on the basis of her previous contributions and workspan, providing it is clear she cannot return to work. The same provision would be available to men also. Single women who are sick would come under sickness benefit arrangements.

Twenty-seven per cent of women aged 60-64 in 1951 were widowed or divorced. Nearly a fifth were at work. The rest may be receiving widows' pension rather than retirement pension but they will get a benefit no less than the present flat-rate insurance benefit. The principle here is that if cover for widowhood is to be provided on the husband's insurance for younger widows then the cover must apply to ages 60-64 also. Such provision need or need not be as generous as the provision for a widow over sixty-five, but clearly the introduction of a national superannuation scheme will entail reconsideration of widows' pensions and other benefits.

Finally, as many as 57 per cent of women aged 60-64 in 1951 were married. Only 7 per cent of them were at work. They fell roughly into the following three categories:

Married Women aged 60-64
16% or 120,000 with husbands aged under 60
47% or 350,000 with husbands aged 60-64
37% or 280,000 with husbands aged 65 and over

It can be seen that over a third would already have husbands drawing a wage-related pension on the substantial scales proposed. (Some would also be still at work.) The rest are not covered by the present national insurance scheme in any case (unless of course they had qualified for a pension on their own rather than their husband's insurance.) About a sixth would have husbands below the age of sixty, nearly all of whom, presumably, would still be active men at work. There remain less than a half with husbands in the same age-group. As nearly 90 per cent of men aged 60-64 are normally at work it is plain that only a small minority are likely to be in any kind of hardship. Their difficulties are met to some extent by the present sickness and other flat-rate benefits. The possibility of allowing some to draw pension early, as suggested above for single women, should, however, be studied — the object being to allow people with permanent handicaps to get national super-annuation between 60 and 65, if necessary.

The conclusion is that the increase in the pensionable age from 60 to 65 for women will affect less than a half of the 1.3 million women aged 60-64. Widows will be provided for separately and up to a third of spinsters will still be in full-time work. (In any event, spinsters form a declining and wives an increasing proportion of the elderly population.)

According to the Government Actuary 16 per cent of women in their sixties were unmarried in 1954, whereas there will be only 9 per cent or 10 per cent in 1979. At least a third of the married women do not qualify for the national insurance pension because (a) their husbands are under sixty-five, *and* (b) they have not earned a pension in their own right.

Most of those who are affected by the change would still be covered by husbands' new earnings-related pensions, and it could be argued that the immediate increase in the pension compensates the wives for their loss of 25s. For these women no special handicaps are likely to arise. Their husbands at sixty-five would be entitled to a substantial earnings-related pension. But the circumstances of spinsters need sympa-thetic consideration and this is largely why a special concession for those who are infirm, allowing them to draw an earlier pension, has been suggested. A more general problem is the availability of work for women of advanced age. Many private schemes in industry have a fixed retiring age of sixty for women. If industry wants to retire women at sixty instead of sixty-five, or is unable to employ women of this age, then fringe benefits for the ages 60-64 can be provided privately.

One of the big advantages of the proposal to increase the age is that there will be a substantial saving in cost which may amount to £45 million a year and which can be used to increase the pension for older pensioners. This estimate covers spinsters between sixty and sixty-four drawing retirement pensions and married women under sixty-five who draw benefits on their husbands' insurance, including the wives below sixty of men over sixty-five. In fact 51 per cent of men aged 65-9 in 1951 and 23 per cent of men aged 70-74 had wives below the age of sixty-five. There may also be a substantial saving in cost eventually by requiring women to qualify for pensions on the same terms as men. Wives who have never been out to work would not be entitled to their own pensions but would have to rely on the husband's. No estimate of such a saving is possible.

Note

1. Although 92 per cent of single women aged 20-24 are in paid employment there are only 66 per cent aged 55-9. The reasons for this falling-off would need to be examined before any final decision were made about the contribution period or pension rights of single women.

Truce on Inequality*

During the last ten years the general image of the Labour Party as presented to the public seems to have undergone a subtle but significant change. The party now seems to be characterized by a diminished attachment to moral and social principle and by a correspondingly greater concern with piecemeal reform, at least in social policy. Its leaders try to give the impression that they are honest, practical men of restraint dealing with the immediate realities of life. They are cautious about what they say they will do when they achieve power and are apt to be discouraged by the expert who tells them that a certain course of action will offend or produce too many technical difficulties. Their strength is their capacity for sustained practical activity; but, as Tawney has said more generally about the failings of the English, they are increasingly unwilling to test the quality of that activity by reference to principle. They seem to have become incurious about theory and therefore about their own destination. They often seem to be rooted in the particular problems thrown up in a particular week or year and do not easily relate solutions of them to a general social objective.

Some such picture, with all the necessary qualifications, must emerge from any study of the recent history of the Labour Party and particularly of the policy documents that have been published since the defeat of 1951. A number of valuable plans and ideas have emerged from the work of various committees set up in the years of opposition; but there has been a strange reluctance either to integrate them into a coherent social philosophy, so that priorities can be decided, or indeed to pursue or spell out in any detail the more imaginative plans which call for hard work and resolution. The best has not been made even of the unco-ordinated programme that now exists, and it is not therefore surprising to find so many people, even those of us most attached to its cause, regarding British socialism as intellectually tame and unadventurous.

Among the reasons for this shift in political character a future historian might well pick out for special attention the fading of interest in the subject of inequality. The main political parties and trade unions, together with economists and sociologists, appear to have called a truce

* First published in the *New Statesman*, 26 September 1959, shortly before the general election (with a reply by Harold Wilson in the following issue).

over inequality. From time to time some efforts, it is true, have been made within the Labour movement to revive the subject, but more because of a nostalgic yearning for the fiery battles of the past than because the issues seem appropriate today. A policy pamphlet on the subject of equality was indeed published two or three years ago but it lacked any serious probing of hard fact and was treated as rather inconsequential.

Why was the truce called? This, I think, is one of the fundamental questions about our post-war society. It hinges on the changing attitudes towards poverty in a society moving towards prosperity, if not affluence. There is first of all the prevalent belief that the 'Welfare State' has lifted the poor out of poverty and, within rough limits, provided equal standards of treatment and income to all citizens. Secondly, there is the belief that incomes and riches have been much more evenly distributed and therefore the differences between the living standards of the working classes and those of the middle and upper classes have narrowed sharply. And thirdly, there is the belief that to step up production is the most important objective in our society because everyone has shared in rising prosperity since the war and is bound to share in any future spoils. All these beliefs are widely held. They are held by socialists as well as Tories, though some socialists hold them in secret. Yet all three are highly questionable.

What precisely did the post-war social legislation bring about? Perhaps the essential feature of that legislation was the creation of an obligation, or contract, to provide all citizens with the basic needs of life in modern society − with certain standards of income security, medical care, housing and education. To a large extent the collective acceptance of this concept of universality was made possible by the war, by the sharing of privations and privileges, by the confrontation, in the armed services, through evacuation and the experiences of the blitz, of one half of society with the other, and by the ideals and high levels of tolerance which the hardships of war aroused in the hearts of men. Rights were created by virtue simply of citizenship; no one was to be excluded because of his wealth, his religion, his colour or his parentage. People's needs were of like value.

But what preceded the acceptance of the concept of universality? What occupational groups were brought in for the first time? How did the changeover affect the recipients − whether health service patients, unemployed, sick or old people? When measured in terms of increases in prices, population trends and proportions of the national income allocated to particular services, what did the changes in fact mean? Were the new standards generous or did they mean simply that people would not be allowed to starve?

As soon as we begin to look at such questions we begin to make the first assault on complacency. Improvements have been slow and uneven. Most of the poorest groups had been covered by national health and unemployment insurance before 1948. Their gains were not remarkable. Expressed as a proportion of average earnings, some of the insurance benefits even of 1959 compare very unfavourably with those of 1938. Some provisions for dependants were new but the bulk of social security legislation did not bring any really marked or sudden enrichment in material benefits. For the poorest sections of the community the crucial thing was the disappearance of the poor law test and the appearance of more humanity in administration. As Titmuss has said, 'This is what universalism really meant to the working classes: some decline in discrimination'.

Some better-off sections of the population did however gain in material benefits on extremely easy terms — especially pensions and sick pay. To achieve universalism in social security it was necessary in the first instance to favour these sections of society. Recent studies have demonstrated for some other social services that the right of free access has benefited the middle classes more than the working classes. For example, Vaizey has shown that the middle and upper income groups have gained most from the changes wrought by the Education Act, especially for their older children at school and university.

Without regard for the facts the various changes brought about by the post-war legislation have been called 'egalitarianism'. The essential thing here is not to confuse universality with egalitarianism. The national insurance scheme is universal — subject to a test of contributions. Yet the benefits it confers are so low that the poorest are driven to seek help from the National Assistance Board and the richest regard them simply as convenient supplements to much more substantial benefits they may obtain from employers or from insurance companies. A major mistake in many discussions since the war has been to regard the so-called public social services as self-contained entities remote from what goes on under the tax system and in industry.

Economists and sociologists did not allay the misapprehensions which grew up about the achievements of the Welfare State. In the decade before the war there were more than a dozen published surveys of poverty — in London, Birmingham, York, Southampton, Merseyside, Sheffield and elsewhere. Much information was brought before the public. Poverty, or the threat of poverty, overshadowed the lives of a large proportion of the population — a vocal and active proportion. In the thirteen years or so since the end of the war there has been only one survey of poverty — and that a rather mismanaged one. The subject has gone backstage.

It is clear, of course, that poverty no longer threatens the majority of the most active and vocal sections of the population. The poor are a voiceless minority. Yet they comprise a large number of people. There are millions depending almost solely on inadequate social insurance and national assistance benefits — the old, the sick, the unemployed, the widows with young children; there are many hundreds of thousands of chronic sick, infirm and socially handicapped persons living in institutions and at home; and there are millions of people, especially those with large families, living on low wages. Although the statistics are difficult to interpret the fraction of the population covered by these categories seems to be closer to one fifth than one tenth — ranging from 5 to 10 million. The scattered and all too few investigations that have been made of their circumstances and living standards make the more extravagant claims for the achievements of the Welfare State seem derisory. By tradition one of the chief functions of the Labour Party has been to speak for the underdog. But today it still seems inhibited from the outright criticisms necessary to fulfil that function: it is impelled to claim too much for the magic years after 1945.

Poverty is not the only subject to have attracted little attention in recent years. Before and during the war all the classical doctrines of the redistribution of income were at the forefront of intellectual thought and political debate. Today these doctrines are often treated with amused indulgency by many intelligent people. They no longer appear to matter. Really, the arguments suggest, didn't we deal with all that old stuff during and after the war? Haven't we all but abolished poverty? Look at the statistics about wage-earners and salaried earners. Look at the results of 'punitive' taxation and of death duties.

To go quietly through what scraps of evidence there are is to make another assault on complacency. Whatever 'redistribution' may mean it is plain that most of it occurred in the war. As early as 1947 the first important step was taken to increase regressive, and lighten progressive, taxes. Since that time, by a process which we may call 'piecemeal amelioration' the lot of the middle- and upper-income groups has gradually improved. I am referring here not only to the more obvious steps taken to relieve surtax-payers in one of the latest budgets or the general switch in emphasis from direct to indirect taxation, but to a series of big and small measures, from the removal of food subsidies to the tax relief granted to the parents of university students. The 1956 Finance Act, for example, allowed £50 million a year in taxes to be lost to the Exchequer so that contributors to private superannuation might enjoy more generous tax concessions. That £50 million was equivalent to the total sum then being paid to old age pensioners by the National Assistance Board. The rich have gained most from the changes because they were most affected by taxation in the first place. The fiscal system is the biggest, if the most silent social service we have.

The changes outside the tax system have been even more important. Comparisons between two persons' incomes tell us little about the real differences in their standards of living. All kinds of indirect subsidies are received by some people — meal vouchers, subsidized and free housing, salaries paid in full during sickness, free travel and so on. This is why some of the traditional statistics about the relative earnings of wage- and salaried earners have become uninformative. The last Blue Book on national income made a quiet change in one of its footnotes, to the effect that the proportion attributed to business expenses of the total spent on wines and spirits in the country had been raised from 5 per cent to 10 per cent. Ten per cent on the business account is nearly £40 million a year for a tiny fraction of the community. This is but one small hint of our need for a penetrating survey of the living standards of different occupational groups.

In tracing the reasons for the current lack of interest in inequality we cannot be content with examining the exaggerated claims for the achievements of the Welfare State and of taxation in bringing about a more equitable distribution of income. We must look to the values of society. There is near unanimity between Tories and Socialists on the desirability of ever-increasing production. Why have a war of attrition between different sections of society about inequality and the redistribution of income when all can share in increasing wealth? Once those in poverty become, in Britain no less than in America, a voiceless minority, why bother with the classical doctrines of socialism? In an advanced country increased production is an alternative to redistribution and is not associated with the same social tensions. Moreover, when the poor form a comparative minority why should they remain at the centre of the politician's interest? As Galbraith has said, 'It becomes easy, or at least convenient, to accept the use of the conventional wisdom which is that the rich . . . are highly functional and also much persecuted members of the society . . . To comment on the wealth of the wealthy, and certainly to propose that it be reduced, has come to be considered bad taste. The individual whose own income is going up has no real reason to incur the opprobrium of this discussion. Why should he identify himself, even remotely, with soapbox orators, malcontents, agitators, Communists and other undesirables?'

Yet look at the consequences. If public opinion, including the Left, puts expanding production first, then almost automatically there is a psychological obligation to subscribe to the importance of capital investment and of building so-called incentives into the tax system. In the policy documents of the Labour Party there is a noticeable shifting of feet whenever there is the slightest suggestion of using taxation as a weapon for social ends. Now we begin to understand part of the embarrassment of present-day socialism. For, as Galbraith points out, the conventional defence of inequality rests basically upon its functional role as an incentive and as a source of capital.

The facts seem to be inescapable. It is not the changes in social insurance, not any radical redistribution of income, which has brought about the diminution of poverty in Britain. Full employment, and the increase in output of recent decades, have brought the increase in well-being of the average man. And subscription to the virtues of expanding output has sapped the moral fibres of the Left. Not only, it is thought, will wage-earners benefit, everyone will benefit, and there will be an end to poverty. Yet this, as much as the hoped-for diminution in inequality, is not at all self-evident. On the contrary the evidence suggests both that a substantial minority of the population live in destitution or near destitution and that they have few prospects of improvement at a time when the wealth of some sections of the population is increasing rapidly.

This is the real challenge facing the next Labour Government, which many of us earnestly hope will be taken up. Can it stomach the thought that the social legislation of its 1945 predecessor could be bettered and, what is more, should now be critically reviewed? Can it make sure that the evidence necessary to formulate policy on such subjects of national importance as poverty and the living standards of different groups is being collected, either by a better financed research and information department of its own, or preferably, by some independent body? Can it disengage itself from the cloying attentions of those who think it better to invest in machinery rather than people? And can it end the truce over inequality? To do so, it must apply social principles which radically improve the income and living conditions of the poor and handicapped and — at the small cost of limiting the individual's ability to secure advantages outrageously in excess of those available to other citizens — enlarge his freedom to choose what kind of life he shall lead.

Freedom and Equality *

In the social history of most nations there are periods when factional enrichment and self-interest outweigh collective endeavour. Private extravagance and public parsimony tend to become the ruling principles and begin to threaten the common good. It would be hard to deny, at least by comparison with the years 1906-11 and 1942-8, that Britain has been living through just such a period. The recent history of social policy partly illustrates this.

For the best part of a decade after the election of 1951 the Tory Government was very defensive in its attitude to the social services inherited from the post-war Labour Government. There was little evidence of electoral support for a policy of dismantling them. Health, education and welfare services had been completely recast, and it would have seemed irresponsible to insist on major administrative reforms before they had been given the chance to settle down — especially when they were so popular. Moreover, some of the building, recruitment and social security programmes which were under way had acquired a momentum that was difficult, at least for a few years, to deflect. This explains why for so long few changes appeared to be made in the general balance and structure of these services.

In the first years of power the Tories found it necessary to claim that the Welfare State was partly of their own making. They wanted to feel their way gently through an uncertain political situation. From time to time they imposed restrictions on costs and withdrew, or reduced, particular subsidies, invoking, it must be admitted, a few unfortunate precedents set by the Labour Government between 1949 and 1951. This had consequences which have been insufficiently appreciated. In a period of rising national income and rapid social change even a 'holding' operation can in practice lead to some withering away of public services, simply because the private sector can develop at a much faster rate.

They also made subtle adjustments in the methods by which social security and other services were financed, with the long-term effect of reducing the redistribution of income from rich to poor. They therefore found financial control to be a strong and most acceptable weapon. Without appearing to meet the Labour Party in a head-on collision

* First published in the *New Statesman*, 14 April 1961.

over the principles of welfare they could put into reverse the equalitarian trends of the war and immediate post-war years.

This is however only a small part of a complex story and a part which makes the events of 1961 little different from those of the previous ten years. The middle generation of Tory leaders who had been guided into power by Mr Butler had tried to come to terms with the modern world and therefore with the Welfare State. In 1951 they accepted the public social services partly because they saw it was politically expedient to do so but also because they wanted Conservative policies to be more positive in some respects than they had been in the past. They began to realize that there might be some connexion between the quality of public education and industrial productivity. They also felt that gentlemen should object to intolerable slum conditions, whether in houses or in hospitals. They talked of 'decent' or 'civilized' standards.

While they certainly did not believe in equality some of them felt that the State had to provide limited services for all citizens in medical care, education and some fields of welfare. Keynes and Beveridge had persuaded them that there might be some virtue in the concept of a national minimum. They tended to draw the minimum at a low level, for they wanted individuals to have room for manoeuvre to add to State provision by their own efforts. There had to be no disincentive to individual enterprise, no strict limits imposed on the freedom of employers, the big corporations and the insurance interests. So although they never succeeded in producing a coherent statement of this 'new' conservatism they appeared to be reconciled to the view that the State should provide some minimum services for *all* citizens.

Today this short-lived and admittedly uncertain attachment to a philosophy of limited universal services seems to be threatened. A different and much older philosophy is again on the march. With the 1959 election over and the Labour Party in disarray, many Tories no longer feel so inhibited from speaking their minds about social objectives. It is true that for a number of years writers like de Jouvenel, Hayek and Colin Clark have urged the abandonment of the principles generally accepted after the war, but their influence was for a long time inconsequential. Lately however Liberals such as Walter Hagenbuch and Professor Alan Peacock, and right-wing authors of pamphlets and books issued by the Conservative Political Centre, the Bow Group and the Institute of Economic Affairs, a quasi-research body, have taken up their pleas. As Mr Geoffrey Howe writes in the latest publication of the Bow Group: 'Over the whole field of social policy our firm aim should . . . be a reduction in the role of the state.' Or as Professor Peacock puts it: 'the true object of the Welfare State, for the Liberal, is to teach people to do without it.'

What are the main features of this philosophy? There are of course shades of meaning and emphasis but broadly it may be said to start with the idea that the individual should be master of his own destiny; that he should be free to spend his income as he thinks best and to add to his private property; and that he should be responsible for his own and his family's needs. It goes on with the argument that the nation is becoming more and more prosperous. As a result, many of the problems for which the social services were set up have been solved and a much higher proportion of the population no longer needs protection or subsidy. They can stand on their own feet. Instead of regarding the social services as permanent institutions, we should, as Mr Arthur Seldon has put it, regard them like crutches which can be thrown away as soon as we learn how to walk. The object then is to see how many services can be returned to the private sector.

For those services which cannot be dismantled immediately one of two principles should be applied. Each individual should pay a weekly or monthly sum as close as possible to the cost of the benefits he enjoys. Or the services should be restricted to persons who, according to a test of means, cannot afford to provide for themselves. Following these theories we have had a crop of suggestions that pensions should only be given to those who pass a test of low income, that a lodging fee should be paid by hospital patients and an education fee by the parents of children in State schools. And that subsidies for housing and school meals should be abolished.

Essentially this philosophy is a reversion to the unrepentant Tory individualism of the nineteenth century. As then, it has never been cogently expressed. The assumptions are unclear, as are the steps in the argument and the translation of the argument into a rational and effective programme of political action. I can but raise some general questions.

Freedom for Whom?

First, the concepts of 'freedom' and 'individual responsibility' are used uncritically in this context. To some extent we may sympathize with the idea that an individual should be free to spend his money as he thinks fit and to be responsible for himself and his own family. But freedom implies choice, and responsibility, knowledge. Suppose an individual has no State taxes or contributions to pay for his security in sickness, old age, and so on. How else can he obtain security? One answer is that his firm might have a pension and a welfare scheme and help him in many different ways. Yet these are social services, rather similar in purpose to those run by the State — the only difference being (though not one we can lightly pass over) that they do not cover several million workers. But what freedom does the individual have to influence the shape of these schemes? Or to contract out of them if he thinks them unfair? Does he retain his right to a pension or to some other benefit if he has to leave his employment?

Another answer is that he can privately insure himself and his family. He will pay a premium. But if there is a history of tuberculosis in his family what freedom does he have to get adequate private insurance or to get it on the same terms as an average person in a trouble-free family? Will he pay an extra premium for the unlikely risk of contracting cancer in his forties? There are a thousand and one unlikely hazards he may have to consider. What happens if through protracted illness or unemployment he cannot keep up his payments? Can he responsibly choose which insurance company would give him the best terms and where does he get the information on which to take a decision? How far are insurance companies indeed accountable for their decisions? Such questions make us realize how limited is the area of real choice or how uncertain the exercise of responsibility. It is the employer, or the insurance official rather than the individual, who possesses the main share of freedom and power.

There is a second misconception. The individualists tend to talk and write about the social services as if they were a dispensable artefact of society. Sometimes they describe them as unnecessary indulgences or luxuries. Yet employers who want greater productivity aim to prevent strikes and keep morale and health standards high. They try to keep their experienced workers. They therefore improve working conditions, pay wages during sickness and set up health pensions and welfare schemes. As a general rule, even if they pursue these aims fitfully, they tend to achieve greater prosperity and efficiency than their fellows. By analogy the same argument applies to the national economy as a whole. From this point of view social services are an integral and indispensable part of modern society. Far from being a handicap to industrial efficiency and economic advance they are a condition of it.

The recent Crowther Report supplies an instructive example. The committee certainly based some of its arguments for a big expansion in education for those aged 15-18 on the principle of wider opportunities. But others it based on the principle of national efficiency, or of economic growth and competitiveness. We were providing too few technically qualified workers and managers. Both Russia and the United States were outstripping us in educational advances and technological ingenuity. How could we be more efficient? By *collectively* investing more in public educational services.

A third misconception is that in a relatively prosperous society most individuals have the capacity to meet any contingency in life. Only a poor and handicapped minority need special protection or help. This ignores the infinite diversities and changing conditions to be found in any population. Men gain or fall in status and living standards; at one stage of their life their dependencies are minimal, at others unduly onerous; sometimes they need exceptional help to achieve qualifications and skills held to be desirable by society; and at all times they are susceptible to the vicissitudes of prolonged ill-health, disability, redundancy or unemployment, and bereavement, which they are usually powerless to control or even reasonably anticipate. Unanticipated adversity is not the peculiar experience of one fixed section of the working class.

The individualistic philosophy about the Welfare State is weakest of all in its narrowness of scope. Intelligent discussion of the social services has been bedevilled since the war by a refusal to look farther than those provided by the Government at public cost. It is simply not enough in the 1960s to look narrowly at *State* education, the *national* health service, *national* insurance and so on. As Richard Titmuss pointed out in what is perhaps the most important post-war comment on social policy ('The Social Division of Welfare' in his book *Essays on the Welfare State*), the definition of a social service 'should take its stand on its aims; not on the administrative methods and institutional devices employed to achieve them'.

There are thus two systems other than the one commonly recognized. The first is the occupational welfare system, whereby employers provide pensions, child and educational allowances, health and welfare services, season tickets, meal vouchers and medical expenses. This probably costs around £1,500 million a year. The term 'fringe benefits' is becoming inappropriate. The other is the fiscal welfare system, whereby individuals are given tax allowances and reliefs for wives and children, aged, incapacitated and infirm relatives, housekeepers, and life assurance and superannuation. The total cost is likely to be of the order of £1,000 million. These two systems have grown enormously since the war. Tory and Liberal philosophers have not called for their abolition. They rarely mention them. Yet both are designed to meet certain dependent needs of the individual and his family — just like the national health service and national insurance. And both are collectively provided services.

The individualistic philosophy can be criticized in terms of its own basic assumptions and scope, as well as the more traditional arguments about inequalities and injustices which involve millions of persons who are sick, handicapped, aged, supporting large families on low incomes and working in declining industries or small firms which cannot introduce welfare schemes. Yet the Government seems to be edging towards it. The arguments put forward in Parliament for the health service charges and contributions show this. So does Mr Brooke's new proposal to put pressure on local authorities to adopt differential rent schemes for council housing. But the new pension scheme provides an even better example.

The present retirement pension is paid for in part by flat-rate contributions from both the employee and the employer and in part by the Exchequer. A second scheme has now started which will entitle some people to an additional pension. All those earning £9 a week or less pay nothing and receive nothing. They number six million workers or about a quarter of the working population. The self-employed are also left out. Those employees earning more than £9 a week are doing one of two things. If they already belong to a scheme run by their employers which offers them terms at least as good as the Government, their employers have had the choice of contracting them out of the Government scheme. This seems to be applying to about four million people. The others are paying 4¼ per cent of each pound (or ten pence) over the 9th and up to the 15th of their weekly earnings. They may not earn as much as £15 but if they do they will pay 4¼ per cent of each of the six pounds from the 10th to the 15th, adding 5s. 1d. Their employer adds an equal amount.

A man now aged sixty and earning £11 a week will get an extra shilling when he is sixty-five. If he earns £15 a week he will get 5s. Even if he is only fifty now and pays contributions for the next fifteen years on earnings between £9 and £15 he will add only 13s. to his pension. In 1966 the maximum extra pension will be 4s; in 1986 it will be 22s; and in 2008, 41s. This 41s. is what a youngster of eighteen will get when he is sixty-five, providing he earns £15 in every week in every year of the forty-seven before his sixty-fifth birthday. Periods of sickness and unemployment are not credited. This is not exactly a breathtaking scheme. The Government has assumed conservatively that the real level of earnings will increase 2 per cent per annum. This means that in the year 2008 the average wage is likely to be £38 per week. The maximum extra pension of 41s. in that year will be trifling in relation to this figure. In terms of today's wages it would be equivalent to about 16s.

The Tory Plan

Why, then, did the Government go to so much trouble to produce such a mouse? One explanation is that in 1957 the Labour Party published a much more ambitious plan for national superannuation which on the whole was greeted with such enthusiasm that before the 1959 election the Tory Party deemed it expedient to produce a rival. During the ensuing period of heart-searching some Tories appeared to agree with some of the motives of the Labour plan. They were troubled by the amount of poverty in old age and by the fact that occupational pension schemes were not expanding in the form or at the rate which would guarantee a sufficient supplement in retirement for several million older workers for a number of years hence.

At this point the individualists seem to have entered the discussion and it is clear that, in collusion with the Treasury, they all but won the ensuing battle. In October 1958, the Government's plan was announced and its prime object was 'to place the national insurance scheme on a sound financial basis'.

This was an ambiguous way of describing an extraordinary political manoeuvre. A young worker starting to pay these new contributions could buy commercially from an insurance company, with the same contributions, an annuity at least three times greater than he is promised under the Government scheme. The profit is used to help finance the flat-rate pension. This is the crucial point. In the first year the new contributions will bring in £186 million and almost nothing will be paid out. In the tenth year £304 million will be collected and only £15 million spent. And in the fortieth year £544 million will be collected and only £214 million spent. These are facts about the scheme as at present constituted, not political arguments. As Professor Lafitte has said, 'essentially [the purpose of the Act] is to alter the *financing*, not to transform the *benefits*, of national insurance'. And this new burden bears much more heavily on workers earning between £10 and £15 a week than on those earning large sums.

The New Strategy

The increased health service charges and contributions recently approved by Parliament form another part of this intensified strategy to relieve the Exchequer of its financial share of the cost of the social services and place a heavier burden on either the low-paid contributor or the recipient. Since 1957 the health service contribution has been increased twice and in July of this year it goes up again to 2s. 8½d. a week. To more than treble a single poll-tax in a period of four years is certainly more than a straw in the wind.

The belief in equal participation by all citizens in the social services is also crumbling away. Already we have moved a long way from comprehensive social security, first by default, in allowing occupational and fiscal arrangements to make nonsense of the Beveridge scheme, second by deliberate Government manipulation of the finances of income security and now by deliberate restrictions in the scope of social insurance. The flat-rate social insurance benefit has never reached a level upon which people could live without other resources. (This is the principle which Beveridge promulgated and which, in the war, everyone agreed on. For years both Labour and Tory Governments halfheartedly subscribed to it, without putting it into practice.) That is why the numbers of people resorting to national assistance were never the residual few thousands originally intended.

Then, in 1954, came the first explicit rejection of the principle. The Government claimed only that the benefit provided a minimum and that individuals were expected to get additional income to achieve subsistence. Many salaried workers would have generous sickness pay or occupational pensions. But many wage-earners in time of trouble would have to turn to the National Assistance Board.

The Government therefore adopted the strategy of minimizing the role of comprehensive social insurance and leaving its benefits at a low level. It decided to lay emphasis instead on selective national assistance. This was much cheaper. In 1959 it announced that those receiving assistance were going to enjoy some share in rising national prosperity. The meaning of this is unclear. The new rates are an increase of 7 per cent for a single person and less than 6 per cent for a married couple over the rates introduced in September 1959. In this time average industrial earnings have already increased by 9 per cent or 10 per cent and are still rising. Social insurance is therefore restricted in scope and function, and national assistance beneficiaries are not getting their full share of advancing prosperity. The prospect is one of widening inequalities.

What do these decisive changes in social policy mean in practice? We may take the example of two men who retire. One is the wage-earner with no private pension who now receives a retirement pension of 57s. 6d. at sixty-five. This is 19 per cent of average earnings. If he gets any further earnings over a small amount his pension is progressively reduced. If he cannot live he goes to the National Assistance Board so that he can pay his rent. He is one of millions of single and widowed persons and married couples in this country living on £3, £4 or £5 a week.

The other, a civil servant, a former permanent secretary of a government ministry, is reported to have retired from the civil service at sixty, obtained a substantial lump sum of a few thousand pounds, and also a £1,500 a year pension, which was not subject to reduction if there were further earnings. He is now on the Board of one of the nationalized industries at a salary of £2,500 a year plus nearly £1,000 for entertainment expenses. We may note the qualifying age of sixty; the tax-free lump sum; the pension of around half final salary; and the lack of an earnings rule. We may wonder whether the principles of State pensions, or indeed, for that matter, of social security, make sense.

Many people shy away from the issue of pensions and other social security benefits because it seems complex — a matter for actuaries and other experts. Yet the issue is basically a simple one. Are we to accept the perpetuation of two nations, of first- and second-class citizens, in our society? This is what is implied by a philosophy which applies the rigorous concept of the means test or of the subsistence minimum, through the public social services, to a large section of the population, while condoning the application of completely different principles and standards, through private and occupational social services, to a much smaller and more privileged section of the population.

The central choice in social policy lies in fact between a national minimum and equality. To choose the first may be well-meaning but short-sighted, for by clinging to a formula which was more appropriate to the conditions of the past the needs and conditions of the present may be overlooked. Paradoxically, inequalities may become wider rather than narrower. The differences between the Labour Party and one wing of the Tory Party will then really be differences of degree and emphasis rather than of principle. Justice cannot be achieved by looking narrowly at the so-called public social services. Their problems cannot be solved in isolation from those of the occupational or the fiscal social services. Standards of need, or minima, cannot be decided only by investigating the poor section of society or the working classes. Any measure only makes sense by reference to what is happening in the rest of society. For poverty, or human need, is not an absolute condition, except perhaps in terms of bare physical survival. Individuals belong to families, to small communities and to the wider society. They therefore have material, psychological and social needs which can only be measured or met by comparison with the full range of conditions found in society as a whole.

The implications for policy therefore begin to fall into place. The Labour Party has already adopted a plan to reduce the fall in income on retirement. This plan could be extended to embrace the whole of social security — including sickness, unemployment, widows' and industrial injuries benefits. The employer should perhaps be obliged to pay full wages for the first months of sickness.

Privilege and Welfare

It would be pointless to embark on such a radical transformation of social security without also overhauling tax concessions and employers' allowances for children and other dependencies, so as to avoid the private undermining of principles collectively accepted. Greater improvements in the living conditions of poorer people can be achieved partly by restricting the opportunities of the better-off to gain privileges which are 200 per cent or 1,000 per cent greater. We want freedom, freedom perhaps to diversify the State pension scheme, the State health scheme or the State education scheme, but not freedom to jeopardize collective well-being. Contracting out is an alternative to diversification but only on strict conditions in the public interest. An individual who contracts out must continue to make his contribution towards maintaining the standards available to all citizens — that goes without saying. But he must not be able to secure advantages outrageously in excess of those available to other citizens.

In its education policy, for example, the Labour Party tends to ignore private education and talks vaguely of gradually squeezing the public schools out by so improving State education that the competition becomes too tough for the Headmasters' Conference. That, in the present situation, is an empty claim. If we concede the right of the individual to choose an alternative form of schooling for his children we must also make sure that the public schools satisfy certain conditions of approval — in their financing, entitlement to tax reliefs and pupil-teacher ratios. This is the only means of discouraging the continuation and growth of privileged islands in society. It is difficult to ignore the result of appeals for endowments and covenants, which have allowed more rapid capital extensions in many private than in most State schools, or the way firms now help salaried employees to pay fees for children in private schools. It may be feasible to link private schools with a regionalized system of State schools and grant them a semi-autonomous status. This is one way both of showing that society cares as much about, and is prepared to spend as much on, the secondary modern child as the young Etonian, and of improving the overall quality of education.

The object of a social democracy is to enlarge the individual's freedom of choice. But this cannot be achieved by devising modest principles for some conventional sector of State activity any more than by retreating into a philosophy of individual salvation. In social policy it can be achieved only by devising principles which apply to all institutionalized methods of meeting need — to industrial, voluntary and private associations as well as central, regional and local government services — and therefore to all members of society. In the last analysis to pursue individual freedom is to pursue social equality.

It will be one of the supreme paradoxes of history if social inequalities become wider instead of narrower and poverty more widespread during the term in office of the present Labour Government. Yet the likelihood of this happening is far from remote. Here is a political movement whose egalitarian ideals were nurtured by the degradations which millions of men, women and children endured during the nineteenth century in mines, factories and slums. These ideals are vigorously expressed today on the shop floor, and within the trade unions, at ward meetings and at party conferences. Men have come to regard the achievement of equality as the essence of socialism. Much that is important and indeed noble in the search for a humane social order — unselfishness, partnership, solidarity, fair shares, common responsibility and, above all, the elimination of poverty — is crystallized in the concept. This central motivation carried the Labour Party to power in 1945 and played a big part in the victories of 1964 and 1966.

Given the history and ideals of the Labour movement how is it possible to conceive, therefore, that the problems of poverty and inequality might be growing? Brian Abel-Smith has discussed already the shortcomings of forward planning and has shown in terms of this country's recent experience and developments in other industrial countries that the social services are being starved of resources.[1] Richard Titmuss has shown that the private market is incapable of solving the problem of poverty, discrimination and unequal access to education, social security and medical care.[2] I shall argue first that the problem of poverty in modern society is different from conventional or traditional interpretations, and that it is big and is growing. It therefore demands more comprehensive action to solve than might be supposed if the traditional interpretation were followed. Secondly, I shall argue that even by conventional standards the extent of poverty in Britain has been and is underestimated; and thirdly, that the Labour Government has as yet done little to meet such poverty. Finally, I shall try to suggest the kind of measures which have to be given priority for socialist objectives to be reached.

* First presented as a Fabian autumn lecture in November 1966 and published by the Fabian Society in January 1967.

1. The Need for a New Conception of Poverty

There are many different conceptions of poverty.(3) The individual may feel he is poor, in relation to the people around him, the job he is expected to perform or his past experience. Collective or conventional views tend to be reflected in the minimum standards of social security benefit which are adopted in different countries. Those with less income than the minimum rates of benefit are regarded as in poverty. Within a single country different organizations may hold conflicting views. For example, local authorities in Britain vary widely in the means tests they apply in educational, home help and housing services. A single organization, too, may apply different conceptions simultaneously. The Government's definition of subsistence varies from around £50 a week for class A employees working temporarily in Paris, £21 per week for employees or consultants on official business in this country, to around £5 10s. a week (including average rent) for citizens on national assistance.

Is there an objective or scientific approach? Historically, much has been made of a basic 'subsistence' level — meaning, in its restricted sense, the minimum resources needed by a man or a family to get enough to eat and maintain physical health. The trouble with this approach is that contrary to common supposition nutritional needs cannot be strictly defined and to a large extent are relative to the social and occupational conditions in which they arise. If men are expected to expend their energies in steelworks or mines rather than look after a herd of camels they need more to eat and drink. But practically no scientific study has been made of variations of diet according to both social and occupational environment. Whether those in sedentary occupations, like clerks, pass their evenings and weekends in violent physical exercise — playing football and ballroom dancing — while the miners have their feet up in front of a television set is unknown. Secondly, even in agricultural societies there are psychological and social needs as basic as nutritional or physical needs which can be met only by the expenditure of resources in money or kind. Thirdly, in industrial societies the individual and the family plainly have to meet new obligations which are thrust upon them — whether by local housing or education authorities, the state, modern technology and marketing or simply changing social norms and values.(4)

Human needs arise by virtue of the kind of society to which individuals belong. We can therefore consider them meaningfully only in relation to the social groups and systems to which they belong — ranging from households, families, local communities, national societies to, finally, international society. Any rational definition of poverty must be relative. Consequently, if it is to be applied at different points of time during periods of economic and social growth it must be upgraded, and not merely repriced.

This helps to explain inconsistencies which arise in the world today. United Nations and other experts have produced standards of subsistence for some developing countries far in excess of the resources commanded by the average wage-earner in those countries but far below the standards adopted in advanced industrial countries.(5) The national income per head in India, Bolivia, the Congo and Pakistan, when translated into U.S. dollars, is *on average* less than 100 dollars a year. The amount required by the *poor* to survive is far less. Yet the standard officially adopted in the United States, below which people are described as in poverty, ranges from about 1,500 dollars a year for a person living alone to about 700 dollars a head for large families.(6)

There is a reluctance to accept evidence that so-called 'subsistence' standards are dramatically higher in advanced industrial than in developing countries, and there is an equal reluctance, at least in Britain and the United States, to accept the evidence that such standards have been or ought to be upgraded in the course of time. There are political as well as social and psychological reasons for this. The subsistence or national minimum has a hallowed history. In Britain the basic rates payable by the Supplementary Benefits Commission and Ministry of Social Security are distantly related to the levels advocated in the Beveridge Report in the war, which in turn reflected the standards used in measuring poverty by Rowntree and others before the war. Many people like to believe the national minimum has a scientific basis. First of all, when used as a measure of poverty only a minority of the population are found in fact to be exposed to this problem. Wages in industrial countries are usually enough to maintain physical efficiency. Secondly, if the same measure is applied in later years the proportion in poverty is found to diminish. This is very comforting for politicians.(7) But if the standard is adjusted only for price increases the diminution is inevitable. Since real incomes in industrial countries tend to rise, the proportion of the population 'left behind' is almost bound to shrink. Thirdly, the whole concept of a national minimum invites selective, ameliorative and isolated rather than universal and reconstructional policies to relieve poverty. Social and economic reforms, it is supposed, do not have to be drastic. Provided welfare can be concentrated among the pockets or islands of the population where it is needed all will be well. The rich, the middle-income groups, the status, income and class hierarchies of society and the values and standards of many professional and voluntary associations will not be threatened. Minor adjustments alone are needed.

The subsistence standard or national minimum has an ideological rather than a scientific basis. It reflects the separatist social philosophy flowing historically from the less-eligibility principle of the English Poor

Law. The income-levels of the poor, it is supposed, have to be determined differently from those of the rest of the population — as if they were a race apart. Sargent Shriver, director of the U.S. President's War Against Poverty, has complained of the tendency in the United States for many to speak of 'we the people' and 'they the poor'. Broadly, the poor are allowed living room on a 'floor' at the bottom of the hierarchical social structure, above which they are expected to rise by their own efforts. They have to struggle for a foothold on the ladders to the more affluent levels of society, irrespective of the fact that there are places enough on neither the ladders nor the upper storeys for more than a few more of them and irrespective of the fact that chutes from the upper storeys are regularly transporting individuals and families to the nether levels.

It is only in terms of a modern version of Brueghel's Tower of Babel, as representing hierarchical society, that we can perceive the limitations of the 'national minimum' approach to poverty. Each level of society may be on an escalator of socio-economic growth, and there may be machinery for slightly reducing or increasing the distance between levels. But the structure determines poverty. In relation to the resources commonly sought after and commonly acknowledged to be necessary there is a section of the population which is deprived of commanding them.

What is the alternative approach? Individuals and families can be defined as in poverty when they lack or fall seriously short of the resources required to share in the customs and style of life approved and commonly available in society. This might, of course, be discussed at great length but two matters deserve special attention. The idea of what constitutes individual or family 'resources' in modern society has to be revised. We can no longer talk about poverty only in terms of the money coming in week by week. There are people with small incomes but substantial other resources (including assets) and vice versa. The ownership of assets can be important in maintaining living standards, especially among the middle-aged and old. There are not only assets like savings and housing, but also cars, boats and household possessions. Some people have powers to distribute the realization of assets over time.(8) Then there are fringe benefits — such as luncheon vouchers, educational endowment, superannuation payments and travel and housing expenses. Recent estimates suggest that the cost of fringe benefits to employers is over 14 per cent of the earnings bill in Britain and still rising.(9) In one study fringe benefits accounted for an extra 31 per cent of the £7,000 average earnings of company managers but 11 per cent of the £1,000 average earnings of those at the foot of the salary scale.(10) For some families income in kind (e.g. gifts and services from relatives and neighbours) is of major importance.

Account must also be taken of current consumption of public social services and private possession of public assets, such as the use of free or subsidized housing and office-space and the possession of assets such as educational qualifications. Too readily in the past it has been supposed that universal public services have automatically conferred equality of access as well as equality of rights. The wealth dispensed by government is, as Charles Reich has argued, the new property.(11) Who owns this property and how such ownership is measured are important questions. More middle-class than working-class children gain university degrees at State expense.(12) National Health Service lists and school classes tend to be larger in working-class areas.(13) Many of the poorest people seem not to qualify for subsidized council housing or are obliged to leave it for far worse and usually more costly privately rented housing.(14)

Other groups may not have access to welfare. Many migrants, especially from overseas, cannot qualify for years for admission to housing waiting lists. Of men who were unemployed in August 1966 nearly half did not receive unemployment benefit and half of the latter received national assistance. Some of those getting unemployment benefit did not qualify for the full rate.(15) Separated wives and widows may not qualify for supplementary benefits.(16) These are the kind of issues with which we will increasingly be obliged to deal.

Families vary in their command of these kinds of resources. A family may be in poverty in terms of all or only some of them. It may have low monetary income, no liquid assets, no educational capital, access only to a dilapidated hospital and an overworked general practitioner partnership; the children may go to a slum school and the home itself may be a slum. Alternatively, only some of these deprivations may apply. The distinction between total and partial poverty is one which must be made in industrial society. Both kinds of poverty are significant. This analysis also suggests that some of the people who are excluded in surveys of income and expenditure, such as children in children's homes and adults in long-stay hospitals and residential Homes, may be found to be in poverty. Isolated institutions can too quickly fall behind the standards of living being attained by the population in private households. By comparison with standards of living enjoyed by people of the same age in the general community, there is evidence of the inmates of many psychiatric hospitals, hospitals for chronic disease and welfare institutions being in poverty.(17)

The second matter which is crucial to a revised conception of poverty is the level of resources at which it is justified to begin talking of 'poverty'. In descending the various scales of resources it is in principle possible to establish when there are significant departures from social norms and conditions. For example, in many surveys the proportion of household expenditure devoted to food has been found to be fairly constant for middle-income groups but increases sharply below particular levels of income. The point at which the proportion changes could be treated as the point below which people may be found to be in poverty. Future research might establish other indices of exclusion from participation in particular social customs and relationships, such as inability to take holidays away from home, keep children at school, replenish stocks of clothes, have regular cooked meals and entertain guests and treat friends at home or outside the home. President Johnson's advisers have sometimes recognized the problem and have searched for formulations going beyond the traditional conception of poverty. In his message on poverty to Congress in 1964, for example, the President asked, 'What does this poverty mean to those who endure it?' First, he gave the traditional interpretation. 'It means a daily struggle to secure the necessities for even a meagre existence.' But he then went on, *'It means that the abundance, the comforts, the opportunities they see all around them are beyond their grasp'* (my italics).(18)

2. The Scale and Nature of Poverty

We are struggling to identify and measure these new forms of poverty. In Britain it could be argued that they began to be recognized around the mid 1950s. Earlier the Labour movement and the general public assumed that through its Welfare State policies the Attlee Government had consolidated the greater social equality ushered in by the war. In the words of the chairman of the National Food Survey Committee, published as late as 1960, we had witnessed the 'virtual elimination' of poverty.(19)

At first the problem was thought to apply to a substantial section of the aged but to relatively few other persons in the population. In writing of the United States, where unemployment was heavy in some areas, Galbraith referred to 'islands' of poverty.(20) It was difficult in both countries to believe that despite high employment and rising prosperity there remained large-scale hardship. Yet a gradually accumulating literature on the aged, widows, the sick and the unemployed in Britain,(21) and a few income studies in the United States led to a partial realization of the size of the problem. Finally a quantitative measure was obtained of what at least was conventionally regarded as 'poverty'. In the United States 38 million people or 22 per cent were found to have incomes below those thought necessary to secure a reasonable minimum diet.(22) In Britain the proportion of subsistence poverty was found to be smaller but still substantial. An analysis of income data collected for 1960 by the Ministry of Labour suggested that between seven and eight million persons, or around 14 per cent, were living below a specially defined 'national assistance' standard (i.e. a standard incorporating the basic national assistance rates and average rent plus a margin, 40 per cent, to cover income which was disregarded by the N.A.B., and discretionary additions which were commonly granted).(23) The studies in both countries revealed the unpalatable fact that hardship existed among a substantial number of families of wage-earners.

Not only are the numbers of the poor large. They are almost certainly growing. There have been relative increases in some groups in the population who have been at an economic disadvantage in the years since the war. For some years it has been generally recognized that 'on the whole . . . the economic inequalities between developed and underdeveloped countries have been increasing'.(24) The possibility that a similar process may have occurred within some of the developed countries is just beginning to dawn. In many of them there has been a shift in structure of the adult population towards the older age groups; a revival of the birth-rate together with an increase in the number of families with four or more children; and small increases in the numbers of chronic sick, disabled and handicapped among the middle and older age-groups. Certain forms of dependency may in fact increase in advanced societies. Secondly, the differential development of state and private welfare schemes has reinforced social divisions. The growth of occupational sick pay and superannuation schemes has made a mockery of the equal flat-rate benefits of national insurance. The real value of family allowances has been eroded while that of children's tax allowances has increased. The teaching and facilities in far too many secondary modern schools has remained abysmal while that in many independent direct grant and grammar schools, and perhaps also in the new comprehensive schools, has greatly improved. Thirdly, it is possible that flagging demand for unskilled workers, together with the continuing increase in the employment of married women and the greater opportunity for certain workers to maintain two jobs has held down the wage-rates of some male employees and thrown a number into premature retirement. These are some of the critical factors.

The Character of the Problem

What therefore was the problem faced by the Labour Party when it achieved power in October 1964? Among those in poverty are the following:

1. Families in which the head is in full-time work but has either a relatively low wage or several children or both (the estimated number of persons living below a national assistance standard, including rent and a margin of 40 per cent extra to allow for income disregards and discretionary additions,(25) is three million

of whom rather less than a million have incomes below the basic national assistance rates, including average rent paid).

2. Persons of pensionable age, whether living alone, as married couples or with others in the household (the estimated number living below a national assistance standard is about 2½ million, of whom about 850,000 have incomes of less than the basic national assistance rates, including average payment for rent).

3. Families composed of a mother and dependent children but no father (estimated number of persons below the standard being around ¾ million, of whom possibly as many as 300,000 have incomes of less than the basic national assistance rates).

4. Families in which one parent, not necessarily the head or the father of a family, is disabled or has been sick for three months or more (estimated number of persons living below the standard being about ¾ million including ¼ million with incomes of less than the basic national assistance rates).

5. Familes with a father who is unemployed (estimated number of persons living below the standard being at least ½ million at the present time, of whom at least ¼ million have incomes of less than the basic national assistance rates).

Although these groups are not exhaustive they are the principal ones and are discussed below.

Wage-Earner Families

Too little is yet known about living standards in these families. The Ministry of Social Security's survey of households drawing family allowances is eagerly awaited. A pilot study of families in London with five or more children has shown that nearly a quarter have incomes below the basic supplementary benefit rates and another sixth only up to 20 per cent more than these rates.(26) The man's wage is below the total that would be allowed under the national assistance or what is now the supplementary benefits scheme. Some families' incomes do not reach the total even when the wife takes paid employment to supplement the wage.

The problem is by no means confined to large families. A small minority of wage-earner households with one, two or three children falls below national assistance or supplementary benefit levels but they account for the majority of families found to be in hardship.(27) A disproportionately large proportion of men with low wages are disabled or have histories of ill-health and disability. In October 1960, when the average wage was £14 3s. 0d., a survey of manual earnings in selected manufacturing industries carried out by the Ministry of Labour showed that as many as 10 per cent of men aged twenty-one and over were receiving less than £10 a week. About 30 per cent had earnings of less than 80 per cent of the average.(28) The survey had severe limitations. (29) Nonetheless the survey was the most comprehensive yet carried out by the ministry.

A recent report of the Family Expenditure Survey allows us to go farther — though the precision of the data is still uncertain.(30) An analysis of the earnings of male employees aged twenty-one and over who were covered by the 1965 Survey showed that 8 per cent, representing more than a million, were earning under £12 a week, or less than 60 per cent of the average earnings, which were then nearly £20. About 41 per cent, or 6 million, had earnings of less than 80 per cent of the average. Employees in manufacturing industry tended to earn rather more. Few of them had earnings of less than 80 per cent of the average (the figure for *manual* workers being 22 per cent, compared with 30 per cent in the 1960 special inquiry). The report shows that there are substantial proportions of manual workers in the extractive and service industries earning considerably less than the average, and also that there are some non-manual workers with very low earnings.(31)

Without further information about the regularity of earnings, household composition and other sources of household income it is difficult to judge the meaning of these earnings data. Some people with low earnings live in households where there are other earners. The number of wives in paid employment has been rising steadily since the war and is now around 4½ million. Despite this increase the number of households with more than one earner has been falling. At the 1961 Census 42 per cent of all households in England and Wales had more than one earner, and 13 per cent three or more earners.(32) This compared with 46 per cent and 15 per cent respectively at the 1951 Census. The increase in married women in paid employment seems to be more than balanced by the increase in numbers of 'retirement' households, the falling number of composite households and more adolescents in households who stay on at school.

Retired Persons

A series of local and national studies allows us to be fairly precise about the income levels of the aged. The incomes of a majority are low. In 1962 nearly 1¾ million men and women aged sixty-five and over (or about half of all single and widowed persons) had total incomes of less than £4 a week, and 400,000 couples (or just under a quarter of all couples) less than £6 a week. They accounted for well over half the total of nearly 6 million persons of this age and corresponded roughly with those whose incomes derived wholly from the State together with those who had no more than £1 a week in addition to State benefits.

The median income of the retired is about half that of younger persons in the population who have no dependants.(33)

There is another way of expressing the relatively low incomes of the majority of the elderly. A quarter of retirement pensioners, or around 1½ million, receive national assistance but at least another ¾ million do not receive assistance and yet would seem to qualify for it. A further million do not qualify but are only marginally better off. Social scientists who made cautious estimates of these numbers in the 1950s (34) were derided by Government ministers and by the chairman of the National Assistance Board and yet eventually vindicated. The Allen Committee of Inquiry into the Impact of Rates on Households (35) and The Ministry of Pensions' survey of Retirement Pensioners both concluded that there were between half a million and a million retirement pensioners who were eligible for national assistance and were not receiving it.(36)

Another common assumption must also be questioned. Occupational pensions add significantly to the incomes of only a minority of the retired — two thirds of whom, it should be noted, are women. Forty-eight per cent of men, 24 per cent of women on their own insurance and 11 per cent of widows draw such pensions. A third of the men, a quarter of the women and a half of the widows receive less than 30 shillings a week. Moreover, three quarters of those with pensions from the private sector have not received an increase since they first started getting them.(37)

Fatherless Families

The Census of 1961 shows that for England and Wales there were approximately 400,000 families in which there were dependent children under sixteen years of age but only one parent, usually the mother — accounting for a million persons, including 600,000 children.(38) About 6 per cent of all children are in such families and the Family Expenditure Survey shows that their incomes are low. For example, in 1953 - 4 8 per cent of all children in Britain were in households living below a defined national assistance standard but as many as 36 per cent of children in households consisting of one woman and two or more children were living at this standard.(39) To take another index of comparison, in 1953-4 average expenditure of households consisting of a woman and two or more children was 160 shillings; whereas the average expenditure of a household containing a man, woman and one child was 240 shillings, 50 per cent more.(40) A pilot study by Dennis Marsden at the University of Essex reveals that compared with widows, separated and divorced wives with children tend to be poorer and unsupported mothers of illegitimate children are poorest of all. Not only do they feel stigmatized socially; their incomes are more insecure and irregular, based as they are on national assistance and court orders; they do not receive state benefits as of right and stringent earnings rules are applied when they receive assistance.(41) The 1965 report of the National Assistance Board shows that there are 104,000 women separated permanently from their husbands and receiving assistance of whom 50,000 have neither court orders nor out-of-court agreements. There are 43,000 with court orders, only 21,000 of whom receive maintenance regularly; 15,000 receive no payments at all.(42)

The Sick and Disabled
About 456,000 persons below pensionable age have been off work for three months or more and are dependent on sickness benefit (as many as 310,000 of whom have been off work for twelve months or more). (43) In addition there are 275,000 persons receiving war disablement pensions with 30 per cent or more disablement (three fifths of them in the First World War or subsequently) and another 90,000 with industrial injury disablement pensions, also with 30 per cent or more disablement.(44) Finally, there are 139,000 incapacitated persons receiving supplementary benefit (national assistance) allowances only. Most of these have been incapacitated since birth or early childhood.(45) Although the exact numbers drawing both sickness benefit and war or industrial injury pensions are not known it seems that there are in the population at least 750,000 people under pension age who are disabled or long-term sick. About 240,000 receive national assistance in some form and perhaps another 50,000 to 100,000 might qualify for supplementation or basic assistance. If we add dependants these figures become, respectively, around 400,000, and 120,000 to 240,000.

The Unemployed
In November 1966 approximately 575,000 were unemployed, of whom 160,000 had been unemployed two months or more.(46) The Ministry of Labour carried out a special survey of the unemployed in October 1964 and found that half of the women and 60 per cent of the men were 'poor placing prospects on various personal grounds'. This categorization is highly ambiguous if not prejudicial but those on the list included many who were disabled or who had a history of ill-health. As many as 8 per cent of the women and 10 per cent of the men were registered disabled persons. In December 1965 as many as 112,000 unemployed persons received assistance. Together with their dependants they numbered 272,000. Of these about 88,000, nearly a third, were in households affected by the wage-stop.(47)

Widening Inequalities in Britain

The problem in 1964 was not, however, one just of scant monetary resources. At a time of growing demand for higher education how could the proportion of working-class children reaching the sixth forms and going on to university be increased? Broadly speaking, inequalities of educational opportunity have not been greatly reduced over a generation.(48) How is it possible to steer enough resources to the secondary modern and primary schools to prevent them falling even farther behind the new comprehensive as well as the independent, direct grant and grammar schools? What can be done to increase dramatically the numbers of young working-class people benefiting from further education services?

There are many other spheres in which there are sharp contrasts in facilities and opportunities. How is it possible to upgrade ancient hospitals, particularly for the chronic sick and mentally ill, when the general and teaching hospitals are insisting on more space and better equipment? How can the proportion of slum and sub-standard housing which cannot be replaced in the next twenty years be renovated or modernized? And how can the division of resources between different regions be prevented from remaining as unequal as it is or from becoming more unequal, despite the actions of recent governments? In many different spheres therefore there is a problem not only of how to allocate additional resources but how to reallocate existing resources.

Some economists have suggested that emigration of labour from certain areas may have secondary depressing effects which perpetuate or even widen disparities between regions in rates of unemployment.(49) Sociologists too have begun to call attention to these disparities. Over a period of eight years up to 1961 the number of long-term unemployed was on average ten times greater in the Northern Region than in the Eastern and Southern Regions. There was also a higher rate of sickness and incapacity, markedly lower average earnings and markedly fewer children staying on at school beyond the age of fifteen.(50)

In some respects, as I have suggested above, the problem of poverty in Britain has been growing. We might begin with low earnings. Unfortunately it is difficult to say much about the trends in the *distribution* of earnings over the past twenty years. But *average* earnings in low-paid industries are rising less quickly than in other industries. In 1960 the Ministry of Labour listed average earnings in 128 industries. There were twenty-four with average earnings of less than £12 10s. In seventeen of these industries earnings rose during the next six years (April 1960 to April 1966) by less than the average of 44 per cent. Earnings in agriculture, which are also relatively low and which were excluded from this analysis, also rose less than average.(51)

Secondly, the value of family allowances has fallen. For a family with four children, for example, they have fallen from 12 per cent of average earnings in 1956 to 6 per cent of average earnings in 1966.(52)

Thirdly, social security beneficiaries have continued to be subject to principles of 'minimum' treatment, despite the development in this century of fringe benefits and fiscal welfare, despite more public awareness of the deprivations of environment and opportunity and despite the more rapid growth of social security in other countries. Levels of benefit have remained low. Between 1950 and 1960, as Mr Tony Lynes has shown, average disposable income per head rose faster than national assistance rates.(53) Increases in benefits in 1961, 1962 and 1963 slightly redressed the balance, but not enough to do more than mildly improve the relative level of living of beneficiaries. And the position has worsened again since the latest increase which was made in March 1965.

Fourthly, the relative increase in dependence within the social structure, particularly children and the elderly, has swelled the numbers with low incomes. The numbers of children in large families and of persons of advanced age have increased disproportionately.(54) Sociologists have begun to write of an 'underclass' in industrial societies and have also begun to appreciate that periodic increases in immigration can postpone the need to make structural adjustments in the economy and in the status hierarchy. Racial prejudices may displace but also in some ways reinforce existing social prejudices. White natives who occupy the same kind of areas and kind of jobs as coloured immigrants can easily be regarded as inferiors too and gradually they experience a fall, relative to others, in living standards. There is therefore the possibility of poverty growing in two forms — that of a dependent 'underclass' of people who are found in all regions of the country, and that of immigrant and native-born families living in communities in areas of bad housing where the unemployment rate is high.

Many illustrations of the consequences of these trends might be given. Households in the report of the National Food Survey are divided according to composition and social class into a number of groups. The proportion of children living in groups of households which consume a diet which *on average* fails in at least two particulars to reach the minimum levels recommended by the British Medical Association increased between 1960 and 1964 from 36 per cent to 43 per cent. Those in households failing to reach the minimum levels in three or four respects (protein, calcium, energy value and riboflavin) increased slightly from 16 per cent to 19 per cent.(55) These household groups consist of man and wife and three or four children and adolescents and children and they include two groups in the highest-income class, and not only groups in the middle- and lowest-income classes. I wish it were possible to express these findings more directly and more cogently. It is a public scandal that the National Food Survey Committee has as yet made no effort to establish the numbers and kinds of families markedly *below* the average. A national food survey has been carried out annually at considerable public expense for many years. Its most important conclusion has been buried in statistical minutiae. Although the conclusion was disinterred recently by curious social scientists and brought into public view(56) the committee has not felt it proper either to present the findings in the most revealing form or to undertake urgent inquiries to develop our knowledge about these large sections of the population who are living at inferior nutritional levels. Perhaps the Ministers of Social Security, Labour and Agriculture can combine to put pressure on the committee to answer the simple question which has been waiting to be answered for at least a decade — how many families (and how many children and adults in those families) have diets which are 10 per cent or 20 per cent or more below the minimum levels recommended by the British Medical Association?

3. Intentions and Performance

By the late 1950s the Labour Party had begun to develop a coherent strategy for dealing with poverty. Of the statements published in the few years before October 1964, the most radical was probably *Signposts for the Sixties*. Measures were required to achieve two major objectives — the elimination in so many departments of national life of the disjunction between private affluence and public squalor, and the dispersal of new forms of privilege or power that were concentrating among a small ruling élite. What were the remedies? They were, briefly, to transfer the freehold of building land to public ownership, repeal the Rent Act, repair and modernize private rented houses and build more houses, introduce redundancy payments, completely re-cast national insurance by introducing 'a system of all-in wage-related social security', reduce the size of school classes, reorganize secondary schools along comprehensive lines, 'broaden the present narrow apex of higher education', establish a trust to integrate private with state schools, introduce a capital gains tax and re-grade family allowances steeply according to age.(57) Later statements added or reaffirmed plans for regions within a national economic plan, the introduction of an incomes guarantee and a rates rebate scheme, the abolition of prescription charges and the expansion of community care services. Writing at the time of the 1959 election, the present Prime Minister acknowledged the fact that 'many' of the British people faced 'real, bitter poverty'. He went on, 'the co-existence of conspicuous wealth and avoidable poverty is a distortion of the moral laws of civilized society'. He admitted that Labour's was a 'piecemeal' programme but that it was 'on a broad front' and corresponded with the complexities of human needs. Piecemeal though it was it represented 'the unifying and transforming influence of a Socialist approach'.(58)

Whether these proposals were indeed sufficiently far-reaching and sufficiently integrated to meet the problem can of course be disputed. They were at least constructive and implied a shift of resources from rich to poor and from private to public sectors. But it must be emphasized that in the event the Labour Government has so far failed to implement some of the most important of these measures and has implemented others in a much milder form than originally intended. In some instances the situation is clear. Measures like improved family allowances just have not been introduced. Measures like the Land Commission Bill, the Rent Act, the Capital Gains tax, the Corporation tax and the Social Security Act seem to be small in their effects. The Land Commission Bill turns a plan for the automatic acquisition of land for development (which meant stabilizing rather than reducing the price of land) into one primarily involving a betterment levy. Power to acquire land in certain circumstances is vested in the commission but in the absence of evidence that it can be used extensively we must assume it will be used sparingly.(59) The Rent Act has damped down the increase in number of extortionate rents, but by leaving initiative with tenants and creating a system of rent assessment which in some ways is biased against tenants it has so far had a surprisingly small result. Moreover, many of those entitled to benefit under the new rates rebate scheme are not applying. The capital gains tax replaces the short-term levy introduced by Selwyn Lloyd. The maximum rate of 30 per cent (20 per cent for amounts up to £5,000) is low and is lower than the effective rate of income tax and surtax that is applicable to high incomes. This is not a wealth tax. It is an intermediate kind of tax which allows room for argument about some capital values at the time the Finance Act was implemented and therefore the amount of gain to which the rate of tax up to 30 per cent is applied.

The incorporation of the income guarantee scheme within the Social Security Act is a particularly intriguing example of a paper lion which has turned into a lamb. For a long time the Labour Party had been searching for a way of abolishing the means test in national assistance, at least for the great majority of recipients, and simultaneously raising the standards of living of those who had been accustomed to drawing assistance. While in opposition in 1963 it stated, 'As a result of the Government's policy, what was the exception has become the rule ... The means test, which it was the aim of the 1946 Act to abolish, has been built into the Government's system of social security, as one of its main instruments for distributing relief.'(60) In 1963 the party therefore not only reaffirmed its previous support for a national superannuation scheme but firmly committed itself to extending the change 'from flat-rate pensions to half-pay on retirement' to all forms of state benefits and, to ensure 'fair play' for existing pensioners, an income guarantee was to be introduced. The guarantee involved giving a supplement to pensioners and widows to raise their incomes to a certain level 'well in excess' of the present level of retirement pension. It would be paid automatically — through simplified tax returns.

The Social Security Act of 1966 attempts to preserve this proposal, but it is a pale shadow of its former self. Nominally the National Assistance Board has been abolished by the merger with the Ministry of Pensions. In its place is the Supplementary Benefits Commission. Efforts are being made to improve the image and encourage more people to apply for supplementary help. In some ways it is still too early to comment on administrative procedures. But the opportunity to make a clean break with restrictive and narrow-minded attitudes enshrined in the National Assistance Act of 1948 was lost. Some important steps in the direction of establishing the rights of non-contributory beneficiaries could have been taken. For example, it is a pity that the right of a person to know in writing how his supplementary benefit has been calculated or why his application for benefit has been refused was not written into the act.(61) The effect of a symbolic clause upon relations between officers of the new Commission and the public might have been considerable. Instead, much of the apparatus of the act passed eighteen years previously was preserved in a too bureaucratic form.

Secondly, the qualifying conditions for supplementary help were liberalized. The amounts of capital and income which can be 'disregarded' in assessing needs was increased. A standard rate of 9s. a week was added to the supplementary grants of old people and the sick. The idea was that this would be an automatic supplement for long-term beneficiaries. But for the great majority of existing recipients it made little or no difference to the amounts they received. Seventy-three per cent of supplementary pensioners at the end of 1965 were already receiving discretionary additions averaging 10s. 1d. per week. Fifty-seven per cent of the sick received amounts averaging 11s. 8d.(62) The 9s. supplement does of course limit the amount of discretion that an officer can exercize at present to add to a particular rate of assistance. This is good but because the amount is so small it does not change the existing situation drastically. There will remain a large number of people whose incomes will in part depend on official discretion. And the opportunity of reviewing the rationale for the basic rates was not taken.

Thirdly, and most importantly, the income guarantee was not applied outside the customary spheres of operation of national assistance. The

Labour leaders wanted to fuse income tax and income security. But after they approached one of Britain's most implacable institutions, the Board of Inland Revenue, they retreated. Officials of this Board and of the National Assistance Board persuaded them to change their minds. Perhaps their momentum for reform had already been lost. The fact is that the Board of Inland Revenue felt it was outrageous for the Board actually to hand out money. They were a taxation department, not a social service department. To bring together the functions of taxing income and making it more secure seemed to them improper. Yet their reaction may have been a blessing in disguise, because the Labour Party had not begun to perceive the likelihood that in any form it could be implemented, the income guarantee would resemble traditional means-tested services.

The verdict of history is likely to be that the Social Security Act of 1966 has achieved little more than extending national assistance, or supplementary benefit, to a larger number of the lower middle classes, (63) while distinguishing rather more sharply between old and young. It has also served the purpose of saving face for the Labour Party — which is not perhaps the strongest reason for reform.

The act also discriminates against the unemployed. One discriminatory practice against those with large families, the wage-stop, is preserved. Another, against the long-term unemployed, is introduced. Unlike the retired, who receive it at once, and unlike the sick, who receive it after two years, none of the unemployed receive the long-term benefit of 9s. a week.

What has happened to the complementary and even more important plan — the wage-related scheme of social security, incorporating national superannuation? I believe it can be argued that with a little more determination on the part of the Government we might have had this on the statute book by the end of 1965. In November 1964, soon after the election, the Government took a major decision. It announced big increases in existing benefits, raising the retirement pension of a single person by 12s. 6d. to £4 a week and of a married couple by 21s. to £6 10s. This was, it is true, a substantial improvement on existing rates but was carried out within the structural inadequacies of the existing scheme and was quickly overtaken by increases in earnings.(64) Moreover, the employees' flat-rate contributions which, according to the Labour Party only a year earlier, had 'already reached a level where they constitute a savage poll tax on the lowest-paid worker'(65) were increased by 17 per cent, from 11s. 8d. to 13s. 8d. a week. One view was that the needs of the poor were urgent and that a comprehensive review would take time. But the work of Lord Beveridge's committee in the war from the start to the publication of the actual report was accomplished in eleven months and the Labour Government already had a head start afforded by the deliberations and publications of its Study Group on Security and Old Age, which had been sitting since the mid-fifties. Another view is that it had difficulty in getting on with a socialist programme with such a tiny parliamentary majority and in such a grave economic crisis. But the social productivity, if we may call it such, of the Labour Government has been if anything smaller since March 1966 than before that date and the National Plan, as Brian Abel-Smith has pointed out, brazenly adopted the assumption that a major new scheme would not be introduced before 1969.

In fact, what was planned to be a consistent and concerted attack on poverty has turned into haphazard skirmishes on a wide front. The Government has given little impression from its actions that it has adopted an overall strategy. By increasing benefits along conventional lines early in 1965 it took the edge off demands for reform. By then introducing a redundancy payments act and later earnings-related benefit in unemployment and sickness for the first six months it allowed itself to be diverted from giving priority to poverty to giving priority to redeployment. The earnings-related scheme for the unemployed and sick does little for those with low earnings. Men and women with less than £9 a week do not qualify. A man with £12 a week gets a supplement of £1 in addition to his flat-rate benefit of £4 but if he has a wife and four children only 8s. because the act has introduced a maximum total benefit of 85 per cent of earnings and, with a flat-rate of £9 16s., he would otherwise exceed this maximum. If he is unlucky enough to have been unemployed or sick for a total of twelve weeks in the preceding tax year, by no means a rare eventuality, he will receive no supplement at all.(66)

The scheme does nothing for the man with long-term benefit. The supplement is paid after two weeks' unemployment but ceases after a further six months. Those who have become accustomed to receiving fairly substantial earnings-related supplements will then experience a sharp reduction in level of living or they will have to apply for means-tested supplements. If they happen to be sick and they go on to means-tested supplementation they will have to wait another eighteen months before they qualify for a standard supplement of 9s. a week. This is not planning. It is helter-skelter chaos. There are a number of connected problems. The Government has failed to wind up the Conservative Government's graduated pension scheme, after proclaiming, rightly, that it was a disgraceful 'swindle'.(67) It has also failed to introduce transferability of pension rights, which means incidentally that it has not removed an important obstacle to redeployment.

Instead of a coordinated and consistent scheme of social security we run the risk of building up a fragmented, piecemeal set of measures which bristle with anomalies and between which many groups in the population fall. It should perhaps be recalled that the original aim of the Labour Party's national superannuation plan, and hence of the comprehensive wage-related social security plan, was to bring about a dramatic immediate increase (50 per cent for single retirement pensioners) in national insurance benefits by rationalizing the principles and practices of existing employers, private and public schemes within a single wage-related scheme which the mass of the population might find personally attractive as well as socially just.(68) The scheme would simultaneously reduce by over a million the number having to depend in any form on means-tested assistance. The introduction of a single co-ordinated scheme would also allow more flexibility to eliminate anomalies than a succession of piecemeal measures. Perhaps the most indefensible anomaly is the payment of different rates of benefit to those disabled in war, industry and civil life.

Let me refer briefly to one other plan. Has much been done to carry out the modernization and repair of sub-standard housing? According to the Denington sub-committee on standards of housing fitness, which reported in November 1966,

'there are many, many houses which are below any standard that can be considered satisfactory in the second half of the twentieth century. About three quarters of a million are below the present minimum fitness standard. Something like 3 million lack one or more of the basic amenities of W.C., cold water tap, hot water supply and bath. While some of them will be demolished in the next few years, others must serve for a longer period, however fast new homes are built. These must have some degree of improvement, according to the length of time they will remain in use. Sound houses must be maintained in good repair and improved where practicable. Successive Governments have tried to secure the voluntary modernization of these houses but the response has been inadequate and disappointing. Present measures of compulsion, which apply in limited circumstances to tenanted property, have proved ineffective, perhaps because of the cumbersome and time consuming procedure. *In our view there is a need both for effective compulsion to improve and maintain the better old houses and for more pressure for early clearance of the worst'.(69)*

Although about 120,000 improvement grants a year in England and Wales are made, only about a third are made to private landlords. The principal beneficiaries are middle-class owner-occupiers.

While some Government actions have not lived up to pre-election plans others may actually have reinforced social inequalities and poverty. For example, soon after awarding Members of Parliament, ministers and judges huge proportionate pay increases, and university teachers, general practitioners and senior civil servants increases ranging from 10 to 25 per cent, the Government expected the trade unions to accept happily a wage-policy holding down increases to 3 to 4 per cent. The restoration of traditional differentials of pay can be invoked to justify most of these increases. But in terms of Socialist strategy as well as the immediate need to secure support for an incomes policy they were inept.

Again, by imposing harsh controls on the entry of immigrants and by simultaneously refraining from introducing any really positive measures for racial integration, the moral authority of the Labour Party, so carefully established by Hugh Gaitskell in the famous parliamentary debates of 1961 and 1962, was lost in one reckless step. The position of the coloured minority is still very different in Britain from what it is in the United States but social scientists are beginning to wonder how far we will follow the pattern established there of increasing inequality in living standards and employment status between white and coloured sections of the population.(70) If so, then Britain will have, if it has not already, a group of new poor.

By adopting a non-existent or at most a weak policy on the integration of coloured immigrants the Government has surrendered more than it probably realizes. Acquiescence in racial inequality tends to have a corrupting influence on general attitudes towards social inequality.

4. Future Policies

1. Raising Minimum Standards

This analysis clearly implies certain priorities in policy. First of all, measures to raise low standards of living are required. The most urgent action is required to increase family allowances at least threefold and extend them to only and first children in the family;(71) introduce general pensions and allowances including constant attendance allowances, for the long-term sick and those disabled in civil life as well as in industry and war;(72) provide regular State maintenance allowances for all fatherless families; abolish the wage-stop in supplementary benefits and also the benefit limit imposed on those with less than average earnings in the earnings-related unemployment and sickness scheme; and bring forward the more comprehensive plan for wage-related social security. A major repairs and modernization programme is badly needed, particularly for housing,(73) as I have argued, but also for schools and hospitals, quite apart from a scheme for new buildings which involves an expenditure closer to the proportions of gross national product being spent by some other countries.(74) A variety of measures to strengthen the threadbare sections of our social services are also required. Examples of these are under-doctored areas and under-developed community-care services, under-staffed schools, particularly secondary modern schools where there is a high turnover of staff, and under-staffed hospitals, particularly for long-stay patients.

2. Universalism

Because the new minimum levels can be defined only in relation to the resources, customs and institutions of the community certain complementary measures must simultaneously be adopted to reallocate those resources and modify those customs and institutions. This will inevitably form part of general domestic policy. It means challenging the kind of view put forward by the Minister of Social Security at the 1966 Labour Party Conference when she said that further improvements in social security depended on economic productivity. Other social service ministers have made similar statements. The argument was put forward in the Labour Party Election Manifesto of 1964. In fact, of course, there is considerable scope for redistribution, of both an aggregate nature from one public service to another as well as of a vertical nature between well-off and poor, even at a time of economic crisis. Fundamentally redistribution must also be reinforced by change in political and administrative institutions.(75)

The tax system must become more progressive. Its total effect is in fact regressive at the lowest incomes and then proportional even up to quite high incomes at present.(76) Real income re-distribution does not seem to have markedly changed since before the war.(77) If tax allowances for children are reduced, and direct family allowances increased, and if wage-related contributions replace flat-rate contributions in social security some but not all of the inequalities will be reduced among low and relatively low income groups. Other measures to strengthen the progressiveness of the tax system become necessary. It is possible, in the history of tax policy, that when certain groups in the population are taxed more heavily they respond by asking for larger pay differentials and by resorting more frequently to legal and illegal methods of avoiding tax, by pressing for larger fringe benefits and by converting income into capital. Much of this therefore implies that egalitarian objectives must be pursued more vigorously through fiscal policy but also through measures designed to elicit information particularly from companies, corporations and trade unions and impose limits on their powers to exploit privilege. The new Companies Act is a mild step in this direction.

I am arguing, in effect, that some form of incomes policy is necessary less for economic than for social reasons. Minimum wage legislation might be helpful in raising the standards of those with the lowest wages, but only if it is wide in scope and if the levels are not merely linked automatically with average earnings but deliberately designed to *rise,* relative to the average, over a number of years.(78) One assumption upon which a new national plan should be based is that minimum wages and minimum social security benefits will in future rise faster than average earnings. Poverty must be tackled through a wages or incomes policy as much as through a better fiscal or social security policy.

This amounts therefore to an argument for a deliberate policy of securing a levelling up of wage and income levels through a concerted incomes, fiscal and social security policy. It means bringing certain government departments together which are not accustomed to working with each other. It also means professionalizing the Civil Service and improving the information at our disposal. Earlier I complained about the analyses offered by the National Food Survey Committee. There is little doubt that far better analyses of income distribution could be provided through the Board of Inland Revenue and the Ministry of Labour than are at present published. We are just beginning to produce the kind of data which are needed by a modern society if it is to have humanitarian and socialist objectives. This needs emphasizing for it is no academic foible. If the Ministry of Pensions had had a substantial Statistical and Research Department in the past the reluctance of hundreds of thousands of beneficiaries to apply for assistance, or the poverty of children in large families and of the disabled, might have been revealed a lot earlier. Perhaps the newly-appointed director of the Central Statistical Office can, with suitable support from ministers, breathe sweetness and light into the innermost recesses of the Government's information services.

3. Limitation of Privilege

Finally, however, this strategy of achieving equality through integration cannot be effective unless it is recognized that adjustments have to be expected of social elites. If poverty is relative then standards are partly determined by the incomes, wealth, living conditions and expectations of the rich. The relief of poverty is secured by lower managerial and professional incomes, relative to the average, as much as by higher minimum wages and benefits. It is not that the rich can pay sufficient new taxes to finance, say, a major increase in the retirement pension. It is doubtful whether they could finance a five shilling increase. Their resources and incomes provide the starting point from which the rest of the social hierarchy unfolds, and this is crucial. No doubt the difficulties of embarking upon such a strategy are immense. History might lead us to suppose that although there are periods of greater social equality the traditional lines of division between classes and income groups reappear in the long run. Guy Routh made a detailed study of occupational and pay structure in Britain between 1906 and 1960 and concluded that over a period of fifty years 'the most impressive finding was the rigidity of the inter-class and inter-occupational relationships'.(79) Barbara Wootton has brilliantly described the apparently irrational but fundamentally social determination of differentials of pay.(80)

The problem, moreover, is no longer narrowly national. The 'brain drain' and the emulation by élites in developing countries of Western standards of living reminds us that the inequalities of pay structures have outside determinants as well. But difficult as it is the problem must be faced. Government ministers should have relatively lower salaries than they do today. So should permanent secretaries, university professors, hospital consultants and company directors. If maximum wage-legislation is felt to be remote from political practicalities I believe it will in time come to be taken seriously. In struggling to establish the principle of making public the remuneration of company directors and managers, Peter Shore, among others, has recognized that incomes policy must start at the top.(81) The moral point which I want to impress is that if it is the highly skilled, managerial and professional classes who gain from present differentials it is the aged, the low-wage-earners, the children in large families, the sick and the disabled who lose.

In advanced industrial societies inequalities are maintained by the educational system, by the institutions of property and inheritance, by the professions and the trade unions, and by popular ideas or beliefs about status, responsibility and rights. The process of structural change can introduce new inequalities as well as reduce existing ones. Every salary increase that is larger than the average wage-increase, even when accepted by national sentiment to retain the professional manpower, say, of doctors and scientists, widens inequalities and may indirectly increase the extent of poverty. One is linked to the other. The privileges at the exclusive public school are gained at the cost of worse conditions in a secondary modern school in one of our big cities. One is in equilibrium with the other. So perhaps the critical criterion of socialist strategy, which the Government has yet to meet, is a relative diminution of the citadels of privilege. When honours are no longer conferred, and managers earn only two or three times as much as dustmen, and, cruellest of all, public schools really are integrated rather than given a new lease of life by Flemingism, the millennium may begin to dawn.

I have been extremely critical of the Government's record in the first two years of office. It would be unfair to neglect the list of reforms which have been adopted — the abolition of prescription charges, the tax on betting, the restriction on business expenses, protection from eviction and others in addition to some which I have discussed. Good deeds have been done. But they are no more than hot compresses on an ailing body politic. I have tried to call attention to the need for a more single-minded and large-scale strategy to achieve greater social equality and have tried to make a number of suggestions. Greater equality is not dependent on economic growth. Indeed, it would be possible to go further and argue that greater equality is a pre-condition for rapid economic growth. National morale can be raised and the right sense of national purpose created. Improving social security could be one means of persuading people to accept severe restraint on wage and salary increases. Another could be further control of upper-income fringe benefits and tax avoidance practices. These suggest what would be a practical immediate policy as well as one concordant with ultimate socialist objectives. The Labour Government is compromising too readily with entrenched interests, is avoiding the need to confront racial and social prejudice with moral authority, is failing to introduce institutional change and is forgetting that in this growingly more complicated world it must, like Alice, run even faster to stay in the same place and to preserve, still less extend, existing human rights.

Partly our problem is one with which it is irresponsible to pretend that Government ministers must wrestle alone. Tawney reminded us, 'Nothing could be more remote from Socialist ideals than the competitive scramble of a society which pays lip service to equality, but too often means by it merely equal opportunities of becoming unequal.' He warned against 'the corrupting influence of a false standard of values, which perverts, not only in education, but wide tracts of thought and life. It is this demon − the idolatry of money and success − with whom, not in one sphere alone but in all, including our own hearts and minds, Socialists have to grapple.'(82)

Notes

1. Abel-Smith, B., *Labour's Social Plan,* Fabian Tract, 369, December 1966.

2. Titmuss, R.M., *Choice and 'The Welfare State',* Fabian Tract, 370.

3. There is a rapidly growing literature. Among recent publications, see, for example, Abel-Smith, B., and Townsend, P., *The Poor and the Poorest,* Bell, 1965; *Low Income Groups and Methods of Dealing with their Problems,* papers for a trade union seminar, Report and Supplement, O.E.C.D., Paris, 1966; Goodman, L.H. (ed.), *Economic Progress and Social Welfare,* Columbia University Press, New York and London, 1966; Ornati, O., *Poverty Amid Affluence,* The Twentieth-Century Fund, New York, 1966; Miller, S.M., and Rein, M., 'Poverty, Inequality and Policy', in Becker, H.S., *Social Problems,* John Wiley, New York, 1966.

4. A vivid instance of the insistence of society that individuals conform to modern

standards was a case in New York of an old man who was denied welfare because he refused to give up sleeping on rags in a barn. The court's considered opinion included this gem: 'Appellant also argues that he has a right to live as he pleases while being supported by public charity. One would admire his independence if he were not so dependent, but he has no right to defy the standards and conventions of civilised society while being supported at public expense.' Quoted by Reich, C.A., 'The New Property', *Yale Law Journal*, vol. 73, no. 5, April 1964.

5. See, for example, United Nations, *Assistance to the Needy in Less-Developed Areas*, Department of Economic and Social Affairs, United Nations, New York, 1956.

6. Orshansky, M., 'Counting the Poor: Another Look at the Poverty Profile', *Social Security Bulletin*, vol. 28, January 1965.

7. Seebohm Rowntree liberalized the measure of poverty which he had used in York in 1899 when he undertook a second survey in 1936 and again when he undertook a third survey in 1950, but not to the same extent as real increases in wages. Partly (though not wholly) as a consequence he found fewer people in poverty — the percentage falling from 28 to 18 and then to 2 at the three dates, Rowntree, B.S., and Lavers, G.R., *Poverty in the Welfare State*, Longmans, 1951. Similarly, by applying its standard of subsistence, the Social Security Administration of the United States has found an encouraging reduction in poverty from 22 per cent to 18 per cent during five recent years. As the 1964 *Economic Report of the President of the United States* declares with pride (p. 110), 'five years of prosperity and continued economic expansion have contributed significantly to reducing the number of people who live in poverty. Between 1959 and 1964, the number of persons defined as poor decreased from 38.9 million to 34.1 million.' But the failure to revise the measure in accordance with wage increases and social changes largely invalidates the result.

8. A full account is given by Titmuss, R.M., *Income Distribution and Social Change*, Allen & Unwin, 1962.

9. Reid, G.L., and Robertson, D.J., *Fringe Benefits, Labour Costs and Social Security*, Allen & Unwin, 1965.

10. A study by Hay, M.S.L., Management Consultants, *The Times*, 11 August 1966.

11. Reich, C.A., op.cit.

12. Committee on Higher Education, Report on Higher Education (the Robbins Report), Appendix 2, Students and their Education, H.M.S.O., 1964.

13. The Newsom Report describes in particular the disadvantages of the schools in slum areas. Seventy-nine per cent of them, compared with 40 per cent of secondary modern schools generally, are in buildings which are seriously inadequate. The turnover of staff is much higher. Fewer pupils stay on an extra term or two beyond the minimum leaving age and fewer belong to school clubs and societies. Ministry of Education, *Half our Future*, A Report of the Central Advisory Council for Education (England), H.M.S.O., 1963, Chapter 3.

14. The Milner Holland Committee on Housing in Greater London has vividly described the rigidities in housing supply and the difficulties of various classes

of tenants. 'The people who suffer most from housing stress are those with the lowest incomes, those with average incomes and large families, and many of the newcomers to London.' *Report of the Committee on Housing in Greater London,* Cmnd. 2605, H.M.S.O., March 1965, p.91 (see also pp.127-31). In France 'the poorest families cannot get into the low-rent flats for letting which in theory are designed for them ... In the present state of the law, low-income families are therefore inexorably forced into slum neighbourhoods, squalid furnished accommodation or "the grey areas" on the outskirts of the town.' When slums are torn down 'the destruction of their neighbourhoods involves the destruction of a whole network of relationships and communications, drives them further from their place of work, deprives them of their accommodation with its very low rent and the last remaining amenities (running water, for example).' Parodi, M., 'France', *Low Income Groups and Methods of Dealing with their Problems,* op.cit.

15. The Supplementary Benefits Commission has powers to refuse benefit to a mother when it believes it has evidence of her living with another man. Anonymous letters are sometimes acted upon. There are individual officers who have responsibility for investigating fraudulent claims. Some mothers report instances of officers searching rooms and cupboards without permission in attempts to check whether or not there are men present or articles of men's clothing lying around. These inquiries do not appear to be as ruthless as those in some parts of the world. In certain areas of the United States, for example, special investigation teams pay surprise visits in the middle of the night and search the house for any sign of a man, with unnerving effects on the entire family. See, for example, Greenleigh Associates, *Facts, Fallacies and the Future,* A Study of the Aid to Dependent Children Program of Cook County, Illinois, 64, 1960.

16. *Ministry of Labour Gazette,* October 1966.

17. Sheldon, J.H., *Report to the Birmingham Regional Hospital Board on its Geriatric Services,* Birmingham R.H.B., 1961; Brown, G.W., and Wing, J.K., 'A Comparative Clinical and Social Survey of Three Mental Hospitals', *Sociological Studies in the British National Health Service,* The Sociological Review: Monograph no. 5, 1962; Jones, K., and Sidebotham, R., *Mental Hospitals at Work,* Routledge & Kegan Paul, 1962; Townsend, P., *The Last Refuge,* Routledge & Kegan Paul, 1962.

18. *The War on Poverty: The Economic Opportunity Act of 1964,* United States Senate, U.S. Government Printing Office, Washington, 1964.

19. See the preface to the Annual Report of the National Food Survey Committee, *Domestic Food Consumption and Expenditure, 1958,* H.M.S.O., 1960.

20. Galbraith, J.K., *The Affluent Society,* Hamish Hamilton, 1958, Chapter 23.

21. See, for example, Marris, P., *Widows and Their Families,* Routledge & Kegan Paul, 1958; Shaw, O.A., and Bowerbank, M., 'Living on a State Maintained Income I and II', *Case Conference,* March and April 1958.

22. Orshansky, M., op. cit.

23. Abel-Smith, B., and Townsend, P., op. cit. In real terms the American 'poverty line' is much higher than the British but judged in relation to average earnings is about equal. In fact more of the poor in the United States than in Britain are markedly below the line.

24. Myrdal, G., *Economic Theory and Underdeveloped Regions*, Methuen University Paperbacks, 1963, p.6.

25. See Abel-Smith, B., and Townsend, P., op.cit.

26. Land, H., 'Provisions for Large Families', *New Society*, 24 November 1966.

27. See *Circumstances of Familes*, H.M.S.O., 1967.

28. *Ministry of Labour Gazette*, April and June 1961.

29. It did not cover earnings in agriculture, transport, docks and mining, for example, did not extend to clerical, technical and supervisory staff, and referred to only 73 per cent of the total number of manual workers employed in the selected industries.

30. As with preceding income and expenditure surveys the response rate was low and it is possible that fewer of those with low earnings than with average or high earnings responded.

31. Ministry of Labour, *Family Expenditure Survey, Report for 1965*, H.M.S.O., 1966, pp. 3 and 4. Average earnings of men 21 years and over were £20 6s. in April 1966, according to the *Ministry of Labour Gazette*, October 1966, p.697.

32. Census, 1961, England and Wales, *Household Composition National Summary Tables*, H.M.S.O., 1966, Table 4.

33. Townsend, P., and Wedderburn, D., with Korte, S., and Benson, S., *The Aged in the Welfare State*, Occasional Papers on Social Administration, no. 14, Bell, 1965.

34. For example, see Cole Wedderburn, D., with Utting, J., *The Economic Circumstances of Old People*, Occasional Papers on Social Administration, no.4, 1962.

35. The committee estimated that there were 800,000 *households* with retired heads (containing over a million retired persons) who were 'apparently eligible for national assistance but not getting it'. Even allowing for some understatement of incomes they concluded that about half a million households were eligible. *Report of the Committee of Inquiry into the Impact of Rates on Households* (The Allen Report), Cmnd. 2582, H.M.S.O., 1965, p.117.

36. The ministry's study showed that 34 per cent of widowed and unmarried female retirement pensioners were receiving national assistance, that another 21 per cent were provisionally entitled to it and that only 19 per cent had a net available income exceeding needs (as defined by the national assistance scale rates) by £1 a week or more. The corresponding figures for widowed and unmarried male pensioners are 22, 13 and 33; and for married pensioners 18, 11 and 50. Ministry of Pensions and National Insurance, *Financial and Other Circumstances of Retirement Pensioners*, H.M.S.O., 1966, pp. 20 and 83-4.

37. ibid., pp. 154-63.

38. Census, 1961, England and Wales, *Household Composition National Summary Tables*, H.M.S.O., 1966.

39. Abel-Smith, B., and Townsend, P., *The Poor and the Poorest*, op.cit., p.32.

40. Ministry of Labour, *Report of an Enquiry into Household Expenditure in 1953-4*, H.M.S.O., 1957.

41. Marsden, D., *Mothers Alone*, Penguin, 1973.

42. *Report of the National Assistance Board for the Year ended 31st December 1965*, Cmnd. 3042, H.M.S.O., 1966, p.27.

43. Ministry of Social Security, personal communication (referring to the year 1964-5).

44. *Report of the Ministry of Pensions and National Insurance for the Year 1965*, H.M.S.O., 1966, pp.97 and 146.

45. *Report of the National Assistance Board for the Year ended 31st December 1965*, Cmnd. 3042, H.M.S.O., 1966, pp. 6-8.

46. Altogether probably 150,000 people have experienced six months' unemployment during the past year. Some experience recurrent short spells of unemployment rather than long spells.

47. *Report of the National Assistance Board for the Year ended 31st December 1965*, op.cit., pp. 30 and 61.

48. In the 1950s only ½ per cent of the children of unskilled and semi-skilled manual workers were reaching the universities, about the same proportion as in the late 1930s and 1940s. About 14½ per cent of the children of professional, managerial and intermediate occupational groups were doing so, compared with 6 per cent in the 1930s and 1940s. In recent years one in every four of the non-manual middle-class children entering a grammar-school-type course at the age of eleven, but only one in every 15 to 20 of unskilled manual workers' children entering such a course, have eventually gone on to a university. Little, A., and Westergaard, J., 'The Trend of Class Differentials in Educational Opportunity in England and Wales', *British Journal of Sociology*, 1964. We should also remember that in comparing utilization of educational facilities there has been a rapid expansion in university courses for graduate students, the majority of whom are middle-class.

49. For example, Archibald, G.C., 'Regional Multiplier Effects in the United Kingdom,' *Oxford Economic Papers*, spring, 1967.

50. Sinfield, R.A., *Unemployed in Shields* (unpublished).

51. Ministry of Labour, *Statistics on Incomes, Prices, Employment and Production*, no. 18, September 1966, pp. 26-7.

52. This downward trend is true not only of Britain, where the allowances are relatively low, but also of some other countries where they are relatively high, for example, France.

53. Lynes, T., *National Assistance and National Prosperity*, Occasional Papers on Social Administration, no. 5, Codicote Press, 1962.

54. Between 1953 and 1965, for example, the number of children in families drawing family allowances in Britain grew by 25 per cent. But the number of fourth children attracting allowances in families grew by 50 per cent, fifth children by 63 per cent and sixth or later children by 84 per cent. *Reports of the Ministry of Pensions and National Insurance for the Years 1953 and 1965*, Cmnd. 9159 and Cmnd. 3046, H.M.S.O., 1954 and 1966. Also, between 1953 and 1965 the number of retirement pensions in payment increased by 54 per cent. This rate of increase was faster than the increase in numbers of persons

of pensionable age, which itself was much higher than the increase in the population of all ages. Two further points are worth noting. First, there has been a disproportionate increase in the numbers of persons aged eighty and over among the elderly; between 1951 and 1961, for example, their numbers increased by 40 per cent. Second, the Registrar General's estimates of population suggest that during the next ten years the numbers of children under fifteen and persons of pensionable age will increase by 15 or 16 per cent, but the population aged 15-59 will increase by only 2 per cent.

55. This trend has not been consistent throughout the last ten years. In 1956, for example, the number of children in families which on average failed to reach the minimum levels in two or more respects was 36 per cent, but in three or four respects 29 per cent. There has been a slow upward drift in the nutritive content of the average diet of all groups of families but (a) the poorest and largest groups of families has not gained on the richest and smallest families, (b) the poorest and some of the middle-income large families and those with adolescents and children have still to attain the B.M.A. levels, and (c) relatively *more* of the children in the annual survey are now to be found in larger households. Ministry of Agriculture, Fisheries and Food, *Domestic Food Consumption and Expenditure: 1964 and 1960.* Annual Reports of the National Food Survey, H.M.S.O., 1966 and 1962.

56. For example, Lambert, R., *Nutrition in Britain 1950-60,* Occasional Papers on Social Administration, Codicote Press, 1964.

57. 'We should reorganise family allowances, graduating them according to the age of the child, with a particularly steep rise for those remaining at school after the statutory school-leaving age.' *Signposts for the Sixties,* 1961.

58. Wilson, H., 'The War on Poverty', *New Statesman,* October 1959.

59. The commission is to be voted £45 million for acquiring and managing land and this would be extended to £75 million with parliamentary approval. These are very small amounts by comparison with land values or capital investment programmes. It is still of course too early to pronounce on the total effects of the bill, for much will depend on the policy which is in practice followed by the commission, but the prospects of it becoming a major instrument of controlling development in the public interest are not dazzling.

60. The Labour Party, *New Frontiers for Social Security,* 1963, p. 9.

61. The minister gave assurances in committee that administratively 'as soon as possible, at least those getting a supplementary pension [not *benefit*] will receive written explanation. Others, if there is a refusal, or if they are not clear, or if they do not think that the amount they are receiving is sufficient will right from the beginning be able to ask for a written explanation, as they can do at the moment'. *Hansard,* 17 June 1966, col. 1906.

62. *Report of the National Assistance Board for 1965,* op.cit, p. 18.

63. The amounts of capital and income which can be 'disregarded' in assessing needs have been increased.

64. The increase in early 1965 represented the largest *absolute* increase in national insurance benefits up to that time, though some increases in earlier years were relatively larger. The benefits of early 1965 represented increases in benefit of

18.5 per cent for a single person and 19 per cent for a married couple. But between May 1963 and August 1966 average industrial earnings rose by 20 per cent. Between May 1963 and August 1966 retail prices increased by 13 per cent. *Ministry of Labour Gazette,* October 1966.

65. The Labour Party, *New Frontiers for Social Security,* p.11.

66. Adrian Sinfield also points out that 'the implication of calculating gross *weekly* earnings from a gross *annual* income for the assessment of the supplement seems to have been overlooked. Although the use of a gross annual income has administrative advantages, it also lowers the value of the supplement for men with previous recent experience of unemployment, sickness or any other absence from work'. op cit.

67. The benefits are very small indeed in relation to contributions. The Government's 'profit' on the scheme is growing. In 1962-3 the excess of income over expenditure was £182 million, in 1964-5 it was £277 million. (Parliamentary written answer by Mr Norman Pentland, *Hansard,* 6 July 1965).

68. The Labour Party, *National Superannuation,* 1957.

69. Ministry of Housing, Central Housing Advisory Committee, *Our Older Homes: A Call for Action,* Report of the sub-committee on standards of housing fitness, H.M.S.O., 1966, p.5.

70. Research has shown that in the years since the war the economic gains of the non-white population in the United States have been less than proportional to those of whites and that the relative position of a significant majority of non-whites has worsened. Ornati, O., op.cit., p.59.

71. In a survey of 62 countries with some form of family allowances system, only 12 were found not to make a payment to the first or only child in the family. United States Department of Health, Education and Welfare, *Social Security throughout the World,* 1964, Washington, 1966.

72. The Disablement Income Group has been bringing the needs to the attention of the public. The anomalies of social security benefits have been discussed recently by Phyllis Willmott in a book written otherwise by disabled individuals. Hunt, P. (ed.), *Stigma: The Experience of Disability,* Chapman, 1966.

73. Ministry of Housing, Central Advisory Committee, *Our Older Homes,* op.cit.

74. See, for example, Political and Economic Planning, Broadsheet no. 490, *Housing in Britain, France and Western Germany,* 1965; United Nations, *Statistical Indicators of Housing Levels of Living,* 1959.

75. 'A new Government unhappily does not mean a new Civil Service élite . . . The Civil Service is too narrowly based on Oxbridge. It lacks expertise. The specialists it has are not put in the right places; its personnel lacks experience in the industrial, financial and social service fields in which it has to operate; there are high institutional barriers to outside recruitment; it neglects to train', Shore, P., *Entitled to Know,* MacGibbon & Kee, 1966, p.164.

76. In 1964 a family of man and wife and two children with an original income in the lower middle range of £676-815 paid about 28 per cent of that income in taxes (national insurance contribution 9 per cent, income tax 1 per cent and indirect taxes 18 per cent), while a similar family with an income of £1,448-

1,751 paid 27 per cent (national insurance 5 per cent, income tax 7 per cent and indirect taxes 15 per cent). For a family of man and wife and one child the figures are 32 and 32 respectively and for a man and wife and three children 25 and 24 respectively. For families of similar composition *direct* taxes are mildly progressive up to 100 per cent above and below mean income, *indirect* taxes are mildly regressive and national insurance contributions sharply regressive. These figures are based on Tables D, 1d and 2b in 'The Incidence of Taxes and Social Service Benefits in 1963 and 1964', *Economic Trends*, no. 154, August 1966. In calculating the percentage of original income taken in indirect taxes, I have taken the total average figure for indirect taxes and have divided it proportionately between the income remaining after taxes and insurance contributions have been paid and income represented by social service cash benefits (family allowances and national insurance benefits).

77. 'There appears to have been little increase in the amount of vertical redistribution between 1937 and 1959, but the extent of the increase, if any, depends on how much the estimates of the amount of redistribution in 1937 would have been reduced if they had been made on the same basis as our estimates for 1959'. Nicholson, J.L., *Redistribution of Income in the United Kingdom in 1959, 1957 and 1953*, Bowes & Bowes, 1965, p. 61.

78. Economists have come to mixed conclusions about minimum wage legislation. For example, a review of the 1956 American legislation suggested that *temporary* improvements were secured in low-wage industries at the cost of some displacement of labour and a reversion before long to former differentials. Douty, H.M., 'Some effects of the 1 dollar minimum wage in the United States,' *Economics*, May 1960.

79. 'According to our calculations, the average for semi-skilled men was 86 per cent of the all-class average in 1913 and 85 per cent in 1960; for unskilled men, the percentage was the same in both years. The women's average was 63 per cent of the all-class average in 1913 and 64 per cent in 1960'. Routh, G., *Occupation and Pay in Great Britain*, Cambridge University Press, 1965, p. x. Certain comparative figures drawn from the same source are equally interesting. In 1913/14 the unskilled worker received approximately 19 per cent of the average earnings of 'higher' professional workers (16 per cent of general practitioners' average earnings) and in 1960 26 per cent (21 per cent). In 1913/14 he earned 31 per cent of the average earnings of managers but in 1960 29 per cent. Routh, G., op.cit., calculated from Tables 30 and 47.

80. Wootton, B., *The Social Foundations of Wage Policy*, Allen & Unwin, 2nd ed., 1962.

81. 'The top salary structure [of industry] . . . is today shrouded in secrecy and has never been subject to any serious or rational consideration'. Shore, P., *Hansard*, 21 February 1965.

82. Tawney, R.H., *The Radical Tradition*, Allen & Unwin, 1964, pp. 178-80.

21 Mr Wilson's `Social Advance' *

The Prime Minister took as the thesis of his address to the Labour Party
Conference the great social advance which has occurred under the Labour
Government: 'In the three years we have been in office we have ended
the slide to social inequality and public neglect. We have put in hand a
dramatic deployment of resources in favour of those in greatest need,
in favour of the under-privileged, on all fronts of social action.'

It is just this redistribution of social resources which the Child Poverty
Action Group and other organizations say has not taken place. Good
things have been done, since October 1964, such as the abolition of
prescription charges, leasehold reform, redundancy payments, the direction of more resources to the development of comprehensive schooling.
But the cold truth is that in three years of office the Labour Government has failed to take a really major step in the war against poverty.
And it is not the economic situation which has prevented this step from
being taken.

The Government accepts that there is still poverty. Information collected by the Ministry of Labour for 1960 showed that 7½ million
people in Britain were at or below a national assistance standard of
living. They comprised five principal groups: (1) wage-earners with children who had a low wage or a large family; (2) the aged; (3) the disabled
and chronic sick; (4) fatherless families; and (5) the unemployed and
their families.

Social scientists have since shown, for the United States as well as
for this country, that the first three of these vulnerable minorities have
been increasing disproportionately to population. Two recent official
reports from the Ministry of Social Security have presented in scarifying
detail how depressed are living standards among some of these minorities. Many of the families are not eligible for public assistance (or
supplementary benefit as it is now called) according to existing rules.
Substantial proportions who *are* eligible do not apply.

---

* Address given to the Child Poverty Action Group during the Labour Party
Conference at Scarborough in 1967, a version of which was published in *Tribune*,
13 October 1967.

Wage-Earners with Children

What then has the Government done for these minorities? First, in face of unanswerable evidence about poverty among children it dithered for two years before announcing this summer that family allowances would be increased in two stages this winter by a derisory 7s. Yet these allowances have not been increased since 1956. They have been held down for more years, so far as I am aware, than any wage-rate or allowance of a substantial section of the population.

Between 1957-8 and 1967-8 the estimated gross cost of family allowances for the United Kingdom as a whole rose from £128 million to £160 million — because of the increase in families eligible for allowances; yet the cost of income tax and surtax relief for children rose in the same period from £230 million to £630 million — increases of 25 per cent and 174 per cent respectively. There is nothing to prevent the Government recognizing the needs of child dependency on the principle of increasing direct allowances very substantially and reducing tax allowances, and it would not even be necessary to make any family with an income up to the surtax-paying level worse off as a consequence. This is the reform being urged by the Child Poverty Action Group.

This adjustment in state support for child dependency is feasible and would illustrate perfectly the thesis of 'putting in hand a dramatic deployment of resources in favour of those in greatest need'. But not only is the Government proposing to add only a miserable 7s. to the allowance for the second child and subsequent children; it is proposing simultaneously to increase the costs of school meals by 2s. 6d. a week.

The Department of Education accepts that there will be a significant reduction in the numbers of children paying for meals at school. And many of the children who qualify for free meals are not at present getting them. Some people will even be worse off as a result of the package deal. For a man with average earnings who has two children at school, the extra 7s. for the second child may be worth as little as 4s. 8d. after tax, and he will have to pay 5s. extra per week for school meals.

The Aged

Secondly, there is poverty among the aged. The Government has not introduced its national superannuation scheme, the main object of which was to allow a dramatic increase in existing pension levels in exchange for higher proportional contributions towards higher eventual pensions. Although a detailed outline of the scheme was available in 1964 the public learns that legislation may not be introduced until the end of the life of this Parliament, in 1969 or 1970.

Why five or six years' delay? No adequate explanation has ever been put forward. The scheme worked out several years ago by Richard

Crossman and a backroom committee was carefully vetted and fully supported by Harold Wilson, Hugh Gaitskell and Anthony Crosland in turn, before being enthusiastically endorsed at a Labour Party Conference. The scheme was a social reform on the scale of Beveridge's wartime plan. It still offers a novel and attractive means of raising revenue with the support of the general public.

The mystery is why the Government did not introduce it in 1965 or 1966 as one of the major measures which would help bring the economic crisis under control. Increased proportional contributions would have reduced demand, so helping to stabilize prices, without leading to pressure for increased wages, and in the early years a surplus of £300 million or more per annum would have greatly helped the Chancellor of the Exchequer in his attempts to steady the pound and adapt the tax structure to secure confidence at home and abroad. To guard against a possible inflationary effect of increased employer's contributions, the Government could have made simultaneous selective tax concessions to industry, particularly the export industries.

The tragedy is that, like the proposal for reforming family allowances, national superannuation may be emasculated in the process of delay and consequent loss of enthusiasm. Far from standing four-square behind major reform, it seems that the Labour Cabinet has to be persuaded by a tiny minority of visionary members to adopt even a number of small and poorly co-ordinated measures.

The Prime Minister said last week that the flat-rate retirement pension had been raised substantially since Labour was returned to office. The single person's pension, which is being increased for the second time from 30 October, will then have been raised by the Labour Government by 33 per cent. But since May 1963 (when benefits were last increased by a Tory Government) average industrial earnings have already increased by about 32 per cent.

Since pensions tend only to be increased every two years, earnings are certain to outstrip the new pension rates during 1968 and 1969. So the Labour Government cannot even claim to have ensured parity between social security benefits and earnings throughout its term of office, still less to have substantially reduced the gap. Miss Margaret Herbison resigned from her post of Minister of Social Security in the summer of this year, probably over this very failure.

The Prime Minister also referred in his speech to the supplement of 9s. which retirement pensioners qualifying for supplementary benefit are now eligible to receive automatically. But before the bill introducing the supplement was debated in the House of Commons early in 1966, 73 per cent of retirement pensioners who qualified for assistance were already then receiving an average of over 10s. per week as a discretionary addition. Justified as the new supplement may be, the cost is therefore primarily a book-keeping transaction.

The Disabled and Sick
Thirdly, the disabled and chronic sick. The Disablement Income Group has pressed hard for a disability pension scheme of the kind operated in Sweden, where around 2 per cent of the population under sixty-five benefit. In Britain there are outrageous anomalies as between people with equivalent disabilities who receive widely varying incomes according to whether they qualify as war disablement pensioners, industrial injury pensioners, sickness beneficiaries or, like some housewives, for no benefit at all.

For the first six months of sickness and unemployment the Government has now started a wage-related scheme, but it does little for the man or woman with low earnings. Men and women with less than £9 per week do not qualify. A man with £12 per week gets a supplement of £1 in addition to the present £4 but only 8s. if he has a wife and four children. The act introduced a maximum benefit to which people would be entitled of 85 per cent of earnings. If a wage-earner with £9-12 happens to have had several weeks' sickness or unemployment in the year he barely receives any supplement under the scheme. If a man with higher earnings falls sick he loses the wage-related supplement after six months and depends solely on the flat-rate benefit, unless he is eligible to apply for assistance to the Supplementary Benefits Commission. After another eighteen months he qualifies for the automatic supplement of 9s. So his income falls after six months and rises marginally after two years.

It is difficult to write or speak with forbearance about this plainly makeshift set of arrangements. The Government seems to have made small progress with its 'long-term review', so far as the disabled are concerned. Judith Hart and Richard Crossman made it clear at conference that they were aware of the problem and had ideas about how to solve it.

What could be done to remedy the situation? The Government should declare that it intends to introduce new pensions for all kinds of disabled persons, including children, according to degree of disability, and without discrimination according to the place or origin of the disability, or as between men and women. It should immediately launch a national study to establish the numbers of disabled in the population, including the mentally handicapped, and appoint an expert committee to work out a modern method of assessment and review the social services for the disabled.

In the early 1950s the Piercy Committee did not get very far in exploring the problem in modern terms. The Government should immediately introduce two interim measures — reimbursing Selective

Employment Tax for all disabled employees, and extending constant attendance and hardship allowances from war pensioners and industrial injury pensions to other disabled persons.

Fatherless Families and the Unemployed

Fourthly, fatherless families. It was the previous, and not the present, Government which increased disproportionately the allowances for the dependent children of widows. The long-term review has shown no signs of producing a proposal to introduce a guaranteed maintenance allowance either for the children or for the mother in fatherless families. Yet several hundred thousand children are involved, and they and their mothers often experience particularly acute forms of poverty.

Finally, the unemployed. There are ominous signs that, despite protestations to the contrary, the Labour Government may be reconciled to accepting a higher percentage of the work-force who are at any given time unemployed than its supporters believed possible. There are redundancy payments and wage-related supplements for the first six months of unemployment, but it is often forgotten that many of those who become unemployed are men who do not qualify for these payments or supplements.

In November 1966 only 24 per cent of those getting unemployment benefit were drawing any wage-related supplements. And, as it is well-known, many men do not qualify for flat-rate unemployment benefits and have to resort to national assistance (now called supplementary benefit — which rather adds to the confusion).

Here the wage-stop can be penal. Many thousands of families have state help cut to below the subsistence level so that such help shall not exceed their previous earnings at work. What should be understood is that not only is the wage-stop principle inequitable: there is no possibility of making it equitable. How can one allow for the overtime element in previous earnings, for the loss since the start of unemployment of the opportunity to work overtime because of a local or national recession, for changes in the earnings levels of particular industries, for fluctuating piece-work earnings, and so on?

The solution to this problem must involve at least three measures: abolition of the wage-stop, general improvements in family allowances, and the introduction of a percentage disability pension payable in work or out of work. Evidence is accumulating that people who are liable *both* to unemployment and low wages tend to be chronic sick or disabled. The most practicable way to help them may be through the combination of a disability pension and family allowances rather than by the much more complex and less certain alternative of introducing a minimum wage.

Stigma of Public Assistance

Is there other evidence of social advance? The Prime Minister chastised the Conservative Party for seeking to restore to the British people all the indignities of a Public Assistance Society. He proclaimed that since the last conference the 'Government has abolished the stigma which attached to the old National Assistance'. But what in fact has happened? The name 'national assistance' has been changed to 'supplementary benefit'. The levels of the allowance have been raised. A few changes have been made to the rules about income and capital disregards.

The Prime Minister assumes that because there was a surge of new elderly applicants after these changes, they were numbered among the 500,000 to 1 million old people established in an official survey as eligible for national assistance, but who would not apply for it. It would be unwise to jump to this conclusion. Changes of name for 'poor relief' and 'public assistance' have been made before. The staff are largely the same. The offices are the same. All historical and sociological evidence would teach caution in expecting minor changes in procedure to lead to dramatic changes in public attitudes.

The more likely explanation is that because benefit rates were raised and income and capital disregards were relaxed, *some* of those who had not previously been eligible but who could now claim allowances applied. All previous evidence has shown that in addition to the 40-45 per cent of the retired who are at or below supplementary benefit rates, another 20 per cent or 25 per cent have an income only £1 or £2 higher. The Ministry of Social Security itself has shown that 35 per cent of the new applicants own the dwellings they live in and nearly 40 per cent have capital assets of £300 or more. It seems pretty clear that the great majority of those very poor people formerly reluctant to make themselves known to the National Assistance Board are not yet submitting to the blandishments of the Supplementary Benefits Commission.

Increase in Social Expenditure

The Prime Minister has drawn attention to sharp increases in social expenditure, and he dwelt on the fact that between 1963-4 and 1967-8 expenditure on the public social services increased by 45 per cent (and included in that figure education, 42 per cent; health and welfare, 45 per cent; housing, 55 per cent and social security, 44 per cent). Prices increased by 15 per cent. However, the figures must be placed in perspective. In industrial societies some degree of growth and of inflation seems to be normal. Every few years it is possible to claim considerable absolute increases, therefore, in public expenditure. The statistics show that in the four years up to 1963-4 (the year which the Prime Minister took as his base-line) the Tory Government increased social expenditure by almost as much as the Labour Government, and during a period, moreover, when prices did not rise by so much. The increase in expenditure on the social services between 1959-60 and 1963-4 was 43 per cent (included in that figure education, 53 per cent; health and welfare, 35 per cent; housing, 47 per cent and social security, 40 per cent).(1) Prices increased by 11 per cent. Moreover, increasing dependency in the social structure should be borne in mind. The proportions of the aged and the disabled and possibly even of fatherless families are increasing and in recent years this has also been true of children. Even if *rates* of expenditure per person did not rise, we would expect total expenditure to rise.

International comparisons are also instructive. Expenditure on education, health, welfare and social security is rising relative to national income or gross national product in most countries for which there is information. As more of the population reach higher education; as staff are better paid; as increases in the cost of surgery and drugs accelerate and as a better-educated public makes demands for all these goods and services, the proportion of national income taken up by the 'Welfare State' increases. This is the 'price' of building really advanced industrial societies, and, despite knock-about political arguments, the advance is taking place remorselessly in all countries. Whatever the political complexion of government the trend is the same.

But under a Labour Government is the pace of advance as good as in, say, France, or Germany, or Sweden or Australia? This is the real measure of advance. Social scientists have been urging again and again that we have fallen behind in some major respects in recent years. West Germany spends 10.4 per cent of its gross national product on social cash benefits (social insurance, public assistance, and family allowances); Austria, 9.2 per cent; Sweden, 9.1 per cent; Belgium, 8.8 per cent; France, 8.3 per cent; Italy, 7.9 per cent and the Netherlands, 7.7 per cent. We are near the foot of the league with 6.4 per cent.

Measures of advance in social expenditure as a whole in other countries are also chastening. The Prime Minister made much of an increase of 45 per cent in four years. Bur after years of introducing reforms, Sweden still maintained a rise of 42 per cent in a recent period of four years, and the figures for Norway and Denmark (excluding education) are 55 per cent and 61 per cent respectively.

Much of the increased expenditure is going to the middle-income groups, the new managers, the children of the middle-classes, who largely account for the growing cost of higher education, and the educated consumers who expect high standards in medical care. The real test of social advance is how far a substantial proportionate shift of resources to the lowest income groups has occurred. There is little evidence that this has yet happened in Britain.

The momentum of the problem of poverty in our society, which had been allowed to grow throughout the 1950s and early 1960s, has not been properly checked in the period since October 1964. The surprising fact is that the Labour movement has been so muted in criticism of the Government, and has not given vociferous support to ministers who want to introduce more reforms. There is a high level of unemployment, and there are five major groups who are in poverty. This summer the Government published a major survey and then dared to do nothing effective about the poverty it revealed. The time has come to cry halt, to get priorities right, and to regain the respect of socialists, both young and old.

The Prime Minister has quoted a previous speech of his in which he said 'Among civilized men greatness among nations is judged not by a country's battleships, its supersonic bombers, its arms or its H-bombs, or by the speed and efficiency with which it can mount an imperialist military excursion. It is judged by its treatment of the least privileged of its citizens, its young children, its old folk, its war disabled, and those injured in factories or in the mines.' These words have a faintly hollow ring when the record is consulted. If the record is to be transformed in the life of this Parliament some very quick action will have to be taken.

Note
1. Source: for 1959-60 to 1963-4, *Annual Abstract of Statistics;* for 1963-4 to 1967-8, the Prime Minister, 4 October 1967.

Official statistics are exposed to many different political and social influences whether they are the by-product of routine administration or the outcome of recurrent or occasional research. This thought is prompted by a new Government Report.(1) In the forms in which they are collected, presented and distributed official statistics reflect national values and help to define the scope of what is regarded as useful political discussion about policy. Those in charge of statistical information services may respond sensitively to changes in government direction or style. An opposition party which has come to power promising to meet a particular problem may find in office that confirmation can be found for its assessment of the scale of the problem. For example, a survey report published by the Ministry of Pensions and National Insurance confirmed that there were around a million retirement pensioners not receiving but eligible for national assistance.(2) Alternatively, if a party has become committed to an ideology of self-help and economies in public expenditure the statistical information services adapt bravely to post-electoral conditions. Departments find that economies can be made in the publication of statistical series which are, in the Government's view, redundant or unhelpful. Recent examples include the statistics of personal income distribution (3) and of social security.(4) Categories may be redefined so that trends can no longer be clearly followed or, indeed, may be left as previously defined despite criticisms from outside agencies or individuals which remain unanswered or which may even be unanswerable. Above all, texts which touch on controversial issues like redistribution, wealth or inequality seem to have been lovingly compiled by civil servants in order to neutralize dissension. They lend themselves to contradictory interpretations. These texts may be so sparing in the elucidation of a jungle of statistical tables that they baffle and confuse the unwary and a kind of swamp stretches in front of the pilgrim in search of truth. The reports of the Family Expenditure Survey, including some of the follow-up reports in *Economic Trends*, furnish examples. The tables are not always clear; the choice of absolute categories for the ranges of income make trends from year to year hard to perceive; and the text

* First published in the *Political Quarterly*, January 1972.

fails to mention some of the most important conclusions that can be drawn from the tables, or tells a slightly different story.

Bureaucracy and Statistics

It would be wrong to discuss official statistics only in terms of their sensitivity to political opinion and government. Bureaucracies have vested interests in producing information which, so far as possible, is non-contentious and expressed in forms which are familiar and acceptable to prevailing values. This is not just because this imposes least stress on working routine and everyday management. It also conforms with public expectations of the civil service. The government services of most nations are supposed, for example, to be politically impartial although directed by political masters. Despite the fact that there are other aspects of bureaucracy, such as recruitment, training, organization, management and accountability which help to sustain this belief, the statistical information services clearly play their part. By a variety of consciously or unconsciously motivated strategies they reduce potential social conflicts and reflect a common denominator of agreement. Bureaucracies also have vested interests in defining problems for which they are largely responsible in forms which, when applied in research, show that these problems are of 'manageable' proportions. From the viewpoint of bureaucracies it is more satisfactory if problems are found to be of a kind and size with which they can deal than if they imply an upheaval of administrative structure.

Although information systems respond to technological innovation it is important to remember that these systems possess rigidities due to staffing, programming, capacity and procedures which prevent them from handling certain kinds of information. But there are organizational as well as technical constraints. All organizations, and hierarchical organizations in particular, impose restrictions on the types of information which circulate internally as a basis for decision-making and externally as a basis for evaluating the work of the organization. When the functions of administration and intelligence are served by the same department, the latter will tend to be distorted by the former. If this were not so it would be difficult, for example, to explain the dearth of information in the annual reports of the Supplementary Benefits Commission about the wage-stop, variation between areas in the award of discretionary allowances, and the number of unemployed whose benefit is terminated — all these subjects being of considerable public interest in recent years.

The more contentious and far-reaching a social problem appears to be, the more difficult it is to obtain unambiguous statistical evidence about that problem. The best example is the statistics of the distribution of incomes and of wealth, which Richard Titmuss exposed so mercilessly a few years ago in his book, *Income Distribution and Social Change.* Despite his and others' criticisms, comparatively few improvements have been made to Board of Inland Revenue data. The first issue of *Social Trends* in 1970 was disappointingly reticent on this subject. For the last decade as much as for other periods of history it would be difficult not to conclude that the development of knowledge about social conditions has been muffled for a variety of very complex political and social reasons.

A more positive example of the pressures that are brought to bear on statistical evidence is the evidence about strikes, which Professor H. A. Turner has recently examined.

It appears, in sum, that the assumptions as to the frequency, character and costs of strikes in Britain, on which all three of the Conservative Party 1968 statements on industrial relations, the Report of the Royal Commission on Trade Unions, etc., and the Government White Paper on early 1969 were based, are (to say the least) highly dubious. The evidence that the pattern of industrial conflict in Britain is in some way different to that in other countries, as taking the form of frequent small strikes rather than a few big ones, is quite unconvincing. The suggestion that the United Kingdom is unique in having a majority of its strikes occur as unofficial or unconstitutional ones is largely unsupported. . . One can perhaps add that what seems currently a widespread public assumption that Britain is notably strike-prone appears to have little justification.(5)

The sociologist must therefore adopt the view that official statistics may bear only an indirect or partial relationship to an objective representation of a phenomenon under study. They are produced by bureaucratically organized agencies which are invested with social control functions and the statistics are one potent (though controlled and sometimes even censored) source of ideas about society and its problems. They therefore cannot be set aside but must be understood and explained like any 'objective' data.(6) What has to be conceptualized is the possibility, if not the actuality, of some alternative body of data with which they can be compared and their limitations revealed and understood. In principle a distinction has to be made between statistics which are the outcome of social conceptions and processes and those which are produced on the basis of criteria which are 'independent', 'external' or 'objective'.

Statistical Trends in Poverty

Some of the general characteristics of official statistics are illustrated by a recent Government report on *Two-Parent Families*. The most important conclusion that can be drawn from this report is that in the 1960s and in December 1970 there were, according to the Department of Health and Social Security, around 100,000 families in which there were 300,000 children of men in full-time paid employment, or unemployed men drawing supplementary benefit but wage-stopped, who were living on incomes below the basic Government poverty standard. Discussion of the reasons and remedies for this situation would seem to be of over-riding importance.

But the evidence presented about trends in poverty is inconclusive and calls in question the scope, timing, methods of analysis and presentation of this report. For it raises central questions of principle about the technical handling and the political implications of Government research and information about poverty. It would be naive to suppose that its production has been a detached operation entirely divorced from the political scene.

The history of it is that in 1968 the Government was under strong pressure from a number of sources, including the Child Poverty Action Group, to acknowledge the large dimension of poverty and do more about it. One Government survey of retirement pensioners carried out in 1965 and published in 1966 and another of families with two or more children carried out in 1966 and published in 1967 had revealed extensive poverty and large numbers apparently eligible to apply for national assistance (supplementary benefit), but who were not, in fact, receiving it. Research of wider scope was called for. In 1968 Mrs Judith Hart, then Minister of Social Security, undertook 'as a matter of urgency' to prepare a report on all aspects of poverty on the basis of data collected in the Family Expenditure Survey (F.E.S.). This was preferred to new research for the speed with which results could be prepared. Government Ministers were aware that any results which applied to the situation in late 1968 and 1969 would reflect increases in family allowances introduced in three stages in 1967-8 and in pensions and other national insurance scales, as well as supplementary benefits, in the autumn of 1968. By the autumn of 1969 interest in the date of publication began to become acute. On 6 March 1970 Mr David Ennals, Minister of State for Social Security, said that the results 'will be published as soon as possible', and after repeating this undertaking in a formal speech on 19 April 1970 he said that the Government was in fact working on a 'prototype' analysis. 'Although we ourselves need these figures badly, and the pressures for publication are bound to increase, we are determined not to release them until we have made sure, humanely speaking, that they are completely reliable.'

Towards the end of January 1970 the Child Poverty Action Group (C.P.A.G.) had presented a memorandum to the Secretary of State for Social Services on poverty among the low-paid, unemployed, disabled, elderly and fatherless families, arguing that measures introduced since 1964 had not been as effective as supposed by the Government, and that poverty was increasing relatively, at least among some groups. Not least among its complaints was that adequate information about poverty was very slow in reaching the public. The chief conclusion was that although the Labour Government 'introduced a number of reforms, poverty remains on a considerable and perhaps even greater scale than when it assumed office'. It called for prompt action on a wide front. After this was published, vigorous debate was joined with Government Ministers. Mr Ennals in particular attempted to rebut the main conclusion in detailed articles in *Tribune* (13 February, and 6 March).(7) The Conservative Opposition took up the criticisms in Parliament, led on at least two occasions by Mr Heath, and when Mr Wilson announced an election for June turned them to electoral advantage. Poverty had increased under Labour, they said.

Publication of the long-awaited report was expected in the autumn of 1970 but in fact it did not materialize until July 1971, although data for 1970 had been speedily incorporated. There was a political stake in the results on either side. Those with Conservative sympathies probably felt that if the electoral charge that poverty had become worse under Labour was not confirmed it would be just as well for a decent interval to elapse before the report was published. Those with Labour sympathies probably felt that even if their worst fears had not been confirmed there were no figures in the report which could be turned to positive political advantage. Those in Government departments who had to prepare successive drafts of the report (and there is reason to believe that at least by the late spring 1970 a paper was circulating in Whitehall, and a revised draft in August 1970) cannot have been impervious to the strength of political interest and feeling on either side. A number of key decisions about the scope of the report and the assumptions on which estimates could be built about the extent of poverty could transform its nature.

Statistical Defects

There are a number of features of the Government's report which require critical discussion and which make it difficult to draw any precise conclusions about trends in poverty. I shall set these out in turn. The conclusion must be that the F.E.S. clearly does not, at least as presently administered, provide the data required, and special surveys of poverty need to be carried out.

1. *Unsatisfactory treatment of 1966 data*. The report concludes that 'the evidence suggests that there may have been a decline in the numbers of families [living below their supplementary benefit level] between December 1966 and 1968, after which the estimates of numbers are stable.' Considerable emphasis was placed on this in D.H.S.S. press statements. But there are three odd facts about this conclusion. First, it is based not on the June 1966 figures, when the survey was actually carried out, but on a re-working of those figures to take account of increases in supplementary benefit scales late in the year (which inevitably placed more families below the new levels). Secondly, although the 'needs' of families are adjusted to take account of the increases in rates between June 1966 and December 1966, their resources are not similarly adjusted. This is inconsistent and misleading because the D.H.S.S. adjusts resources of people interviewed in the F.E.S. during 1968, 1969 and 1970 to 31 December, according to industry group. A weak excuse is given which scarcely justifies the failure to make the adjustment and certainly does not justify the emphasis in the conclusion. This reads: 'However, as earnings increased only slightly between June and December 1966 the extent of overstatement in the December 1966 estimate will be slight, and had such an adjustment been made, then the evidence would probably have suggested that the numbers of such families declined between December 1966 and December 1968, and remained stable subsequently.' Thirdly, the report actually states that 'exact comparisons between 1966 and later years are not possible without re-processing the 1966 data', and yet it proceeds in the following two pages to give a detailed statistical comparison for these years.

2. *Failure to use F.E.S. data for 1966 and earlier years*. In the report the F.E.S. data for 1968-70 are compared with the *Circumstances of Families* data for 1966. Since the latter were obtained by different methods and by a different Government body it is remarkable that comparisons with the corresponding F.E.S. data for the same year are not made. Although the sample was smaller in that year than in the late 1960s it was large enough for reliable results to be obtained at least for smaller families.

3. *Self-employed excluded*. The D.H.S.S. report states in effect (p.3) that since information about the incomes of the self-employed collected in the F.E.S. is not very reliable, the self-employed have been excluded from the count of the poor. But the Department of Employment and Productivity has not admitted the unreliability of this information and indeed has included the self-employed in all its previous reports on the survey, as has the Central Statistical Office (C.S.O.) in its reports on the

redistribution of income. Perhaps someone in the D.H.S.S. doubts the evidence of the *Circumstances of Families* report and elsewhere that the incidence of poverty among the self-employed is up to four times higher than among the employed. Included among the self-employed are shopkeepers, tinkers, small-holders and farmers. Unless there is some basis in knowledge for the contention that the proportion of self-employed found in surveys to be poor is greatly exaggerated it is hard to understand why the statistics should be adjusted. Moreover, the omission of the self-employed affects trends in poverty as well as its level. With the introduction of the Selective Employment Tax self-employment increased after 1966 as a proportion of all employment.(8) Since a higher proportion of the self-employed are poor this would tend to *increase* the overall rate of poverty.

4. *Incomes adjusted to end of year.* In the F.E.S. households are surveyed throughout the year. Instead of comparing incomes with the supplementary benefit scales at the approximate time of interview the D.H.S.S. adjusted earnings 'by an index of average earnings in the industry group of the employee to a December 31st position'. The Department also took the benefit scales in force at that date. But this can seriously distort comparisons from year to year. For example, if family allowances happen to be raised late in the year the vast majority of families interviewed earlier in the year will all be credited with the increases as if they had been receiving them for twelve months. The criteria by which the D.H.S.S. had adjusted incomes other than earnings to the end of the year are not explained. The adjustment of housing costs also present a number of conceptual difficulties.

5. *Pooling over years of information for large families.* The F.E.S. sample includes about 200 households each year with two parents and four or more children but the D.H.S.S. has stated that this is 'not sufficiently large for reliable estimates of their net resource distribution to be obtained'. The source of embarrassment appears to be that the number of families with four or more children and negative net resources was estimated on the basis of the survey to be 14,000 in 1968, but 42,000 in 1969 and 12,000 in 1970. But the decision of the D.H.S.S. to add the *average* of four-child families with negative resources in the three years 1968-70 to the yearly totals for families with one, two or three children seems very arbitrary, particularly since the *number* of four-child families in the sample, about 200, is not unrespectable. Categories with similar numbers have frequently been presented in percentage distributions in previous Government reports. Moreover, the relatively small number of large families in the sample

does not seem to be the source of the problem of fluctuating results. The report shows that the number of one-child and two-child families with incomes below the supplementary benefit level also varies widely and in an opposite direction between 1969 and 1970. Finally, the report states on page 5 that there is approximately a one in three chance that the actual 1970 figure is more than 15,000 above or below the observed figure. However, for 1969 'much of the difference' between the actual figures (85,000 for all families) and the pooled figure (66,000) 'can be explained in terms of sampling error'. Yet this could only happen with a chance of much less than one in three — in fact, nearer one in six.

6. *Inappropriate use of absolute values in analysing trends.* The report shows numbers of families with net resources with up to £5 and up to £2 above the supplementary benefit level for different years. The numbers tend to be smaller in the later years. But the value of the pound has fallen rapidly both in relation to prices and to earnings. It is particularly surprising that the D.H.S.S. has presented pooled data for three years (e.g. Table 2) on this basis. This method has an in-built bias towards showing a decline in the population who are represented as living on the margins of poverty. Much of the information about trends in personal income presented by Government Departments, particularly the C.S.O. and the Board of Inland Revenue, need to be put on to a relative basis.

7. *Incomplete analysis of wage-stopped families.* The report states that 'in order to obtain estimates of the number of families with negative net resources it is necessary to add the estimate of the number wage-stopped [to the total].' After 1966 the number of men who were unemployed for long periods and whose supplementary benefit was reduced so that their total benefit did not exceed their former wage increased. But the corresponding number of men who were receiving unemployment benefit but not supplementary benefit because the application of the wage-stop made them ineligible for such benefit, despite the fact that their incomes were below the basic scale rates, must also have increased. Those receiving supplementary benefit but wage-stopped represent an 'iceberg' phenomenon. There are many more below the visual level. The report does not deal with this aspect of poverty among unemployed men with families (nor indeed sickness or disability in relation to poverty).

8. *No adjustment for differential changes in prices.* During a period of rapid inflation and changes in the subsidy policy of the Government,

changes can occur among certain groups in their relative living standards, even when differentials net of tax remain the same. After a preliminary increase for four-child families in the autumn of 1967 family allowances were increased in two steps in 1968, but in announcing the autumn 1967 and April 1968 increases Mr Gordon Walker (26 July 1967) made it clear that a large part of the increase was to compensate families for a reduction of the subsidies for school meals and welfare milk. The D.H.S.S. report makes no reference to this.

9. *Insufficient information on non-response and representativeness*. The F.E.S. of 1968, 1969 and 1970 had a response of 69 per cent, 67 per cent and 69 per cent respectively, compared with one of 90 per cent for the survey of *Circumstances of Families*. No special tests to show whether non-respondents differ from respondents have been published. Moreover, comparisons between family structure in the F.E.S. and the Census would help to indicate why results of the F.E.S. fluctuate from year to year.

Conclusions

The Government's report on family poverty illustrates some of the limitations of official statistics. The report is a slim document of eighteen pages. Its scope is severely restricted to working families and wage-stopped families. Reservations may need to be made about the possibilities of measuring poverty among fatherless families and the long-term sick on the basis of the F.E.S. sample, for example, because of their small representation, but such reservations do not have to be made about the elderly and other groups. The Government still seems to be holding back from making as much immediate use of the F.E.S. as it might.

The results of the analyses of the data for 1968, 1969 and 1970 are, however, disconcerting from a methodological point of view. It is not easy, for example, to 'explain' the findings for 1969 or 1970 about families with one child or with four or more children. The authors of the report seem to have chosen to amalgamate certain of the results for different years rather than undertake a much more rigorous examination of the representativeness of the F.E.S. and the possibilities of strengthening the fieldwork on poorer sections of the population. It would seem better to publish unadjusted results while calling attention to the limitations of the data and adopting supplementary research procedures to reduce these limitations. The D.H.S.S. clearly regard the F.E.S. as much more limited in value than does, say, the Department of Employment or the C.S.O. For example, W.F.F. Kemsley in his admirable Government booklet on the F.E.S. describes it as a 'multi-purpose inquiry, serving a wide variety of needs and providing an invaluable supply of economic and social data' including data on the redistributive effects of taxation. But the D.H.S.S. choose to say that 'the F.E.S. sample is designed primarily to provide weights for the retail price index', and that 'it is not designed to produce estimates of the distribution of families by net resources.' Together with the statistics presented, this lack of enthusiasm implies that special surveys of the distribution of resources need to be mounted.

In Table 1 the data compiled by the D.H.S.S. are compared with data obtained from other official sources in the 1960s. The view adopted here is that unadjusted survey findings should be reported and studied for the detection of trends unless the grounds for adjustment rest on secure knowledge — like the failure of a particular sample to fully represent the numbers in the population of a particular type of family. The findings should also relate to the period of their collection. Since the *Circumstances of Families* survey was carried out in June 1966 the data for that time are preferred to the estimates obtained by (partial) projection to the end of the same year. But it is true that one-child families were not included in that survey and the Ministry of Social Security added a very rough estimate of the number with inadequate resources to the findings for other families. Altogether the first two columns of the table seem to represent the best summary that can be given on the basis of official survey data of trends over the decade in the number of two-parent families and of individuals in those families with resources less than the supplementary benefit level.

The data which emerge for 1968, 1969 and 1970 from the D.H.S.S. report do not suggest that poverty among families of men in full-time work substantially increased, as C.P.A.G. and others feared. Nor do they suggest it diminished. Sampling variations and the problems of allowing for non-response as well as measurement bias make any more emphatic conclusion impossible. Moreover, trends among the unemployed, the sick and disabled, fatherless families, the elderly and single and married people at work but lacking children, remain to be investigated, and some of these trends have certainly worked towards increasing the extent of poverty. The rate as revealed by official statistics appears to have fluctuated for different years, as the evidence in the accompanying table shows, and the fluctuations cannot easily be related to events. None of the statistical estimates have been adjusted for certain factors affecting living standards, principally differential changes in the cost of living. In particular, the full increase in family allowances is included in income although part of that increase, as Mr Gordon Walker announced, replaced the subsidy withdrawn from

Table 1 Number of families (and people in those families) of a father in full-time work or wage-stopped with resources of less than the supplementary benefit level (thousands)

Year	No. of families in full-time work (no. of people in brackets) Unadjusted	In full-time work and wage-stopped		
		Unadjusted	Adjusted by D.H.S.S.(4)	
		Families (no. of people in brackets)	All Families	Families with 2 or more children only
1960 (1)	85 (370)	—	—	—
1966 June (2)	95 (470)	110 (552)	—	72
1966 December	—	—	—	114
1968 (3)	73 (334)	102 (500)	100	73
1969 (3)	96 (527)	122 (677)	92	76
1970 (3)	74 (336)	105 (505)	105	74

(1) Abel-Smith, B., and Townsend, P., *The Poor and the Poorest*, Bell, 1965.
(2) *Circumstances of Families*, H.M.S.O., 1967.
(3) D.H.S.S. Statistical Report Series No. 14, *Two Parent Families*, H.M.S.O., 1971 (Tables 2, 10A and 10B). The estimates are the same as those publicized by the D.H.S.S. except that an estimate for the self-employed has been restored (in the columns of unadjusted estimates). In the absence of actual data from the samples the number estimated on the basis of the Government survey in 1966 (see *Circumstances of Families*, p. 39) has been incorporated for each of the years 1968, 1969 and 1970. The figure has not been increased proportionately in line with an increase in the proportion of self-employed.
(4) Three adjustments were made by the D.H.S.S. to the estimates based on the surveys. First, estimates of families with four or more children and resources below the supplementary benefit level were averaged for the three years 1968-70 and added to the other estimates for those years. Secondly, the estimate of the self-employed below the level was replaced by an estimate in the same proportion as for the employed. Thirdly, some other adjustments were made to the 1966 estimate.

school meals and welfare milk. A concerted effort needs to be made by research organizations to ensure that reliable information about trends can be produced.

Finally, the operational definition of poverty being used by the D.H.S.S. may be much too stringent, with the result that poverty has been estimated to be much smaller than it really is. The level of need is taken as the basic supplementary benefit scale rate for the family plus the appropriate rent allowance. In practice, the Supplementary Benefits Commission often awards an additional weekly allowance for exceptional circumstances. It also disregards certain types and amounts of income in calculating a family's resources. Neither of these 'practical' modifications are built into the D.H.S.S. measure. If they had been incorporated the estimated number in poverty would have been higher.

However, these points are inconsequential in relation to the use of supplementary benefit scale rates to define the income required to surmount poverty. These scale rates have been raised from time to time since the war to keep pace with inflation and rising earnings. But their basic rationale has not been examined either by a Government body or by an independent commission. They therefore derive from the thinking set out thirty years ago in the Beveridge Report of 1942. Lord Beveridge appointed Seebohm Rowntree as a consultant and adopted a modification of the Rowntree subsistence standard, which was originally worked out and applied in York in 1899. The sub-sistence standard has been used nationally to define poverty and to justify the rates paid in benefit. It represents a 'social' but not necessarily objective or scientific conception of poverty. The D.H.S.S. admit in this report that 'such a definition does not consider the whole complex of environmental and social circumstances relevant to an exhaustive study of poverty' but do not appreciate that the definition is itself a conventional one, representing a 'national minimum' rather than a conception which has some basis in objectively validated criteria. Social scientists must escape the trap of discussing poverty only as defined by the Government.

Notes

1. *Two-Parent Families: A Study of their Resources and Needs in 1968, 1969 and 1970,* Department of Health and Social Security, Statistical Report Series, no. 14, H.M.S.O., 1971. The author wishes to acknowledge the valuable help provided in compiling this note by Professor A.B. Atkinson, Colin Bell, Nicholas Bosanquet, Geoffrey Hawthorn and Adrian Sinfield.

2. Ministry of Pensions and National Insurance, *Financial and Other Circum-stances of Retirement Pensioners,* H.M.S.O., 1966.

3. The National Income Blue Book for 1970 announced the suspension of publi-cation of tables giving the distribution of personal incomes. 'The table included in earlier Blue Books has been dropped because of the increasing amount of estimation required to produce calendar year figures on a national accounts basis'. *National Income and Expenditure,* H.M.S.O., 1970, p.97.

4. The amalgamation first of the National Assistance Board and the Ministry of

Pensions and National Insurance and then of the Ministry of Social Security and Ministry of Health led to a substantial reduction in statistical information published in annual reports. See the appropriate reports for 1965-8. Although supplementary statistical digests can now be obtained they do not continue some statistical series and are not so accessible to the public.

5. Turner, H.A., Is Britain Really Strike Prone?, University of Cambridge, Department of Applied Economics, Occasional Papers 20, Cambridge University Press, 1969, p.44.

6. A useful discussion of the problem in relation to the statistics of deviance will be found in Kitsuse, J.I., and Cicourel, A.V., 'A Note on the Use of Official Statistics,' Social Problems, 1963-4, pp.131-9.

7. The C.P.A.G. memorandum, and the ensuing discussion with Mr Ennals, are printed in Poverty and the Labour Government, Child Poverty Action Group, 1970.

8. For example, the percentage of men paying national insurance contributions who were self-employed increased from less than 8 per cent in 1965 to about 9 per cent in 1969.

3 The Social Underdevelopment of Britain 1970-74 *

27 October 1970 was a black day for the poor of Britain. After a period of gestation following the June election, the unveiling of the mini-budget marked a turning point in social history and was tantamount to a declaration of class warfare. It represented a return to the more authoritarian and doctrinaire principles of Tory social philosophy, which no Tory administration of the post-war years had dared espouse and to which the Heath administration has obstinately clung. This budget laid the framework of thought for all the major subsequent measures — the successive budgets and mini-budgets of 1971-3, stages I, II and III of incomes policy, the Housing Finance and Social Security Acts of 1972 and 1973, the reform of personal income taxation and introduction of VAT, the Tax Credit Scheme and the reorganization of the National Health Service.

When every allowance is made for the muddled intentions of some parts of its social strategy, for the new forms of help it has given (at small financial cost) to certain minorities, and for the tendency to exaggerate the effects of new Government policies, as distinct from other influences, on the broad distributions of current public expenditures and living standards, the verdict must stand. The Government must be indicted for introducing greater social inequality and dissension and for threatening the basic stability and quality of British life.

The social policy of any Government can be evaluated in different ways — in relation to long-established Party objectives and principles; the expression of those objectives and principles in the Party manifesto; the internal consistency of the statement of objectives and the means chosen for fulfilling these objectives; the standards and tests for policies which it perceives and accepts; and more objective standards of social need or condition.

The Tory administration was faced in 1970 with the task of defining the strategy which would put the aims of its manifesto into operation. 'A Better Tomorrow' already included the ingredients for a more divisive strategy, such as the commitments to cut income tax and surtax, reduce public expenditure, extend private and occupational pension schemes, introduce an Industrial Relations Bill, encourage private indus-

* First published in the *New Statesman*, 25 February 1974.

try, change the housing subsidy system, sell council houses, establish
further controls over immigration, and take 'firm action to deal with
abuse of the social security system . . . so as to prevent the whole system
from being brought into disrepute by the shirkers and scroungers'. But
in deference to the poverty lobby the harsh implications of the manifesto were tempered by unspecific promises to protect pensioners' living
standards, improve benefits for the ill and disabled, give priority to
community services, 'tackle the problem of family poverty and ensure
that adequate family allowances go to those families that need them'.
Iain MacLeod had committed the Party in May 1970, a few months
before his death, to an increase in family allowances, and in a letter to
the Child Poverty Action Group on 1 June Mr Heath stated, 'We accept
that . . . the only way of tackling family poverty in the short term is to
increase family allowances and operate the clawback principle' (i.e.
simultaneously reducing the value of tax allowances for children to
standard rate tax-payers).

Although the auguries were ominous there were therefore grounds
for supposing, especially when the Party failed to secure a majority of
the votes of the electorate, that the inegalitarian and authoritarian pre-
dispositions of Tory social strategy might be moderated in practice.
Much depends on the final definition of the scope and degree of effect
of new policies, like actual tax rates and amounts of expenditure. Politicians are inclined to be expedient. Much also depends on the countervailing effects upon living standards of different policies and how they
may be transformed by movements in earnings, property values and
prices. After all, the Tory administration of 1959-64 had, for example,
maintained a higher rate of increase annually in social service expenditure in real terms than previous post-war Administrations and a higher
rate, if housing is included, than that achieved subsequently under
Labour (5.5 per cent compared with 4.9 per cent). Developments in
education, hospital building, housing, community care and even the
1963 pension increase do not, for example, bear out conventional stereo-
types of Tory retrenchment.

Mr Barber threw down the gauntlet in his first mini-budget. Income
tax was substantially reduced and public expenditure cut by £330 million in 1971-2, rising to £1600 million in 1974-5. Cheap welfare milk
was abolished, prescription, spectacles, dental and school meals charges
raised, free school milk for children over the age of seven discontinued,
and a cut of £100 million to £200 million in housing subsidies and
£150 million in agricultural support promised. At the same time the
pledge to raise family allowances was set aside and, instead, the Family
Income Supplement scheme was announced to help low income families on test of means.

The three principal ingredients of Tory social strategy throughout the period 1970-4 were duly established: (1) Resources and power were to be shifted further to the deserving rich, on grounds that they were crucial to the economy and the future stability of Britain's social order. (2) Private industry was to be given greater freedom and its management principles adopted more emphatically in the administration of government, on grounds of social and economic efficiency and the benevolent administration of welfare. In the words of the Chancellor, 'Our object is to lessen Government interference ... extend the opportunities for profitable investment, and widen the area within which industry rather than Government will take decisions'. The slow encroachment of democratic procedures of public control, arbitration, consultation, consumer representation and participation, and complaints machinery upon business and professional values was to be halted, and even the numbers of civil servants reduced or levelled off. (3) The management of the social services and social security in particular was to be more strongly infused with the principle of conditional welfare for the few; on grounds not just of cutting progressive taxes and Government subsidies and so creating better material incentives for investors and managers, but also that industry rather than society was best equipped to define the right to income and that the number among the population in genuine need was, anyway, few. Through means-tested benefits the prosperous working class would be obliged to 'fend for themselves' and 'stand on their own feet', and the undeserving poor, the so-called workshy, cohabitees and deceitful immigrants would be properly vetted and controlled. For the small class of deserving poor, on the other hand, new forms of national charity should properly be developed and dispensed.

The strategy reaffirmed, in short, the paramountcy of the values of the market. Its character and scale deserve to be better understood. For that would pave the way for a counter-strategy by Labour on a scale undreamed of in 1964-70. Tax reliefs in excess of £600 million have been granted in the last three years to those with incomes of £5,000 a year and over. These reliefs include increases in the exemption limits for estate duty, coupled with an easing of the scale of the rates, an increase in surtax limits, an increase in earned income relief, the effect of a cut in corporation tax on personal holdings of shares, the reduction of the standard rate of tax and disaggregation of a child's investment income from the income of his parents. Even without any account being taken of the huge gains in property values in the last three years or the pre-existing scale of inequality and privilege the figure effectively demolishes the well-publicized supposition that taxation of the rich offers little scope for the finance of substantial measures for the poor.

Each of the major social measures enacted in the 1970-74 Parliament illustrates the strategy. Through the Housing Finance Act the Government is seeking to turn council housing into a profit-making enterprise. By raising rents to so-called 'fair' levels and reducing subsidies the Government's intention is to produce a surplus, before rebates are paid, on housing revenue accounts. The total annual rent incomes of the local authorities are to be drawn upon to meet the costs of rebates to poorer tenants. If there is a deficiency only three-quarters of the deficiency is to be met by the Exchequer. If, however, there is any surplus it will go first to offset any subsidy in rent allowances made by the Government to private tenants, and will go second in equal measure to the central government and back to the local authority's rate fund. One consequence is that the rebate scheme for poorer council tenants is to be financed largely from the rents paid by better-off tenants instead of from general taxation. Another is that the latter may also be subsidizing the rent allowances of poorer private tenants and even local and central expenditure on non-housing projects. A third is that local councils have a direct incentive to place poorer tenants in areas with poorest housing and lowest rents, thus grading housing classes more finely.

The Act fails in any way to deal with the accumulating privileges of owner-occupation. In 1970-71 local and central subsidies amounted to about £39 per council house. Tax relief on mortgage interest amounted in the same year to £61 per mortgaged house. Even this latter figure is small in relation to the real savings of owner occupiers in comparison with other members of the community. For example, it does not include any estimate of the saving in not paying tax on the capital gains made on their homes by owner-occupiers in recent years. Nor is the figure as high as the estimated saving in not paying tax on imputed rental income. Schedule A tax was withdrawn, it should be remembered, in 1963. Too much attention is concentrated on the problems faced by intending owner-occupiers in buying a house and not enough on the privileges of established mortgagees, particularly the richer rather than the poorer section among them. In the *National Westminster Bank Review* for May 1972 Harrington showed that the combined effect of tax relief and inflation was to make the real rate of interest on loans actually *negative* in some recent years. In the *Housing Review* for May-June 1973 Hare showed on modest assumptions about inflation that after initial purchase in 1970 the real housing costs of average buyers and council tenants in Scotland are rapidly becoming less unequal. Before half the usual term of mortgage repayment is completed the buyer will be paying *less* absolutely than the council tenant for his housing. And with house prices outstripping retail prices the buyer who sells his home after as little as six years will have spent less altogether on his housing than the average council tenant.

The tax reliefs, improvement grants and part of the capital gains which are received by owner-occupiers are financed directly and indirectly from public funds.'They contribute to the scarcity of housing as well as gross inequalities in housing. The recent boom has encouraged owners of highly priced accommodation to compete for more spacious and well-endowed homes. They make disproportionate claims on the building industry. But must homes of an affluent minority be further enriched, or should limits be placed on such enrichment so that more of the growing numbers of homeless and deprived can enjoy reasonable living conditions?

The false pieties of the market are also writ large in the Government's reconstruction of earnings-related pensions in 1972. The Act represents a surrender to the power of commercial insurance and the occupational pensions lobby. Occupational pension schemes have always been inequitable. Substantial pensions and lump sums are paid for, in effect, not only by the taxpayer but by people who leave their jobs and lose their pension rights or only receive the accumulated and not the investment value of their own and not their employers' contributions. Substantial initial pensions are also financed indirectly by the reduction during inflation of the value of pensions in payment. There is rarely any cover, still less adequate cover, for widows. Administratively the schemes are extremely wasteful.

No serious attempt was made by the Government to knock this commercial lottery into equitable shape. The size of the pension funds is now of inestimable importance in controlling the affairs of the City. Every financial encouragement has been given to the schemes, despite the disquieting evidence in the 1971 report of the Government Actuary about the inequality between manual and non-manual employees, and the flagging coverage and low benefits for the former. The so-called State Reserve pension scheme has been deliberately constructed to be as poor as possible in relation to occupational schemes. There are no rights to protection from inflation up to the date of retirement, disability or widowhood, contrary to all inflation proofing of pensions in Europe. As Professor Chester has pointed out, a man retiring in 1995 after 20 years' contributions can expect a pension from this source of only 8 per cent of his last computable earnings. Again, this is far inferior to the State schemes of most European countries.

The reorganization of the National Health Service illustrates the second part of the Government's strategy to extend managerial rule. A multi-tier hierarchy amost totally controlled from above has been introduced on grounds of efficiency. The power of the former Regional Hospital Boards has been extended to cover planning decisions affecting the general practitioner and other community health services and they have been renamed Regional Health Authorities. Each authority has about 15 members, all of whom are appointed by the Secretary of State. Few of those appointed are manual workers or consumers. A third are businessmen — bankers, company directors, business executives, property developers and brokers. Most of the rest are doctors (usually consultants), solicitors and accountants. They are to plan the regions and supervise Area Health Authorities, which will also consist of 15 members, 11 of whom are appointed by the Regional Health Authorities and only four by the local authorities. The chairman of each Area Health Authority is appointed by the Secretary of State. The bottom tier of new community health councils will have almost no rights. Half of their members will be appointed by the local authorities, a third will represent local voluntary organizations and the remainder are to be appointed by the Regional Health Authorities. In such a structure the voices of the hospital consultant and health administrator will dominate, and those of the patient, the representative of the local population and the advocate of community health will be muted.

Selective welfare is the final element in the Government's social strategy. In history three different policies for ending poverty might be distinguished — *conditional welfare for the few, minimum rights for the many,* and *distributional justice for all.* The first was enshrined in the Poor Law Report of 1834 of Senior and Chadwick, and applied thereafter with differing degrees of enthusiasm, more resolutely in the 1870s and 1880s, say, than the middle of the nineteenth century. It is characterized by the means test, charity and low public expenditure. The second began to emerge with the legislation of the first decade of the twentieth century and was spelt out in the Reports of the Poor Law of 1909, particularly the Minority Report of the Webbs and their notion of the national minimum, but was applied with renewed emphasis from the appearance of the Beveridge Report of 1942. It is characterized by universal benefits and rights up to a subsistence or other minimum and across a highly restricted range of State and local services. It implies underpinning rather than reconstruction of economic and social institutions.

Since the war both policies have been pursued, the Tories tending ideologically to favour the first and Labour the second, whatever the correspondence between them when in office. Despite occasional flirtations with the third policy, which is characterized by the destratification of society through occupational and community reorganization and equal distribution of all kinds of resources, it could be argued that the choice between the second and third has never been squarely faced by Labour.

The three policies must not be regarded as different methods of dealing with a problem whose nature is generally perceived and agreed. Each policy involves a different conception of the problem, different evaluation of the evidence and different explanations of poverty. Any attempts to ameliorate or reduce poverty contains an implicit explanation of its cause and implicit assumptions about its definition and scale.

Mr Barber had no doubts about the objectives of policy. They were to 'confine the scope of free provision more closely to what is necessary on social grounds. In the social services we shall establish more sensible priorities. We shall expect that where the user can afford it, he should bear more of the cost and the taxpayer less; but we shall give help to those who need it'. The last claim is not easy to test. The Government provides inadequate means of monitoring changes in living standards of the poor and not much information is yet available for 1973 or 1974. The latest analysis of the Family Expenditure Survey by the Central Statistical Office shows little change throughout the 1960s and early 1970s in the level of income of the poorest fifth of different types of families, relative to the median.(1) Slight fluctuations in the figures from year to year could be accounted for by sampling variation. On these figures the Government cannot claim to have given 'help to those who need it'.

For the five year period 1968-72 the Central Statistical Office found a tendency for the original incomes of the lowest quintile to fall relative to the median, partly explained by the rise in unemployment, but this seemed to have been offset by tax changes and wider dependence on social security benefits.

The trouble with these figures is first that measures of 'lowest quintile incomes' do not provide a good guide to the incomes among the twenty per cent of households distributed below those levels. The Reports of the Family Expenditure Survey now include data about the lowest decile but do so only for 1971 and 1972. They do not suggest much change taking place in the incomes of the poorest tenth, relative to the median or the highest decile, though among three-child and four-child families there seems to have been a fall. Indeed, despite the introduction of the Family Income Supplement, the expenditure of the poorest families with three and four children was £23.40 and £23.22 respectively in 1972, only marginally greater than for families with two children (£23).(2)

Second, the figures do not reflect the differential effect upon poor and rich of price changes. According to the latest report of the National Food Survey 33 per cent of the incomes of the poorest families with one child and 39 per cent with four or more children was devoted to food, compared with only 18 per cent and 23 per cent respectively of the incomes of the richest families. Between the beginning of 1970 and the end of 1973 food rose in price by 56 per cent, whereas other items rose by only 34 per cent. Again, the introduction of VAT in April 1973 put up the prices of 'necessary' items such as beds, prams and cots and lino although the prices of 'luxury' items, such as cameras and colour television sets, were lowered. These trends force one to conclude that there was a significant fall (which I estimate conservatively at about 3 per cent) in the living standards of the poorer families relative to richer families during this period.

Throughout the life of the Government lip service has been paid in its documents on incomes policy to the low paid and pensioners. The measures necessary to give them priority have not been understood, elaborated or implemented. The latest Department of Employment report on its survey of earnings show that the earnings of the lowest decile of male manual workers, expressed as a per cent of the median, was 67.3 in 1970, 68.2 in 1971, 67.6 in 1972 and back again to 67.3 in 1973. The value of the single rate of pension has still not been restored even to the level of between 20 and 21 per cent of average industrial earnings, which it had attained briefly in 1963, 1965 and 1967, and has been fluctuating around 18 per cent and 19 per cent since 1970.

In a meticulous study of the living standards of people at work during 1972-3, which is to be published next week, Tony Atkinson and Chris Trinder conclude, 'Although the Stage II formula was designed to give larger percentage increases to the low paid there were other forces working in the opposite direction. The low level of the tax thres-hold, the failure to increase family allowances, and the faster increase in the price of necessities all meant that the advantage of the low paid worker was eaten away'. And even this was to suppose the faithful implementation of the Stage II formula.(3)

The neglect of family allowances is the most indefensible part of the whole story. They were last increased in 1968 and have steadily declined in value, whereas pensions and other rates have increased five times and prices by 50 per cent. Hardship during inflation has thereby been con-centrated upon working families with children. As long ago as April 1971 even *The Times* declared that an increase in the allowances 'was the most urgent priority of all for family poverty. Without it the Govern-ment cannot claim to have met their social responsibilities.'

The Government has spurned the general welfare of children, parti-cularly the poorest. Yet the Department of Health has lately become concerned about the slow decrease in the death rate of infants between one month and one year and a report from the Scottish Home and Health Department called attention in 1973 to the fact that in the last 20 years England and Wales has slipped from fifth to eighth place, and Scotland from eighth to twelfth in the ranking of countries by infant mortality.(4) The rate for social classes IV and V is still much higher than for social class I and the gap has not been reduced in recent years. According to other indices of health and well-being, such as height of schoolchildren, there also remain pronounced inequalities between the social classes.

The Government abolished cheap welfare milk and free school milk for older children in primary schools in April 1971. The latest report of the National Food Survey concludes, 'In households which were affected both by changes in welfare milk and school milk the average decrease in overall consumption was 0.4 pints per person per week . . . The overall decrease in consumption appears to have been slightly greater in the lower income groups than in the higher.' The report also points out that in 1971 there was a *decrease* in the nutritional level of poorest families. Among the poorest families with four or more children intakes of protein and iron were lower than in any of the previous five years and the energy value of their diet remained significantly below the standard set by the Department of Health.(5)

The Government will claim it introduced the Family Income Supplement and enlarged the scope of other means-tested welfare. But at the last count FIS reached only a tiny fraction of working families and its total cost was a derisory £12 million a year, despite anguished attempts to employ business advertising techniques. The Government has been forced to admit that only half the estimated number of families eligible for benefit are receiving it. Even this is likely to be an overestimate. No adequate basis for estimating the numbers who are eligible has been published. Up to now the Government have depended upon estimates of low earnings at *particular dates* which have been compared with the numbers receiving FIS. This ignores the fact that the earnings of many of the latter will have changed since their needs were first assessed. The rules of FIS depend on the production of pay slips covering a few weeks before the start of 12 months benefit. This is only one of the ways by which the deficiencies of a means-tested strategy, of conditional welfare for the few, have to be remorselessly exposed.

The Government has been hounded by the pressure groups and local and national research studies into conceding two major weaknesses, even in its own terms, of its anti-poverty strategy. Means-tested benefits do not reach all, and often not even a majority, of those who are eligible for them. And the poverty trap created by that strategy is incontestable. How can a Tory Government argue that a limitation of the disincentives of marginal rates of tax releases the productive energies of the rich but not the poor? Hoist with its own petard it gives the impression of writhing about for a respectable solution which will yet correspond with its own perception of need.

The Government will also claim that it is introducing the Tax Credit scheme. In some respects this scheme is an unknown quantity, an empty frame which remains to be filled with flesh and blood. The method of financing the credits, and the actual rate of credit, for example, which are ultimately chosen will have an important effect on the distribution of net benefits. But searching examination by various critics has revealed that it is limited in coverage; inflexible in being unable to accommodate varying rates of credit for different categories of need; does not concentrate resources on the poorest groups; will worsen the net incomes of some groups, including certain pensioners, who are living just above the poverty line; will lead to discontinuity in the receipt of weekly benefit by some groups entering and leaving employment; and will proliferate the administration of benefits among the D.H.S.S., the D.E. and thousands of employers, without leading to the replacement of any existing schemes. It is governed by the desire to escape more progressive rates of taxation and institutionalize a constant rate, and to shift, at a cost of crudity, unfairness and over-simplification, the administration of both taxation and welfare from public departments to employers. In the course of the study of the scheme by a Parliamentary Select Committee, one constructive outcome was to force the Government to concede that the children's credit would be paid to all mothers through the Post Office. Except for the name this amounts to a commitment to develop the present family allowance system, which the protracted discussion of the scheme had put into cold storage. We have come full circle since 1970. These payments to mothers have nothing to do with the principles of Tax Credits and might be legislated in advance of the introduction of the scheme, as even Tory backbenchers have argued. Moreover, the decision on the way children are to have rights to 'credits' is tantamount to a rejection of the principles of the rest of the scheme.

The neglect of the disabled has been another major defect of Tory strategy. In the mid and late 1960s support grew for a comprehensive system of allowances or pensions for the disabled. In 1968-69 a national survey of the adult disabled was carried out and a report published early in 1971. Nearly three years later no commitment even in principle has been made by Sir Keith Joseph. He has retreated into the formula of completing a departmental review by the autumn of 1974. The introduction of invalidity and attendance allowances and the improvement in invalidity pensions cover small numbers and cost very little, and he has admitted that they represent only a 'beginning'.

Sir Keith's grudging approach to the problems of handicapped children is particularly revealing. Accurate estimates of their numbers do not exist and in October 1973 a proposal for a Government survey was rejected. Sir Keith said it was impracticable to apply to children the definitions and tests of handicap applied to adults. This ignores the fact that there are functions like eating, sleeping and communicating which children find as necessary as adults to perform and ignores too the specialised literature on child handicap, as for example of the National Children's Bureau, and Rutter and Tizard. Sir Keith also said that since children necessarily come into contact with the education system their needs are less likely than those of adults to be overlooked. But this certainly does not apply to children under 5 and ignores the evidence of neglect by the educational and other services of a variety of the needs of handicapped children and their parents. For one who strives so hard to project an image of compassionate ministerial concern such reasoning smacks of hypocrisy. In whose interests does it lie not to discover the exact scale and severity of the problem? Is the Government frightened of sponsoring inquiries which might demonstrate how paltry are its own expenditures?

When public interest in handicapped children was at its height in 1973 over the 400 thalidomide children, Sir Keith had an opportunity to commit the Government to developing a new and equitable statutory system of allowances, grants and services for another 300,000 or 400,000 children handicapped as a result of chronic disease or accidents at home or on the roads. Instead he provided a tiny grant of £3 million in the first instance to the Joseph Rowntree Memorial Trust for the limited category of children who are seriously congenitally handicapped.

All Governments encounter difficulties in shaping society according to their wishes and are subject to internal conflicts and external pressures and constraints. A full policy analysis would have to reflect all the major cross-currents and inconsistencies. Yet with such qualifications the administration of 1970-74 followed a social policy whose aims and means were better integrated and concerted than any of its post-war predecessors. By the tests of social justice, democracy, satisfaction of need and elimination of poverty, that policy must be damned. It has strengthened the rich, emphasized hierarchical and managerial values and resurrected the most abrasive nineteenth-century principles of conditional welfare for the few.

The lessons are long and hard for the Labour Party. There is no short cut to the creation of a just society or even the elimination of poverty while retaining the market society. Those goals are to be achieved, in the end, only through the diminution of the resources and powers of the rich. 'What thoughtful rich people call the problem of poverty', wrote Tawney in 1913, 'thoughtful poor people call with equal justice the problem of riches.'

Notes

1. *Economic Trends,* November 1973.

2. *Report of the Family Expenditure Survey for 1972,* H.M.S.O., 1973.

3. Atkinson T. and Trinder C., 'Real Incomes of People at Work' in Young M. (ed.), *Poverty Report 1974*, Temple Smith, 1974, p.54.

4. Scottish Home and Health Department, *Towards an Integrated Child Health Service,* Joint Working Party on the Integration of Medical Work, Edinburgh, 1973, p.8.

5. Ministry of Agriculture, *Household Food Consumption and Expenditure: 1970 and 1971*, A Report of the National Food Survey Committee, H.M.S.O., 1973, pp. 44-5 and 53.

Inequalities in living standards, the worsening problem of poverty and the failure to integrate society through much bigger investment in the social services are perhaps the three dominant social policy problems of contemporary Britain. Indeed, they are dominant problems in nearly all industrial societies and need to be documented and discussed in great detail if more comprehensive and effective policies to meet them are to be developed. I shall attempt to summarize some of the evidence about these three problems in turn, and go on to suggest in outline, in the fourth part of this paper, a strategy for meeting them.

The Problem of Inequality

An overall view of the kind of society we want to create depends on understanding its present structure and the changes that have been taking place in that structure in recent years. Living standards comprise only one, but an important, aspect of such structure. They depend on the price of goods and services that are available to different sections of the population. They also depend on resources in the form of cash incomes, assets, industrial 'fringe' or welfare benefits and free and subsidized public services. And it is difficult to reach hard and fast conclusions about trends in living standards while methods for measuring the distribution of cash incomes remain rudimentary and few reliable data exist about the distribution of other types of resources. The process of analysis is not so much one of amalgamating the statistical distributions for different sectors and reviewing the weights to be attached to each sector as it is one of making shrewd use of crude indicators to bridge the large gaps in the information we have.

Two stages have to be identified in any historical account of living standards in Britain since the 1930s. First, there was a marked levelling of standards during the war. Secondly, there was a partial reversion to former inequalities during the 1950s. Altogether the country was becoming more prosperous but some groups could not keep up — or the number of people in some low-income groups were swelling. By the middle 1960s, indeed, there were signs that a third phase may have begun, in which low-income groups were not so much losing advantages

* Extended version of a series of four articles in *The Times,* 8 – 11 March 1971.

recently won as being denied access to new kinds of resources. The high priority being accorded to economic growth, and therefore to the value of certain professional, managerial and technological skills, together with an associated rise in the number of dependants in the population, is presenting a prospect of accelerating inequality. An increase in the proportion of the population in the upper-middle-income group is being accompanied by a corresponding increase in the proportion in the poorest income-groups, and there may also be some widening of differentials in real living standards. It is still too soon to be sure that a third phase can be properly identified. However, these three phases could still be regarded as short-run fluctuations within a more stable and continuing inequality.

While there has been common agreement about the first phase (though not about its extent) there has been a lot of controversy about the second. In the period immediately following the Second World War the increase in employment of women as well as high levels of employment for men, the introduction of promised social reforms and continuing high levels of taxation caused many people to believe that Britain had abolished poverty and had created a much more equal society. The differences between rich and poor, it was widely supposed, had been sharply reduced. Moreover, some interpretations of the statistics suggested that 'levelling' was continuing into the 1950s. In a well-known paper in the *Journal of the Royal Statistical Society* for 1959, Harold Lydall concluded, 'A study of the period 1938-57 reveals a continuous trend towards greater equality in the distribution of allocated personal income. . . For the future, unless there is a catastrophic slump, the trend towards equality is likely to continue, though probably not as fast as in the past twenty years.'(1) In particular, he found that the tendency towards reduced inequality of pre-tax incomes seemed to have been accelerating.

In his book, *Income Distribution and Social Change,* Professor Richard Titmuss questioned the statistics on which such early analyses were based. Recipients of income were ill-defined, and included a heterogeneous collection of individuals and income units. The proportionate increase of incomes in the middle range between 1938 and 1955 might be attributed to decreased unemployment and to more employment of married women rather than to any reduction of earnings differentials or more egalitarian effects of fiscal policies. The apparent levelling of pre-tax incomes might be attributed not just to a fall in incomes from investment and rent but the employment of tax-evasion techniques — for example, passing on wealth to members of the family to escape death duties, sometimes while they continued to live in the same household. Because changes were taking place in the structure of the general and employed population, as well as in the kind and use during life of resources, it was difficult to pin down the changing dimensions of inequality. Even if post-war was more equal than pre-war society the change was much less dramatic than asserted by some and the evidence for a continued trend after 1950 was very partial.(2)

During the 1950s salaries advanced slightly faster than wages. The earnings of certain professional and managerial groups rose markedly. Property incomes from rents, dividends and interest increased between 1955 and 1965 by 139 per cent, compared with 84 per cent for earned incomes.(3) Tax concessions in successive budgets and increases in certain tax allowances tended to favour the higher income groups, even if their effects were partly counter-balanced by the higher taxes paid on earnings which continued to rise during this period of inflation. A trend in the admittedly incomplete statistics of income distribution had come to a halt.

In a paper written in 1967 which he has subsequently brought up to date, R.J. Nicholson found that the proportion of income after tax received by the top 10 per cent of income-recipients decreased at some stage between 1949 and 1957 but with minor fluctuations the proportion remained about the same between 1957 and 1967. One per cent of income recipients with the highest incomes continued to receive about 5 per cent and the next 9 per cent 19-20 per cent of the aggregate of all personal incomes after tax. But the incomes of the 30 per cent with the lowest incomes continued to diminish during both periods, from nearly 15 to about 12 per cent of aggregate income. Correspondingly, there had been little change, except at the lowest levels of income, in the general structure of pre-tax incomes. The reduction in inequality of personal incomes appeared to have come to an end in the mid-1950s.(4)

By the late 1960s even those who had spoken of a 'continuing' post-war trend towards equality of personal incomes were beginning to reverse their opinions. In an important book Harold Lydall assessed a wide range of international evidence about employment incomes and concluded that in ten of eleven countries for which there was information the distribution of pre-tax incomes had not merely remained stationary during the 1950s but had actually widened. They included France, Germany, Sweden, Australia, Canada, New Zealand and the United States, as well as the United Kingdom. This tendency to widen did not apply to the earnings distribution of male manual workers in some countries, but was particularly marked for the distributions of non-manual and female employees in most countries.(5)

These assessments do not tell the whole story, however. The statistics about personal incomes for the United Kingdom include no allowance for increased valuations of capital assets, differential movements in prices, or the effects of indirect taxation and free or subsidized social services. R.J. Nicholson, for example, accepted the possibility that if certain 'tax-avoidance' incomes and other claims on wealth outside personal income had increased in the late 1950s and early 1960s 'the distribution of incomes on some wider definition may have moved towards greater inequality.'(6)

The best source of information about changes in the real distribution of resources, and one which could be further improved, is the Family Expenditure Survey. The non-response rate is disturbingly large and fluctuations attributable to sampling errors reduce the opportunities of reaching precise conclusions about trends from year to year. It is particularly difficult to generalize clearly about trends affecting the richest and poorest groups in the population. Nonetheless, Table 1, which is based on an analysis of the surveys in *Economic Trends,* shows first that, except for the lagging of households with one child and the faster growth of households with three adults and two children, the 'final' incomes of different types of family have been rising at roughly similar rates since 1961. Secondly, the levels of income of most types of family remain in roughly the same relationship as they were in 1961 (the family with three children, for example, having 150 per cent more income than the one-person household after paying all taxes and receiving all benefits, compared with 148 per cent eight years previously). Finally, among the families within each type there has been no pronounced change in the dispersion of incomes, the poorest 20 per cent being in 1969 at about the same and if anything a little below the level of income they had reached in relation to the median income in 1961. There is no evidence of a trend towards equality at low levels of living, but if anything a faint reverse trend. Compared with a very slight relative improvement in the incomes of the poorest couples with two children there has been a slight deterioration in the incomes of the poorest couples with one child and four or more children and households comprising three adults and one child and three adults and two children. The figures dip for seven out of ten categories and although the fluctuations due to sampling must be remembered the trends were broadly the same in 1968.

These results allow for the effects of indirect as well as direct taxes. The Family Expenditure Survey data show not only that indirect taxes take a larger proportion of low than of high incomes but that among low-income families with children indirect taxes have increased sharply as a proportion of income, particularly between 1965 and 1968. Recent increases in indirect taxes and national insurance contributions seem to have more than counterbalanced any progressive

Table 1 Income after all taxes and social service benefits of different types of household

Type of household	Income as per cent of						Per cent of median income below which 20% of each category live		
	Income in 1961			Income received by one adult					
	1961	1965	1969	1961	1965	1969	1961	1965	1969(2)
One adult (excl. pensioners)	100	131	160	100	100	100	70	72	72
Two adults (excl. pensioners)	100	120	153	181	167	173	70	72	69
Two adults, one child	100	124	147	206	194	189	74	75	73
Two adults, two children	100	120	158	230	210	227	73	75	76
Two adults, three children	100	126	162	248	238	250	78	73	78
Two adults, four children	100	121	158	276	254	271	86	77	79
Three adults	100	121	156	255	235	249	74	75	73
Three adults, one child	100	118	148	291	261	270	80	76	79
Three adults, two children	100	135	170	294	303	311	80	76	77
Four adults	100	121	155	333	306	322	81	78	78
All households	100	(123)(1)	(156)(1)	208	192	196	56	55	54

Notes: (1) Estimated in terms of 1961 distribution by size of households.
   (2) The figures published in Table 4, *Economic Trends*, February 1971, have been slightly adjusted to conform with income as defined for 1961 and 1965.

Source: Based on *Economic Trends*, February 1970, Tables 2 and 5, and February 1971, Tables 4 and 5. Further information supplied by the Central Statistical Office.

effects of income tax and surtax. The British tax system overall is very unprogressive. In the dry words of the authors of *Economic Trends*, 'For each type of family, direct and indirect taxes combined form a remarkably stable proportion of income over a wide range of incomes.'(7)

But the results allow inadequately for the value to families of the social services. Actual cash benefits are allocated to personal incomes but only imputed average National Health Service and education benefits. Because of higher rates of illness and disability some low-income families may in fact obtain more value than average from the National Health Service. On the other hand, when the children of high-income families attend grammar schools and universities, they may benefit to a greater extent than average from the public subsidy. During the past fifteen years the middle-income groups have gained substantially from the disproportionate expansion of higher education. Some benefits that are received predominantly by the middle − and high-income groups, such as housing improvement grants, are not taken into account at all. Other benefits may be worth more than their face value. Between 1963-4 and 1969-70 the value of tax reliefs to private owner-occupiers increased from £90 million to £215 million. The average value per recipient, taking no account of capital appreciation, was about £48 in the latter year.

Industrial fringe benefits are now of considerable importance and, as Lydall remarks, may offset the equalizing effects of progressive income taxes in many countries. Recently they were estimated to add 20 per cent to managerial staff salaries of around £4,000 and over 30 per cent to salaries in excess of £7,000.(8) Although the scope of such benefits has widened in recent years they are more common among the middle- and upper-income groups and are of greater relative value.

It is difficult to come to firm conclusions about trends in the distribution of wealth. Since the war there has been some decrease in the holdings of the richest one per cent, but this has been largely balanced by an increase in the holdings of the next 9 per cent, so that the concentration of wealth remains considerable. Indeed, wealth is distributed more unequally in Britain than in most other industrial countries. According to the Board of Inland Revenue data the richest 10 per cent own nearly three quarters of total personal wealth. According to survey data the poorest 50 per cent have no liquid assets at all or very few.(9)

Finally, price increases have affected the poor more than the rich. Since it was started the Retail Price Index for Pensioners has kept slightly ahead of the general index. More generally, for the period 1955-66, D.G. Tipping has shown that at the lowest levels of income prices increased by 4.3 per cent more than they did for the highest levels of income — mainly because of the disproportionate rise in rents and the costs of fuel and light.(10)

The fact that differentials in pre-tax and post-tax incomes seem to have changed comparatively little in recent years is in some respects puzzling. Even Britain's slow rate of economic growth has been accompanied by a big change in the distribution of occupations. Between 1955 and 1969 the national salary bill increased by 198 per cent but the wages bill by only 106 per cent. As a proportion of all salaries and wages the former grew from 34 per cent to 42 per cent.(11) But there is no evidence of a depreciation of salaries relative to wages. The average salary has remained substantially larger than the average wage. How can this be explained? It would seem that some groups among wage-earners have not kept pace with the rise in real earnings and that the shift towards expensive salaried employment has been financed by the growth of inexpensive un-employment and retirement, including premature retirement, as discussed below.

It is, therefore, reasonably certain that despite social and incomes legislation greater equality of real incomes was not achieved between the mid-1950s and 1970. On the contrary, there seems to have been a shift in the reverse direction which is understated if attention is paid only to the conventional statistics of personal income distribution or even to the broader measures of the Family Expenditure Survey.

This conclusion contradicts a good deal of popular, and political, supposition. The problem is not appreciated quite so keenly as that of inequalities between rich and poor nations. Unless properly docu-mented and understood we may continue to fail to adapt our policies to bring about greater social justice and hence greater social cohesion and, it may be argued, economic prosperity.

The Problem of Poverty

There are at least two senses in which the problem of poverty in Britain might be said to be getting worse. The first is that the propor-tion of the population living in poverty or on its margins might be increasing, and the second that some groups of the poorest people might be, compared with middle-income groups, increasingly worse off. The evidence for these two propositions is admittedly incomplete and stronger for the first than for the second. The first, if not the second, also seems plausible in the context of general movements in the pattern of income distribution. Both propositions depend on a relative concept of poverty, such that every society creates the needs, whether dietary, occupational or social, that individuals try to satisfy, and which change and become more elaborate as society itself changes and becomes more prosperous. Although it is far from being ideal, because it is conventional rather than objective or scientific, the best measure available is the poverty line defined by the Supplementary Benefits Commission in the basic scale rates which are paid to the poor.

Five dependency groups — retirement pensioners, long-term unemployed, middle-aged disabled, fatherless families and families with four or more children — have grown substantially or slightly in proportion to population in recent years. They cover a total of over 13 million people, or more than the membership, say, of the trade unions. The first three groups, at least, seem destined to increase during the 1970s. All of them are particularly liable to experience poverty. Even should the Government act to improve the incomes of people in one or more of these groups the total effect could be not to diminish the total numbers in poverty but prevent them increasing. It would be surprising if those with incomes less than the supplementary benefit scales numbered fewer than 3½ million at the beginning of 1971, or a million more than in 1966.

The rise in numbers of people of pensionable age, from 13 per cent of the population just after the war to 16 per cent in 1970, is well-known. The proportion is now levelling off. But the steep increase in retirement and the emergence of a fourth as well as a third generation are facts which are less well understood. As late as 1959 only 47 per cent of men retired at the age of sixty-five but ten years later the the figure stood at over 70 per cent.(12) If this is one indirect method of financing a larger salariat then as the supply of retirees of pensionable age runs out more pressure may be put on men in late middle age to retire. Old people in their late seventies and eighties who are poorer and more infirm than people already retired in their sixties have also become a larger and more distinct group in the population.

More people are retiring prematurely and fewer than expected are entering work. Since 1966 the numbers employed have contracted from figures originally projected for 1970 by about one million. The unemployment rate has grown from 1½ per cent to nearly 3 per cent. Ten per cent of those on the disabled persons' register are unemployed. For the three years 1967-9 the number of men wholly unemployed for more than two months averaged about 250,000. During 1970 the number was close to 300,000. Whether or not these trends are short-term or long-term they mean that disabled workers have been dislodged, some of them perhaps finally, from a precarious employment; the working lives of some men have been shortened; the chance of supplementing low incomes has been ruled out for some women;

improvements in the lowest rates of pay have been discouraged and more families have found themselves in poverty.

During the ten years up to 1969 the number of men aged 55-64 and sick for six months or more rose by 68,000 or from 5.7 per cent to 7.2 per cent.(13) Between 1961 and 1966 the number of fatherless as a proportion of all families increased very slightly from 7.3 to 7.5 per cent. Such families include nearly ¾ million children.(14) The number of families with four or more dependent children increased between 1961 and 1966 by 17 per cent but by only a further 4 per cent between 1966 and 1969. These families now account for a quarter of all children.(15)

Compared with other sections of the population the living standards of these groups have been improved by some events and reduced by others. The value of benefits has fluctuated. For example, the rates for retirement pensions were raised approximately every two years during the 1960s. An attempt to reduce the differences between these rates and earnings was made both in 1963 and 1965, but the gains were quickly eroded. During most of the decade the single person's pension fluctuated in value around 19 or 20 per cent of average gross industrial earnings but fell to about 17 per cent by the end of 1970, as Table 2 shows. During 1971 the lowest relative values were reached since early 1958.

The pension that is paid does not alone, however, determine the standard of living. More pensioners now have small graduated pensions and increments for deferred retirement; 28 per cent now have supplementary benefit, compared with 22 per cent in 1965. The Government put up the basic scales of national assistance, excluding rent, in 1965, to a level which was slightly higher relative to earnings than the figure achieved in May 1963 and broadly maintained it for a few years. But the increase in November 1970 failed to restore the scales to previous levels of value.

Another source of income for pensioners who draw supplementary benefit is the long-term automatic addition of 50p. per week (9s or 45p. per week in 1966). In practice this new supplement has not added to the real incomes of most people drawing supplementary benefit, because 73 per cent of old people who were helped by the former National Assistance Board in 1965 received discretionary additions averaging 10s. 1d. or just over 50p. per week.(16) According to A.B. Atkinson the introduction of the supplementary benefits scheme reduced the numbers of pensioners not applying though eligible for assistance by between 100,000 and 200,000 (17) but between half a million and three quarters of a million remain.

Altogether there is evidence from the Family Expenditure Survey

Table 2   Benefit rates as per cent of average industrial earnings

	Single Pension	Supplementary benefit for single person	Family allowances for four children
1948 October	18.9	17.5	10.9
1961 April	19.1	17.8	9.3
1962 April	18.4	17.1	8.9
1963 May	20.8	19.5	8.6
1964 April	19.2	18.1	8.0
1964 October	18.7	17.6	7.7
1965 April	21.2	20.1	7.4
1965 October	20.4	19.4	7.1
1966 April	19.8	18.8	6.9
1966 October	19.7	20.0	6.9
1967 April	19.4	19.7	6.8
1967 October	21.0	20.1	7.7
1968 April	20.2	19.3	11.9
1968 October	19.6	19.8	12.6
1969 April	18.8	19.0	12.1
1969 November	20.0	19.2	11.7
1970 April	19.0	18.3	11.3
1970 November	17.6	18.3	10.2

that as a percentage of the incomes of other one-person households the incomes of pensioners living alone fell from 51 in 1961 and 52 in 1962 to around 44 in 1964 but climbed again to 52 in 1968. Pensioner couples gained ground a little more evenly on households consisting only of two young adults, their incomes rising from 45 per cent to 48 per cent of the latter between 1963 and 1968.(18) Fringe benefits for the employed are not included in these figures and would certainly reduce the slight upward trend in the late 1960s. Prices also rose faster for pensioners over this period, marginally for most goods and services but rapidly, it would appear, for housing. For example, the rents paid to pensioners receiving a supplementary benefit increased by 35 per cent, compared with 22 per cent for general housing costs between 1965 and 1969.

The big gap in living standards between pensioners and others has thus not been substantially narrowed. There are at least two forms of poverty. There is the poverty — which is accepted but has not been properly documented since 1965 — of that large number of pensioners eligible for supplementary benefits but not claiming them. There is also the poverty of aged, and usually widowed and infirm, pensioners who obtain supplementary benefit but who have extra disability needs and have lived on small sums for so long that they have been unable to replace stocks of clothing and furniture.

Some other groups have fared worse. Despite publicity about the disabled and evidence of large numbers not registered and not receiving adequate incomes little progress has been made towards a comprehensive disability pension scheme. The Chronically Sick and Disabled Persons Act of 1970 has had little impact on local authorities because extra resources were simply not made available by the Government. The hardship of fatherless families has only lately led to the setting up of the Finer Committee and not yet to a new system of allowances.

The fortunes of the unemployed have been mixed. An earnings-related benefit scheme was introduced in 1966 but it is not redistributive between low and high-paid and, because of a new form of wage-stop, some low-paid men with children are paying contributions without receiving any benefits. Because very short-term and long-term needs are not covered only about one in six of the unemployed are receiving these benefits at any single time. The Supplementary Benefits Commission has been severe towards the unemployed. A special review of the wage-stop in 1967 has had small results and the numbers of people in families whose incomes are reduced below the scale rates is approximately 100,000. In 1968 tough rules terminating the benefit received by some single and married men after short periods were introduced. Between 1965 and 1969 the numbers dependent on unemployment benefit who received discretionary additions to the basic rates paid to them by the Commission fell from 16 per cent to 7 per cent. Even the absolute number getting such additions diminished during a period when the number of long-term unemployed nearly doubled. In these senses, and quite independently of any qualitative deterioration there may or may not have been in public and official attitudes towards them, some of the unemployed were relatively poorer than their predecessors.

Finally, there are the low-paid with children. Rates of pay seem to have lagged, as Table 3, based on reports of the Family Expenditure Survey, shows. The report of a survey by the Department of Employment and Productivity for April 1970 contains no evidence of improvement. Authoritative studies, like that on the *Circumstances of Families* carried out by the Ministry of Social Security in 1966, show that in addition to the families actually living in poverty there are more than twice as many who have an income of only up to £2 above the official poverty line. Any postponement of increases in family allowances, any increase in regressive taxes or any differential increase in prices (for example local authority rents, or even 'fair' rents under the new legislation) puts them at risk.

Table 3 Per cent of median earnings below which are the poorest 10 per cent of manual wage-earners (men, 1964-9)

1964	71.6
1965	69.7
1966	68.6
1967	69.7
1968	68.9
1969	68.4

Source: Annual Reports of the Family Expenditure Survey.

Unlike national insurance benefits family allowances have not been increased every two years to catch up with prices and earnings. Present levels in relation to earnings are below those of 1946. The increases in 1968 were offset not only by reduced tax allowances but by increases in the price of school meals and welfare milk, the withdrawal of free milk in secondary schools and the reintroduction of prescription charges. Flat-rate insurance contributions, which had been raised as lately as October 1967, were raised by a further 1s. in May 1968. The tax allowances for single persons and married couples was increased in the budget of April 1970 but though this helped the man with children it did not help him more than it did the man without children, and indeed helped far more people without than with children. As a redistributive measure it was clumsy. It was far less efficient in reducing poverty, and far more inequitable, than raising family allowances.

Family poverty therefore remained extensive in 1970. The evidence from the annual Family Expenditure Survey shows no marked decrease or increase during the late 1960s, when due allowance is made for sampling variations (see p.342 above). Including an estimate for one-child families a Government survey found in 1966 that there were 95,000 families of men in full-time work and 15,000 of unemployed men subject to the wage-stop, as well as other groups like one-parent families, who were living below the level of the national assistance scales.(19) Sir Keith Joseph gave comparable figures for the summer of 1970, allowing for the latest earnings data as well as increases in rates of supplementary benefit, of 110,000 and 24,000 respectively, who would qualify for help under the new Family Income Supplement scheme, beginning in August 1971. He went on to admit that the scheme would not help all working households living below the supplementary benefit level. Despite pressure in Parliament for more precise information, as, for instance, on 15 February 1971, he said only that the scheme would help between one half and two thirds of working households in poverty.

Poverty is certain to increase sharply during 1971. Prices are rising quickly. The reduction in the standard rate of tax will bring small help to poor families. Some earners below the poverty line will actually continue to pay tax. The Conservative Government is introducing higher charges for school meals, prescriptions and dental and opthalmic services, withdrawing cheap welfare milk and withdrawing free milk in primary schools for children aged seven and over. There is no evidence that more than a small fraction of working families theoretic-ally exempt from paying new charges will in fact claim exemption. The Government admits that none of the very large numbers of families on the margins of poverty will be helped by the F.I.S. scheme. About half in poverty are estimated as likely to get help, and some experts consider that this estimate is over-generous. Wage-rates will be higher by the time that the scheme comes into effect. Many of the few who will get help will not receive sufficient help to take them out of poverty. Even on the Conservative Government's most optimistic assumptions the F.I.S. scheme is unlikely to reduce family poverty even to the numbers of the late 1960s.

Underinvestment in the Social Services

Between 1959 and 1969 public expenditure in the United Kingdom on the social services grew in real terms by 66 per cent, or an average of 5.2 per cent per annum (Table 4). During the five years 1959-64 expenditure grew by 31 per cent and during 1964-9 by 27 per cent.

Throughout the periods covered by different political administrations, therefore, the growth of the public social services has been more rapid than of the economy as a whole (under 3 per cent per annum).

Table 4 Annual percentage rate of increase in public expenditure (current and capital) at constant prices

	1951-9	1959-64	1964-9	Forecast 1970-71 to 1974-5 (2)
Education	4.9	5.9	4.7	3.3
National Health Service	1.9	3.2	3.3	3.3
Housing	−2.3	10.3	2.9	−0.4
Social Security (1)	5.4	4.9	6.5	2.1(3)
Welfare and child care	2.7	7.4	5.6	5.9
All social services	3.3	5.5	4.9	2.5
Social services less housing	4.3	4.8	5.3	2.8

Notes: (1) Including subsidies for schools meals, milk and welfare foods.
(2) Excludes Northern Ireland. Local welfare included with N.H.S. and child care, and social work in Scotland counted only under 'welfare and child care'.
(3) No allowance made for increases in benefits in real terms.

Source: Estimates based on National Income and Expenditure 1970, H.M.S.O., 1970; Public Expenditure 1969-70 to 1974-75, Cmnd. 4578, H.M.S.O., 1971; Social Trends, No. 1., 1970; P.E.P. The Cost of the Social Services 1938-1952, Planning, No. 354, June 1953, and information privately supplied by the Treasury and the Central Statistical Office. Method of revaluation based on official indices.

The remorseless growth of such public expenditure in face of apparently sincere attempts on the part of successive administrations to restrain it is one of the ironies of the whole post-war era. The reasons for such growth do not appear to be understood, least of all at the Treasury. Perhaps the momentum, in other countries as much as our own, has not been adequately analysed. Perhaps, instead of starving the social services of proper resources, we would have willingly invested far more if the national momentum and the needs had been so analysed and discussed. Perhaps objectives of social stability and cohesion would be served better not by bigger, but better-controlled, expansion.

How sustained has the growth been? In 1938 the cost of the public social services represented just under 11 per cent of Gross National Product. In 1947, before the introduction of the National Health Service, they represented just under 13 per cent. Despite a huge fall in unemployment the effects of the change in age-structure of the population were beginning to be felt. The subsidies introduced in the war for school meals, welfare milk and foods were being maintained and the housing programme was in full swing to make amends for the lack of building since 1939. In 1951 the social services jumped to 16 per cent of G.N.P., mainly because of the transfer from the private to the public sector of health expenditure.(20) But the failure to grasp this fact and correctly forecast the real extra costs, together with a failure to examine trends in other countries, led to restrictions on health service expenditure from which the report of the Guillebaud Committee in the mid-fifties only partly rescued the nation. During the early 1950s the social services grew very slowly and in the late 1950s more quickly to 17 per cent of the G.N.P. but then the rate quickened again and they grew steadily during the 1960s to a total of nearly 24 per cent by 1969. A large part of the total does not however represent a direct use of resources. If transfer incomes are excluded the total would be 13 per cent, as Table 5 shows. There are, however, advantages in comparing all forms of public expenditure on the social services with G.N.P., to examine trends and cross-national differences. The U.N. agencies follow this convention.

Only to a small extent does this extra 7 per cent of G.N.P. during the decade represent an improvement of standards or a relative gain on the part of those with low incomes. Nearly one per cent is due to relatively more pupils of fifteen years of age and over staying on at school and more students going into further and higher education. The establishment of new colleges and universities has led to a demand for resources that is going to be difficult to control. And a substantial part of the rise in the per cent of G.N.P. devoted to the National Health Service represents disproportionately higher costs — of medical and other salaries, drugs and equipment.

A substantial part of the expansion, perhaps half of the additional 7 per cent, is explained by demographic change. Nearly 2 per cent, for example, can be estimated to be due to the rise in the number of social security allowances in payment. Retirement pensioners and children eligible for family allowances both increased in number during these ten years by more than a million and a half. Much of the additional housing expenditure is due to population increase and, in particular, to the rate of formation of new married households and the disproportionate increase because of an ageing population in the rate of formation of one or two-person households. The disproportionate rise in numbers aged five to nineteen lifted education costs. And more home help and welfare services were required just to maintain the proportion of elderly and disabled, and particularly the proportion of people over seventy and eighty, receiving care.

Table 5 Expenditure on social services as per cent of Gross National Product

	1951	1959	1964	1969	£m. 1969
Education	3.1	4.0	4.8	6.0	2,328
National Health Service	3.8	3.7	3.9	4.7	1,813
Housing	3.1	2.0	2.8	2.9	1,118
Social Security	6.0	7.1	7.6	9.6	3,723
Welfare and Child Care	0.24	0.25	0.31	0.42	163
All social services	16.2	17.1	19.3	23.7	9,145
Current exp. on goods and services	6.6	7.2	7.8	9.7	3,754
Capital expenditure	3.3	2.3	3.5	3.6	1,388
Transfer incomes	6.3	7.5	8.0	10.4	4,003

Sources: As for Table 4.

The improvements are, therefore, modest in scope and degree though real enough. They include relative increases in the numbers of medical and nursing staff in hospitals, a reduction in the number of overcrowded classes in schools, the modernization of parts of the capital stock of health, welfare and education services, and a slight relative increase in the rates of benefit received by some groups living on social security. (Between 1959 and 1969 social security payments increased from 7.0 per cent to 8.8 per cent of personal income, or from 8.3 per cent to 8.8 per cent if the 1969 ratios of numbers of allowances to personal incomes are applied to the earlier year.) Against these improvements has to be set the emergence of new problems and growth of old ones – such as racial disturbances, environmental pollution, the social problems of motorway planning and high flats, and new forms of homelessness, disabled living and isolation.

The U.K. rate of social service growth is by no means high. Indeed, the signs are that it is rather low. Nor is it unusual for such growth to exceed economic growth. Excluding education and housing, reports by the International Labour Organization show that in the mid as well as the early sixties social service growth was faster in Austria, Belgium, Czechoslovakia, France, Italy, Japan, the Netherlands, Sweden and New Zealand, for example, than in the U.K., and ranged from 7 per cent to 11 per cent per annum, compared with less than 5 per cent for a comparable definition for the U.K.(21) Calculations based on a Scandinavian study show that the annual real rate of growth during 1964 to 1967 was 13 per cent in Denmark, 11 per cent in Sweden and Finland, and 6½ per cent in Norway for social services other than education and housing, compared with 6½ per cent for these services in the U.K. By 1967 these services represented between 16 per cent and 19 per cent of G.N.P. in all four countries, compared with under 14 per cent for the same services in the U.K.(22) While expenditure on education is also difficult to compare between countries, Debeauvais points out that in nearly all industrial countries growth of such expenditure is much faster than of the economy as a whole, sometimes more than twice as fast. In 1955 11 countries spent more than the U.K. in terms of G.N.P. and in 1965, 13.(23) The fact is that all advanced countries are having to make increasing provision for social dependency, the escalating costs of medical care for the acute sick, and the rapid extension of higher education to more people aged 17-25.

But more social dependency can mean more people living at very low income levels, including redundant and prematurely retired people, drawn especially from the ranks of the unskilled and semi-skilled. More provision for the acute sick and for special surgery can lead to a diminishing share of new resources for the chronic sick. And a disproportionately large extension of higher education which falls far short of being universal amounts to being a big switch of national resources to the middle-income groups.

Certain kinds of growth in spending on the social services can therefore have unfortunate side-effects. That is because the functions of the social services have become more complex and perhaps more conflicting. No longer can the services be conceived to be primarily for the working classes and any expansion of them an automatic contribution to the reduction of inequality. There have been three recent phases. Until after the Second World War most of the social services were used by the low-income, or by low-income and low-middle-income groups. The post-war social security and health service reforms did indeed help those groups among the poor (like dependants in health insurance) who had not previously been eligible for benefits. But they brought in middle-class groups, sometimes, as in the case of ten years' contributions for the full retirement pension, on favourable terms. The role of flat-rate contributions in financing social security was increased and of direct taxation decreased. The employed working classes largely financed the sick and dependent working classes, as did the earning middle classes their dependants. The second phase, then, was marked by universal 'flat-rate' coverage. Recently the direct benefits to the middle-income groups of the expansion of higher education and the growth of the social service professions have been rising fast. The more highly paid working class have benefited from the introduction of redundancy and earnings-related unemployment and sickness schemes, while the increase in numbers of means-tested schemes has concealed the fact that the majority of the poor who are entitled to benefit from them fail to utilize them. In this third phase the social services are operating in practice to perpetuate as well as reduce inequalities.

In 1968, according to a special analysis of the Family Expenditure Survey, families of man and wife and two children with under £1,000 per year obtained £330 in value from the social services, and similar families with £3,100 or more obtained £336. Families with these incomes but three children obtained £440 and £457 respectively.(24) These instances are exceptional but successive surveys show that prosperous families obtain as much or nearly as much in absolute value from the public social services as do the poorest working families.

Once the value to the middle- and higher-income groups of fiscal and industrial social service benefits are added to estimates such as these, the inconsistencies and shortcomings of Government social policy become more apparent. Fiscal and industrial welfare have become major distributors of national resources. They serve similar – in some cases identical – functions. Lump sums upon retirement and occupational pensions are paid for partly by the generality of tax-payers and earnings in sickness largely by the generality of consumers. Tax reliefs on mortgage interest are a housing subsidy and tax allowances for children a form of family allowance. The fiscal and industrial welfare systems are more likely than the direct public social services to squander national resources or withhold them thoughtlessly for want of adequate public scrutiny.

It would be difficult to explain some of the capricious acts of the Government, like the introduction of the Family Income Supplement scheme, or the abolition by stages of free school milk, except in the absence of social planning. The Robbins Report and ten-year plans for hospitals and community services were published in the early 1960s. Later the Department of Economic Affairs and the National Board for Prices and Incomes were established (and then wound up), certain central departments amalgamated and the Central Statistical Office reorganized. Planning in certain sectors has improved although in others has proceeded in fits and starts. But there has been little or no forward planning of a concerted kind on the allocation of resources. The National Plan of 1965 was not followed up and even in that plan the provision for social service growth was meagre and poorly analyzed and presented. Such growth was regarded then as now as a by-product of economic growth and not a stimulant.

Instead of reaching its promised fulfilment in the mid-1960s social planning largely degenerated into misconceived Treasury control of public expenditure. The White Papers on public expenditure of December 1969, October 1970, and January 1971 contain little evidence of serious thinking about social aims and strategies.(25) No sign is given of lessons learnt from the experience of other countries. Neither does the full impact upon expenditure of demographic change appear to have been grasped. The 1971 White Paper on public expenditure unwisely makes no allowance for future increases in the real levels of social security benefits. In terms of recent experience the Government's predicted rates of growth for the 1970s can be criticized as unnecessarily low and unrealistic, at least for education, social security and housing, as Table 4 shows. If a rising share of G.N.P. is already committed to the maintenance of present standards for a proportionately larger dependent population then it is all the more necessary to educate the public into realizing that this will mean putting taxes up instead of down. But the problem is much deeper. Resources are needed in addition to reduce the gap in living standards between the poor and the rest of the population — for families living on low incomes and living in slum conditions in hospitals as well as ordinary homes. There is a major task ahead of urban regeneration and of income support. Resources are also increasingly required to alleviate the social problems brought about by scientific innovation and technical change. It is through social policy that the reunifying influences made necessary by job specialization and the growth of industry and the professions can be exerted. Otherwise society will disintegrate into incomprehension and conflict. Nothing short of massive collective investment in the concept of the good society will be enough. The problem is not to reduce public expenditure or hold it proportionately steady, but to allocate a rising share of resources according to a strict though inspired sense of national priorities.

Social Planning in the 1970s

How can we begin to meet the related problems of inequality, poverty and ill-balanced development of social services? The evidence testifies to the fact that they are disconcertingly large and deep-rooted. They are like cancers which sap the working efforts and vitality of society and embitter its character. Whether we are fired by noble aspirations and want to create a society which is the envy of the world for its fairness, tolerance, unity and vigour, or cynically realistic about the need to bridge class, racial and community divisions for the sake of a fragile prosperity, the scale of the challenge remains daunting. The Government needs to act with greater moral authority than it has done at any time in the past twenty years. That must seem a very remote possibility.

On what principles can it proceed? Social policy must be comprehensive. It cannot be confined to the interests of the five public social services — education, health, housing, social security and welfare. It must cover those aspects of fiscal and incomes policy which have aims and functions which are predominantly social. It must cover the welfare rights of employees and facilities at work. And it must help to extend information, consumer and legal services to the whole population.

The administration of social policy must be unified. The lines of responsibility between local authorities and central departments, hospital management committees and local authorities and among different central departments are sometimes obstructing the fulfilment of major priorities. While a redefinition of areas of responsibility is almost certain to produce new problems for a future generation they may help to meet shorter-range objectives and may be risks worth taking.

The aims and priorities of policy must also be better formulated. Government ministers are inclined to speak ambiguously, and with different voices. Experts from universities and planning departments shrink too often from 'the best view' and they don't like brawling with the public. Time given up to discussion of the general conclusions that should be drawn from erudite evidence about needs and arguments with the public about priorities and procedures is time well-spent.

What, then, should the priorities be? Their choice depends on an assessment of need which, as I have argued, can mainly turn on the criteria of inequalities of resources and relative deprivation. Their choice depends also on the extent to which any of the measures which are proposed are likely to reduce that need while encouraging national unity and discouraging stigmatizing behaviour. This argues in favour of systems which apply to all or to all in certain social categories, such as children or the disabled, irrespective of income. Services for all ensures that all who need services get them. It is for the tax system to help those who have good incomes to pay at least as much from those incomes as they receive in benefits.

There is a strong case for adopting five major priorities. First, priority in incomes policy for the low-paid. Priority was supposed to be given to the low-paid by the previous Government but no detailed policy was worked out and 'priority' was no more than pious hope, as the evidence shows. Instead of being passed to an inter-departmental committee, as they were by the Labour Government, proposals for minimum-earnings legislation should be looked at more imaginatively and determinedly. Wages councils which cover three million workers should be greatly strengthened and bigger penalties introduced for employers who do not honour recommended rates. Above all, the earnings and fringe benefits of management and the professions should be brought into consistent public scrutiny by means of new legislation which control levels and principles of payment, even at the risk of losing a few skilled people to overseas countries. The earnings structure is pyramidal, and, as Barbara Wootton has argued, the control of earnings at the apex is more likely to reduce inequality (partly because it induces a greater readiness in the public and among the unions to respect the aims of an incomes and prices policy) than the cumbersome and herculean task of squeezing the base.

Increases in earnings should favour the low-paid. It has long been a mystery why the nation has come to accept wage increases of a fixed percentage as natural, even though 5 per cent means only £1 for the man on £20 per week, but £2 for the man on £40 and £5 for the man on £100. The chances of implementing an acceptable formula, say, the high-paid getting 10 per cent less than the average percentage increase and the low-paid 10 per cent more, might be explored. In this instance, a standard rise of 10 per cent would mean 9 per cent for the high-paid and 11 per cent for the low-paid. The poor conditions of work of many of the low-paid and their lack of fringe benefits should be exposed. A law requiring employers to pay wages during the first two weeks in any spell of sickness should be introduced. This would also save at least £100 million from national insurance benefits for other purposes. And any overall policy on behalf of the low-paid would depend substantially, in the final analysis, on a supporting policy of full employment.

Secondly, priority for the taxation of wealth and the more progressive taxation of incomes. A modest wealth tax of a kind introduced in other countries would raise £300 million annually and a gifts tax a similar amount. Alternatively a capital receipts tax as proposed by J.E. Meade and others (26) which is paid on a progressive basis throughout life could soon reach £600 million annually. This would help to reduce the wasteful accumulation of a disproportionate share of new national resources by a tiny percentage of the population. Steeply progressive rates for such taxes should be adopted and though there are administrative problems of collection they are no larger than those posed by capital gains, corporation and selective employment taxes for the Board of Inland Revenue in recent years. The substitution of earnings-related for flat-rate social security contributions will not only help the low-paid but make it politically possible to raise the funds to narrow the gap in standards of living between social security recipients and the rest of the population. The partial or total replacement of earned income relief at two ninths by a flat amount would again help the low-paid and contribute towards the progressiveness of the tax system. Tax reliefs for children and the aged would be reduced so that higher direct allowances could be paid. Tax relief for interest on mortgage payments would be phased out. Measures such as these could realize an additional amount well in excess of £1,500 million a year (equivalent to 3-4 per cent of national resources) to finance a dramatic improvement of community services and living conditions among the poor.

Thirdly, a large-scale social programme to deal with the worst forms of poverty. Means-tested and negative income-tax schemes must be discarded on grounds of inefficiency, dampening effect on low wages and work incentives, and social stigma and divisiveness. The single most effective measure would be to double family allowances and extend them to the first or only child in each family. This would put the U.K.'s system of family support up to a level comparable with much of Europe. It could be financed by adjusting the tax system in such a way that the poorest without children would also be helped. Table 6 shows the net gain or loss to different families of combining three proposals. (i) a family allowance of £2 for all children, including the first, taxing only £1 of this amount (roughly the present amount); (ii) the withdrawal of child tax allowances, and (iii) the substitution of earned income relief of two ninths of income by relief of £175 plus one ninth.(27) The net cost of this in a full year could be less than £100 million. This would ensure that everyone in the low-income groups was better off, including the poorest without children, but families with children would receive most, and would still gain from the operation up to high levels of earnings. The family allowance would in fact vary according to the age of children but would average £2.

A reform of almost as much significance would be the introduction of a disability pension scheme, not just for the 100-150,000 most severely disabled people under pension age but for the hundreds of thousands of moderately as well as severely disabled people of all ages. A high proportion of the low-paid are partly disabled, including men who have had an accident outside their work or are suffering from bronchitis and have been obliged to seek a less well-paid job. A substantial proportion of the most impoverished old people are the oldest and most infirm. For each of these groups a 10, 20 and 30 per cent or higher pension worth £1 for each 10 per cent of assessed disability would greatly improve living standards. For the latter this scheme might have to be simplified in the form of 'partial' or 'full' disability supplements worth £1, £2, or £3 payable initially only to those aged seventy and over. In addition to these two schemes a change to earnings-related social security contributions would permit (a) some increase, relative to earnings levels, of the existing pension, (b) the introduction of allowances for fatherless families, (c) allowances for families in which there is a physically handicapped or mentally handicapped child, and (d) the development of national superannuation for future generations of old people.

Table 6　Increase in net income per week achieved by paying a family allowance of £2 for each child, abolishing tax allowances and replacing earned income relief of two ninths by £175 plus one ninth.

	Earnings per week (£)							
	10	12.50	15.0	17.50	20.0	25.0	30.0	50.0
Single person	0.50	0.80	0.70	0.60	0.50	0.25	0.05	−0.80
Married couple	—	0.20	0.70	0.60	0.45	0.25	0.00	−0.80
Married couple + 1 child (aged 8)	2.00	2.00	1.40	1.35	1.20	1.00	0.80	−0.10
Married couple + 2 children (6,8)	3.10	3.05	2.20	1.80	1.70	1.50	1.25	0.40
Married couple + 4 children (6, 8, 10 and 12)	5.10	4.30	3.45	2.60	2.50	2.25	2.05	0.80

Fourthly, a community development programme. The E.P.A., urban aid and community development plans have been started on a small scale and have not been properly related either to the housing or community welfare services. Although the building programme, after declining since 1967, should be expanded, the main effort must be in a modernization and repairs programme, detailed for each area and and going far beyond the contribution so far achieved by the Housing Improvements Act of 1969. It should be backed by central supervision and control. Special local authority teams of construction and repairs workers should be created and the worst housing taken over by the local authority, although some groups of housing might be placed at a later stage under voluntary housing associations or, better, co-operative ownership. Responsibility for certain environmental facilities, like playgrounds and play centres, might also be entrusted by the local authorities to these area teams and communities, and this would permit more grass-roots participation. Housing subsidies should be personal but flat-rate. The means-tested allowances apparently now being considered by the Government are an unsatisfactory alternative. Flat-rate rent allowances should be payable to all the disabled, say £1 or £2 per week according to degree of disability, and to families with more than two dependent children, say £1 for each dependent child after the second. This scheme would cost about £200 million and would largely, but not wholly, replace the present system of subsidies.

Finally, there would be priority for family and community care instead of institutional care. Far too many of the patients in chronic sick and psychiatric hospitals and nursing homes and the residents of homes for the old and disabled live in poor and overcrowded conditions. Despite campaigns on behalf of the old and the mentally handicapped successive Governments seem to have decided that the vested interests of some hospital superintendents cannot be overruled and that local policy cannot be influenced, even to the extent of co-ordinating a reduction of beds in hospital with an increase in community services. The Seebohm Committee did not qualify the resources needed and define clearly the objectives of the re-organized community welfare services. A big expansion of manpower is needed but assistant workers even more than expensive professional personnel. Resources for a dramatic increase of home help, meals, sheltered housing and visiting services, sheltered workshops and day centres for the handicapped are required, perhaps through a new percentage grant or a central 'community care' programme. For five or ten years part of the expected increase in long-stay hospital costs could be transferred by the Government to the accounts of the local authorities in proportion to the decrease in hospital population.

The coherence of any plan must be represented in its direction and administration. Responsibility for children's services is being transferred from the Home Office to the Department of Health and Social Security, though responsibility for race relations is, strangely, being retained. Community welfare should be granted a much larger administrative wing. Yet at some stage the federal department should be amalgamated with the Department of Education and the Ministry of Housing. Despite the dangers of an overblown bureaucracy there can be enormous gains in flexibility of adjustment and power to control priorities. A central policy review unit has been set up in the Cabinet

Office under the Prime Minister. Its functions have still to be made clear. A Social Advisory Council, possibly overlapping in membership with an Economic Advisory Council, should be set up with direct responsibility to the Prime Minister. Served by a substantial research and information staff it would be responsible for converting the social aims of government into operational programmes. It would review social conditions and needs and the effects of changes in incomes, social service and tax policies and compile forward plans.

Any attempt to outline a social plan will seem over-ambitious. It will leave many questions unanswered. But it may serve the purpose of showing how serious is the morass into which the nation has stumbled and how fundamental and far-reaching must be the policies to escape from it.

Notes

1. 'The Long-term Trend in the Size Distribution of Income', *Journal of the Royal Statistical Society*, Series A (General), Part 1, 1959, p.35.

2. Titmuss, R.M., *Income Distribution and Social Change*, Allen & Unwin, 1962.

3. *National Income and Expenditure*, H.M.S.O., 1970, Table 2.

4. Nicholson, R.J., 'The Distribution of Personal Income', *Lloyds Bank Review*, January 1967.

5. Lydall, H., *The Structure of Earnings*, Oxford University Press, 1968.

6. Nicholson, R.J., op.cit., p.18.

7. *Economic Trends*, February 1970, p.xvii.

8. Report of a Hay-M.S.L. Management Co. Survey, *The Times*, 11 August 1966.

9. See, for example, Lydall, H., *British Incomes and Savings*, Basil Blackwell, 1955, p.3.

10. Tipping, D.G., 'Price Changes and Income Distribution', *Applied Statistics*, no. 1, 1970.

11. Calculated from *National Income and Expenditure*, H.M.S.O., 1970, Table 19.

12. D.H.S.S. *Report by the Government Actuary on the Financial Provisions of the National Superannuation and Social Insurance Bill*, Cmnd. 4223, H.M.S.O., 1969, p.21.

13. Information supplied by the Department of Health and Social Security.

14. *Social Trends*, no. 1, 1970, p.59.

15. ibid., p.101.

16. *Report of the National Assistance Board for 1965*, Cmnd. 3042, H.M.S.O., 1966, p.74. Some also now receive an 'exceptional circumstances addition'. But the number fell from 24 per cent in 1967 to 19 per cent in 1969 (averaging 5s.7d.). *Annual Report of the D.H.S.S. for 1969*, Cmnd. 4462, H.M.S.O., pp.331-2.

17. Atkinson, A.B., *Poverty in Britain and the Reform of Social Security*, Cambridge University Press, 1969, pp.75-6.

18. Based on *Economic Trends*, February 1970, p.xliii, *Economic Trends*, July 1968, p.xxxi, and information supplied for 1960 and 1961 by Central Stat. Office.

19. *Circumstances of Families*, H.M.S.O., paras, 22 and 40. To the figure of 70,000 families with a father in full-time work is added the estimate of an additional 25,000 families with only one child (para. 40).

20. For estimates for pre-war and post-war see Political and Economic Planning, *The Cost of the Social Services, 1938-1952*, Planning, no.354, June 1953.

21. I.L.O., *The Cost of Social Security*, 1964-66, Geneva, 1971; Wedel, J., 'Social Security and Economic Integration – II', *International Labour Review*, December 1970.

22. *Social Security in the Nordic Countries*, Copenhagen, 1970.

23. Attention is called to the difficulties of allowing properly for varying definitions of educational services and differential changes in prices. Debeauvais, M., *et al., Comparative Study of Educational Expenditure and its Trends in O.E.C.D. Countries since 1950*, Background Study no. 2, Conference on Policies for Educational Growth, O.E.C.D., 1970. For the 1950s Edding also shows that the rate of expansion of expenditure on education was lower in the U.K. than a number of other countries. Edding, F., 'Expenditure on Education, Statistics and Comments' in Robinson, E.A.G., and Vaizey, J.E. (eds.), *The Economics of Education*, Macmillan, 1966, p.40.

24. *Economic Trends*, February 1970, pp.xxix-xxx.

25. *Public Expenditure 1968-69 to 1973-74*, Cmnd. 4234, H.M.S.O., December 1969; *New Policies for Public Spending*, Cmnd. 4515, H.M.S.O., October 1970, and *Public Expenditure 1969-70 to 1974-75*, Cmnd. 4578, H.M.S.O., January 1971.

26. Meade, J.E., *Efficiency, Equality and the Ownership of Property*, Allen & Unwin, 1964; Atkinson, A.B., 'The Reform of Wealth Taxes in Britain', *Political Quarterly*, January-March 1971.

27. The reduced allowance of one ninth upon earnings of over £4,005 would also be abolished.

Index of names

360

Prest, A.R., 158

Radcliffe-Brown, A.R., 21, 26
Rankin, G., 234
Reddin, M., 146, 156n.
Rehin, G.F., 59
Reich, Charles A., 271, 290n.
Reid, G.L., 291
Rein, M., 24, 290n.
Revell, J., 37
Rex, John, 12, 25, 96, 97, 117
Robb, B., 197, 234
Robertson, D.J., 291
Robinson, E.A.G., 356
Robinson, G., 157
Robson, W.A., 23n.
Roby, P., 24
Rose, H., 114
Roth, Martin, 195
Routh, Guy, 35–6, 289
Rowntree, B. Seebohm, 32, 45, 269, 291, 317
Robinson, Kenneth, 127n., 234
    and AEGIS affair, 194–5
    and mental health services, 161, 189
    and selectivity, 121
Russett, Bruce, 23n.
Rutter, Michael, 329

Sainsbury, S., 233
Samuel, R., 114
Sandys, Duncan, 90
Schorr, Alvin L., 24, 30, 44n., 120
Scott, S., 115
Seldon, Arthur, 158, 259
Senior, Nassau, 324
Shanas, E., 25, 45, 182, 216–17
Shaw, L.A., 159, 292
Shearer, A., 184
Sheldon, J.H., 195, 292
Shenfield, B., 158
Shore, Peter, 289, 296
Shriver, Sargent, 270
Sidebotham, R., 181, 191, 292
Sieve, J., 24
Silburn, R., 118
Simon, Sir John, 88
Sinfield, R.A., 294, 296, 317
Skeet, M., 233
Skinner, F.W., 233
Slater, F., 114

Smelser, N.J., 13, 14–15, 17, 25
Smigel, E.O., 24
Smith, G., 119
Smith, T., 119
Spencer, Herbert, 13, 18
Spencer, K., 116
Spengler, Oswald, 18
Speth, J.G., 157
Stacey, M., 25, 218
Stein, B., 160
Stein, Z.A., 166
Stevens, R., 220, 234
Stores, G., 166

Tawney, R.H., 251, 290, 329
Taylor, W., 196
Timms, N., 234
Tipping, D.G., 37, 336–7
Titmuss, Richard, 127n., 156n., 291
    and analysis of incomes, 332
    his work, 33
    on definition of social service, 24, 261
    and selectivity, 121
    and statistics of income and wealth, 308
    and welfare problems, 267
Tizard, J., 181, 184
    and community care, 176
    and mentally handicapped children, 161, 165–6, 329
Tobin, James, 128
Todd, J., 120
Tönnies, F., 14
Tooth, G.C., 59, 187
Townsend, Peter
    academic history, 1
    Family Life of Old People, The, 158
    Labour and Inequality, 46, 119
    Last Refuge, The, 86, 181, 182
    Legal Rights of Low Income Families, 220
    'Means Tested Social Services', 118
    'Need for a Social Plan, The', 196
    Poor and the Poorest, The, 159, 290n., 292, 293, 316
    Poverty in the United Kingdom, 26
Toynbee, Arnold, 18
Trinder, Chris, 326
Turner, H.A., 308
Turnstall, Jeremy, 235

moral defectives, 182–3
physical handicap and mental
    ability, 164
personal incapacity, 168
research on, 161–2
social planning for, 161–80
subnormal intelligence, 163–7
unsuitability of hospitals for, 172–5
variations in prevalance of, 170–71
Milner–Holland Report, 101, 110

National assistance, change in attitudes
    to, 125
Labour policy on, 281
National Assistance Board, 121,
    145, 253, 277, 282
pensioners and, 339
poverty and, 272–7, 303
Tory Government and, 264
unclaimed, 144, 306, 309
and unemployment, 302
National Food Survey, 279–80, 327
National Health Service (*see also*
    Hospitals *and* Mental health
    services), *A Hospital Plan for
    England and Wales*, 68
and class structure, 271
contributions to, 263
and the elderly, 67
exemption from charges for, 147
expenditure on, 141, 225, 303,
    345
and G.N.P., 345
improvement in, 346
and low-income families, 336
prescription charges, 121, 263,
    342, 343
under Tories, 320, 323–4
National Insurance, contributions, 342
Labour policy on, 121, 280
and poverty, 253
and social security reform, 123
Tories and, 262–5
National Plan of 1965, 27, 51, 56,
    57–8, 284
Negative income tax, abuse of, 133
author's view of, 134
and equity, 131–2, 141–2
explained, 128
and incentives to work, 130–31
inefficiency of, 352
problems of, 129–30

purpose of, 142
selectivity and, 125
and universal social security; 141
in U.S.A., 30, 131, 142, 157
Newsom Report, 34

Old people (*see also* Pensioners),
A.E.G.I.S. affair, 194–5
attitude to social change, 17
care of, 65, 67, 68
community care for, 71, 204–5,
    218, 354
domiciliary services for, 71–4,
    216, 346
hospital planning for, 68–70
housing, 74–5, 77, 78, 107, 212
inequality and, 37, 38–9, 72–3,
    235–8
institutions, 75–7, 204, 218
MoH plans and, 58–9
mental health services and geriatrics,
    189, 190
and pensions, 29, 353
poverty, 272, 275–6, 298,
    299–301, 338
social services, 212
and unclaimed benefits, 144, 203

Pensioners (*see also* Old people),
attendance allowances, 246–7
increase in number of, 37, 338,
    345
and national assistance, 144, 306,
    309
and poverty, 338–41
supplementary, 282
and supplementary benefits, 125,
    144–5, 339
and Tax Credit scheme, 328
Pensions, differentiation in, 29
disability, 66, 238, 277, 301, 328,
    341, 352–3
earnings and, 300, 301, 326, 339
Labour policy on, 236–7, 284
national superannuation plan,
    236–7, 262, 282, 283–5,
    299–300
and poverty, 286
retirement, 235–8, 262, 339, 348
single or widowed persons', 44n.
state and occupational, 236, 261,
    276

Skeffington Report, 219
Social planning, definition of, 44
    and improvization, 123
    'incomprehension' of, 138
    in the 1970s, 349–55
    under Labour, 50, 51
    need for, 56–66
    P.P.B.S., 60–1, 124
    proposed Department of, 62, 64
    two-stage procedure for, 207–8
    Seebohm report, and, 191–3
Social policy, 1–23
    definition of, 2–8
    dominant problems of, 331
    and economic doctrine, 122
    historical trends in, 137
    Labour Party's, 121
    for the mentally handicapped,
        175–80
    relief policies, 150–1
    reorganization of, 47–55
    social objectives and, 9–13, 31–9
    and social planning, 44, 208
    and social services, 29, 43
    structure of, 9–10
    'universality' in, 137
Social security, 'compensatory', 155
    and the economy, 122
    expenditure on, 225, 303, 304
    Labour and, 50, 281–2, 287
    post-war universality, 252–3
    proportional contributions, 64,
        352, 353
    slow progress in, 48
    social control and, 153
    and taxation, 141, 143
    Tory Party and, 262–5, 321
    women and, 239–50
Social services, 135–56
    Barber on, 325
    conflicting functions of, 347–8
    and economic criteria, 62
    and economic vitality, 57
    expenditure on, 49, 51, 56–7,
        138, 303–4, 320
    future of, 27–44
    and G.N.P., 345, 349
    and industrial efficiency, 260
    Labour policy on, 121
    misconceptions about, 27–8
    purpose of, 28

selectivity in, 136
selective services, 139–42
and social needs, 211–12
social policy and, 29–30
subdivision of, 16
Tory Party and, 258–9, 320, 321–4
of U.K. compared with other
    countries, 347
underinvestment in, 343–9
universal services, 137, 141
Social structure, affluence and, 12–13
    change and, 20–21
    dependency and, 37
    deviance, 169–70
    differentiation, 14–15
    and health of schoolchildren, 327
    inequality and, 22
    personal incapacity, 168
    and poverty, 270, 288–9
    and public expenditure, 304
    selectivity and, 127
    and social services, 347–8
    subnormal intelligence, 163–7
    'under-class', 38, 279
Social workers, British Association of,
    223, 231–2
    and community development,
        229–30
    functions required of, 40
    group practice, 230–31
    training, 77–8, 206
    Younghusband on, 231
    Younghusband Committee and,
        210–11
Statistics, bureaucracy and, 307–8
    on incomes, 332, 333–4
    and information about trends,
        315–16
    interpretation of, 306–7
    presentation of, 7
    statistical defects, 311–14
    and trends in poverty, 308–10
Strikes, 308
Supplementary benefits, and housing,
    107
    increase in scope of scheme, 139
    initiative to claim, 132
    and measure of poverty, 317
    non-application for, 298, 303, 341
    payment of, 51
    pensioners and, 339